Dedicated to Margaret and Mary and Harold and to all of the parents in the world who are the most influential teachers of the young child.

Copyright © 1981, James Flood and Diane Lapp

Printed in the United States of America

Macmillan Publishing Co., Inc.
866 Third Avenue
New York, New York 10022

Collier Macmillan Canada, Ltd.


Library of Congress Cataloging in Publication Data

Flood, James Edward.
    Language/reading instruction for the young child.

    Includes bibliographies and index.
    1. Language arts.  2. Children—Language.
    3. Language acquisition.  4. Bilingualism.

I.  Lapp, Diane, joint author.  II. Title.
LB1575.8.F54  1981          372.6          79–17259

ISBN 0–02–338470–0


Printing:  1 2 3 4 5 6 7 8          Year:  1 2 3 4 5 6 7

# Language/Reading Instruction for the Young Child

**James Flood**
*Boston University*

**Diane Lapp**
*San Diego State University*

Macmillan Publishing Company
*New York*
Collier Macmillan Publishers
*London*

# Preface

This book has been designed to assist you in developing the language abilities of young children. Few texts deal with instructional issues as they relate to the teaching of language/reading for the young child. This text, however, contains important background information about the overall development of the child, the child's environment and some very practical ways that children can be helped to develop their language abilities.

The book is divided into five sections to facilitate your reading. Section I, "Historical Background of Early Childhood Education," offers some comments on the past and speculates on the future of early childhood education.

Section II, "The Development of the Young Child" provides some important background information related to the norms for child development in the areas of physical growth, cognitive development, and language acquisition/development. A chapter on "play," as an important part of the young child's life, has been included to help you in understanding the behaviors, thoughts, creative impulses, and desires of young children.

Section III, "Curriculum Models for Developing Language/Reading Programs for Young Children," presents several ways in which educators have attempted to design reading/language programs for young children. This section suggests a language experience base as the most appropriate mode of instruction. This section also includes many activities and suggestions for implementing a language experience program.

The role that parents can play in the education of their young children is explained in detail in this section. Practical suggestions to help parents in teaching their young children are explained, and games and activities are presented for parents to use with their children.

Section IV, "For Those Who Are Ready: The Reading Process," introduces you to the processes that you will need to understand as you teach children to read. This section includes definitions of reading, historical perspectives about reading in content areas, and numerous activities that will help you to reinforce your teaching strategies.

Section V, "Developing a Language/Reading Program for Every Young Child," includes important information about teaching children who are learning English as their second language. Your program design and its implementation and management are discussed in detail.

This book will help you to perform society's most valuable and important task—the education of its young.

In an effort to facilitate readability, we have used the editorial "he" throughout the text. Its use as a referent in no way is intended to denigrate our female colleagues and students.

## Acknowledgement

The authors wish to thank their excellent typist Susan Melanson, their exquisite photographer Linda Lungren, and their emotional mainstay, Sharon Ryan Flood.

James Flood
Diana Lapp

# Contents

# Section

# I

# Historical Background of Early Childhood Education

# 1

# Historical and Contemporary Perspectives of American Early Childhood Education

*Figure 1.* Many programs such as day care centers and Head Start Programs are the result of social and political forces of the 1960s. Educators hoped that these programs would provide an effective developmental foundation in the early learning years. (Photo by Linda Lungren)

The intellectual, emotional, and social development of young children has been studied by many great educators. Comenius, Pestalozzi, Froebel, Basedow, Piaget, and Montessori have all studied the child and his world. The early endeavors of these educators have been continued through the efforts of contemporary educators like Gesell, Ilg, Zirbes, Hymes, and Havinghurst.

Although there is an extensive body of literature on the development of the young child, the education of children of this age was virtually ignored within the public school and in the general American community before 1960. During the 1960s some public schools offered half-day kindergarten programs, and the Lanham Act, instituted during World War II, provided financial assistance for the children of mothers who worked in strategic war industries. Until the 1960s, programs for the education of young children were quite rare. Although the first early childhood programs may not have provided quality education for all young children, they should be credited for introducing group child care and guidance for a large strata of the American population.

## Why Early Childhood Education?

Today, early childhood education programs that provide educational training for children from birth to the age of eight are found in nursery schools, day care centers, Head Start programs, kindergartens, and primary classes. Many of these programs are the result of social and political forces of the 1960s. Social commentaries of the 1950s and 1960s such as *Why Johnny Can't Read*, *Education and Ecstasy*, *Our Children are Dying*, *Death at an Early Age*, *How Children Fail*, and *The Way It 'Spozed To Be*, coupled with a cry for relevance from the urban and Appalachian populations of America, roused national concern for the development of early childhood intervention programs.

The impact of the literacy explosion of the 1960s exposed the educational discrepancies between the affluent and the poor in America. National concern caused many researchers to investigate the causes of these discrepancies. Many educators concluded that America's technological expansion after World War II caused many unskilled laborers to be replaced by complex machinery. Ironically, this technology provided increased financial and social benefits for the skilled and professionally educated people who were increasing in demand. This situation resulted in an extremely stratified population.

In an effort to minimize this stratification, many prominent educators proposed the implementation of early childhood intervention programs as a remedy for the social and educational dilemma that they were witnessing.

They hoped that these programs would provide an effective developmental foundation in the early learning years that would result in measureable positive effects in the primary, middle, and secondary school populations of the 1970s, 1980s, and 1990s.

The 1976 results of the National Assessment of Educational Progress (NEAP) in reading suggest that their hopes were well founded. Children who could have been affected by any early intervention programs were the nine-year-olds who were tested in the 1976 survey. It was reported that

> Nine-year-olds during the second assessment read significantly better than did 9-year-olds four years earlier. The improvement was recorded in all reading skills but was most noteworthy in reference skills.
>
> Black 9-year-olds improved even more dramatically than did 9-year-olds as a whole. Reading specialists suggested that both increases might be attributed to successful reading intervention programs in the primary grades.
>
> (NAEP report, 1976, p. xi)

Several reading experts who participated in the 1976 NAEP assessment attribute the success of the nine-year-olds, at least, in part, to early intervention programs:

> Nine-year-olds are doing so well because we're placing more instructional emphasis here. We espouse the idea that reading should be taught throughout the 12 grades, but we really don't teach it.
>
> (NAEP report, Chapman, 1976, p. 26)
>
> Another hypothesis is that, after being exposed to Sesame Street and other good television shows, kids are coming to school able to do more.
>
> (NAEP report, Farr, 1976, p. 26)
>
> Kindergarten is also becoming more universal. A lot of federal and state funds have been funneled toward programs at this level.
>
> (NAEP report, Blanton, 1976, p. 26)
>
> Nine and 13-year-olds are doing very well—much better than I anticipated—on the items that measure basic literal comprehension. Even though the increase isn't large, over such a short period, it is statistically significant. I would hypothesize that the reason for the greater increase at the 9-year-old level is that most of the reading intervention programs have taken place in the primary years.
>
> (NAEP report, Farr, 1976, p. 10)
>
> The reading panel members, who attributed the general increase in performance of 9-year-olds to the many reading intervention programs conducted at the primary level, pointed out that improvement at this level is extremely important because it supplies individuals with a foundation for further reading development. The improved scores of black 9-year-olds—which, according to the panel, might be attributed to integrated schools, greater funding in impacted areas, and to social factors outside the school—could signal progress toward equalization of educational opportunity.
>
> (NAEP report, 1976, p. 25–26)

## The Evolution of Early Childhood Education Programs

The development of many of the 1960s early childhood intervention programs was intended to provide environmental stimulants that would facilitate the optimal development of the child by providing the experiential background needed to ensure a successful transition into the elementary grades. The majority of these programs included provisions for
1. The identification and remediation of physical problems.
2. The development of receptive and expressive discourse skills.
3. Social class interactions.
4. Multi-ethnic interactions.


### *Kindergartens*

In Germany during the early nineteenth century, Friedrich Froebel developed the first kindergarten. It was based on a religious philosophy that stressed the integration of the individual with God, nature, and others. The curriculum of the Froebelian kindergarten included:

1. The *Gifts* that were soft, manipulative balls, blocks, and sticks used to develop sensory and perceptual skills, symbols of the universe, and geometric representations.

2. The *Occupations* that consisted of activities such as paper cutting and folding, cardboard construction, painting, sewing, clay modeling, and other tasks, which represented the work of the early primitive people.

3. The *Mother's Plays* that were songs, games, marching, and dancing activities taken from the early examples of playful interactions between peasant mothers and their young children.

4. The *Nature Experiences* that involved the child in outdoor play and explorations of nature.

Teachers were forbidden to introduce any formal reading, writing, or mathematics instruction in the kindergarten. This type of curricula was intended to distinguish the phenomenon of childhood learning from classical elementary programs. The content of these early programs was heavily related to the life experiences of the child. This personalized model of curriculum was based on the following three principles of Froebelian philosophy:

1. The child is not a miniature adult, but, rather, a unique developing human organism.

2. Self-activity and involvement must be inherent in the learning process.

3. The value of play as a learning vehicle is paramount.

As the concept of early childhood programs expanded throughout Germany, training institutions began to accept women as well as men into their programs. Many of these trained teachers immigrated to the United States during the mid-nineteenth century. As a result of this widespread immigration to America, the first kindergarten was established by Margarette Schurz in Watertown, Wisconsin in 1855. She invited the children of her relatives to her home to join her own children in a series of educational activities that she had learned in a German training institute. Throughout the 1850s and 1860s similar German-American kindergartens were established throughout the United States.

*Figure 2.* Kindergartens allowed the child to take his place in the company of his equals, to learn his place in their companionship, and still later to learn wider social relations and their involved duties. (Photo by Linda Lungren)

The first English-speaking kindergarten was established by Elizabeth Peabody in 1860 in Boston. Peabody, through her interactions with Schurz, became interested in kindergarten education because it allowed "the child to take his place in the company of his equals, to learn his place in their companionship, and still later to learn wider social relations and their involved duties." Tuition at the Peabody kindergarten was fifty dollars per term. Whereas this was a school for children from wealthy families, the American concern for immigrant children of lesser wealth opened the doors of the kindergarten to all children.

In 1870 Kate Wiggin, author of many children's books including *Rebecca of Sunnybrook Farm*, headed a settlement kindergarten in San Francisco. The supporters of settlement kindergartens believed this was the place to begin the development of good American citizens. As Riis pointed out:

> The real reform of poverty and ignorance must begin with the children. The little ones, with their new standards and new ambitions, become in a real sense missionaries of the slums, whose work of regeneration begins with their parents.
>
> (Riis, 1895, p. 92)

It was believed that urban reform would occur through reaching the young children, who, in turn, could reach the parents. Time schedules were designed to facilitate this transfer; children spent one-half day in school, and during the remaining one-half day, the teacher visited their homes and parents in an attempt to better understand the uniqueness of each individual and family. Social interaction between teachers and parents was the prime intent of these daily schedules.

Opponents of these programs leveled several criticisms. They suggested that these programs were:

1. Too expensive to maintain.

2. A nonsense program full of fun, not learning.

3. Not diverse enough to encourage the development of children whose families were not poor immigrants.

4. Too involved with individuals, thus, neglecting socialization within groups.

These reservations, coupled with the popular literature of the early 1700s that questioned the learning capabilities of poor children, led to the development of separate kindergarten programs for poor and wealthy children. Programs for the less wealthy children were classically structured. Although the children were very young, the basics of reading, writing, and mathematics skills were introduced.

It was believed that the relevance of these subjects would become apparent to the student only after he had reached greater maturity and after the other categories of knowledge had been revealed to him. For the moment, he must accept the material without question and place a high priority on the principle of "deferred gratification," a distinctive characteristic of the classical model of education (Lapp, et al., 1975, p. 22).

The classical curriculum was intended to ready the less wealthy child for entrance into the elementary school:

> ... to discipline and subdue his emotions so that they are proper and can serve order. So freed, the student's mind is then capable of penetrating, through the skill of logic, into the hidden realities of the world. Once he has acquired this skill, he will be introduced into the "great conversation" of Western tradition, joining such minds as Aristotle, Shakespeare, and Freud. Throughout his education, the student

will habitually see beyond surface confusion into the permanent order. Strengthened by this new insight, he then acquires confidence and poise, and can enjoy security in every situation and respond correctly to whatever challenge is offered. Education, then, is a search for the meaning of life; a journey to the center of reality from which all knowledge radiates.

(Lapp, et al., 1975, p. 29–30)

"Disciplined learning" became the theme that characterized the kindergarten curriculum of the financially impoverished child. Creativity and independent learning experiences continued to be part of private or affluent public school kindergartens.

The social-class division and revision of the American kindergarten hindered social reform by addressing cognitive life in school and ignoring the relevancy of its application to social life situations. Reading readiness became the focal point of the curriculum, replacing the introductory philosophy of the American kindergarten that had stressed the integration of the individual with God, nature, and others. The kindergarten of the early and middle 1900s stressed intellectual readiness instead of social readiness as a vehicle for social change.

### Nursery Schools

The first nursery schools, designed by Rachel and Margaret Macmillan in the slums of London, provided social, physical, emotional, and intellectual health care to children of the poor, aged three to five. Nursery school programs were designed to nurture the "gestalt" or whole child, and the nursery school teachers were responsible for every aspect of the child's development including physical cleanliness and neatness.

The original English nursery was a large one-story building with French windows that opened into gardens. Children's play was welcomed in these gardens. Although programmatic inclusion of play may have been a result of the teachings of Froebel, the Macmillan sisters were greatly influenced by Edouard Seguin, a French educator who pioneered the importance of sensory education in his work with retarded children. Stressing mastery of the *observable* rather than the *symbolic*, the Macmillan nursery school emphasized the social, emotional, and cognitive development of the child more than the child's religious development. The curriculum of the Macmillan school included activities designed to encourage reading, writing, mathematics, and science skill development as well as sensory, rhythmic and language development. Grace Owen, a friend of the Macmillan's, objected to the inclusion of reading, writing, mathematics, and science activities in an early learning program; she designed a London nursery school that stressed unstructured play activities. These free play activities included work with nonstructured materials such as water, sand, paper, and art supplies.

Because of the success of the Macmillan school, England passed the Fisher Act of 1908; it encouraged the widespread establishment of nursery schools in all local English school systems. The Fisher Act may have been a sign of support, but necessary funds were never provided, and expansion of the nursery school program was severely constricted.

Grace Owen and several other teachers who had worked with the Macmillan sisters immigrated to the United States in the early twentieth century. By 1920 their influence was observable in the development of the Merrill Palmer School of Motherhood and Home Training and a nursery school at Columbia University. These early American nursery schools often emphasized cognitive skill development over social or emotional learning. Unlike the London nursery schools for children from deprived areas, the United States nurseries were viewed as "the place" designed to train women in home management and motherhood techniques.

Although American nurseries were similar in educational concept to the London nurseries, they were designed for children from affluent families; tuition charges were standard. Because the United States programs were established for children from affluent families, there was little emphasis on health care. During the 1920s the concept of nursery school education spread slowly throughout the United States. The depression of the 1930s produced great unemployment among nursery school teachers and the elimination of many programs. In an attempt to alleviate the economic burden of the vast numbers of unemployed teachers, the federal government in 1933, through the Federal Emergency Relief Act (FERA) and the Works Project Administration (WPA), provided funds for the development of nursery schools that provided many jobs for unemployed teachers.

Using these WPA funds, many communities designed nursery school programs that provided educational training for children and educational expansion for the nursery school movement. The affluence of post-depression years and the onset of World War II, a period in which many women were employed in war-related work, were major factors in the decrease of the number of unemployed teachers. The Lanham Act of 1941 provided federal support for child care centers that educated the children of mothers involved in war work. However, at the end of the war, federal monies for nursery school education were withdrawn.

Parent-cooperative nurseries, originally begun in the 1920s, flourished during the 1950s. The curriculum of privately owned parent-cooperatives often included courses designed to extend the parents' knowledge of child development and child rearing practices. Although private parent-cooperatives still exist, the Economics Opportunity Act and the Elementary and Secondary Education Act of the 1960s again provided federal support for the development of preschool educational experiences.

## Montessori Schools

> I succeeded in teaching a number of the idiots from the asylums both to read and write so well that I was able to present them at a public school for an examination together with normal children. And they passed the examination successfully. . . . While everyone was admiring the progress of my idiots, I was searching for the reasons which could keep the healthy children of the common schools on so low a plane that they could be equalled in tests of intelligence by my unfortunate pupils.
>
> (Montessori, 1964, p. 38–39)

> I became convinced that similar methods applied to normal children would develop or set free their personality in a marvelous and surprising way.
>
> (Montessori, 1964, p. 33)

These statements of Maria Montessori characterize the philosophy of the *cosa dei bambini*, or Italian nursery school, which developed during the same period that the Macmillan sisters developed the English nursery school. Modifying the methods of Jean Itard and Edouard Seguin, Montessori first directed her teaching efforts toward financially poor Italian children who had been labeled "mentally deficient" and housed in the State Orthophrenic School.

In 1907 Montessori accepted a position as the director of a slum housing project day care center in San Lorenzo, Italy. This experience began her work with "normal" children of financially poor and illiterate parents. The only educational materials available to her were the sensory materials she had used in her earlier work with mentally retarded children.

Instruction took place in one of the rooms in the apartment building. The room was sparsely furnished with office furniture. Although Montessori did not particularly espouse any one method of instruction, she was interested in "normal" children's reactions to the materials she had used with the mentally retarded children. She was anxious to learn if the responses of younger children of "normal" intelligence were similar to the reactions of older retarded children.

Montessori did not structure a scientific experiment because she believed that an artificial environment would hinder the natural reactions of the children. The children of the Montessori school were instructed in a "natural environment," which was defined as "one where everything is suitable for his age and growth, where possible obstacles to his development are removed, and where he is provided with the means to exercise his growing faculties" (Lillard, 1972, p. 4).

As Montessori observed children from three to seven years of age working with these sensory materials in a natural environment, she was amazed by the extent of their concentration and decision-making abilities. Because of the pleas from the illiterate mothers of her students, Montessori began to incorporate early reading and writing experiences into the curriculum. Four- and five-year-olds were given sandpaper letters to feel and to trace. They enthusiastically received these letters and added sounds to them; eventually, the children were reading words and then books.

By 1909, use of Montessori's sensory approach to early learning was being used by most orphan asylums and children's homes in southern Switzerland. In 1912 Maria Montessori visited the United States and gave her first American lecture at Carnegie Hall. Subsequently, Margaret Wilson, sister of Woodrow Wilson, and Mrs. Alexander Graham Bell started the American Montessori Association.

Montessori schools met with great enthusiasm until 1914 when William Kilpatrick, an influential educator and follower of Dewey, published *The Montessori System Examined*, which characterized the Montessori approach as one adhering to outdated educational practices.

> The didactic apparatus which forms the principal means of activity in the Montessori school affords singularly little variety, by its very theory presents a limited series of exactly distinct and very precise activities, formal in character and very remote from social interests and connections. So narrow and limited a range of activity cannot go far in satisfying the normal child. . . The best current thought and practice in America would make constructive and imitative play, socially conditioned, the foundation and principal constituent of the program for children of kindergarten age.
> (Kilpatrick, 1914, p. 27–28)

He further criticized the sensory/tactile materials of the Montessori curriculum when he stated, "On the whole, the imagination, whether of constructive play or of more aesthetic sort is but little utilized. . . it affords very inadequate expression to a large portion of child nature." (Kilpatrick, 1914, p. 28–29)

Kilpatrick also characterized Montessori's attempts to introduce writing, reading, and mathematics skills to children under six as "unnecessary." As a result of such criticism, the majority of American Montessori schools closed by 1918, and the concept of the Montessori sensory approach for early learners was virtually undiscussed for forty years.

By the early 1960s America was startled by an increase in the number of children who could not read, an increase in the number of high school dropouts, and the successful launching of spacecraft into outer space by the Soviet Union. Because of these problems, American educators began to reinvestigate the theories of Montessori as an innovative technique that might possibly remedy the American educational problems.

### Day Care Centers

The early *creche,* translated as crib, often referred to as a day care center, was established in Paris in 1844, and in the United States in 1854 to fight infant mortality and to provide services for working mothers. Day care centers originally began as a result of the Industrial Revolution, a time when many women began working outside the home. The physical needs of young children of the middle and lower classes with working mothers were attended to in the day care center, whereas the children of the wealthy were cared for by family servants or "nannies." Infants, toddlers, and nursery school age children were often so crowded together in a day care setting that neither space nor opportunity was available for educational activities.

In 1920, as a result of the introduction of the nursery school movement, many day care centers began to include limited educational experiences for their children in addition to attending to the physical needs of children. During the late 1930s and early 1940s, working mothers began to demand quality educational programs for their children. These demands and the funds provided by the Lanham Act of 1941 contributed to the refinement of day care center facilities and curricula. Unfortunately, many of these centers were forced to close in 1946 when the Lanham Act was terminated.

### Head Start Programs

*Project Head Start* was designed in 1965 with funds provided from the United States Office of Economic Opportunity for the development of preschool educational programs for poor, minority children, often referred to as "disadvantaged." Project Head Start was the first American mass preschool program for economically impoverished children. It was an attempt by the U.S. Office of Education to implement "a war on American poverty," by providing services for approximately six million American children.

A variety of program models were designed and implemented throughout the United States. An analysis of these models demonstrated the need for additional programs. A one-year program was believed to be inadequate for providing the readiness skills needed by the target children for successful entrance into first grade. *Project Follow Through* was similar to Head Start because it was supported by USOE funds, but it differed from Head Start because it contained a home-parent component. Like the Head Start Programs, Project Follow Through exemplified the curricular attempts to provide cognitive, physical, medical, social, nutritional, and health services to young children.

In 1972 funds were provided for the education of handicapped young children. Children enrolled in these early education programs were to be selected from one of the following categories:

1. Physically handicapped.
2. Gifted.
3. Speech impaired.
4. Hearing disabled.
5. Visually handicapped.
6. Mentally retarded.
7. Socially deprived.

8. Economically disadvantaged.
9. Learning disabled.
10. Emotionally retarded.

The inclusion of all of these children in one classroom required a wide range of knowledge and skill on the part of the teacher. Although, in some cases insufficiently trained personnel staffed these programs, the initial measurements of these programs, such as the 1976 *National Assessment of Educational Progress Report*, are beginning to show positive cognitive gains.

### British Infant Schools

The British Infant School serves children from five to seven years of age. The British Infant School curricula, which is tightly structured and flexibly administered, provides early learning experiences in mathematics, reading, writing, sensory, aesthetic, and social experiences. Many different materials and methods are used to teach these academic subjects.

The British Infant School concept spread rapidly through Britain after World War II and throughout the United States in the late 1960s and early 1970s. The implementation of the British Infant School concept was hastened by the release of the 1967 *Plowden Report*, officially titled *Children and Their Primary Schools*. It was a study of the existing British primary school system. It was documented in the Plowden Report that the "open" classroom had replaced approximately one third of all fixed curriculum schools. Further insights regarding the characteristics and successes of the British Infant School came to the attention of American educators through the writing of Joseph Featherstone. In America the British Infant School was often referred to as an "open" classroom designed to foster the social and cognitive development of young children, especially those who had completed a Head Start program.

The following features characterize the British Infant School and the American "open" classroom:

1. A room functionally divided into open, flexible working areas.
2. Multiple learning resources of many types.
3. Well managed and sequentially structured curriculum.
4. Student participation in decision making regarding learning activities.
5. Teachers interacting with individuals alone or in small groups.

The works of Piaget formed the theoretical base of the open classroom. Similar to Montessori, Piaget suggested that early learning must be related to the child's sensory experiences. It was argued that early learning experiences must encourage the child to:

1. Manipulate objects and symbols.
2. Explore language through creating and answering questions.
3. Interact with others in social situations.

*Figure 3.* A feature of the American "open" classroom is a room functionally divided into open, flexible working areas with multiple learning resources of many types. (Photo by Linda Lungren)

The teachers begin with the assumption that the children want to learn and will learn in their fashion; learning is rooted in first-hand experience so that teaching becomes the encouragement and enhancement of each child's own thrust toward mastery and understanding. Respect for and trust in the child are perhaps the most basic principles underlying the Open Classroom.

From the application of these principles derive the most notable characteristics of learning in such a classroom: a general atmosphere of excitement; virtually complete flexibility in the curriculum; interpretation of the various subjects and skills; emphasis on learning rather than teaching; focus on each child's thinking and problem-solving processes, and on his ability to communicate with others; and freedom and responsibility for the children. (Gross and Gross, 1970, p. 71–72)

The success of a program that required so much flexibility on the part of the child and the teacher could only be successful if the teacher had a workable understanding of classroom management skills. In an attempt to disseminate information about classroom management, the Educational Development Center (EDC), a nonprofit curriculum development center in Newton, Massachusetts, conducted workshops and sponsored consultant services for many teachers, administrators, and parents throughout the United States.

Although the efforts of EDC were felt in many classrooms in many states, most American teachers had not been taught management skills, and "open chaos" frequently replaced the open classroom. The results of the open classroom concept were described by Oettinger, 1969. He suggested that it was too rapidly implemented and it fell short of its philosophical intention.

## Contemporary Early Childhood Education Programs

The exactness of an historical review of an existing institution is often politically debatable; however, the contemporary debate regarding the significance of preschool education closely parallels the historical debate that characterized its evolution. Early attempts to implement preschool programs were made as social measures to equalize housing, health facilities, and educational opportunities among America's immigrants. These attempts at social equalization still reflect the underlying philosophy of contemporary federally funded preschool programs.

Parental involvement, individualized attention, and social and cognitive curricula have consistently represented the pedagogical innovations of preschool educators. Public and private nursery school and day care centers abound. Aid for Dependent Children or Work Incentive programs have provided funds for the early education of less financially able children. Depending on the interest and commitment of each presidential administration, funds for such programs are either extended, diminished or eliminated.

Although this historical review may initially seem depressing, it is intended as a commentary of enthusiasm because of the soundness of educationally philosophy, methods, materials, and practices that have characterized early childhood education programs throughout American history.

The schools have never been able, however, to solve the social problems that have plagued America since its origin. If we wish for improved cognitive growth scores among the less financially able, the majority of citizens, not just educators, must be committed to substantial community, economic, and health care reforms. Societal programs, coupled with existing preschool programs, may provide the means for eliminating existing poverty and discrimination.

## BIBLIOGRAPHY

Ames, L. B., and F. L. Ilg, *School Readiness*. New York: Harper & Row, Publishers, 1972.

Basedow, J. B. (1724–1790) *Auszewahlte padazozische Schriften*. Besorzt von A. Reble Paderborn, F. Schoninzh, 1965.

*Children and Their Primary Schools*. A Report of the Central Advisory Council for Education (England) Vol. 1 and II. This is the 1967 Plowden Report published by (HMSO) Her Majesty's Stationery Office, British Information Services, Sales Section, 845 Third Avenue, New York.

Comenius, J. A. *John Amos Comenius on Education*(With an introduction by Jean Piaget). New York: Teachers College Press (1967, © 1957).

Comenius, J. A. *The Great Didactic of John Amos Comenius*. Trans. into English and ed. by M. W. Kestinze. London: A & L Black, 1907–10.

Comenius, J. A. *A Reformation of Schools, 1642,* Menston, England: Scolar Press, 1969.

Davis, M. D. *Nursery Schools: Their Development and Current Practices in the United States*. Bulletin, 1932, No. 9, U. S. Office of Education Washington, D.C.: Government Printing Office, 1933.

Dewey, J. *Democracy and Education*. New York: Macmillan Publishing Co., Inc. 1916.

Dewey, J. *The Child and the Curriculum*. Chicago: University of Chicago Press, 1956.

Evans, E. D. *Contemporary Influences in Early Childhood Education*. 2nd ed. New York: Holt, Rinehart and Winston, Inc., 1975.

Featherstone, J. "Schools For Children," *The New Republic*, (August 10, 1967).

Featherstone, J. "How Children Learn," *The New Republic*, (September 2, 1967).

Featherstone, J. "Teaching Children To Think," *The New Republic*, (September 9, 1967).

Fisher, L. "Report of the Commissioner of Education," in Vanderwalker, *The Kindergarten in American Education*. New York: Macmillan Publishing Co., Inc., 1908.

Froebel, F. "The Young Child," in *F. Froebel: A Selection From His Writings*. Ed. by Irene M. Lilley. Cambridge: Cambridge University Press, 1967.

Gesell, A. *The First Five Years: A Guide to the Study of the Preschool Child*. New York: Harper & Row, Publishers, 1940.

Goodlad, J. I., M. F. Klein, and J. M. Novotney. *Early Schooling in the United States*. New York: McGraw-Hill Book Company, 1973.

Gross, B. and R. Gross "A Little Bit of Chaos," *Saturday Review*. (May 16, 1970), 71–73, 84–85.

Havinghurst, R. *Human Development & Education*. New York: Longman, Inc. 1953.

Hymes, J. L. *Behavior & Misbehavior: A Teacher's Guide to Action*. Englewood Cliffs, N. J.: Prentice-Hall, Inc., 1955.

Hymes, J. L. *A Child Development Point of View*. Englewood Cliffs, N. J.: Prentice-Hall, Inc., 1955.

Hymes. J. L. *Before the Child Reads*. Evanston, Ill.: Row, Peterson, 1958.

Hymes, J. L. *Teaching the Child Under Six*. Columbus, Ohio: Charles E. Merrill Publishing Company, 1968.

Hymes, J. L. *Effective Home-School Relations*. Sierra Madre: Association for the Education of Young Children, 1974.

Ilg, F. L. *School Readiness: Behavior Tests used at the Gesell Institute* (Gesell Institute of Child Development, New Haven). New York: Harper & Row, Publisher, 1972.

Ilg, F. L., A. L. Gesell, L. B. Ames. *Infant and Child in the Culture of Today: The Guidance of Development in Home and Nursery School*. New York: Harper & Row, Publishers, 1974.

Ilse, F. *Preschool Education: A Historical and Critical Study*. New York: Macmillan Publishing Company., Inc., 1927.

Itard, J. *Wild Boy of Aveyron*. New York: Appleton-Century-Crofts, 1962.

Kilpatrick, W. *The Montessori System Examined*. Boston: Houghton Mifflin Company, 1914.

King, I. A. *Preparing Enrollment.* Washington, D. C.: Government Printing Office, 1975.

Klein, J. W., and L. A. Randolph. "Placing Handicapped Children in Head Start Programs," *Children Today,* 3:6 (November-December 1974), 7–10.

Lapp, D., H. Bender, S. Ellenwood, and M. John. *Teaching and Learning: Philosophical, Psychological, Curricular Application.* New York: Macmillan Publishing Co., Inc. 1975.

Lazerson, M. "Social Reform and Early Childhood Education: Some Historical Perspective," in *As The Twig is Bent: Readings in Early Childhood Education.* Eds. R. H. Anderson, and H. G. Shane. Boston: Houghton Mifflin Company, 1971.

Lazerson, M. "Urban Reform and the Schools: Kindergarten in Massachusetts, 1870–1915." *History of Education Quarterly.* (Summer 1971), Vol. XI, no. 2, 115–142.

Levin, T. "Preschool Education and the Communities of the Poor," in *The Special Disadvantaged Child,* Vol. 1, ed. by J. Hillmuth, Seattle: Special Child Publishers, 1967.

Lillard, P. P. *Montessori, A Modern Approach.* New York: Schocken Books, Inc., 1972.

Maccoby, E. E., and M. B. Zellner. *Experiments in Primary Education: Aspects of Project Follow-Through.* New York: Harcourt Brace Jovanovich, Inc., 1970.

Montessori, M. *The Montessori Method.* New York: Schocken Books, Inc., 1964.

National Assessment of Educational Progress. *Reading in America: A Perspective on Two Assessments.* Reading Report No. 06-R-01, Denver, Colorado, October 1976.

Oettinger, A. *Run, Computer, Run: The Mythology of Educational Innovation.* Cambridge, Mass.: Harvard University Press, 1969.

Osborn, K. "Project Head Start," *Educational Leadership,* (November 1965), 98–102.

Peabody, E. *Lectures In the Training School for Kindergartners.* Boston: D. C. Heath & Company, 1893.

Pestalozzi, J. H. *Pestalozzi's Leonard & Gertrude,* translated by E. Channing. New York: Gordon Press, 1977.

Piaget, J. *Plays, Dreams, and Imitation in Childhood.* New York: W. W. Norton & Company, Inc., 1962.

Piaget, J. "Development and Learning," in *Piaget Rediscovered.* Ed. by R. E. Ripple and V. N. Rockcastle. Ithaca, N.Y.: Cornell University Press, 1964.

Prescott, E. and E. Jones. *The "Politics" of Day Care,* Vol. I. Washington, D.C.: National Association for the Education of Young Children, 1972.

Riis, J. "Children of the Poor," in *The Poor in Great Cities.* Eds., Woods, R. A. et al. New York: Charles Scribner's Sons, 1985, 92.

Riles, W. C. "ECE in California Passes the First Test." Phi Delta Kappan, 57, No. 1 (September 1975), 3–7.

Seguin, E. *Idiocy and Its Treatment.* Albany, N.Y.: Press of Brandon Printing Co., 1907.

Steinfels, M. O. *Who's Minding the Children? The History and Politics of Day Care in America.* New York: Simon & Schuster, Inc., 1973.

Ward, F. E. *The Montessori Method and the American School.* New York: Macmillan Publishing Co., Inc., 1913.

White, J. *Montessori Schools.* London: Oxford University Press, 1914.

Wiggin, W. K. D. *My Garden of Memory.* Boston: Houghton Mifflin Company, 1893, 105–107.

Williams, R. *"Reading in Informal Classrooms."* Free pamphlet published by Educational Development Center, 55 Chapel Street, Newton, Massachusetts, 1969.

Zirbes, L. *Comparative Studies of Current Practice in Reading, with Techniques for the Improvement of Teaching.* N.Y.: Teachers College, Columbia University, 1928.

Zirbes, L. *Encouraging Creativity in Student Teaching*. Cedar Falls: Association for Student Teaching, 1956.

Zirbes, L. *Spurs to Creative Teaching*. New York: G. P. Putnam's Sons, 1959.

# Section

# II

# The Development of the Young Child

This section has been designed to introduce you to important theories about the psychological, biological, linguistic, and cognitive development of the child. An understanding of this background information is critical for designing and implementing appropriate early learning experiences for young children.

The information that is contained in these three chapters is often complex and may cause you some difficulty when you read it for the first time. However, this information is so important that it is worth reading and rereading. It will help you to understand your students, and it will help you to become a fine teacher for every young child who comes into your classroom.

# 2

# Understanding the Physical and Cognitive Growth of the Child

*Figure 4.* Understanding the Physical and Cognitive Development of the Child. (Photo by Linda Lungren)

> The eye—it cannot choose but see,
> We cannot bid the ear be still;
> Our bodies feel, where'er they be,
> Against or with our will.
>
> *Wordsworth*

## PHYSICAL/BIOLOGICAL GROWTH OF THE CHILD

### The Newborn

The first two weeks of a child's life are commonly referred to as the *neonatal period*. The child during this time makes the dramatic transition from intrauterine existence when he depended entirely upon his mother to an extrauterine life. Although the neonate will continue to depend on adults to a great extent, he has begun his own unique path of physical, emotional, and intellectual development.

The neonate's body weight fluctuates as much as 10 per cent of his birth weight as a result of gain and loss of fluids during this two-week period. He may be hairy for a few days until the fuzzy prenatal body hair disappears. He may also be light in color for he has not yet developed full skin pigmentation or thickness of skin texture. Over a few days time, the vernix caseosa, an oily covering that protects the infant against infection, dries naturally.

Because of the partial molding that allows the head to pass through the pelvis, the newborn's head may be elongated and misshapened. It may also be proportionately larger than it will be later in life. As the newborn's skull bones are not yet fused, this temporary molding is possible. The newborn has six fontanels, or soft spots, on the head. These are places where the bones have not yet grown together; they are covered by a tough membrane. Because the nose cartilage is also malleable and may have been affected during the birth process, the newborn's nose may look squashed for a few days.

The first few weeks of life are more a transitional period between two drastically different modes of existence than they are a time of growth, for the human newborn has been only partially prepared for life outside the womb. Life outside the womb depends upon the functioning of vital mechanisms that were not previously in use. The typical vaginal delivery may have been exhausting for the child, especially when labor is prolonged or complicated. The fact that the newborn sleeps a great deal during the postnatal weeks may be related to tiring during the birth process.

When the child is born, he begins to actively initiate interactions with his environment, and he begins to use his senses. As the mechanisms for his vital functions become needed for extrauterine life, his existence requires more effort. The umbilical cord served for passage of oxygen and carbon dioxide in prenatal life, but now the newborn must use his own respiratory system. The blood of the fetus was circulated through the umbilical cord to the placenta, and clean blood was carried back. Outside the womb, the neonate's own circulatory system must take over and do the work that the umbilical cord was doing before his birth.

In the uterus, the umbilical cord brought food from the mother and carried waste matter away; the infant's own body will take over these functions at birth. Temperature was constant in the uterus, but the neonate must be able to keep his body temperature constant in spite of air fluctuations. Layers of fat beneath the skin enable the full-term infant to regulate body temperature.

The neonate's behavior is controlled by the spinal cord and lower brain centers at first because the cerebral cortex, which controls perception, thought, and memory, is not fully mature at birth. Generally, within the first two weeks, the healthy, full-term newborn adjusts to postnatal life. The premature baby usually requires more time to make these crucial adjustments.

In the following table several characteristics of prenatal and postnatal life are compared:

| Characteristics | Prenatal Life | Postnatal Life |
|---|---|---|
| Environment | amniotic fluid | air |
| Temperature | relatively constant | fluctuates with atmosphere |
| Stimulation | minimal | all senses stimulated by various stimuli |
| Nutrition | dependent on mother's blood | dependent on external food and functioning of digestive system |
| Oxygen Supply | passed from maternal bloodstream via placenta | passed from neonate's lungs to pulmonary blood vessels |
| Metabolic Elimination | passed into maternal bloodstream via placenta | discharged by skin, kidneys, lungs, and gastrointestines |

Source: P. S. Timiras, *Developmental Physiology and Aging*. New York: Macmillan Publishing Co., Inc. 1972, 174.

### Reflex Behaviors

During his first weeks and months of life the newborn exhibits many primitive reflex behaviors that decrease by the end of the first year. These bits of behavior (such as grasping, sucking, occasional glancing at nearby objects) have been discussed by Jean Piaget in the analysis of the development of his own three children. The reflexes operate briefly and mechanically and are not deliberately controlled by the infant. The appearance of these reflexes has been attributed to the subcortical control of the child's nervous system. As the cerebral cortex matures, it inhibits expression. Such reflexes as coughing, sneezing, yawning, and eye-blinking are protective reflexes that do not decrease. Examination of the infant's reflexive behaviors allows assessment of the level of cortical functioning and the normalcy of neurological development.

## Sensory Capacities

The newborn is capable of certain visual activities at birth, such as his eyes blinking at sudden increases in light intensity. The speed of his pupillary response corresponds to the intensity of the light. His eyes become increasingly sensitive to contrasts in brightness during the first few weeks of life, even though his retinal structures are incomplete and his optic nerve under-developed.

The newborn is sensitive to some aspects of sound within the first few hours after birth; experiments have shown that the cortex functions to some degree from the first day of life. The very young infant can discriminate differences between sounds and between differences in pitch, which indicates the auditory system is operating and well developed at a very early stage.

The neonate's olfactory system is developed well enough for the distinction of different odors. Experiments measuring the newborn's body activity and respiration brought about varied responses to a change in odor stimulus, indicating that the infant is able to discriminate among various odors at this very early stage.

There has been little research on the infant's sensitivity to taste. Most experiments that have been conducted on taste show the new infant has a relatively insensitive palate.

As discussed earlier, the newborn has the ability to regulate body temperature; the full-term healthy neonate can usually maintain normal body temperature when the room temperature is dropped slightly.

Limited research shows that with each day of life, the infant gains sensitivity to pain. There is a great deal of questioning as to whether it is ethical to subject young children to painful experiences because of the far-reaching negative effects such experiments may have.

## Behaviors

The newborn manifests a strong desire to sleep most of the day and night. Periods of wakefulness slowly increase with each day during the first few weeks of life. The newborn may also show quick mood changes, as he becomes easily irritated. He can shift from a state of great distress to a state of comfort quite abruptly. Of course, there may be great variability among babies in the area of irritability.

The newborn shows special sensitivity to sharp noises, bright lights and sudden movements. He is not able to focus on nearby objects until about five or six weeks, at which time the infant begins to focus on his moving hand. At about six weeks of life, the infant's motor control has increased markedly. He is able to follow moving objects more successfully, and he can hold his head upright for increasing periods of time; he can also control his arm and hand movements.

*Figure 5.* The newborn infant is not able to focus on nearby objects until about 5 or 6 weeks, at which time the infant begins to focus on his moving hand. (Photo by Jonathan Sutton)

## Physical Changes

The course of growth and development is unique for each individual. Although the ranges within which certain characteristics should become evident are wide, certain basic developmental patterns can be expected. During the first three years of life, the child's height, weight, and body proportions change drastically. The child's head size becomes increasingly more proportionate. Height and weight growth during the first year is far more rapid than during the second year of life, and changes are even less drastic during the third year of life. One must realize, however, that the child's height and weight can be influenced by many factors, including heredity, nutrition, general physical and emotional health, and environmental conditions.

The following tables, developed by Watson and Lowrey in the mid 1960s, are still among the most frequently used sources for charting the normal development of children.

The Development of the Young Child

## Weight and Height Percentile Table:
## Boys (Birth To Age 18)

| WEIGHT IN LB | | | WEIGHT IN KG | | | AGE | HEIGHT IN IN. | | | HEIGHT IN CM | | |
|---|---|---|---|---|---|---|---|---|---|---|---|---|
| 10% | 50% | 90% | 10% | 50% | 90% | | 10% | 50% | 90% | 10% | 50% | 90% |
| 6.3 | 7.5 | 9.1 | 2.86 | 3.4 | 4.13 | Birth | 18.9 | 19.9 | 21.0 | 48.1 | 50.6 | 53.3 |
| 8.5 | 10.0 | 11.5 | 3.8 | 4.6 | 5.2 | 1 mo | 20.2 | 21.2 | 22.2 | 50.4 | 53.0 | 55.5 |
| 10.0 | 11.5 | 13.2 | 4.6 | 5.2 | 6.0 | 2 mo | 21.5 | 22.5 | 23.5 | 53.7 | 56.0 | 60.0 |
| 11.1 | 12.6 | 14.5 | 5.03 | 5.72 | 6.58 | 3 mo | 22.8 | 23.8 | 24.7 | 57.8 | 60.4 | 62.8 |
| 12.5 | 14.0 | 16.2 | 5.6 | 6.3 | 7.3 | 4 mo | 23.7 | 24.7 | 25.7 | 60.5 | 62.0 | 65.2 |
| 13.7 | 15.0 | 17.7 | 6.2 | 7.0 | 8.0 | 5 mo | 24.5 | 25.5 | 26.5 | 61.8 | 65.0 | 67.3 |
| 14.8 | 16.7 | 19.2 | 6.71 | 7.58 | 8.71 | 6 mo | 25.2 | 26.1 | 27.3 | 63.9 | 66.4 | 69.3 |
| 17.8 | 20.0 | 22.9 | 8.07 | 9.07 | 10.39 | 9 mo | 27.0 | 28.0 | 29.2 | 68.6 | 71.2 | 74.2 |
| 19.6 | 22.2 | 25.4 | 8.89 | 10.7 | 11.52 | 12 mo | 28.5 | 29.6 | 30.7 | 72.4 | 75.2 | 78.1 |
| 22.3 | 25.2 | 29.0 | 10.12 | 11.43 | 13.15 | 18 mo | 31.0 | 32.2 | 33.5 | 78.8 | 81.8 | 85.0 |
| 24.7 | 27.7 | 31.9 | 11.2 | 12.56 | 14.47 | 2 yr | 33.1 | 34.4 | 35.9 | 84.2 | 87.5 | 91.1 |
| 26.6 | 30.0 | 34.5 | 12.07 | 13.61 | 15.65 | 2½ yr | 34.8 | 36.3 | 37.9 | 88.5 | 92.1 | 96.2 |
| 28.7 | 32.2 | 36.8 | 13.02 | 14.61 | 16.69 | 3 yr | 36.3 | 37.9 | 39.6 | 92.3 | 96.2 | 100.5 |
| 30.4 | 34.3 | 39.1 | 13.79 | 15.56 | 17.74 | 3½ yr | 37.8 | 39.3 | 41.1 | 96.0 | 99.8 | 104.5 |
| 32.1 | 36.4 | 41.4 | 14.56 | 16.51 | 18.78 | 4 yr | 39.1 | 40.7 | 42.7 | 99.3 | 103.4 | 108.5 |
| 33.8 | 38.4 | 43.9 | 15.33 | 17.42 | 19.91 | 4½ yr | 40.3 | 42.0 | 44.2 | 102.4 | 106.7 | 112.3 |
| 35.5 | 40.5 | 46.7 | 16.1 | 18.37 | 21.18 | 5 yr | 40.8 | 42.8 | 45.2 | 103.7 | 108.7 | 114.7 |
| 38.8 | 45.6 | 53.1 | 17.6 | 20.68 | 24.09 | 5½ yr | 42.6 | 45.0 | 47.3 | 108.3 | 114.4 | 120.1 |
| 40.9 | 48.3 | 56.4 | 18.55 | 21.91 | 25.58 | 6 yr | 43.8 | 46.3 | 48.6 | 111.12 | 117.5 | 123.5 |
| 43.4 | 51.2 | 60.4 | 19.69 | 23.22 | 27.4 | 6½ yr | 44.9 | 47.6 | 50.0 | 114.1 | 120.8 | 127.0 |
| 45.8 | 54.1 | 64.4 | 20.77 | 24.54 | 29.21 | 7 yr | 46.0 | 48.9 | 51.4 | 116.9 | 124.1 | 130.5 |
| 48.5 | 57.1 | 68.7 | 22.0 | 25.9 | 31.16 | 7½ yr | 47.2 | 50.0 | 52.7 | 120.0 | 127.1 | 133.9 |
| 51.2 | 60.1 | 73.0 | 23.22 | 27.26 | 33.11 | 8 yr | 48.5 | 51.2 | 54.0 | 123.1 | 130.0 | 137.3 |
| 53.8 | 63.1 | 77.0 | 24.4 | 28.62 | 34.93 | 8½ yr | 49.5 | 52.3 | 55.1 | 125.7 | 132.8 | 140.0 |
| 56.3 | 66.0 | 81.0 | 25.54 | 29.94 | 36.74 | 9 yr | 50.5 | 53.3 | 56.1 | 128.3 | 135.5 | 142.6 |
| 58.7 | 69.0 | 85.5 | 26.63 | 31.3 | 38.78 | 9½ yr | 51.4 | 54.3 | 57.1 | 130.6 | 137.9 | 145.1 |
| 61.1 | 71.9 | 89.9 | 27.71 | 32.61 | 40.78 | 10 yr | 52.3 | 55.2 | 58.1 | 132.8 | 140.3 | 147.5 |
| 63.7 | 74.8 | 94.6 | 28.89 | 33.93 | 42.91 | 10½ yr | 53.2 | 56.0 | 58.9 | 135.1 | 142.3 | 149.7 |
| 66.3 | 77.6 | 99.3 | 30.07 | 35.2 | 45.04 | 11 yr | 54.0 | 56.8 | 59.8 | 137.3 | 144.2 | 151.8 |
| 69.2 | 81.0 | 104.5 | 31.39 | 36.74 | 47.4 | 11½ yr | 55.0 | 57.8 | 60.9 | 139.8 | 146.9 | 154.8 |
| 72.0 | 84.4 | 109.6 | 32.66 | 38.28 | 49.71 | 12 yr | 56.1 | 58.9 | 62.2 | 142.4 | 149.6 | 157.9 |
| 74.6 | 88.7 | 116.4 | 33.84 | 40.23 | 52.8 | 12½ yr | 56.9 | 60.0 | 63.6 | 144.5 | 152.3 | 161.6 |
| 77.1 | 93.0 | 123.2 | 34.97 | 42.18 | 55.88 | 13 yr | 57.7 | 61.0 | 65.1 | 146.6 | 155.0 | 165.3 |
| 82.2 | 100.3 | 130.1 | 37.29 | 45.5 | 59.01 | 13½ yr | 58.8 | 62.6 | 66.5 | 149.4 | 158.9 | 168.9 |
| 87.2 | 107.6 | 136.9 | 39.55 | 48.81 | 62.1 | 14 yr | 59.9 | 64.0 | 67.9 | 152.1 | 162.7 | 172.4 |
| 93.3 | 113.9 | 142.4 | 43.32 | 51.66 | 64.59 | 14½ yr | 61.0 | 65.1 | 68.7 | 155.0 | 165.3 | 174.6 |
| 99.4 | 120.1 | 147.8 | 45.09 | 54.48 | 67.04 | 15 yr | 62.1 | 66.1 | 69.6 | 157.8 | 167.8 | 176.7 |
| 105.2 | 124.9 | 152.6 | 47.72 | 56.65 | 69.22 | 15½ yr | 63.1 | 66.8 | 70.2 | 160.3 | 169.7 | 178.2 |
| 111.0 | 129.7 | 157.3 | 50.35 | 58.83 | 71.35 | 16 yr | 64.1 | 67.8 | 70.7 | 162.8 | 171.6 | 179.7 |
| 114.3 | 133.0 | 161.0 | 51.85 | 60.33 | 73.03 | 16½ yr | 64.6 | 68.0 | 71.1 | 164.2 | 172.7 | 180.7 |
| 117.5 | 136.2 | 164.6 | 53.3 | 61.78 | 74.66 | 17 yr | 65.2 | 68.4 | 71.5 | 165.5 | 173.7 | 181.6 |
| 118.8 | 137.6 | 166.8 | 53.89 | 62.41 | 75.66 | 17½ yr | 65.3 | 68.5 | 71.6 | 165.9 | 174.1 | 182.0 |
| 120.0 | 139.0 | 169.0 | 54.43 | 63.05 | 76.66 | 18 yr | 65.5 | 68.7 | 71.8 | 166.3 | 174.5 | 182.4 |

## Weight and Height Percentile Table:
## Girls (Birth To Age 18)

| WEIGHT IN LB | | | WEIGHT IN KG | | | AGE | HEIGHT IN IN. | | | HEIGHT IN CM | | |
|---|---|---|---|---|---|---|---|---|---|---|---|---|
| 10% | 50% | 90% | 10% | 50% | 90% | | 10% | 50% | 90% | 10% | 50% | 90% |
| 6.2 | 7.4 | 8.6 | 2.81 | 3.36 | 3.9 | Birth | 18.8 | 19.8 | 20.4 | 47.8 | 50.2 | 51.0 |
| 8.0 | 9.7 | 11.0 | 3.3 | 4.2 | 5.0 | 1 mo | 20.2 | 21.0 | 22.0 | 50.4 | 52.8 | 55.0 |
| 9.5 | 11.0 | 12.5 | 4.1 | 5.0 | 5.8 | 2 mo | 21.5 | 22.2 | 23.2 | 53.7 | 55.5 | 59.6 |
| 10.7 | 12.4 | 14.0 | 4.85 | 5.62 | 6.35 | 3 mo | 22.4 | 23.4 | 24.3 | 56.9 | 59.5 | 61.7 |
| 12.0 | 13.7 | 15.5 | 5.3 | 6.2 | 7.2 | 4 mo | 23.2 | 24.2 | 25.2 | 59.6 | 61.0 | 64.8 |
| 13.0 | 14.7 | 17.0 | 5.9 | 6.8 | 7.7 | 5 mo | 24.0 | 25.0 | 26.0 | 60.7 | 64.2 | 67.0 |
| 14.1 | 16.0 | 18.6 | 6.4 | 7.26 | 8.44 | 6 mo | 24.6 | 25.7 | 26.7 | 62.5 | 65.2 | 67.8 |
| 16.6 | 19.2 | 22.4 | 7.53 | 8.71 | 10.16 | 9 mo | 26.4 | 27.6 | 28.7 | 67.0 | 70.1 | 72.9 |
| 18.4 | 21.5 | 24.8 | 8.35 | 9.75 | 11.25 | 12 mo | 27.8 | 29.2 | 30.3 | 70.6 | 74.2 | 77.1 |
| 21.2 | 24.5 | 28.3 | 9.62 | 11.11 | 12.84 | 18 mo | 30.2 | 31.8 | 33.3 | 76.8 | 80.9 | 84.5 |
| 23.5 | 27.1 | 31.7 | 10.66 | 12.29 | 14.38 | 2 yr | 32.3 | 34.1 | 35.8 | 82.0 | 86.6 | 91.0 |
| 25.5 | 29.6 | 34.6 | 11.57 | 13.43 | 15.69 | 2½ yr | 34.0 | 36.0 | 37.9 | 86.3 | 91.4 | 96.4 |
| 27.6 | 31.8 | 37.4 | 12.52 | 14.42 | 16.96 | 3 yr | 35.6 | 37.7 | 39.8 | 90.5 | 95.7 | 101.1 |
| 29.5 | 33.9 | 40.4 | 13.98 | 15.38 | 18.33 | 3½ yr | 37.1 | 39.2 | 41.5 | 94.2 | 99.5 | 105.4 |
| 31.2 | 36.2 | 43.5 | 14.15 | 16.42 | 19.73 | 4 yr | 38.4 | 40.6 | 43.1 | 97.6 | 103.2 | 109.6 |
| 32.9 | 38.5 | 46.7 | 14.92 | 17.46 | 21.18 | 4½ yr | 39.7 | 42.0 | 44.7 | 100.9 | 106.8 | 113.5 |
| 34.8 | 40.5 | 49.2 | 15.79 | 18.37 | 22.32 | 5 yr | 40.5 | 42.9 | 45.4 | 103.0 | 109.1 | 115.4 |
| 38.0 | 44.0 | 51.2 | 17.24 | 19.96 | 23.22 | 5½ yr | 42.4 | 44.4 | 46.8 | 107.8 | 112.8 | 118.9 |
| 39.6 | 46.5 | 54.2 | 17.96 | 21.09 | 24.58 | 6 yr | 43.5 | 45.6 | 48.1 | 110.6 | 115.9 | 122.3 |
| 42.2 | 49.4 | 57.7 | 19.14 | 22.41 | 26.17 | 6½ yr | 44.8 | 46.9 | 49.4 | 113.7 | 119.1 | 125.6 |
| 44.5 | 52.2 | 61.2 | 20.19 | 23.68 | 27.76 | 7 yr | 46.0 | 48.1 | 50.7 | 116.8 | 122.3 | 128.9 |
| 46.6 | 55.2 | 65.6 | 21.14 | 25.04 | 29.76 | 7½ yr | 47.0 | 49.3 | 51.9 | 119.5 | 125.2 | 131.8 |
| 48.6 | 58.1 | 69.9 | 22.04 | 26.35 | 31.71 | 8 yr | 48.1 | 50.4 | 53.0 | 122.1 | 128.0 | 134.6 |
| 50.6 | 61.0 | 74.5 | 22.95 | 27.67 | 33.79 | 8½ yr | 49.0 | 51.4 | 54.1 | 124.6 | 130.5 | 137.5 |
| 52.6 | 63.8 | 79.1 | 23.86 | 28.94 | 35.88 | 9 yr | 50.0 | 52.3 | 55.3 | 127.0 | 132.9 | 140.4 |
| 54.9 | 67.1 | 84.4 | 24.9 | 30.44 | 38.28 | 9½ yr | 50.9 | 53.5 | 56.4 | 129.4 | 135.8 | 143.2 |
| 57.1 | 70.3 | 89.7 | 25.9 | 31.89 | 40.69 | 10 yr | 51.8 | 54.6 | 57.5 | 131.7 | 138.6 | 146.0 |
| 59.9 | 74.6 | 95.1 | 27.17 | 33.79 | 43.14 | 10½ yr | 52.9 | 55.8 | 58.9 | 134.4 | 141.7 | 149.7 |
| 62.6 | 78.8 | 100.4 | 28.4 | 35.74 | 45.54 | 11 yr | 53.9 | 57.0 | 60.4 | 137.0 | 144.7 | 153.4 |
| 66.1 | 83.2 | 106.0 | 29.98 | 37.74 | 48.08 | 11½ yr | 55.0 | 58.3 | 61.8 | 139.8 | 148.1 | 157.0 |
| 69.5 | 87.6 | 111.5 | 31.52 | 39.74 | 50.58 | 12 yr | 56.1 | 59.8 | 63.2 | 142.6 | 151.9 | 160.6 |
| 74.7 | 93.4 | 118.0 | 33.88 | 42.37 | 53.52 | 12½ yr | 57.4 | 60.7 | 64.0 | 145.9 | 154.3 | 162.7 |
| 79.9 | 99.1 | 124.5 | 36.24 | 44.95 | 56.47 | 13 yr | 58.7 | 61.8 | 64.9 | 149.1 | 157.1 | 164.8 |
| 85.5 | 103.7 | 128.9 | 38.78 | 47.04 | 58.47 | 13½ yr | 59.5 | 62.4 | 65.3 | 151.1 | 158.4 | 165.9 |
| 91.0 | 108.4 | 133.3 | 41.28 | 49.17 | 60.46 | 14 yr | 60.2 | 62.8 | 65.7 | 153.0 | 159.6 | 167.0 |
| 94.2 | 111.10 | 135.7 | 42.73 | 50.35 | 61.55 | 14½ yr | 60.7 | 63.1 | 66.0 | 154.1 | 160.4 | 167.6 |
| 97.4 | 113.5 | 138.1 | 44.18 | 51.48 | 62.64 | 15 yr | 61.1 | 63.4 | 66.2 | 155.2 | 161.1 | 168.1 |
| 99.2 | 115.3 | 139.6 | 45.0 | 52.3 | 63.32 | 15½ yr | 61.3 | 63.7 | 66.4 | 155.7 | 161.7 | 168.6 |
| 100.9 | 117.0 | 141.1 | 45.77 | 53.07 | 64.0 | 16 yr | 61.5 | 63.9 | 66.5 | 156.1 | 162.2 | 169.0 |
| 101.9 | 118.1 | 142.2 | 46.22 | 53.57 | 64.5 | 16½ yr | 61.5 | 63.9 | 66.6 | 156.2 | 162.4 | 169.2 |
| 102.8 | 119.1 | 143.3 | 46.63 | 54.02 | 65.0 | 17 yr | 61.5 | 64.0 | 66.7 | 156.3 | 162.5 | 169.4 |
| 103.2 | 119.5 | 143.9 | 46.81 | 54.2 | 65.27 | 17½ yr | 61.5 | 64.0 | 66.7 | 156.3 | 162.5 | 169.4 |
| 103.5 | 119.9 | 144.5 | 46.95 | 54.39 | 65.54 | 18 yr | 61.5 | 64.0 | 66.7 | 156.3 | 162.5 | 169.4 |

## Motor Development

Maturation, primarily, and environment, secondarily, contribute to early motor development. Maturity of the cerebellum between the age of six months and a year and one half enhances the child's motor control. The child naturally performs a new motor behavior and continues to practice it until achieving mastery. When mastery of one motor activity has been achieved, the child progresses to the next skill level. As with Jean Piaget's stages of intellectual development, the child cannot move on to the next level of development until he has mastered the activities of the previous stage. The child's age may vary, but the sequence of skills is constant for all babies.

In the following chart the rate of motor development from birth through the first year is illustrated. When reading this chart, assume that the child is also capable of the behaviors that are delineated in each preceding month. Remember that the rate of development of these behaviors is very flexible.

| | |
|---|---|
| Newly born infant | Time spent awake and asleep are hard to differentiate.<br>Inconsistent motor behaviors.<br>Evidences many reflexive behaviors.<br>Head sags when unsupported.<br>Frequently moves head when placed on back.<br>Changes positions often. |
| First month | Fixates on objects for long periods of time.<br>Is still unable to support head when held in an upright position. |
| Second month | Is now able to hold head erect when held.<br>Raises chest when lying flat. |
| Third month | Is able to turn from side to side when lying flat. |
| Fourth month | Opens and closes hands.<br>Observes objects placed in own hand.<br>Is able to sit with support.<br>Plays and chews hands and clothing. |
| Fifth month | Is able to sit with minimal support.<br>Reaches for and grasps objects.<br>Moves from back to chosen side without help. |
| Sixth month | Is able to transfer objects between hands.<br>Willingly drops one object when given another.<br>Uses own hands to support sitting positions. |
| Seventh month | Is able to sit alone.<br>Begins attempts to crawl. |

| | |
|---|---|
| Eighth month | Crawls. |
| | Attempts to stand. |
| Ninth-Tenth month | Begins to stack toys (blocks). |
| Eleventh-Twelfth month | Stands alone. |
| | Walks with some help. |

## The Toddler

The young child begins to walk alone shortly after he is able to stand alone. As we think of children we know we often think of their similarities as well as of their differences. Most of what we know about children suggests that both the chronology and style of the child's motor development are affected by *heredity* and *environment*.

In an attempt to measure the effect of environment, Dennis (1960) studied the motor development patterns of institutionalized children. In two of the institutions he visited, where the children exhibited extremely retarded motor behaviors, he found:

1. Overworked, tired, unsympathetic child attendants.
2. Uncuddled children.
3. Young infants and children who spent much time lying in bed.
4. Infants eating from propped up bottles.
5. Infants never placed on their stomachs.
6. Infants never removed from their beds until they could sit unsupported.
7. No toys.
8. No play equipment or child-size furniture for toddlers.

When these infants were taken from their cribs, they remained in a sitting position and scooted around the floor instead of creeping. This occurred because they had never been placed on their stomachs and had no experience raising their heads or putting their arms and legs under their bodies. Fortunately, their motor retardation was only temporary. When they were removed from the unstimulating environment, their motor skills developed normally.

Dennis (1960) also found that children who lived in institutions experienced normal patterns of motor development if they were

1. Fed in the attendant's arms.
2. Talked to by the attendants.
3. Played with by the attendants.
4. Placed on their stomachs.
5. Propped in sitting positions.
6. Given many toys.

The following chart cites additive motor development behaviors of the toddler aged 13 to 36 months.

| | |
|---|---|
| Thirteenth-Fourteenth month | Is able to climb stairs, sit down, and stand alone. |
| Fifteenth month | Is able to walk alone. |
| Sixteenth-Eighteenth month | Is able to build towers of objects. Runs clumsily. Pushes toys. |
| Eighteenth-Twenty-fourth month | Kicks balls. Plays alone. Runs well. Is able to jump 10 to 12 inches high. Is able to turn the individual pages of a book. Can walk up and down stairs. |
| Twenty-fifth to Thirty-second month | Can walk on tiptoes. Is able to jump from chairs and beds. Has good hand coordination. |
| Thirty-third to Thirty-sixth month | Is able to ride a tricycle. Can stand on one foot. Draws pictures. Can pour from a pitcher. Can manipulate objects. Can button and unbutton clothing. |

Although the rate of development of these behaviors can only be approximated, they are believed to be consistent for the majority of children. Many parents often wonder if motor development can be accelerated. Studies by Gesell (1929) and Zelazo, Zelazo, and Kolb (1972) do suggest that there is a critical period for the development of each motor behavior, but it can be accelerated by environmental factors.

## The Three- to Six- Going on Seven-Year-Olds

By the time young children reach three years of age, their physical growth is no longer so rapid. Height and weight increases are slow but steady. Between the ages of three and five the young child begins to develop more adult-like proportions; the potbelly disappears. Simultaneous development of the muscular and nervous systems also occurs in the three- to six-year-old. Nutrition affects the growth and development of the young child.

Three- and four-year-olds are cute to observe because they still have many of their "baby" actions as they are developing older characteristics. They have developed the ability to walk speedily and steadily, to climb to sometimes frightening heights, to ride tricycles, and to run and jump.

It may appear that the three- to six-year-old never stops to rest, but in reality they do take frequent rests in squatting, sitting, and prone positions. Developing children require frequent rest periods.

During this span of development, children often exhibit dual-handedness. The observance of a child using his hands interchangeably is often a source of concern to parents and some preschool teachers. Fortunately, there is no need for such alarm. The child should be free to experiment with both hands and be gently guided in using the one for which he clearly shows a preference.

A great deal of personal independence occurs between the ages of two and four. The four-year-old is extremely capable of taking full responsibility for his toilet needs and also for feeding himself. Such independence should be supported by the adults in the environment.

*Figure 6.* The young child develops the ability to walk speedily and steadily and to climb to sometimes frightening heights. (Photo by Linda Lungren)

The fifth year appears to be a much more stable one than the sixth year. The five-year-old is cooperative, supportive, and anxious to learn and to try many new things. The six-year-old appears to be in a period of transition, often experiencing mood changes. The six-year-old is often much more quarrelsome than the five-year-old.

Five- and six-year-olds grow approximately two to three inches and gain three to six pounds per year. They are often serious and at times appear to be more mature than their young age allows. The toothless grin of the six-year-old helps the adult remember how very young the child is.

The large body muscles of the five- and six-year-old are usually better developed than those of their hands and fingers. Small-muscle activities such as drawing, sewing, and writing are much harder for them to perform than running, jumping, and climbing activities that involve large muscles.

### The Seven- and Eight-Year-Old

The seventh year is one of relative stability. The physical growth rate of the seven- and eight-year-old is relatively small. At this age children appear to be always in a hurry. Their hands grow larger and their arms lengthen. Their eyes develop their near vision, and they have acquired most of their permanent teeth. They are generally noisy and happy-go-lucky. Although the seven- and eight-year-olds are subject to childhood diseases, they are fairly sturdy and healthy. Small-muscle activities are easier for the child during his seventh and eighth years than they were during his earlier years.

The end of the eighth year may involve a period of transition for the child; his body is now strong and secure. Because he sees himself moving gracefully toward middle childhood, he often resents any encounters in which he must assume a "babyish" role. Eight-year-olds are willing to participate as team members because interest in independent activities is at a minimum during this period of development. They enjoy being part of the group. They are at an age when interaction is fun. They certainly can no longer be thought of as babies. They are strong and sensitive as they await adolescence.

### COGNITIVE DEVELOPMENT

> Mind. . . is the power to understand things in terms
> of the use made of them.
>
> *Dewey*

As one attempts to discuss or measure the most interesting concepts of life (love, creativity, cognition), it becomes difficult to define and formulate all possible dimensions of the topic but still maintain its vast complexity. As we explore the concept of the development of cognition in the young child, we will attempt to maintain flexibility in definition and formulation in an attempt to avoid limitation of meaning.

## A Workable Definition of the Cognitive System

A categorization of the existing literature related to the topic of the human cognitive system would result in the following theories:

1. Behavioristic theory, which views the cognitive system as a structured network of internal/external stimulus-response interactions.

2. Psychoanalytic theory, which views the structure and function of the id, ego, and super-ego.

3. Psychometric theory, which views the organization and structure of intelligence in terms of the variables measured by a standardized IQ test.

4. Structuralistic-organismic theory, which views the development of the cognitive system through its interaction with the environment.

5. Information-processing theory, which views the cognitive system as a complex device with the capabilities of dealing with information in adaptive ways.

The view of cognition that we shall explore in this text will be a combination of both the structuralistic-organismic theory and the information-processing theory.

## The Structuralistic-Organismic Theory of Cognition

The structuralistic-organismic theory of cognitive development draws heavily on the works of Piaget, which suggest that an individual is a very active participant in cognitive interchanges with his environment. Through Piaget's assimilation-accommodation model of cognitive functioning, we are able to view the learner as a critical thinker who screens and interprets information from his environment in an attempt to develop and extend his own world knowledge. As one develops the structure of his world knowledge, he must refine his experiences to be succinct with the parameters of his previously developed cognitive framework. Given this framework, we can view the mind as an internal organism with the potential to build knowledge structures by interpreting, refining, and reorganizing external data. This process of adapting external stimuli to the parameters of one's already existing internal mental constructs is referred to by Piaget as *assimilation*. *Accommodation* refers to the mental process of adapting the internal cognitive structures to the external stimuli.

When the individual encounters something new that does not fit his existing cognitive structure, he *accommodates* the new by modifying the present structure. When the individual internalizes the change so that he can handle the new experience with ease as a part of his own life space, he has been successful at *assimilating* the new. One can understand the accommodation/assimilation process by a single term—*adaptation*. In dealing with children, ample time must be provided for the accommodation process. Ginsburg and

Opper give a prime example of infant accommodation or adaptation.

> Suppose an infant of 4 months is presented with a rattle. He has never before had the opportunity to play with rattles or similar toys. The rattle, then, is a feature of the environment to which he needs to adapt. His subsequent behavior reveals the tendencies of assimilation and accommodation. The infant tries to grasp the rattle. In order to do this successfully he must accommodate in more ways than are immediately apparent. First, he must accommodate his visual activities to perceive the rattle correctly; then he must reach out and accommodate his movements to the distance between himself and the rattle; in grasping the rattle he must adjust his fingers to its shape; and in lifting the rattle he must accommodate his muscular exertion to its weight. In sum, the grasping of the rattle involves a series of acts of accommodation, or modifications of the infant's behavioral structures to suit the demands of the environment. (Ginsburg and Opper, 1969, p. 19.)

As seen from the Ginsburg and Opper quote, a learner can simultaneously accommodate to a particular characteristic of an object and assimilate the object's characteristics to his previously developed cognitive structures. Therefore, in any cognitive/environmental encounter, the processes of assimilation and accommodation are equally important and their occurrence must be viewed as being mutually dependent.

The following example clearly illustrates Piaget's concept of assimilation/accommodation.

> In the situation we are imagining, a young child is playing with his toy boats in the bathtub and suddenly notices in the corner of the soap dish a tiny fragment of wood from a broken pencil. He picks it up, and after some deliberation (he has sailed many a boat, but nary a wood chip), gingerly places it in the water. Upon discovering that it floats, he adds it to his armada, and emerges from his bath some time later a wiser as well as a cleaner child. The question is, in what way wiser, and through what sorts of wisdom-building (cognitive-developmental) processes?
>
> Let us credit him, at the beginning of the bath, with a certain organized body of knowledge and certain abilities concerning the concrete, functional properties of the main entities in the situation (toy boats, small, nondescript objects, and water). He knows much about their characteristic look and feel and also something of their characteristic reactions to his actions upon them. We could say that he has already achieved a certain level of cognitive development with respect to this microdomain of his everyday world and consequently, in Piaget's terms, he assimilates it and accommodates to it in specific ways that faithfully reflect this cognitive-developmental level. As a result of the new things he did and observed during this particular bath, however, that level will have changed ever so slightly, and consequently his future assimilations and accommodations within that microdomain will also have changed ever so slightly.
>
> Let us suppose he has discovered (accommodation) some things he did not know before about what little pieces of wood can and cannot do (float rather than sink, make only a tiny splash when dropped in water, fail to move a big toy boat when they bump into it) and about what one can and cannot do with them (sail them, make them bob to the surface by holding them under water and then letting go, give them rides on top of other toy boats). Additionally, during this process of "minidevelopment," the content and structure of his mind and its capacity to construe and interpret this microdomain (assimilation) has also altered slightly. For example, his functional class of

boat-like entities has now generalized to include at least certain small lightweight objects that do not closely resemble the more typical and familiar instances of this class (e.g., his toy boats). Subsequently, this small change in conceptual structure may permit him to construe (assimilate) still other kinds of objects as novel candidates for boat play. Moreover, the category of boat-like things may now be functionally subclassified for him into big, strong ones and small, weak ones, whereas it may previously have been a more or less homogenous, undifferential class.

Thus, in the course of trying to accommodate to some hitherto unknown functional properties of a relatively unfamiliar sort of object, and of trying to assimilate the object and its properties to existing concepts and skills (trying to interpret them, make sense out of them, test out one's repertoire of actions upon them) the child's mind has stretched just a little, and this stretching in turn broadens slightly his future assimilatory and accommodatory possibilities. By repeated assimilation of and accommodation to a given milieu, the cognitive system evolves slightly, which makes possible somewhat novel and different assimilations and accommodations, with these latter changes producing further small increments of mental growth.

(Flavell, 1977, pp. 9–10)

## The Information-Processing Theory of Cognition

In an attempt to develop a basic understanding of the theory of information processing, you may wish to think of the human mind or information processor as being similar in capability to its electronic counterpart, the computer. Both the human and mechanical information processors are capable of receiving many pieces of information, performing certain operations of the information, storing in memory the results of these operations, altering the contents of the memory when new information is relevant, and reporting the results of the process in a manner that is defined by the user. The user of the human information processor may be *you*, the early childhood education teacher, or any other human being.

> If we examine the fine structure of thought as it shows up in the protocols of human problem solving, we discover that even routine accomplishments appear to involve many steps integrated into complex sequences. Information-processing theories encourage us to investigate in detail the systems of cognitive structures, elementary psychological processes, and higher-order strategies it seems necessary to postulate to account for the behaviors and achievements we observe . . . . the information-processing approach to the study of man follows his purposes and plans as he seeks, does, and creates things, manipulating objects and information to attain his ends.

(Reitman, 1965, pp. 1–2)

Whereas the rules and operations that govern computer information processing are determined by a computer programmer, the rules and operations that govern the human information processor are not definitively known. Many psychologists (Trabasso, 1972; Farnham, 1972; Rumelhart, 1976; Buhl, 1976) offer insights into this process. We believe the insights of Piaget have offered considerable information to this understanding.

## Stages of Intellectual Development

The first stage of intellectual development occurs even before the development of formalized language patterns. This stage is commonly referred to by Piaget (1952) as the *sensorimotor* stage of development. During this stage the young child develops a system or schemata for organizing the information that is being gained through the senses. It is also during this stage of development that the child develops and refines his responses to environmental stimuli.

The sensorimotor stage of development, which lasts from birth until around two years of age, has been described by Baldwin as:

1. The child's ability to coordinate and integrate information from the five senses (sight, hearing, touch, taste, and smell) to understand that the information received from different senses related to the same object rather than to different, unrelated ones.
2. The child's capacity to recognize that the world is a permanent place, whose existence does not depend on the child's perceiving it. This is the schema of the permanent object.
3. The child's ability to exhibit goal-directed behavior. When the child wants something, he is able to perform several different actions, even to construct new actions never before attempted, to get his way. His actions in this period are very concrete, but limited.

(Baldwin 1968, p. 190)

Piaget (1952) offers insights into this stage of development by discussing the "schema of the permanent object." In the early substages of the sensorimotor stage of development, the child does not remember an object that has been taken away; therefore, the child has no schema of a permanent object. When the child begins to search for objects that have been removed from his vision, he has developed a schema of the permanent object. The development of this schema is basic to the child's understanding of space, time, and causality. Once the child has developed this schema, he is able to understand that objects in his environment are separate from his person.

The following chart delineates the substages of the sensorimotor stage of cognitive development.

### Substages of the Sensorimotor Stage of Cognitive Development
### (0 to 24 months)

| Name of Substage | Age | Characteristics |
| --- | --- | --- |
| Stage 1: Reflexes | 0–1 Month | Innate behaviors become adaptive; e.g., sucking which is innate is adapted for survival. |
| | | Intelligent adaptive behaviors formulate the basis for later activity; e.g., someday the child will secure his own nourishment. |

| | | |
|---|---|---|
| Stage 2:  Adaptation of Innate Abilities to Environment | 0–4 Months | Sucking is innate. By accident the child sucks his hand and fingers. It tastes good. The child adapts to his environment and now sucks for fun as well as nourishment.<br><br>The child reaches and grasps for everything and everyone he sees or hears. He attempts to coordinate vision and grasping.<br><br>The child has not yet developed object permanence. Anything that he cannot see, feel, smell, taste, or hear does not exist. |
| Stage 3:  Refined Adaptation | 4–8 Months | The child repeats behaviors to observe their results. The child is no longer totally focused on his own body.<br><br>An experiment conducted by Piaget with his son suggests that the schema of the permanent object has not been developed by this age. At the time of his feeding I show him the bottle, he extends his hand to take it, but, at that moment, I hide it behind my arm. If he sees one end sticking out, he kicks and screams and gives every indication of wanting to have it. If, however, the bottle is completely hidden and nothing sticks out, he stops crying and acts for all we know as if the bottle no longer existed, as if it had been dissolved and absorbed into my arm. (Piaget, 1968) |
| Stage 4:  Accommodating New Experiences | 8–12 Months | The young child now begins to develop the ability to solve new problems. At 0;8 Jacqueline tries to grasp her celluloid duck but I also grasp it at the same time she does. Then she firmly holds the toy in her right hand and pushes my hand away with her left. I repeat the experiment by grasping only the end of the duck's tail; she again pushes my hand away. (Piaget, 1952, p. 219)<br><br>It is during this substage that the child begins to develop the schema of the permanent object. During this substage children begin to search for objects that they see being hidden. |

Stage 5:
Experimenting
and Discovering

12–18 Months   During this substage of development the
child becomes an active participant in the
environment. She now alters the actions
which she has accidently discovered. She
experiments in order to gain new insights.
At 1;2 Jacqueline holds in her hands an
object which is new to her: a round, flat
box which she turns all over, shakes, rubs
against the bassinet, etc. She lets it go and
tries to pick it up. But she only succeeds
in touching it with her index finger, without grasping it. She nevertheless makes an
attempt and presses on the edge. The box
then tilts up and falls again. Jacqueline,
very much interested in this fortuitous
result, immediately applies herself to
studying it. . . . This discovery, instead
of giving rise to a simple circular reaction,
is at once extended to "experiments in
order to see." (Piaget, 1952, p. 272)

During this stage of development the
child can easily follow a series of object
displacements; however, she is still unable
to conceptualize movement that she does
not see.

---

Stage 6: Cognitive
Inventions

18–24 Months   The child fully develops object permanence during this substage. She is able to
search for objects which she did not see
being hidden. She is not able to mentally
picture events and follow their sequence.
She is no longer dependent on trial-error
tests to solve problems. She also begins to
imitate the behavior of those around her.

Here begins the experiment which we want
to emphasize. I put the chain back into
the box, an empty matchbox, and reduce
the opening to 3 mm. It is understood
that Lucienne is not aware of the functioning of the opening and closing of the
matchbox and has not seen me prepare
the experiment. She only possesses the
two preceding schemata: turning the box
over in order to empty it of its contents,
and sliding her finger into the slit to make
the chain come out. It is, of course, this
last procedure that she tries first. She
puts her finger inside and gropes to reach
the chain, but fails completely. A pause

follows during which Lucienne manifests a very curious reaction, bearing witness not only to the fact that she tries to think out the situation and to represent to herself through mental combination the operation to be performed, but also to the role played by imitation in the genesis of representations. Lucienne mimics the widening of the slit.

She looks at the slit with great attention; then, several times in succession, she opens and shuts her mouth, at first slightly, then wider and wider. . . . The attempt at representation which she thus furnishes is expressed plastically, that is to say, due to inability to think out the situation in words of clear visual images, she uses a simple motor indication as "signifies" or symbol. Luciene, by opening her mouth, thus expresses, or even reflects her desire to enlarge the opening of the box. This schema of imitation, with which she is familiar constitutes for her the means of thinking out the situation." (Piaget, 1952, pp. 337-338)

The origin of these substages of development may be attributed to the research of Piaget with his children. However, subsequent studies by others (Uzgiris, 1972; Gratch and Landers, 1971) have reaffirmed his findings.

During these substages of sensorimotor development the infant develops *social cognition* as well as *psychological cognition.*

In the first stage of the ego (i.e., during infancy) the problem is to distinguish self from nonself. This stage can be divided into the presocial and the symbiotic stages. In the presocial or autistic stage, animate and inanimate parts of the environment are not distinguished. In the symbiotic stage the child has a strong relation to his mother (or surrogate) and is able to distinguish mother from environment, but self is not clearly distinguished from mother. The ego can hardly be said to exist prior to the end of this stage. Loevinger, 1966, p. 198)

Social development occurs as the child discovers both his physical and psychological dimensions. The child's social interactions involve attachments to objects and significant others in the environment.

The basic tenet is that any behavior of a child is a function of the level of cognitive development he has achieved. An illustrative derivation of this principal applied to attachment is that: a child cannot develop a specific attachment until he can both discriminate and recognize an individual person. Even after an infant can do these things, however, he still may not know that the person continues to exist when out of sight. The development of object constancy [again, the Piagetian object concept is meant] should introduce a new phase of attachment behavior, for example, signaling [e.g., crying for, calling] when the attachment figure is not in view. When time concepts begin to be mastered, this should mean both that the child will begin to respond to signs of the mother's impending departure (showing anticipatory protest), and that he will be able to anticipate her return during an absence and derive some comfort thereby. Reactions to death of an attachment figure should vary greatly with the age of the child, depending on the level of understanding of the permanence of death.

(Maccoby and Masters, 1970, p. 91)

Social behavior and cognitive growth mediate each other throughout the development of the human being. The rationale for such occurrences is a topic of great fascination to many educators.

The general state of trust . . . implies not only that one has learned to rely on the sameness and continuity of the outer providers, but also that one may trust oneself and the capacity of one's own organs to cope with urges; and that one is able to consider oneself trustworthy enough so that the providers will not need to be on guard lest they be nipped.                                                         (Erikson, 1950, p. 248)

### The Two- to Six-Year Old

The cognitive functioning of the children within this age span allows for a wide range of contrast. Piaget (1952) refers to the mental development of this age of child as *preoperational*. He suggest that this stage of development begins around the age of two and lasts until the child is approximately seven years of age.

This period of development is characterized by early *symbolic functioning*. The child is able to use symbols to represent the concrete objects, places, and people that were part of his sensorimotor development. The child is able to "think about" people, places, and objects that are not in immediate contact with his five senses.

**Time and Space.**   The preoperational child develops a more workable concept of time and space. He is able to divide life happenings into yesterday, today, and tomorrow. He has a rudimentary understanding of "near," "far," "large", and "small." He can classify objects into meaningful categories and is easily able to understand causation.

**Seriation.**   Children have an understanding of serial relationships when they are able to use one or more dimensions to sequentially arrange objects. In an attempt to measure this development in the preoperational child, Piaget (1952) gave ten sticks of various sizes to children and asked them to select the tallest and shortest sticks. Most children were able to complete this task by the time they were four or five years old. Next, Piaget arranged the sticks in ascending size.

*Figure 7.* Children have an understanding of serial relationships when they are able to use one or more dimensions to sequentially arrange objects. (Photo by Linda Lungren)

After the children looked at this arrangement, Piaget handed the children the ten sticks and asked them to develop a similar arrangement. Children between the ages of five and six were able to accomplish this task, whereas four- to five-year-olds designed arrangements according to only the top halves of the sticks.

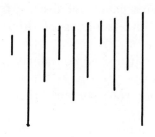

Three-year-olds and some four-year-olds also designed multiple sets.

The five- and six-year-olds who successfully completed the second task and some seven-year-olds were shown the following arrangement

and were asked to insert the missing sticks. The six- and seven-year-olds were able to complete this task but the five-year-olds had much more difficulty. The total relational concept needed to complete a seriation task is not complete until six or seven years of age.

**Classification.**  By the end of the preoperational stage the child becomes very adept at perceiving object characteristics and putting them into categories according to color, size, shape, or other discriminating dimensions. The two and a half- to four and a half-year-old usually disregards individual object characteristics and arranges objects in a straight line or circle. Between the ages four and a half to six and a half years, children begin to sort objects according to more discriminating characteristics. By the time the child is seven or eight years of age he is considered by Piaget to be in the *concrete operational* stage of development, during which time he classifies objects according to several dimensions. However, during the preoperational stage the child has difficulty seeing the relationship between major categories and their subcategories.

### Six and a half- to Eight-Year-Old

Piaget maintains the child becomes *operational* between the ages of five and seven. He is able to engage in abstract mental activities. He is in a stage of development commonly referred to as *concrete operations*. During this stage of development the child is less egocentric. He begins to view himself as part of a larger environment rather than separate and distinct from it.

Piaget measures the child's understanding of the conservation of liquid as follows:

1. The child is shown two equal-sized containers both filled with an equal amount of water.

2. The child is asked if both containers are the same size and hold equal amounts of liquid.

3. The child watches as the liquid from one of the containers is poured into a third taller and thinner container.

4. The child is asked if the amounts of liquid in both containers are still equal.

The child who has not yet entered the concrete operational stage will believe that the amount of liquid was changed. One can then conclude that he is not yet able to conserve liquid. The nonconserver believes that because the thinner glass is taller it has more liquid. He is unable to think beyond the height of the liquid. The conserver may also think that the tall thin container appears to have more liquid; however, he is able to infer that the liquid has not been altered and therefore both containers hold equal amounts

The younger child often bases his decisions on guesses or quick estimates. He appears to be unable to separate the whole into divisible units. The older child engages in much more reasonable thinking. He is able to recognize that the increase in container size was offset by a decrease in width. He is able to engage in *reversible* thinking: what the container gained in height it lost in width. The thinking of the younger child does not mainifest *irreversibility*. The child in the concrete operations stage of development realizes that most problems that are posed have potentially definite solutions. In contrast, the younger child appears only to be able to guess.

The concrete operational child is in the process of establishing a workable knowledge of numbers. He is able to estimate. He no longer has to count every object in every set. He can count by two's, ten's and so forth. He can count in any direction and no longer skips objects or counts them more than once. He is able to compare sets and determine "equal," "more than," and "less than." He is able to duplicate and reproduce sets and he understands length and depth. He is becoming quite skilled. This skillfulness is more thoroughly understood by observing the sophistication of his language patterns which will be discussed in the next chapter.

## BIBLIOGRAPHY

Baldwin, A. *Theories of Child Development*. New York: John Wiley & Sons, Inc., 1968.

Buhl, M. *Information Processing*. Chicago: Science Research Associates, 1976.

Bronfenbrenner, C. "The Changing American Child—A Speculative Analysis." *Journal of Social Issues*. 17:16–18, 1961.

Croake, J. W. "The Changing Nature of Children's Fears." *Child Study Journal*, 3(2):91–105, 1973.

Demos, J. "Developmental Perspectives On The History of Childhood." *Journal of Interdisciplinary History*, 2:315–327, 1971.

Dennis, W. "Causes of Retardation Among Institutional Children: Iran." *Journal of Genetic Psychology*, 96:47–59, 1960.

Elmer, E., and G. Gregg. "Developmental Characteristics of Abused Children." *Pediatrics*, 40:596–602, 1967.

Erikson, E. H. *Childhood and Society*. New York: Norton, 1950.

Farnham, S. *Information Processing in Children*. New York: Academic Press, 1972.

Flavell, J. H. *Cognitive Development*. Englewood Cliffs, N. J.: Prentice-Hall, Inc., 1977.

Flavell, J. H. "Stage-Related Properties of Cognitive Development." *Cognitive Psychology*, 2:421–53, 1971.

Flavell, J. H. and J. F. Wohlwill. "Formal and Functional Aspects of Cognitive Development." In D. Elkind and J. H. Flavell (Eds.) *Studies In Cognitive Development: Essays In Honor of Jean Piaget*. New York: Oxford University Press, 1969.

Freedle, R. O. *Discourse Production and Comprehension*. Norwood, N. J.: Ablex Publishing Corporation, 1977.

Frijda, N. H. "Simulation of Human Long-Term Memory." *Psychological Bulletin*, 77: 1–32, 1972.

Gelman, R. "Logical Capacity of Very Young Children: Number Invariance Rules." *Child Development*, 43:75–90, 1972.

Gesell, A. "Maturation and Infant Behavior Patterns." *Psychological Review*, 36:307–319, 1929.

Gesell, A. et al. *The First Five Years of Life*. New York: Harper & Row, Publishers, 1940.

Gesell, A., and F. Ilg. *The Child From Five to Ten*. New York: Harper & Row Publishers, 1946.

Ginsburg, H., and S. Opper. *Piaget's Theory of Intellectual Development*. Englewood Cliffs, N.J.: Prentice-Hall, Inc., 1969.

Gratch, G., and W. F. Landers. "Stage IV of Piaget's Theory of Infants' Object Concepts: A Longitudinal Study." *Child Development*, 42:359–372, 1971.

Just, M. A., and P. A. Carpenter. *Cognitive Processes In Comprehension*. Hillsdale, N. J.: Lawrence Erlbaum Associates, Publishers, 1977.

Kantowitz, B. H. *Human Information Processing: Tutorials In Performance and Cognition*. Hillsdale, N. J.: Lawrence Erlbaum Associates Publishers, 1974.

King, M. "The Development of Some Intention Concepts in Young Children." *Child Development*, 42:1145–53, 1971.

Klahr, D., and J. G. Wallace. "The Role of Quantification Operators in the Development of Conservation of Quantity." *Cognitive Psychology*, 4:301–27, 1973.

Kohlberg, L. "A Cognitive-Developmental Analysis of Children's Sex-Role Concepts and Attitudes." In E. E. Maccoby (Ed.), *The Development of Sex Differences*. Stanford, Calif.: Stanford University Press, 1966.

Loevinger, J. "The Meaning and Measurement of Ego Development." *American Psychologist*, 21:196–206, 1966.

Maccoby, E. E., and J. C. Master. "Attachment and Dependency." In P. H. Mussen (Ed.), *Carmichael's Manual of Child Psychology*. (Vol. 2). New York: John Wiley & Sons, Inc., 1970.

Piaget, , J. *The Language And Thought of the Child*. New York: Harcourt Brace Jovanovich, Inc., 1926.

Piaget, J. *Judgment and Reasoning In The Child*. New York: Harcourt Brace Jovanovich, Inc., 1929.

Piaget, J. *The Origins of Intelligence In Children*. New York: International Universities Press, 1952.

Piaget, J. *On The Development of Memory and Identity*. Barre, Mass.: Clark University Press and Barre Publishers, 1968.

Piaget, J. *The Child's Conception of the World*. Totawa, N. J.: Littlefield, Adams, and Company, 1969.

Piaget, J. "Piaget's Theory." In P. H. Mussen (Ed.) *Carmichael's Manual of Child Psychology*. (Vol. 1) New York: John Wiley & Sons, Inc., 1970.

Piaget J. *Genetic Epistemology*. New York: Columbia University Press, 1970.

Reitman, W. R. *Cognition and Thought: An Information Processing Approach*. New York: John Wiley & Sons, Inc., 1965.

Reynolds, M. M., and H. Mollay. "The Sleep of Young Children," *Journal of Genetic Psychology*, 43:322–351, 1933.

Rumelhart, D. E. *Toward an Interactive Model of Reading*. Technical Report No. 56, Center for Human Infirmation Processing, University of California—San Diego, 1976.

Simon, H. A., and A. Newell. "Human Problem Solving: The State of the Theory in 1970." *American Psychologist*, 26:145–59, 1971.

Trabasso, T. "Mental Operations in Language Comprehension." *Language Comprehension and the Acquisition of Knowledge*. Washington, D. C.: V. H. Winston, 1972.

Uzgiris, I. C. "Patterns of Cognitive Development in Infancy." *Merrill-Palmer Institute Conference on Infant Development.* Detroit: February 9–12, 1972.

Werner, H., and B. Kaplan. *Symbols Formation: An Organismic Developmental Approach To Language and the Expression of Thought*. New York: John Wiley & Sons, Inc., 1963.

Werner, H. *Comparative Psychology of Mental Development*. Chicago: Follett, 1948.

Wyer, R. S., Jr. *Cognitive Organization and Change: An Information Processing Approach*. Hillsdale, N.J.: Lawrence Erlbaum Associates Publishers, 1974.

Zaporozhets, A. V., and D. B. El'Konin. *The Psychology of Preschool Children*. Cambridge, Mass.: The Massachusetts Institute of Technology Press, 1974.

Zelazo, P. R., N. A. Zelazo and S. Kolb. "Walking In The Newborn." *Science*, 172(4032): 314–315, 1972.

# 3

# Language Acquisition and Development

*Figure 8.* Language is our primary mode of communication. (Photo by Linda Lungren).

Language is our primary medium of communication, and it is through this medium that most instruction occurs. If you as the classroom teacher are to create and/or utilize educational materials most effectively, it is necessary to select materials that suit each child "linguistically"; that is, you must realize the development, needs, and limitations of your children's language in order to establish realistic programs and expectations for each child's learning. The following introduction to theories and research in the field of language acquisition and development will clarify some of the complex features of language theory that exist in the most current literature.

Before we begin the review of relevant information about language acquisition and development, it is important to know that the normal development of language in children is systematic and relatively predictable. The approximate age when children acquire certain aspects of language is presented in the chart below.

| Age | Elements of Language |
|-----|----------------------|
| birth to 1 month | crying |
| 1 month to 2 months | crying and cooing |
| 2 months to 8 months | crying, cooing, and babbling |
| 8 months to 14 months | first words |
| 14 months to 24 months | first sentences |
| 24 months to 48 months | basic syntactic structures of the native language are acquired |
| 48 months to 96 months | speech sounds are correctly articulated |
| 96 months to 132 months | semantic distinctions are refined |

We will review several theories about language acquisition and development in this chapter, and we will divide the review into seven sections:

### 1: A Dictionary of Terms

In order to eliminate the stumbling block of unknown terminology, our discussion of language will be prefaced by a dictionary of terms to clarify the technical language of linguists, which so often confounds readers who are new to the field of language acquisition and development.

### 2: Overview of Language Development Theory

Linguists adhere to a variety of theoretical frameworks. Whereas some linguists emphasize language skills as a part of cognitive development, there are conflicting theories presented by behaviorists, nativists, and psycholinguists. We will look at each of these theories in the next few pages.

## 3: Phonological Development

Phonology is the sound system used in languages; every language has its own phonology. Children learn the sound system of their native tongue before any other stage of language development. Phonological acquisition proceeds in a regular, sequential fashion; it is highly systematic at all points in its development.

## 4: Morphological Development

Morphology refers to the study of the smallest units of meaning in a language. Morphemes are often used by linguists as measures of the development of a child's language.

## 5: Syntactic Development

Syntax refers to the structure of a language, to the manner in which words are ordered in an utterance. Unlike the well-ordered pattern adhered to in phonological development, syntactic development in young children is varied and more complex than phonological development. Despite the controversy and complexity surrounding syntactic growth, there are some universally accepted features of syntactic development and we will discuss these elements in the succeeding pages of this chapter.

## 6: Semantic Development

Semantics refers to word meaning. Knowledge of a child's semantic growth is tantamount to knowing about a child's ever-increasing ability to understand words and their variety of meanings. This is an extremely important area for you as you begin to help each child in his acquisition of new words and his refinement of existing concepts.

7: Implications for Your Classroom

To better relate the study of language acquisition and development to you, the classroom teacher, we will present a number of teaching techniques and approaches which, based on the discussions in the first few sections, coincide with a child's natural progression in the language process. The remainder of this book will deal with the teaching implications of what we know about language development.

## A DICTIONARY OF TERMS

**Behaviorists**   A group of language theorists who hold that language is a result of conditioned limitation.

**Cognitivists**   A group of language theorists who hold that language development is a part of the proper developmental processes of a child.

**Grapheme**   The written representation of phonemes.

**Intonation**   The pattern of rhythmic stress and pitch across an utterance. For example, "Are you going home?" Notice that the rising pitch at the end of a sentence is the usual marker of a yes-no question.

**Language acquisition**   The innate ability to learn language present at birth.

**Language development**   Language growth, which is dependent on the processing of external factors.

**Linguistics**   A manner or language used to talk about language. Linguistics attempts to characterize both a language in particular (English) and language as a general or universal phenomenon.

**Morphemes**   The smallest meaningful elements in a language, for example: the word *cats* consists of 2 morphemes, *cat*, (a free morpheme) and the plural indicator *s* (a bound morpheme). Although the plural cannot stand alone, it is an independent unit that can combine with other morphemes to form a new word.

**Morphology**   The part of grammar dealing with word formation, including inflections, derivations, and the formation of compound words.

**Nativists**   A group of language theorists who hold that there is a biological basis of language which is closely tied to the general maturation of the human organism.

**Phonemes**   A class of sounds that are considered equivalent in one language. e.g., *key, ski*, and *cau* share the /K/ sound, making that shared sound a phoneme of English.

**Phonology**  The sound system of language that proceeds in a regular, step-by-step fashion, which is highly systematic at any point in the acquisition of a language. It is phonology that accounts for the pronunciation of words.

**Psycholinguists**  A group of language theorists who maintain that a child uses language universals that are innate from birth to construct an integral picture of the syntactic process that he acquires from his environment.

**Semantics**  Word meanings that are determined by the context in which they are used; semantics includes the study of idioms.

**Stress**  The accented element of a word such as *de/fíne*, in which the second syllable receives a louder sound and is therefore the stressed syllable.

**Syntax**  The way in which words are put together to form phrases, clauses, or sentences.

These terms will be used throughout this text. It will be important for you to understand these concepts and to know the words that linguists use to describe these concepts.

## OVERVIEW OF LANGUAGE DEVELOPMENT THEORY

The following brief overview of current language development as theorized by behaviorists, nativists, psycholinguists, and cognitivists will help you to become aware of the various positions that are held concerning the origins and development of language. These theories attempt to explain overall language processes; they also provide suitable frameworks by which you may evaluate the specific phonological, morphological, syntactic, and semantic growth of your students.

### Behaviorists

Pavlov (1927), a behaviorist, introduced the concept of classical conditioning in psychological studies. He suggested that a conditioned stimulus in close temporal proximity with an unconditioned stimulus, after a number of treatments, gives rise to a conditioned response. Skinner (1966), in his definition of operant conditioning, stated that a stimulus elicits a response which reinforces a stimulus. Pavlov and Skinner base their theory of language learning on the notion of conditioning, suggesting that language development occurs at a low or passive level as a result of a child's environmental conditioning. Watson (1913), in a parallel theory of classical conditioning, explained language learning in terms of reinforcement of imitative behavior. These conditioned/ imitation theories of language learning are supported by the findings of Bereiter and Engelmann (1966), Osborn (1968), and Hart and Risley (1968), all of whom used conditioning techniques to teach language in varied situations. McNeill (1970), however, found fault with the behaviorist models because they failed to explain how a child faces and overcomes the phenomena of abstractions. Bellugi (1965) also questioned behaviorist models of language development through conditioned imitation because she found students were unable to imitate sentences when they could not comprehend the sentences that they are asked to imitate.

## Nativists

The nativistic theory of language development, forwarded by Lenneberg (1967) and others, suggests that language is closely tied to the child's general maturation. Lenneberg (1967) contended that milestones in language are reached in a fixed sequence; the milestone cannot be accelerated or affected by training or environment. This theory is supported by Ervin and Miller (1963), Ervin-Tripp (1966), and Slobin (1966). This model of language development adheres to a theory of innateness of competency. Carroll (1960) pointed out that one may accept innateness of certain linguistic competencies without being committed to the biological hypothesis explained by Lennenberg. While the nativists theory of language acquisition and development is attractive, the findings of several studies by Hart and Risley (1968), Bereiter and Engelman (1966), and Osborn (1968), in which elements of language were taught through the use of conditioning techniques, cast doubt on the argument that language cannot be taught.

## Psycholinguists

N. Chomsky (1964), a linguist, adheres to the principles of *theory construction* in which a child discovers the theory of his language with only small amounts of data from that language. The child uses language universals that he acquires at birth to construct hypotheses and test features of the child's own language. Through this process the child creates an integral picture of the syntactic processes of the language that he acquires from his environment. Chomsky maintains that this process is more than pure imitation. The learning of language occurs from an interaction of the child with his linguistic environment. It is independent of intelligence and specific experiences. Proponents of this theory (Slobin, 1966; McNeill, 1970) point out inadequacies of behaviorist learning theory to account for the phenomena of language; they maintain that language in its abstract is best explained by Chomsky's theory.

## Cognitivists

Sinclair-de-Zwart (1967), Piaget (1970), and Inhelder (1974) adhere to a cognitive model of language. Cognitive models are unlike behaviorist models that explain language as imitation, nativistic models that suggest language is dependent upon biological elements, or psycholinguistic models that depend upon a belief in the innateness of inherited language abilities. Piaget (1970) and other cognitivists, believe in the inter-disciplinary nature of the development of language; i.e., the interaction of psychological, biological, sociological, linguistic, logical, and epistemological elements. In Piaget's model, he emphasizes that cognitive development is progressive, growth is dependent upon maturation; it is constant in the order of succession that it follows. He maintains that continuous growth, successively staged within the framework of total cognitive activity, occurs in language development in the same way that it occurs in the realm of thought. Piaget maintains that language is structured by logic rather than that logic is structured by language, the view held by Vygotsky (1962). To Piaget, language learning is a part of the broader developmental processes that the child undergoes. Sinclair-de-Zwart (1967) found that the use of linguistic higher-order structures appears as cognitive abilities increase. Ghuman's (1974) data supports this theory; he found that syntactic structures were closely linked with operational levels of thinking, and he suggested that they were interdependent with operational thinking.

## PHONOLOGICAL DEVELOPMENT

The term *phonology* refers to the sound system of a language, a system of regular processes that determines the pronunciation of that language. This sound system, not present at birth, evolves slowly as the central nervous system matures. The schedule for such maturation in English vocalization roughly follows this sequence:

| Age | Proficient Consonant Articulation |
|-----|-----------------------------------|
| 3½  | b  p  m  w  h                     |
| 4½  | d  t  h  g  k  y  n               |
| 5½  | f                                 |
| 6½  | v  j  z  s  l                     |
| 7½  | s  z  o  f                        |

Such a sequence has been established by linguists who have attempted to chart the course of human articulation. Jakobson (1941) found that the development of the phonemic system is the result of the child's attempts to establish a system of oppositions within a sound continuum. The first sounds in this system are: /a/ and /p/. They are in the greatest opposition; /a/ is the most open central, farthest back vowel; and /p/ is the farthest front, stopped consonant. This opposition makes /a/ the optimal vowel and /p/ the optimal consonant. This may account for the widespread occurrence of /papa/ as the first recorded syllable sequence produced by children in many languages of the world. In order to more clearly understand the biological mechanism responsible for sound production, you may find it helpful to examine the chart by Mansoor Alyeshmerni and Paul Tauber on page 57. It illustrates the mechanism involved in sound production and the six major locations where sounds originate.

### Jakobson's Theory

Jakobson (1941), whose theories on phonological acquisition are frequently cited, holds the following positions on phonological development:

1. Phonological development is best described in terms of the mastery of distinctive features.

2. Children do not approximate adult phonemes one by one; rather, they develop their own system of phonemic contrasts, not always using the same features as adults for distinguishing between words. Sometimes children might use the length of vowels to distinguish between words, a feature not used in adult English.

3. The pattern of phonological development in all children is systematic and universal.

However, Jakobson's theories are controversial. Although he has received support from Svachkin (1973) and others, Moskowitz (1973) and Glucksberg and Danks (1975) disagree with Jakobson, suggesting that it is impossible to regard the early stages of phonological development in terms of phoneme contrasts. Rather, they suggest that the child has to develop a fairly sizable, productive vocabulary before developing any consistent phonological system that relates words to each other. They argue that children avoid producing words containing certain sounds and favor other words that consist of sounds they have mastered. The implication of this theory is that children understand many more words than they produce. As children progress past the first two or three years of their lives, phonological development continues. It is during the years between two and eight that children acquire the adult phonological rules of inflectional endings for nouns and verbs.

In addition to the acquisition of sound segments in speech, the suprasegmental aspects of intonation (pitch, stress) are also a part of a child's acquisition

| Articulator | Point of articulation | Position of articulation | Examples |
|---|---|---|---|
| 1. Lower lip | Upper lip | Bilabial | p, b, m |
| 2. Lower lip | Upper teeth | Labiodental | f, v |
| 3. Apex of the tongue and lower teeth | Upper teeth | Interdental | θ (thin)<br>ð (then) |
| 4. Apex of the tongue | Alveolar ridge | Apicoalveolar | t, d, s, z, n, l, r |
| 5. Front of the tongue | Palate | Frontopalatal | č (chip), ǰ (jet)<br>š (ship), ž (azure)<br>y (boy) |
| 6. Dorsum of the tongue | Velum | Dorsovelar | k, g, ŋ (ring), w |

A seventh position, the <u>glottal</u> position, is described as follows: when no organs other than the vocal cords are used in producing a sound, the sounds are called glottal. The <u>h</u> in <u>he</u> and the sound heard between the two parts of the colloquial negative <u>huh-uh</u> are examples of this position in articulation.

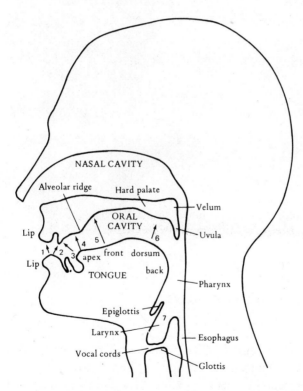

*Figure 9.* The positions of articulation. From *Working with Aspects of Language,* Second Edition, by Mansoor Alyeshmerni and Paul Tauber © 1975 by Harcourt Brace Jovanovich, Inc. and reprinted with their permission.

of phonology. Intonation refers to rises and falls in the voice that indicate questions and statements. Until the age of six months most "babbles" of children are produced with a falling declarative intonation; these "babbles" are then followed by falling and rising sounds in "babbles." At about this time the child begins to imitate the intonation of adults (Nakazima, 1962) and he can discriminate question intonation from statement intonation (Kaplan, 1969). At this point the child, while still acquiring sound segments, seems to possess the basic aspects of the suprasound system—intonation.

*Figure 10.* Until the age of 6 months most "babbles" of children are produced with a falling declarative intonation. (Photo by Jonathan Sutton)

## MORPHOLOGICAL DEVELOPMENT

Morphology is the term linguists use to refer to the study of the smallest units of meaning in language. It is the morpheme, rather than words or phrases, that is used by researchers as a measure of a child's growth in language usage. Morphemes are divided into free morphemes such as *cat* and *dog*, and bound morphemes which cannot exist alone, such as *s* in *cats, dogs*.

The examples below illustrate the number of morphemes in each of the following phases:

|                      | Morphemes |
|----------------------|-----------|
| 1. Hi mom            | 2         |
| 2. My cups           | 3         |
| 3. Stop that now     | 3         |
| 4. Biannual meetings | 4         |

It is believed that as children develop linguistically, the number of morphemes per utterance increases. Although this theory does not account for such factors as content, method of eliciting samples, students, or morpheme types, it does help tabulate and mark increases in language fluency. In order to provide closer analysis of morpheme types used as an indicator of language development, Dale (1976) constructed the table on pages 60–61 from tables designed by Brown (1973).

In this chart he attempted to order specific morphemes according to their order of acquisition, grammatical complexity, and semantic complexity. As you examine this chart, you will notice that the present progressive morpheme is not only acquired before the third-person singular regular morpheme, but it is less grammatically and semantically complex than the third-person singular morpheme. Therefore, it is apt to be present in a child's speech before the third-person singular morpheme.


## SYNTACTIC DEVELOPMENT


The study of syntax is the study of the arrangement of words in a meaningful order within a sentence. Between nine and fourteen months, children produce their first words. They add at least fifty items to their lexicon within the next six months. At this point they begin to combine words to create meaningful syntactic utterances. They often omit articles and auxiliary verbs so their speech sounds like a telegram, for example:

> see truck
>
> drink milk

A short time later children begin to use "pivot" words, that is, fixed words to which other words may be attached, for example, allgone:

> allgone milk
>
> allgone car
>
> allgone candy

## The Acquisition of 14 Grammatical Morphemes of English

| Morpheme | Order of Acquisition | Transformations | Ordering by Grammatical Complexity[a] | Semantic Dimensions | Ordering by Semantic Complexity[b] |
|---|---|---|---|---|---|
| present progressive | 1 | progressive affix | 3 | temporary duration | 4 |
| on | 2.5 | preposition segment | 3 | support | 4 |
| in | 2.5 | preposition segment | 3 | containment | 4 |
| plural | 4 | noun suffix, nominal agreement, article | 7[c] | number | 4 |
| past irregular | 5 | verb agreement | 3 | earlierness | 4 |
| possessive | 6 | (not given in source) | | possession | 4 |
| uncontractible copula | 7 | copula, auxiliary agreement, auxiliary incorporation | 10 | number, earlierness | 8.5 |
| articles | 8 | article | 3 | specific-nonspecific | 4 |
| past regular | 9 | verb agreement, verb suffix | 7 | earlierness | 4 |
| third-person singular regular | 10 | auxiliary agreement, verb agreement, verb suffix | 10 | number, earlierness | 8.5 |
| third-person singular irregular | 11 | auxiliary agreement, verb agreement | 7 | number, earlierness | 8.5 |
| uncontractible auxiliary | 12 | auxiliary incorporation, progressive affix, progressive segment, auxiliary agreement | 12.5 | temporary duration, number, earlierness | 10 |

| | | | | | |
|---|---|---|---|---|---|
| contractible copula | 13 | copula, auxiliary agreement, auxiliary incorporation | 10 | number, earlierness | 8.5 |
| contractible auxiliary | 14 | progressive affix, progressive segment, auxiliary incorporation, auxiliary agreement | 12.5 | temporary duration | 10 |

predictions according to the law of cumulative complexity

present progressive → contractible auxiliary

present progressive → uncontractible auxiliary

past irregular → past regular

past irregular → third-person singular regular

past irregular → third-person singular irregular

third-person singular irregular → third-person singular regular

plural → copula

plural → third-person singular

plural → auxiliary

past → auxiliary

progressive → auxiliary

past singular → third-person

past → copula

third-person singular → auxiliary

copula → auxiliary

[a] Ordering includes thirteen items only, as possessive is not analyzed in source.

[b] Ordering includes ten items; it is assumed that regular-irregular and contractible-uncontractible contrasts are irrelevant to master of semantic content.

[c] The second and third transformations are not involved in all instances of the plural; for this reason Brown bases the ordering on an average of two transformation for the plural.

SOURCE: From Dale, Philip S. Language Development. Second Edition. New York: Holt, Rinehart, and Winston, 1976, 32-33 and from a construction based on Tables 32, 45, 60, 61, and 67 of R. Brown, A first language. Cambridge, Mass.: Harvard University Press, 1973

Gradually, utterance length increases as constructions become either agent-action-object (I see doggie) or two-term-relation expansions, usually of possession, recurrence, or attribution (Brown, 1973), such as "sit daddy chair"; this may mean "sit in daddy's chair." Children then progress to four-word sentences and then to question forming. The first step in this process is the use of intonation. Yes/no questions are indicated by rises and falls in the voice pattern rather than through sentence transformations, for example, "Doggie drink?" rather than "Is the dog drinking?" Only at the second stage of question forming acquisition is a child able to invert sentences into *Wh* question formations, such as, "Who is in the kitchen?" Some explanations for children's syntactic

*Figure 11.* Some explanations for children's language development include theories of imitation, expansion, and reinforcement. (Photo by Linda Lungren)

development include theories of imitation, expansion, and reinforcement. The first theory, that of imitation, is widely disputed. Its proponents maintain that syntax develops as a result of imitation. However, such a theory does not account for a child's ability to generalize beyond what is imitated. The theory of expansion, forwarded from Bloom, et al. (1975), suggests that children pay attention to and learn from input that is slightly more advanced than their own speech. Brown and Bellugi (1964) support this theory, suggesting that expansions supply missing grammatical information for children and help them to retain the content of their utterances. Examples of expansions follow:

### Expansion of Child Speech Produced by Mothers

| Child | Mother |
|-------|--------|
| Baby highchair. | Baby is in the highchair. |
| Mommy eggnog. | Mommy had her eggnog. |
| Eve lunch. | Eve is having lunch. |
| Mommy sandwich. | Mommy'll have a sandwich. |
| Sat wall. | He sat on the wall. |
| Throw daddy. | Throw it to daddy. |
| Pick glove. | Pick the glove up. |

SOURCE: R. Brown and U. Bellugi. "Three processes in the child's acquisition of syntax." Harvard Educational Review, Spring 1964, 34, 141. Copyright © 1964 by President and Fellows of Harvard College.

There is much conflicting data to make us question the expansion theory, for example, Bellugi (1967) reported that children appear oblivious to parent's attempts to correct their language. Feldman (1971) and Cazden (1965) report no difference in the language development of children who receive expansions from their parents and children who do not.

The third theory—reinforcement—suggests that parents reinforce or reward their children for speaking "correctly." In this way, it is argued, grammatical sentences become strengthened and ungrammatically, ill-formed sentences become omitted from a child's repertoire. Although this phenomenon may advance language development, it is surely not rewards and reinforcement that keep us talking. The theory of reinforcement alone is simply insufficient to explain the complexity of language development. In combinations, however, these theories may offer a reasonable explanation of the process.

## SEMANTIC DEVELOPMENT

Semantic development is the growth in a child's ability to assign one or several meanings to a word. In order for word meaning growth or "conceptualization" to occur, the child must first have a series of experiences that are similar to the concept in question. For example, in telling a child what a lion is, one must indicate the range of positive and negative instances—the range of variations that can be found in real lions and the critical respects in which other animals such as tigers and leopards differ from lions. In this manner a child learns words as distinct entities. Children first acquire nouns, then verbs, and finally adjectives. More than 50 years ago, Smith (1926) demonstrated that vocabulary growth in these areas is tremendous in the first six years, as the following chart indicates.

## Vocabulary Growth As a Function of Age

| Age (years, months) | Number of Words | Increment |
|:---:|:---:|:---:|
| 0;8 | 0 | |
| 0;10 | 1 | 1 |
| 1;0 | 3 | 2 |
| 1;3 | 19 | 16 |
| 1;6 | 22 | 3 |
| 1;9 | 118 | 96 |
| 2;0 | 272 | 154 |
| 2;6 | 446 | 174 |
| 3;0 | 896 | 450 |
| 3;6 | 1222 | 326 |
| 4;0 | 1540 | 318 |
| 4;6 | 1870 | 330 |
| 5;0 | 2072 | 202 |
| 5;6 | 2289 | 217 |
| 6;0 | 2562 | 273 |

SOURCE: Adapted from M. E. Smith, "An investigation of the development of the sentence and the extent of vocabulary in young children," *University of Iowa Studies in Child Welfare*, 1926, 3, No. 5.

*Figure 12.* Between the ages of two and six approximately 2,290 word meanings are learned. (Photo by Linda Lungren)

These totals are remarkable when one considers that between the ages of two and six years 2,290 word meanings are learned. Further, when one considers variations in word meaning based on context, the acquisition of 2,290 words in 1,460 days is a staggering feat never to be duplicated again in a person's life.

Because vocabulary development is part of every young child's curriculum, it is necessary to better understand this complex phenomenon. Beyond simple noun/verb/adjective acquisition, children are faced with instruction that uses words dealing with concepts of time (ago, still) and mass (as in the physical sense). Such concepts and the related vocabulary pose problems to children in their early years because these concepts are more abstract in nature than nouns, verbs, and adjectives. They are less easily conceptualized than nouns or verbs. If concrete concepts are inadequately mastered, then problems are likely to arise in the learning of more advanced or abstract concepts because concept mastery appears to be sequential in nature (Carroll, 1960). The implication here is that vocabulary must be taught in a somewhat sequential fashion, moving from the concrete (nouns, verbs, adjectives) to the more abstract (quantity, time, and mass indicators), after the prerequisite concrete concepts have been fully mastered.

## IMPLICATIONS FOR YOUR CLASSROOM

The preceding discussion briefly outlines the current theories regarding language acquisition and development. This summary has been purposefully streamlined in order to supply you with a workable framework upon which you can base your classroom language instruction.

Understanding phonological development clarifies the reasons for a child's confusions, errors, and inabilities at mastering language pronunciation, spelling, and decoding. Morphological development research suggests specific periods during which you may expect your children to acquire language markers such as tense and pluralization. It should be pointed out that such gains may not be realistically expected before the time that the researchers have indicated from their data analysis.

A child's use and understanding of the syntax of sentence structure is vital to comprehension and increases primarily as a product of maturation. This suggests that instructional materials should be selected not only at a childs' vocabulary level, but also as a suitable syntactic level. In the instruction of vocabulary, the developmental process strongly suggests the use of an instructional approach that presents simple and concrete concepts. You should move to the more complex and abstract concepts only after the initial concepts have been mastered.

Research in all areas of language acquisition and development stresses sequential growth. Whether in the area of phonology, morphology, syntax, or

*Figure 13.* Research in all areas of language acquisition and development stresses sequential growth. As a classroom teacher, you must understand this sequence in order to set realistic goals for your young students. (Photo by Linda Lungren)

semantics, it appears that children's progress proceeds in a fairly predictable pattern. As a classroom teacher, you must understand this sequence in order to set realistic goals for your young students. These goals should be consistent with what we know about the normal levels of development for a particular age. In this way, lessons properly geared to current developmental levels will assist rather than confound a child in the language growth process.

The remainder of this book will deal with the implications of current language study by presenting suitable methods for teaching language/reading to every young child. As you read the rest of this book, refer back to these early chapters to help you in your design of a suitable research-based, current, theoretically sound program for each child.

## BIBLIOGRAPHY

Alyeshmerni, M., and P. Tauber. *Working with Aspects of Language.* New York: Harcourt Brace Jovanovich, Inc., 1975.

Anderson, P. and D. Lapp, *Language Skills In the Elementary School*. New York: Macmillan, 1979.

Bellugi, U. "The Development of the Interrogative Structure in Children's Speech Functions." In K. Riegel (ed.), *The Development of Language Functions*. Ann Arbor: University of Michigan Press, 1965.

Bellugi, U. "The Acquisition of Negation." Ph. D. dissertation, Harvard University, 1967.

Bereiter, C., and S. Engelmann. *Teaching Disadvantaged Children in the Preschool*. Englewood Cliffs, N.J.: Prentice-Hall, Inc., 1966.

Bloom, L. M., P. Lightbrown and L. Hood. "Structure and Variation In Child Language." Monographs of the Society for Research in Child Development 40, 1975.

Bloom, L. M., and R. Brown (eds.) "The Acquisition of Language." Monographs of the Society for Research in Child Development 29, No. 92, 1964.

Brown, J. "On Cognitive Growth: II." in J. Bruner, R. Oliver, and P. Greenfield (eds.), *Studies in Cognitive Growth*. New York: John Wiley & Sons, Inc., 1966.

Brown, R. *A First Language*. Cambridge, MA.: Harvard University Press, 1973.

Brown, R. and U. Bellugi. "Three Processes in the Child's Acquisition of Syntax." *Harvard Educational Review*, Spring 1964, 34, 141.

Carroll, J. B. "Language Development." In C. W. Harris (ed.), *Encyclopedia of Educational Research*. New York: Macmillan Publishing Co., Inc., 1960.

Cazden, C. B. "Environmental Assistance to the Child's Acquistion of Grammar." Ph. D. dissertation, Harvard University, 1965.

Chomsky, N. A. *Current Issues in Linguistic Theory*. The Hague: Mouton, 1964.

Dale, P. *Language Development,* 2nd ed. New York: Holt, Rinehart, and Winston, 1976, 32–33.

Ervin, S. M., and W. F. Miller. "Language Development." In H. W. Stevenson (ed.), *Child Psychology*. Chicago: University of Chicago Press, 1963.

Ervin-Tripp, S. M. "Language Development." In M. Hoffman and L. Hoffman (eds.), *Review of Child Development Research*. Vol. 2. Ann Arbor: University of Michigan Press, 1966.

Feldman, C. "The Effects of Various Types of Adult Responses in the Syntactic Acquisition of Two- to Three-Year-Olds." Unpublished paper, University of Chicago, 1971.

Ghuman, A. S. "A Study of Children's Cognitive Operations in Relationship to Their Language." *Indiana Journal of Psychology* (June 2, 1974) 49:149–157.

Glucksberg, S., and J. H. Danks. *Experimental Psycholinguistics: An Introduction*. Hillsdale, N.J.: Lawrence Erlbaum Associates, 1975.

Hart, B. M. and T. R. Risley. "Use of Descriptive Adjectives in the Speech of Preschool Children." *Journal of Applied Behavior Analysis*, 1968,1:109–120.

Inhelder, B. *Piaget and His School*. New York: Springer-Verlag, 1974.

Jakobson, R. *Kindersprache, Aphasie, and Allegmeine Lautgesetze*. Upsala: Almquist and Wiksell, 1941. (English translation: *Child Language, Aphasia and Phonological Universals*.) The Hague: Mouton, 1968.

Kaplan, E. L. *The Role of Intonation in the Acquisition of Language*. Unpublished Ph. D. dissertation, Cornell University, 1969.

Lenneberg, E. H. *Biological Foundations of Language*. New York: John Wiley & Sons, Inc., 1967.

McNeill, D. "The Development of Language." In P.H. Mussen (ed.), *Carmichael's Manual of Child Psychology.* Vol. 1, 3rd ed. New York: John Wiley & Sons, Inc., 1970.

Moskowitz, A. I. "Acquisition of Phonology and Syntax: A Preliminary Study." In *Approaches to Natural Language.* In Hintikka et al. (ed.), Dordrecht, Holland: Reidel Publishing Company, 1973.

Moskowitz, B.A. "On the Status of Vowel Shift in English." In T.E. Moore (ed.) *Cognitive Development and the Acquisition of Language.* New York. Academic Press, Inc., 1973.

Nakazima, S. "A Comparative Study of the Speech Developments of Japanese and American English in Childhood," *Student Phonology,* 2:27–39, 1962.

Osborn, J. "Teaching a Teaching Language to Disadvantaged Children." In M.C. Templin (ed.), *Monographs of the Society for Research in Child Development.* Chicago: University of Chicago Press, 1968.

Pavlov, I. P. *Conditional Reflexes.* Translated by G. V. Amrep. London: Oxford University, 1927.

Piaget, J. "Piaget's Theory." In P. H. Mussen (ed.), *Carmichael's Manual of Child Psychology.* Vol. 1, 3rd ed. New York: John Wiley & Sons, Inc., 1970.

Piaget, J. *Science of Education and the Psychology of the Child.* New York: Orion, 1970.

Sinclair-de-Zwart, M. *Acquisition De Language Et Development De La Pensee.* Paris: Dumod, 1967.

Skinner, B. F. "Operant Behavior." In W. K. Honig (ed.), *Operant Behavior: Areas of Research and Application.* New York: Appleton-Century-Crofts, 1966.

Slobin, D. I. "Comments on Developmental Linguistics: A Discussion of McNeill's Presentation." In F. Smith and G. A. Miller (eds.), *The Genesis of Language.* Cambridge, MA: MIT Press, 1966.

Smith, M. E. "An Investigation of the Development of the Sentence and the Extent of Vocabulary in Young Children." *University of Iowa Studies in Child Welfare,* 1926, 3, No. 5.

Svachkin, N. K. "The Development of Phonemic Speech Perception in Early Childhood." In C. A. Ferguson and D. I. Slobin (eds.) *STudies of Child Language Development.* New York: Holt, Rinehart and Winston, 1973.

Tonkova-Yampol'skaya, R. V. "Development of Speech Inonation in Infants During the First Two Years of Life." *Sov-Psychol.* 7:48–54, 1969.

Vygotsky, L. *Thought and Language.* Cambridge, MA: MIT Press, 1962.

Watson, J. B. "Psychology as the Behaviorist Views It." *Psychological Review,* 1913, **20:** 158–177.

# 4

# Understanding Play: The Work of the Child

*Figure 14.* Understanding Play: The Work of the Child. (Photo by Linda Lungren)

Mommy is typing.
Daddy is cooking.
Jimmy is writing.
Baby is playing.

Mommy is hammering.
Daddy is vacuuming.
Jimmy is dancing.
Baby is playing.

Mommy is  working.
Daddy is working.
Jimmy is working.
Baby is playing.

WHAT IS BABY DOING?


## Understanding Play

It is generally agreed among early childhood educators that play is important for the young child's development. In order to fully understand and appreciate this statement, we will attempt to answer six questions throughout the
remainder of this chapter.

1. What is the historical basis for considering play to be an important
element in children's development?

2. What is play?

3. What is Piaget's view of play?

4. What is symbolic play and what do researchers say about its importance
in the development of the child?

5. What is sociodramatic play and what do researchers say about its importance in the development of the child?

6. What are the implications of research on play for teaching young children?

*Figure A.*

## The History of Research on Play

*Question 1: What is the historical basis for considering play to be an important element in children's development?*

Philosophers, psychologists, educators, linguists, and anthropologists have been fascinated by the activity of young children for centuries. Many of these researchers and scholars have categorized the daily activity of young children under the heading, "play." As early as the fourth century B.C., Plato, in *Laws*, stated: "A child's character will need to be formed while he plays." Plato realized the value of this activity, and he reported that he encouraged children to "play" with various objects in order to discover the principles of addition, subtraction, multiplication, and division.

Comenius (1907) also discussed the significance of play in the education of the child when he stated that a child's sustained interest in objects will provide the framework for his later cognitive achievements. In advancing this position, he observed the way in which he perceived children to acquire the skill of reading: first, the child requires contact with real things; this is followed by pictorial representation of these things, and finally, with their graphemic representations.

In more recent times, psychologists and educators have reexamined the writings of these early philosophers in order to gain valuable insights and to take issue with some of their conclusions. Pestalozzi (1897), for example, objected to Comenius' theory by asserting that children learn about the abstract physical attributes of objects through direct contact with them. However, in carefully analyzing the writings of these two men, it becomes evident that their difference of opinion is the result of their differing definitions of "objects." For Comenius, objects were things that children used in their daily activity: dishes, spoons, boxes. He argued that the daily use of these objects provided the child with early learning experiences. Pestalozzi, however, held the view that objects were expressions of attributes: squares, rectangles, and circles. He maintained that these attributes needed to be taught systematically and directly.

*Figure 15.* Although the organized setting in early schooling provides opportunities for spontaneous play, its curriculum also features structured play suited to the educational needs of young children. (Photo by Linda Lungren)

The debate about the appropriate instructional methodology for the young child within the realm of play continues to the present time. Rousseau (1964), who took a position similar to Comenius' wanted to see the "free" child in a natural environment. In 1921, G. Stanley Hall enlightened these controversial issues by suggesting that appropriate environments could be designed to match the child's natural interests.

*Figure 16.* Contemporary educators have asserted that children as young as two years of age can understand "let's pretend" and are capable of suspending reality functions. (Photo by Linda Lungren)

Child's play has been analyzed from many different vantage points throughout the psychological and educational literature of the twentieth century. Isaacs, in 1933, discussed the social ramifications of play; he maintained that play "offers the child his first effective social education." During sociodramatic play, for example, the child is forced to recognize others and their unique fantasies. Children who participate in sociodramatic play are forced to agree upon roles, "constraints" for role changes, and the permissibility of activities that accompany roles. Contemporary educators have further defined the complexities of play by asserting that children as young as two years of age can understand "let's pretend" and are capable of suspending reality

*Figure 17.* In play, children gradually develop concepts of casual relationships, the power to discriminate, to make judgements, to analyze and synthesize, to imagine and formulate. (Photo by Linda Lungren)

an analysis of the child's activities. Piaget described the developmental stages of play within the framework of a schema on cognitive development. These stages are presented in the chart on page 76.

The first cognitive stage, called the *sensorimotor period*, has six sequential steps; it covers the period from the birth of the child to two years of age. The play of the child during this period is characterized by motor activity, and Piaget refers to the games of this period as practice games. The first step of the sensorimotor period, from birth to one month, is characterized by neonatal reflexes. The child's play during this period is characterized by reflex adaptation.

The second step, from one to four months, is characterized by new and often accidental response patterns. The child's play begins to assume parts of adaptive behaviors and may be manifested by specific motor activities such as grabbing or holding of an adult's finger. In the third step, from four to eight months, the child's sensorimotor development evolves into the coordination of new response patterns. His play is discussed in terms of repeated action on things that will become games, such as shaking a rattle or hitting at a mobile. The fourth step, from eight to twelve months, incorporates complex coordinations. At this time, children begin to search for vanished objects.

### Piaget's Schema on the Development of Play in Children

| Period of Cognitive Development | Age | Games | Characteristics of Play |
|---|---|---|---|
| <u>Sensorimotor</u><br>(imitation, accommodation)<br>Stages: | 0–2 years | practices games | motor |
| 1. neonatal reflexes | 0–1 month | | reflex adaptation |
| 2. new, accidental response patterns | 1–4 months | | assumes part of adaptive behavior |
| 3. new response patterns are coordinated | 4–8 months | | action on things that will become games |
| 4. complex coordination | 8–12 months | search for vanished objects—Where's _____? | (a) application of known schema to new situation |
| 5. means-end manipulation | 12–18 months | | (b) goes from one schema to another, combines unrelated gestures as play |
| 6. beginning of symbolic representation | 18–24 months | ludic symbolism | pretense, make-believe, mime |
| <u>Preoperational</u><br>(egocentric thinking)<br>Stages: | 2–7 years | symbolic games | |
| 1. Preconceptual over-generalized attempts at conceptualization | 2–4 years | Type 1: The child freely uses his individual powers. | solitary |
| 2. Perceptual Intuitive prelogical thinking | 4–7 years | Type 2: The child reproduces the looks and actions of other people. | orderly, precision in imitating, social |
| | | Type 3: The child transposes whole scenes into an inner experience. The emergence of make-believe friends often occurs at this time. | |
| <u>Concrete operations</u><br>(thought that is logical and reversible) | 7–11 years | games with rules | social |
| <u>Formal operations</u> | 11 years upward | | |

Their play is characterized by a two-step progression: first, the application of known schema to new situations, and second, the progression from one schema to another. Examples of their games might include the combining of objects, such as patty cakes, "So Big," throwing/dropping objects on the floor.

During the fifth step of the child's sensorimotor development, from twelve to eighteen months, the child becomes capable of means-end manipulation. His play is characterized by the combining of unrelated gestures as play; examples of play at this time include running and squealing simultaneously.

*Figure 18.* Children's play from 18–24 months is characterized by the beginning of pretense, make-believe, and mime. (Photo by Linda Lungren)

The sixth and final step, from eighteen to twenty-four months, is manifested by the origins of symbolic representation. Children's play during this period is characterized by the beginning of pretense, make-believe, and mime. The child's games begin to contain *ludic* symbolism, for example, a block becomes an airplane.

During the second cognitive stage in Piaget's schema, the child becomes involved in symbolic play. This period of play is the stage that is most frequently and thoroughly discussed in the psychological literature. The second stage of cognitive development, called the *preoperational period*, extends from two to seven years of age and is characterized by the child's egocentric thinking. The play of this period is symbolic, and Piaget refers to the games of this period as symbolic games. It is further divided into two steps: the preconceptual step, from two to four years of age, which is characterized by the child's overgeneralized attempts at conceptualization, and the perceptual or intuitive step, from four to seven years of age, which is characterized by prelogical thinking; for example, the child takes in one attribute at a time without processing a whole picture.

The child's play during the first step, the preconceptual step, from two to four years of age, is characterized by egocentrism and isolation. Symbolic play is at its peak during this time in the child's life. The games of this period progress in three stages:

Type 1 games:  The child freely uses his individual powers.

Type 2 games:  The child reproduces the looks and actions of other people.

Type 3 games:  The child transposes whole scenes into an inner experience. The emergence of "make-believe" friends often occurs at this time.

During the second step, the perceptual or intuitive step, from four to seven years of age, the child's play is characterized by orderliness (coherence, sequentiality), precision in imitating reality, and sociability. The games of this step are moving ever more closely to rule-governed activities.

The third period of cognitive development, *concrete operations* in Piaget's schema, from seven to eleven years, is characterized by logical and reversible thought. The play is social, and Piaget refers to the games of this period as games with rules. The fourth and final period in Piaget's schema, is called the *formal operations* period, which spans from eleven years of age to adulthood. Play during this period is also social and rule-governed.

### Play is the Primacy of Assimilation

Piaget's theory of the nature of play is best summarized by his assertion that play is essentially the primacy of assimilation; it begins with the first dissociation between assimilation and accommodation. The child repeats actions like throwing and dropping solely because he enjoys the challenge of mastering this behavior. Piaget's theory on the development of play asserts that the content of play and the extent of its egocentricity reveal the child's steady progress toward socialized thought. He maintains that the child's growing awareness that objects have numerous properties and that they can be classified along different dimensions is the direct result of his interaction with these objects. He argues that the child needs to perceive reality in his own egocentric manner before he can adapt to an adult system of logical thought. In order for this adaptation to occur, the child must experience and manipulate and experience and interact with other individuals. He argues that play ultimately enhances the development of logical thought because the child must confront other children's perceptions of reality and must accommodate himself to their ideas.

Piaget has presented a comprehensive schema of the development of play in children and has offered an answer to two basic questions: 1) What is the nature of play? and 2) How does it occur in children? He has also proposed answers to another basic question that researchers have continuously asked: What are the by-products of play?

## Differing Viewpoints on the By-products of Play

### Sutton-Smith's View of Play

Sutton-Smith (1971) maintained that children structure their play to make nonsense out of ordinary expectations, thereby developing their divergent thought processes. Sutton-Smith maintains that Piaget's view of the nature of play suggests that children's thought processes in play are convergent, moving in closer harmony with the environment. Furthermore, Sutton-Smith maintains that Piaget's view leads one to conclude that play is the supreme expression of deliberate distortion and disequilibrium, the antithesis of adaptive thought. In Sutton-Smith's model, on the other hand, it is through play that children acquire equilibrium and adaptive thought.

### Psychoanalytic Theory of Play

A second viewpoint on the by-products of play which differs, in part, from Piaget's view is the psychoanalytic theory of play. Proponents of this theory point out that most human emotions are laid bare during play. Love, hostility, anxiety, sympathy, jealousy, and many other human emotions are combined by the child with a great variety of fantasies and defensive maneuvers during play. Psychoanalytic studies indicate that play reflects more than emotion alone. Its emotional, physiological, and intellectual aspects are interwoven and are not easily separable.

Play and reasoning have several similarities. Neither one has direct and immediate consequences in the world. Both contain certain elements of reality which are selected and varied. Isaacs (1933) identified an "as if" orientation in both play and reasoning. A child thinks or plays "as if" the world were ordered in a certain way. This orientation serves to overcome the obstacles of time and space. Peller (1971) maintains that play, like reasoning or thinking, is precipitated by an experience that is not satisfactorily completed. Therefore, play provides opportunities for savoring the pleasant aspects of an experience and for compensating for the unpleasant aspect of that experience.

In fact, psychoanalytic theory has long regarded the young child's play as a reflection of emotional conflicts and a reflection of developing intellectual competence. Erikson (1959) sees children using play to move in a clear developmental direction. First, the young child treats other children as things. Gradually, he learns what play content can be admitted to fantasy, what to play by oneself, and what content can be shared by others. This appears to be an essential step toward the intelligent grasp of ideas other than one's own.

**Symbolic Play**

*Question 4: What is symbolic play and what do researchers say about its importance in the development of the child?*

Although researchers have been interested in every aspect of children's play, the predominant developmental period that has been investigated by scholars has been the period of symbolic play. This period, according to Piaget, ranges from two to seven years and occurs during the preoperational stage of cognitive development. The child's motor skills, language skills, and thinking skills become extremely well developed during this period. Therefore, there are numerous factors that researchers have been unable to unravel when they have attempted to investigate the area of symbolic play.

Piaget classified the components of symbolic play in the following way:

1. a. Projection of symbolic schemes to new objects.
   b. Projection of imitative schemes to new objects.
2. a. Identification of one object with another.
   b. Identification of self or body with other people or things.
3. Symbolic combinations.
4. Collective symbolism—sociodramatic play.

At these early stages the features of symbolic play are quite distinct from exact replicas of reality. Piaget maintains, however, that the roles taken on by the players and the objects that they construct in their dramatic play tend to become more exact and detailed as the child becomes more sophisticated intellectually.

*Psychological Studies on Children's Symbolic Play*

Psychologists, since Piaget, have examined behaviors of children during play situations in order to investigate the progression of behavior. Fenson and

*Figure 19.* Players and objects tend to become more exact and detailed as the child becomes more sophisticated intellectually. (Photo by Linda Lungren)

Kagan (1976) conducted a study which examined the age differences of early symbolic play and examined the age differences in sequentiality of behavior, that is, child's ongoing "stream of behavior." They examined children aged seven months to twenty months and taped a "blow-by-blow" narrative of the individual free-play session of each child. They used a metal tea set for the experiment. They defined three classes of responses: 1) relational acts, relating to the object; 2) symbolic acts such as eating or drinking; and 3) sequential acts.

The results indicated that banging appeared first; it was followed by simple relational acts, then by symbolic acts in which behavior became progressively more sequential. Sequentiality appears to be developed at a slower pace than relationships, and it is not apparent at twenty months of age. In general, the play of both the seven- and nine-month-olds was largely nonrelational and was characterized by close visual and tactual inspection of individual objects (mouthing and chewing). Children who were thirteen months old were more similar in their play to twenty-month-olds than to nine-month-olds.

The following chart illustrates the congruence between the stages of play that Fenson and Kagan have reported and Piaget's cognitive development schema.

| Piaget | | Fenson and Kagan | |
|---|---|---|---|
| Cognitive Stages | | | |
| Age | Sensorimotor | Age | |
| 0–1 month | neonatal reflexes | 7–9 months | prerelational acts |
| 1–4 months | new response patterns | 13–20 months | relational acts and |
| 4–8 months | coordinated responses | | symbolic acts |
| 8–12 months | complex coordinations | after 20 months | sequential acts |
| 12–18 months | means-end manipulation | | |
| 18–24 months | origin of ludic symbolism | | |
| 2–4 years | preconceptual | | |

Markey (1935) completed an extensive study of the symbolic play of fifty-four children ranging in age from twenty-two to fifty months. He used categories similar to those proposed by Piaget and found, as might be expected, that the total amount of symbolic play increased with age. An important finding was the shifts in the types of play activity that appeared at different ages. There was great interest in the make-believe use of materials and personifications for children three years old and younger. After three and a half years of age, these early forms became less common and the make-believe situations of dramatic play became integrated into the child's symbolic play repertoire. They also noted that the younger children engaged in imaginative activities that related to the specific materials before them. The older children, on the other hand, engaged more frequently in complicated make-believe involving relations and themes; they endowed the unstructured materials with functional meanings and combined them in complicated ways.

Many psychologists and educators have attempted to critically examine selected components of symbolic play; more specifically, they have investigated development in the use of symbols during children's play. In investigating the use of symbols, researchers have included the following: use of objects, materials, and gestures.

During the sensorimotor period, from birth to two years of age, the child acts directly on things that are immediately present. The child begins to use materials to symbolize his experiences for himself and to understand the sound patterns of language as a medium for talking about the immediate as well as the distant situation. This is a new way for the child to organize his experience. This use of symbols does not enter all domains of play at the same time; for example, the representational use of material in drawing and painting occurs some time after the use of symbolic objects in play.

Some researchers (Piaget, 1959, Werner and Kaplan, 1963) have noticed that young children during their second year begin to use their bodies in imitation of the motions of persons and the movement of things. Towards the close of the sensorimotor period the child uses his body in depiction of events that have occurred sometime in the past. Werner and Kaplan (1963) and Piaget (1959) view this phenomenon as a highly significant development, indicating the advent of symbolic functioning. About this time, children use parts of their bodies to depict nonkinetic properties of objects; for example, the child arches his back "to be" a bridge. Older children (four and five years of age) can use their body actions to represent patternings in nonbody domains (the child moves his hand in a stepwise ascending motion to show a series of ascending musical tones).

Kaplan (1968) conducted a study on the use of objects with children four, eight, and twelve years of age. They were asked to demonstrate the use of sixteen implements without actually handling them. Kaplan found that four-year-old children tended to use a body part as the implement, whereas the older children would position their hands as if holding the implement and then would enact the correct motions. Overton and Jackson (1971) conducted a similar study in which the overall results were in close accord with Kaplan's findings; they concluded that there is a shift from the use of body part as implement at the younger ages to more purely enactive gestures at older ages.

The Russian psychologist El'Konin (1971) has noted the following progression in the play activities of very young children:

1. Children of one to two years of age can enact such activities as feeding a doll with a cup but cannot carry out this gesture with other objects or without the object.

2. The action can be carried out with a "functional substitute" (a hollow block for a cup).

3. During the third year, objects that have minimal resemblance to their real life counterparts can be used as symbolic substitutes in play (stick = doll).

4. Subsequently, the child will occasionally use enactive gestures in the absence of any object, with an imaginary object.

Sinclair (1970) and Lezine (1971) suggest an earlier emergence of enactive gestures and symbolic use of objects than El'Konin. They maintain that children who are nineteen to twenty-six months old show three kinds of activities that indicate the beginning of symbolic play:

1. The use of animate-type objects as active partners in a play situation.

2. The use of objects "as if" they were other, nonpresent objects (use of a stick as if it were a baby's bottle).

3. Representing nonpresent objects through gesture (child handles empty bottle as if pouring it on his neck, then wipes his neck with the other hand).

## Sociodramatic Play

*Question 5: What is sociodramatic play and what do researchers say about its importance in the development of the child?*

In discussing symbolic play, the period of collective symbolism is of special interest to you, as the teacher of the young child. Collective symbolism, also called sociodramatic play, has been defined as a form of voluntary, social play in which the young child assumes a role and pretends to be a person other than himself by imitating the behavior and language of the assumed person. This play becomes sociodramatic when a selected theme is elaborated in conjunction with one or more other players and the players interact with one another linguistically and behaviorally (Smilansky, 1968). This play is to be distinguished from dramatic play in which the young child may assume a role (carpenter, mother) but does not interact with other players.

*Figure 20.* The young child assumes a role and pretends to be a person other than himself by imitating the behavior and language of the assumed person. (Photo by Linda Lungren)

Sociodramatic play seems to emerge as part of the child's behavior at about the age of three years (Smilansky, 1968; Bühler, 1933; Valentine, 1942; Piaget, 1962). The antecedents to this type of play begin at birth, and specific elements of sociodramatic play are observable as early as the first year. Valentine (1942) suggests that the first clear example of a child's play with an imaginary object appears at about one year, and "direct imitation" is apparent in children's play at the beginning of the second year. Bühler (1933) found that although social interaction with adults begins as early as three to four months, social play does not appear until sometime during the third or fourth year.

Piaget (1960) maintains that real pretending becomes apparent in the play of the child by the end of his second year. At this time the child attempts to engage adults and other children in his play (social play). Piaget explains the evolution of sociodramatic play as a function of the child's emerging verbal abilities; this phenomenon characteristically occurs between the ages of two and four. In general, most researchers agree that sociodramatic play begins somewhere at about the age of three, and it becomes far less frequent at about the age of six, gradually disappearing as games with rules begin to emerge as the primary play activity of the child.

Curry and Armaud (1974) further explain the developmental phenomenon of sociodramatic play in the area of symbolic elaboration of the role. They maintain that the child who is engaging in sociodramatic play is capable of playing out a recent personal or vicarious experience whereas the younger child is able to play out only first-hand experiences. The content of the play seems to change from the younger child's single interest in home and family to an enactment of roles outside the family, such as heroines (Joan of Arc). They also suggest that in sociodramatic play, the child will often displace his aggression in acceptable guises, such as a sheriff shooting the "bad" people, whereas the younger child only thinly disguises his feelings in an effective role, such as a wild horse. At the age of about three or four, they note, the child chooses to cast himself as the "good" person and the other players as "bad." Prior to the emergence of sociodramatic play, the child talks about "playing together" with other children and adults, but the play of the younger child is usually "parallel play." Finally, they note, during sociodramatic play, the child develops an awareness of group membership; the child may say, "Can I play?"

Both El'Konin (1969) and Kohlberg (1969) maintain that there are certain conditions necessary for successful sociodramatic play; a certain independence or differentiation from adults is necessary to participate in this play. El'Konin (1969) explains this as a contradictory condition; the child wants to be independent, yet he also wants to participate in the activities of adults. He explains that the child resolves this contradiction by using adults as major role-playing models. There are, however, several other roles that are frequently enacted by children in sociodramatic play. Fein and Clark-Stewart (1973) list six principal roles that children play: parents, specific adults (grocer), specific children (a little girl), babies, siblings, and animals. From several observational studies, they noted the following rules for the selection of roles.

1. Children play the roles of others who are more or less different from themselves. These can be older, younger, human or infrahuman, real or imaginary. The sociodramatic play of older children encompasses roles that explore complementary relationships: mothers/fathers, babies/siblings, cops/robbers.

2. Early role enactments seem to represent specific others. The enactment of older children seems to represent classes of social others: class of mothers or babies.

3. The role characteristics that a child may choose to enact may be quite discrepant from the characteristics of particular people whom they know; a child may role play a "father" quite discordant with his real father. Children's role playing can often reflect wishes as well as reality.

4. Role playing is both fluid and constrained. There are identifiable techniques for clarifying roles and for maintaining role continuity.

*Figure 21.* The sociodramatic play of older children encompasses roles which explore complementary relationships: mothers/fathers, babies/siblings, cops/robbers. (Photo by Linda Lungren)

In addition to these observations about role selection, El'Konin (1971) pointed out that the younger the child, the more unlikely it will be that he will play "himself." Older children seem to articulate the problem when they say, "How can I play Jack when I am Jack?" They equate role playing with the portrayal of a person other than themselves. The young child also refuses to portray a friend; El'Konin suggests that the young child may be incapable of isolating specific components and, therefore, is incapable of this role enactment.

### Smilansky's Research on Sociodramatic Play

In order to further explain the parameters of sociodramatic play, it is important to examine the works of Sara Smilansky (1968). Currently, her work on sociodramatic play among Israeli children seems to be one of the most frequently cited studies in the field. She maintains that the most important component of sociodramatic play is its imitative element, which she calls the "reality" element. The young child attempts to talk, act, and look like an "other" person, usually an adult. In trying to reproduce the world of the adult, the child experiences limitations caused by his environment which prevent him from imitating the adult exactly. At this point, a second element enters the child's play—nonreality, the make-believe, the imaginative element. The child uses make-believe to enhance his ability to imitate and this imagination enriches the imitation, often adding to the real-life event.

The make-believe, imaginative element of the child's play relies heavily upon verbalization because utterances can direct the action of the play and can substitute for reality. This usually occurs in one of the following ways:

1. Utterances that change the identity of the child; for example, "I am the clerk, you are the customer."
2. Utterances that change the identity of objects; for example, "I am eating an ice cream cone" when the child is gesturing with his fist.
3. Utterances that can be substituted for actions, such as, "Let's pretend I just built a rocket ship and you are stepping into it."
4. Utterances that can be used to describe situations—"Let's pretend you are sick."

These four utterances do not create reality; rather, they provide a context in which the play becomes more lifelike. These make-believe utterances are extremely important because they are the bridge that unites various segments of the child's play. It is the blending of imitative behavior, make-believe utterances, and play-related interaction that constitutes the phenomenon of sociodramatic play.

Smilansky also provided a rationale for studying the phenomenon of sociodramatic play. In explaining her rationale, she argued convincingly that successful participation in sociodramatic play activities foreshadows successful participation in school activities. She believes similar behaviors are required in both of these situations. Problem solving in school, for example, requires make-believe in order to read a dramatic story or to solve a verbal arithmetic problem. In explaining her theory that sociodramatic play advances the child's development in the areas of creativity, intellectual growth, and social skills, she presented fifteen generalizations about the actions and reactions that operate during sociodramatic play and that positively affect the child's development.

### Smilansky's 15 Generalizations About Sociodramatic Play

1. The child creates new situations by combining scattered experiences. He is using imaginative <u>combinations</u>, not an exact imitation of a single behavior.
2. By using a fixed frame of reference, the child draws on experiences selectively. He includes only the behavior that characterizes the role he is enacting.
3. The child learns to act out the main theme of his role.
4. The child learns to concentrate on a theme.
5. The child learns to control himself in relation to his own internalized sense of order.
6. The child learns to discipline his actions within a specific context.
7. The child learns flexibility in his approach to various situations.
8. The child learns how to set his own standards for his actions and to respect the standards of others.
9. The child learns to be a creator.
10. Sociodramatic play helps the child move from egocentrism to cooperation and social interaction.
11. The child is able to observe reality (his surroundings) with the knowledge that at some future date he will use these observations for his own purposes.
12. The child learns new concepts (the concept of "mother" can include behavior patterns that are not necessarily part of his own mother's behavior. In this way, the concept of "mother" is broadened).
13. The child learns to develop advanced stages of abstract thought.
14. The child learns to generalize.
15. The child learns vicariously from the experiences and knowledge of other children.

Smilansky (1968) believes that a child's ability to effectively participate in sociodramatic play increases as his experiences begin to accumulate. She maintains that children who are denied the opportunity to learn sociodramatic play will have less chance to learn how to accept a problematic world; they will be unable to sense the relevance of problems, and they will not be able to participate in school. They lack a generalized capacity to reach for conceptual structures and to operate within their implicit limits. However, children who have engaged in sociodramatic play will profit from school because they have been actors, observers, and interactors. Learning has occurred in a play activity that is in itself rewarding.

*Figure 22.* The effects of sociodramatic play have been described as the means by which the child is able to build a world of shared social relationships. (Photo by Linda Lungren)

In the area of problem solving, researchers have also demonstrated the beneficial effects of sociodramatic play. Smilansky (1968) pointed out that the way in which children organize their sociodramatic play is the same way in which they will have to organize other, more complex problem-solving tasks. The approach is comprehensive and effective. In the case of a particular enactment, "Spaceperson," for example, the child does the following:

1. He selects his stimulus from the environment (Spaceperson).
2. He spontaneously responds ("Pretend this is our spaceship").
3. Others in the environment accept his response ("Let's take it to the moon").
4. He selects cues from other player's responses ("Look, there's a moon crater").
5. He forms new responses to sustain the play ("Let's call headquarters and ask them what to do").

Smilansky (1968) argued that sociodramatic play involves the ability to understand and abstract the salient features of another's role and that it requires empathy and objectivity. Both empathy and objectivity suggest that the child is practicing the operation of reversibility, which Piaget (1962) describes as essential in cognitive structures.

There are several useful implication we can draw from the literature on sociodramatic play. According to several researchers (Smilansky, 1968; Feitelson and Ross, 1973; Singer and Singer, 1974), the most effective training program is one that *includes a participating adult*, who directly involves children and provides immediate feedback to each child's responses. The question of setting and environment also seems to have rather far-reaching implications for the effectiveness of sociodramatic play. In addition to number(s) and availability of props, researchers have reported on the effectiveness of changing the setting to accommodate children's needs and to tap individual experiences and to keep play interesting. Curry (1971) reported on the positive change in Navajo children's sociodramatic play after their housekeeping corner was inadvertently rearranged (for cleaning purposes) to resemble their own homes.

### Rules for Sociodramatic Play

Sutton-Smith (1971) suggested the following rules for sociodramatic play:

1. Teachers must accept the child on the level of development at which he is functioning.
2. Teachers should offer play opportunities that allow for a sensorimotor approach to life. They should provide chiildren with items that stimulate all the sensory modalities and provide opportunities for channeling the direct motor discharge of these sensory impressions.
3. Teachers should allow children to watch activities: for example, a plumber fixing a sink. They should follow up the activity by pointing out the tools that are available for the children to use. This will highlight the potential use of the equipment in sociodramatic play situations.
4. Teachers should have props available that are models of familiar elements from the child's environment.
5. Teachers can provide models by making playful gestures, such as pretending to drink "make-believe" tea.

Although there are disagreements about the precise nature of play development, most educators agree that it is an extremely beneficial activity for children. Therefore, it seems important to briefly review some of the factors that promote and enhance play.

### Materials and Settings for Sociodramatic Play

Several studies have examined the various roles of materials and equipment on children's play. A study conducted by Updegraff and Herbst (1933) found

*Figure 23*. Although there are disagreements about the precise nature of play development, most educators agree that it is an extremely beneficial activity for children. (Photo by Linda Lungren)

that children playing together with clay used more imitation than when they played with blocks. Moyer and Gilmer (1955) found that children played for longer periods of time with toys that were more complex or more novel to them. Pulaski (1970) studied five-year-olds and found that unstructured toys elicited a wider variety of fantasy themes than structured toys. Smilansky's (1968) "advantaged children" seemed to thrive on unstructured materials, whereas the "disadvantaged children" played much more with toy replicas of real-life objects.

Franklin (1970) investigated symbolic play in older children. Four-year-old children were presented two "pretend" situations at two different times, once with a set of realistic play material and once with a set of nonrealistic materials. It was found that the tendency to follow instructions was greater with the realistic toys than with the nonrealistic materials.

After examining young children's play, Stern (1974) developed a comprehensive set of categories that she applied to the analysis of classroom play of three-, four-, and five-year-olds. She found that the three- and four-year-old children engaged primarily in the role play, whereas the five-year-olds showed a marked shift towards using toys and other objects to enact situations. Stern also investigated the "types" of objects that were used symbolically. She reported that realistic toys were the most commonly used at all three age levels. However, it appeared that the older children constructed and used objects of lesser realism during dramatic play than did the younger children.

Schickedanz (1976) proposed several themes that may be appropriate for dramatic play. In the chart on page 93, she lists four different themes and some appropriate props that may enhance play.

### Stress and Sociodramatic Play

There is a general consensus that play is most likely to occur when the organism is free from strong biological drives (Belyne, 1960; White, 1959). Both Erikson (1950) and Pella (1971) have found that play is disrupted when children are under stress; exploratory and manipulative play behavior are affected by conditions which frustrate the child (Barker, Dembo, and Lewin, 1941). Although these studies were conducted in "set-up" situations, Prescott et al. (1967), Johnson (1935), and Jersild and Markey (1935) have conducted studies that give rise to the importance of possible stress-producing factors such as crowding, inappropriate play equipment, and inadequate supervision.

### Language/Reading Development and Sociodramatic Play

In the area of language development, Slobin (1966) found that the acquisition of new words in a child's lexicon might occur more easily in a role-playing situation than in a task-oriented teaching situation.

Wolfgang (1974) conducted a study to explore the relationships between the cognitive area of reading and selected developmental aspects of symbolic play among first-grade males. His results led him to hypothesize that advanced readers have attained an equilibrium between assimilation (play) and accommodation that results in advanced reading performance. The delayed readers were still assimilating freely during fantasy play, suggesting that an interference occurred in their accommodation to reading "signs."

### Thinking Skills and Sociodramatic Play

The role of early play and exploration contributes to the promotion of cognitive growth, according to many developmental psychologists (Bruner 1973; Piaget 1952; White 1959; Sigel 1970).

Piaget (1962) and Vygotsky (1967) both maintain that symbolic play contributes to the development of representational processes and constitutes as a stepping stone toward the development of abstract, logical thinking. Singer

## Dramatic Play Themes and Props

| House Play | Fire Station Play | Doctor's Office Play | Grocery Store Play |
|---|---|---|---|
| 1. Kitchen furniture: a stove, sink, refrigerator, table and chairs, shelves. | 1. Climbing box or building blocks to use in creating a fire station. | 1. Old, white skirts and blouses for use as doctor and nurse dress-up clothes. | 1. A shelving unit. |
| 2. Tablecloth or place mats. | 2. Firefighter hats. | 2. Medical props such as stethoscopes, popsicle sticks or straws (thermometer), strips of white cloth (bandages), plastic syringes, cotton balls, and old flashlights. | 2. Cardboard boxes that can serve as cases for "dairy products" or "produce." (Place smaller box inside larger one to make a raised surface.) |
| 3. Small chest of drawers and doll bed. | 3. Old shirts to use as firefighters jackets | 3. Play telephones. | 3. A large variety of empty containers from foods and other household products. |
| 4. Artificial flowers. | 4. Small lengths of garden hose to use as water hoses. | 4. Dolls and dolls clothes | 4. Plastic fruits and vegetables. |
| 5. Several dolls and stuffed animals. | 5. A bell to use as a fire alarm. | 5. DOCTOR IS IN and DOCTOR IS OUT signs. | 5. Play money. |
| 6. Dolls' clothes, blankets, and bottles. | 6. Old flashlights. | 6. An "appointment" book for the receptionist. | 6. A cash register (toy or old, real one). |
| 7. Old adult clothes: hats, gloves, jackets, neckties, scarves, jewelry. | 7. Play telephones. | 7. Pencils. | 7. Large food sale poster obtained from local grocers. |
| 8. Plastic replicas of fruits and vegetables. | 8. A sign that says FIRE STATION. | 8. Model of clock face with hands that move. | 8. Brown paper bags of various sizes. |
| 9. An assortment of dishes, silverware, pots and pans, and cooking utensils. | 9. Very simple labelled maps of the classroom for use in locating "fires." | 9. An alphabet letter or picture "eye chart." | 9. Newspaper pages containing food ads. |
| 10. Empty containers from food, cleaning products, and toiletry items. | 10. Picture posters with appropriate fire safety messages. | 10. Exposed x-ray films obtained from a doctor. | 10. OPEN and CLOSED signs. |
| 11. Dustpan and small broom. | 11. A large "log" book made with blank sheets of paper. | 11. Poster showing the human skeleton, or body parts. | 11. Old shirts for store employee costumes. |
| 12. Play telephones. | 12. Pencils. | | 12. A kitchen scale to weigh produce. |
| 13. Brown paper bags or plastic net bags to use for "shopping" or "picnicking" trips. | | | 13. A large selection of food and household products coupons clipped from magazines and the newspaper. |
| 14. Container of play-dough. | | | 14. A small pad or small pieces of paper, and pencils. |
| 15. A "cookbook" consisting of a collection of recipe charts used in classroom cooking projects. | | | 15. Magnetic board and letters to use in making signs for special sales. |
| 16. A "telephone book" consisting of children's names, street addresses, and telephone numbers. | | | |
| 17. Paper, pencils, and envelopes. | | | |
| 18. Wall plaques with appropriate sayings such as "Home Sweet Home." | | | |

Schickerdanz, J. "You Be the Doctor and I'll Be Sick." *Language Arts*, 1978.

(Sutton-Smith, 1970–1971). Smilansky (1968) and Sutton-Smith (1970, 1971) have found that specific techniques are used by children to sustain play; they use humor and they change themes in order to keep their play from ending.

That play is an integral part of early childhood programs is certainly not a new concept. Both Froebel (1967) and Montessori (1964) encouraged children to play and to use play to accomplish well-specified goals. Froebel (1967) for example, designed activities and materials to encourage spiritual growth, whereas Montessori used play as a means to develop basic sensory/cognitive understandings. The importance of play is discussed in the following quote from the Report of the Central Advisory Council:

> Play is the central activity in all nursery schools and in many infant schools. This some-times leads to accusations that children are wasting their time in school: they should be "working." But this distinction between work and play is false, possibly throughout life, certainly in the primary school. Its essence lies in past notions of what is done in school (play). We know now that play in the sense of "messing about" either with motivated objects or with other children, and of creating fantasies—is vital to children's learning and therefore vital in school. Adults who criticize teachers for allowing children to play are unaware that play is the principle means of learning in early childhood. It is the way through which children reconcile their inner lives with external reality. In play, children gradually develop concepts of casual relationships, the power to discriminate, to make judgments, to analyze and synthesize, to imagine and formulate. Children become absorbed in their play, and the satisfaction of bringing it to a satisfactory conclusion fixes habits of concentration which can be transferred to other learning. (Central Advisory Council Report, p. 193)

## Definitions of Play

### Question 2: What Is Play?

Several educators have attempted to define children's play. Some of these definitions include the following:

Froebel:  The natural unfolding of the germinal leaves of childhood.

Lazerson:  Activity in itself (free, aimless, amusing, or diverting).

Hall:  The motor habits and spirit of the past persisting in the present.

## Piaget's Research on Play

### Question 3: What is Piaget's view of play?

Piaget answered the question "What is play?" by defining the develop-mental stages through which each child passes. These stages of cognitive de-velopment are manifested by the child's play and can be observed through

(1973) agrees with this view and presents recent research which demonstrates the importance of imagery and verbal coding in children's learning. He believes that imaginative play provides practice in the use of these information-processing skills.

At the age of seven years the child's play seems to indicate the reduction of symbolic play in favor of games with rules. Vygotsky (1962) describes this apparent change in symbolic play as a reintegration of the thought process in which the outward free assimilation of play is internalized as part of the creative thinking process and an equivalence occurs between assimilation and accommodation. As a result, the child can think in more conceptual terms rather than in his previous fantasy-based perceptions of the world.

### Social Interaction and Sociodramatic Play

A topic that is often discussed in detail is the acquisition of roles in children. Children spend a great deal of their time pretending and assuming new roles. Several psychologists, including Piaget, have examined this phenomenon from the perspective of social interaction growth in the young child; they have concluded that there is a sequential developmental pattern in the taking of roles as a vehicle of social behavior.

On the basis of their educational and clinical experience, they have found that role portrayal by children follows certain developmental sequences that appear to contribute to the child's growing mastery of cognitive, affective, and symbolic functions. These sequences may be analyzed along the following dimensions:

1. Symbolic Elaboration of Role—refers to the style or manner in which the child manifests his conception of the role he is enacting. It begins with concrete imitation of perceived actions which the child knows from his own experience. It is strongly linked to the child's cognitive development. It enhances, facilitates, and energizes the attainment of abstract and symbolic mental processes. Conversely, the child's symbolic elaborations reflect important aspects of his current cognitive functioning.

2. Thematic Content—refers to the nature of the behaviors portrayed in association with a specific role. The complexity and elaboration of themes seen clearly related to the child's degree of cognitive sophistication.

3. Integrating of Affect and Intellect—Normally the child can bring rational considerations to bear on how he expresses his feelings. This involves the displacement and channeling of raw affect which is acted out without the consideration of the other person to increasing mediation of expression of more primitive feelings through words and symbolic representation.

4. Enactment of the "Good" Self—encompasses representations of what the child feels is a powerful, safe, and valued role.

5. Distinction Between Reality and Fantasy—children demonstrate their ability to distinguish between real and make-believe by using "pretend" or "make believe." By using these the child gives a cognitive label to a situation which is affect laden.

6. Modes of Interpersonal Transaction—refers to the child's normal developmental movement from solitary, egocentric, personalized play to an increasing awareness of others.

## Implications of Research on Play

*Question 6: What are the implications of research on play for teaching young children?*

The compilation of this information brings us to some most important questions: What are the educational implications of this research? How does this affect you, the teacher, the parent, administrator, or curriculum writer? How can this body of information be used appropriately in order to maximize a child's learning? We shall discuss the implications of this research within three categories: learning environments, materials, and parents.

### Learning Environment

Research suggests that in order to encourage play the physical properties of the learning environment must be different for the child at various points in his development. For example, the child from birth to about eighteen months requires a physical environment that is protective and appropriately stimulating for his age group. An environment that includes only a wide-open space with a jungle gym and a chalkboard would physically limit the child from developing cognition through play. The child, during this period, spends a great deal of time investigating various physical relationships between objects and materials. Therefore, the environment must include mobiles, objects for sucking, and for physical exploration.

During the second period, the symbolic play period, the environment must be created to stimulate the child to investigate, experience, and master all sorts of objects, games, materials, and relationships. The classroom structure must be inviting. If you want a child to play with materials, he must know that they are available, and they must be within his reach. If you want the child to roam freely from one area of the room to another, you have to construct an optimal environment that will be conducive to this behavior.

*Figure 24.* In general, the research seems to support the creation of a classroom structure with several centers where children can play. These students are sharing the gerbil center. (Photo by Linda Lungren)

In general, the research seems to support the creation of a classroom structure with several centers where children can play. The following illustration will serve as a model for an appropriate early learning environment:

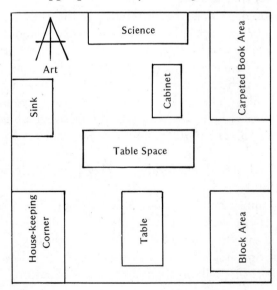

If the environment is designed to encourage several different kinds of play activity, then several different kinds of play activity will probably occur. Conversely, if a classroom is set up with wide-open space, then children will tend to use the open spaces for physical play. A great deal of running, riding,

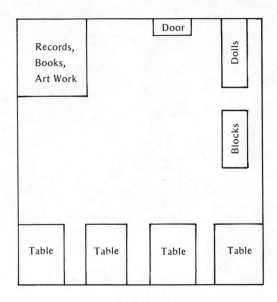

and sliding may occur within the open space area. If the center has the facilities, it may be useful to find an alternate area for this type of play, outdoors or another room. This is not to suggest disapproval of physical play in the form of running and sliding. Obviously, these are extremely important activities; so too are symbolic play, dramatic play, water play, and construction play.

The physical environment affects learning. The child acquires a great deal of his stimulation from the environment; the structure of the classroom can elicit participation in various activities or it can "turn off" the child to certain types of play. Many classrooms are structured in such a way that a passerby could only conclude: "Blocks are all that are important in that room." Often, dolls are strewn about the room, books are ripped and misfiled, and the only area of the room that has clear boundaries is the block area. As Schickedanz (1976) points out, children can learn classroom rules and limits by the structure of the environment. She also points out that rules provide children with greater opportunities for freedom and exploration. It might be that children spend hours in the block corner because they experience great freedom to learn in this area; that is, they know the rules.

It seems obvious that there should be a structured balance within a classroom environment, which will help children elicit and participate in new experiences. Therefore, those who have the responsibility for creating learning environments (parents, teachers, or community leaders) should decide upon the educational objectives and structure the environment accordingly.

*Figure 25.* Children need to experience many different types of materials within their play activity if they are to develop many thinking and coping strategies. (Photo by Linda Lungren)

## Materials

In recent years, many materials have been created for young children. Some of these materials are educationally useful and some are not. Again, it seems to be the responsibility of the purchasers of materials (parents, teachers, or administrators) to determine educational objectives and to establish criteria for the selection of materials to be used in early educational environments.

The research findings presented here seem to suggest that play development can be enhanced greatly through the use of materials. Children need to experience many different types of materials within their play activity if they are to develop many thinking and coping strategies.

The debate over realistic versus nonrealistic materials is in many ways ludicrous. The child will often determine the reality of an object by the way in which he uses it. However, in order not to avoid the seriousness of this question, the data indicate that a combination of materials should be available for the child's use, including "raw" materials, such as blocks, and intricate, realistic materials, such as a miniature tea service. Both types of materials will

*Figure 26.* Manipulative, physical, dramatic, and game-like activities may be part of both spontaneous and structured play activities. (Photo by Linda Lungren)

enhance play; often the raw material provides the child an opportunity to create symbols, and the ready-made materials serve as props for dramatic play.

It is almost axiomatic to say that children will play with materials that are available to them. The community members who are responsible for the education of the child must determine the nature and extent of the materials within a center. These decisions, obviously, should be made from a knowledgeable base. If a goal of the program is to encourage reading skills, then materials must include many books, records, paper, pencils, and crayons. The available materials determine the direction of the entire program.

If you want to encourage a specific type of play, then you must provide materials that will generate that type of play. For example, if you want children to interact with each other, you must provide materials that have the greatest probability for social interaction, such as tea sets, plates, costumes, stores, old clothes, and structured games for two or three children.

*Figure 27.* A combination of materials should be available for the child's use. (Photo by Linda Lungren)

### Parents

The data suggests that adults, caretakers, teachers, and parents can play an important role in the development of play in the young child. Parents can create situations that will produce the play which is beneficial for the child's cognitive development. However, parents cannot be expected to have a knowledge base about play.

### The School's Responsibility to Parents

The school, including administrators and teachers, has some responsibility to inform parents about the possibilities for development that exist within the realm of play.

Schools can inform parents in many different ways. Perhaps the most appropriate vehicle for parent education is a brief, readable newsletter to inform parents about play. A series of one-page newsletters can be produced and distributed to parents on the following topics: why children play, the nature of play, the cognitive benefits of play, the advantages of interaction during play, the construction of materials for play, and the purchasing of games and toys. A more detailed explanation of parent involvement is presented in Chapter 10.

Parents have many questions about play which need to be answered in an appropriate manner. A forum must be established for parents to ask their questions; this can be done in a number of ways: parent meetings, newsletters, question boxes, or conferences. Parents may be concerned about crucial issues and may need some counsel. For example, they may ask such questions as the following:

1. Is it all right for my child to have a pretend friend?
2. It seems that all the school does is let my child play; shouldn't he be learning?
3. Should I give my child guns and Barbie dolls?
4. My child needs special attention, so I don't send him to preschool; does he need other children?

These are important questions that parents ask; they need to be answered if parents are to encourage the development of play in their children.

Parents should be included in the planning and implementation of early education programs. They should be invited to participate in decision making, including the purchase of play-oriented materials.

A further step that schools should take to involve parents and to answer their questions is to invite them to classrooms in order to explain daily schedules and curricula. Parents need information about the relationship between play and learning and the relationship between play materials and learning. Parents can understand that children are learning physical principles about size and gravity when they play with blocks. They can also understand that children can learn to modify their behavior when they play with their peers; they can understand that children learn to extend their thoughts and their language so as to communicate with their peers.

### What Parents Can Do at Home

Parents, after being informed about the benefits of play, can encourage children to be actively involved with play materials at home. Parents can encourage many educational activities, such as sorting, matching, and recognizing one-to-one correspondences. Many activities that parents can use at home are presented in Chapter 10.

Parents should not push their children into play that is beyond their current level of cognitive functioning. However, parents need to realize the component skills of specific tasks before they conclude that a particular task is beyond the scope of the child. Naturally, no one expects a four-year-old child to read *War and Peace*, but there are numerous appropriate prereading tasks for the four-year-old child. Parents (and teachers) should not categorically eliminate "reading" as an inappropriate task for the young child.

*Figure 28.* Parents can help nurture some interest in reading activities early in the child's life. (Photo by Jonathan Sutton)

The parent, far more than the school, is responsible for the education of the young child. It is absolutely crucial for parents to be invited to learn about and to participate in the development of their children.


## BIBLIOGRAPHY

Barker, R. G., T. Dembo, and K. Lewin. "Frustration and Regression: An Experiment with Young Children." *University of Iowa Studies in Child Welfare* (1941) 18; 1–314.

Belyne, D. E. *Conflict, Arousal, and Curiosity.* New York: McGraw-Hill Book Company, 1960.

Bruner, J. S. *Beyond the Information Given: Studies in the Psychology of Knowing.* Selected and edited by Jeremy M. Anglin. New York: W. W. Norton & Company, Inc., 1973.

Bühler, C. *From Birth to Maturity.* London: Kegan, Paul, Trench, Trubner & Co., 1933.

Comenius. J. *The Great Didactic of John Amos Comenius.* Translated into English and edited by M. W. Kestinze. London: H. and L. Block, 1907–10.

Curry, N., and S. Armaud. "Cognitive Implications in Children's Spontaneous Play." *Theory into Practice*, 1974, 13, 273–277.

Curry, N. "Consideration of Current Basic Issues on Play." In *The Child Strives for Self-Realization*. Washington, D.C.: National Association for the Education of Young Children, 1971.

Curry, N. "Dramatic Play As a Curricula Tool." In D. Sponseller (ed.), *Play As a Learning Medium*. Washington, D.C.: National Association for the Education of Young Children, 1974.

El'Konin, D. B. "Some Results of the Study of the Psychological Development of Preschool-Age Children." In M. Cole and D. Maltzman, *A Handbook of Contemporary Soviet Psychology*. New York: Basic Books, Inc., Publishers, 1969, 163–208.

El'Konin, D. "Symbolics and Its Functions in the Play of Children." In W. E. Herron and B. Sutton-Smith, *Child's Play*. New York: John Wiley & Sons, Inc., 1971.

Erikson, E. *Childhood and Society*. New York: W. W. Norton & Company, Inc., 1950.

Erikson, E. *Identity and the Life Cycle*. New York: International Universities Press, 1959.

Fein, G., and A. Clark-Stewart. *Day Care in Context*, New York: John Wiley & Sons, Inc., 1973.

Feitelson, D., and G. Ross. "The Neglected Factor—Play." *Human Development*, 1973, 16, 202–223.

Fenson, L., and J. Kagan. "The Developmental Progression of Manipulative Play in the First Two Years." *Child Development*, 1976, 47, 232–236.

Franklin, M. B. "A Study of Non-Verbal Representation in Middle-Class and Lower-Class Preschool Children." Final Report, Research Division, Bank Street College of Education, New York, 1970.

Freud, S. *Totem and Taboo*. Vienna: Hugo Heller, 1913. Copyright 1950 by Routledge and Kagon. Published in 1962 in New York by W. W. Norton Co.

Froebel, F. "The Young Child." In I. M. Lilley (ed.), *Friedrich Froebel: A Selection From His Writings*. Cambridge, England: Cambridge University Press, 1967.

Hall, G. S. *The Psychology of Adolescence*. New York: D. Appleton and Co., 1904.

Hall, G. S. *Aspects of Child Life and Education*. New York: Appleton-Century-Crofts, 1921.

Isaacs, S. *Social Development in Young Children: A Study of Beginnings*. New York: Harcourt Brace Jovanovich, Inc., 1933.

Jackson, J. "Play As Learning." *Theory Into Practice* 1974, 13:(4), 317–323.

Jersild, A. T. and F. V. Markey. "Conflicts between Preschool Children." *Child Development Monographs*, #21, 1935.

Johnson, H. *Children in the Nursery School*. New York: The John Day Co., Publishers, 1928.

Johnson, M. W. "The Effect on Behavior of Variation in the Amount of Play Equipment." *Child Development*, 1935.

Kaplan, E. "Gestural Representation of Implement Usage: an Organismic Developmental Study," Unpublished doctoral dissertation, Clark University, 1968.

Kohlberg, L. "Stage and Sequence: The Cognitive Developmental Approach to Socialization." In D. A. Goslin (ed.) *Handbook of Socialization Theory and Research*. Chicago: Rand McNally & Company, 1969.

Krown, S. *Three and Fours Go to School.* Englewood Cliffs, N.J.: Prentice-Hall, Inc., 1974, pp. 94–101.

Lazerson, M. "Social Reform and Early Childhood Education: Some Historical Perspectives." In R. H. Anderson and H. G. Shane (eds.), *As The Twig is Bent: Readings in Early Childhood Education.* Boston: Houghton Mifflin Co., 1971.

Lee, J. *Play in Education.* New York: Macmillan Publishing Co., Inc., 1915.

Lezine, I. "The Transition from Sensory-Motor to Earliest Symbolic Function in Early Development." Paris: Unpublished Paper, 1971.

Lieberman, J.N. "Playfulness and Divergent Thinking: An Investigation of Their Relationship at the Kindergarten Level." *Journal of Genetic Psychology*, 107, no. 2 (December 1965) pp. 210–224.

Markey, F.V. "Imaginative Behavior of Preschool Children." *Child Development Monographs*, #18, 1935.

Mitchell, E. and Mason, B.S. *The Theory of Play.* (res. ed.) Cranbury, New Jersey: A.S. Barnes, 1948, 3.

Montessori, M. *The Montessori Method.* New York: Schochen Books, Inc., 1964.

Moyer, K.E. and B.H. Gilmer. "Attention Span for Experimentally Designed Toys." *Journal of Genetic Psychology*, 1955, 87: 187–201.

Omwake, E. "The Child's Estate." In A. J. Solnit and S. A. Provence (eds.), *Modern Perspectives in Child Development.* New York: International Universities Press, 1963.

Overton, W.F., and J.P. Jackson. "The Representation of Imagized Objects in Initited Action Sequences, A developmental study." Paper presented at the bicentennial meetings of the Society for Research in Child Development, Minneapolis, 1971.

Pella, L.E. "Libidinal Development as Reflected in Play." *Psychoanalysis*, 1955, 3: 3–12.

Peller, L. "Models of Children's Play" In B. Sutton-Smith and R.E. Henon's *Child's Play.* New York: John Wiley & Sons, Inc., 1971.

Pestalozzi, J. H. *Leonard and Gertrude.* Boston: D.C. Heath and Co., 1897.

Piaget, J. *Play, Dreams, and Imitation in Childhood.* New York: W.W. Norton & Company, Inc., 1951 (original 1945).

Piaget, J. *The Language and Thought of the Child.* 3rd Ed. New York: The Humanities Press, Inc. 1959.

Piaget J. *The Psychology of Intelligence.* New Jersey: Littlefield, 1960.

Piaget, J. *Plays, Dreams, and Imitation in Childhood.* New York: W. W. Norton & Company, Inc., 1962.

Piaget, J. and B. Inhelder. *The Psychology of the Child.* New York: Basic Books, Inc., Publishers, 1969.

Plato. *The Laws.* Translated from the Greek with an introduction by Trevor J. Saunders. New York: Penguin Books, 1970.

Prescott, E., E. Jones, and S. Kritchevsky "Group Day Care as a Childrearing Environment." Unpublished manuscript, Pacific Oaks College, Pasadena, Calif. 1967. (ERIC No. ED 924453)

Pulaski, M.A. "Play as a Function of Toy Structure and Fantasy Predisposition." *Child Development*, 1970, 41: 531–538.

Pulaski, M. *Understanding Piaget.* New York: Harper & Row, Publishers, 1971.

Rousseau, J.J. *Emile, Julie, and Other Writings*. New York: Barrow's Educational Services, 1964.

Saltz, E., and J. Johnson. "Training for Thematic-Fantasy Play in Culturally Disadvantaged Children." *Journal of Educational Psychology*, 1974, 66: 623–630.

Schickedanz, J. "Structure and the Learning of Limits in Preschool Classrooms." Paper presented at National Association for the Education of Young Children Conference, Anaheim, California, Nov. 1976.

Schickedanz, J. "You Be the Doctor and I'll Be Sick: Preschoolers Learn the Language Arts through Play." *Language Arts*. 55, No. 6 (September 1978).

Sears, S. "The Relationship Between Sociodramatic Play and School Achievement of Second Grade Low Socioeconomic Status Black Children." Unpublished Ph.D. Dissertation, Ohio State University, 1972.

Shaw, M.E. "Psychological Ecology of a Nursery School." *Child Development*, 1963, 34: 979–999.

Siegel, I., "Developmental Theory in Preschool Education." *Early Childhood Education*, Yearbook of the National Society for the Study of Education, 1972.

Sigel, I. "The Distancing Hypothesis: A Causal Hypothesis for the Acquisition of Representational Thought." In M. Jones (ed.) *The Effects of Early Experiences*. Miami, Fl.: University of Miami Press, 1970.

Sinclair, H. "The Transition from Sensory-Motor Behavior to Symbolic Activity." *Interchange*, 1970, 119–126.

Singer, J., and D. Singer. "Fostering Imaginative Play in Preschool Children: Effects of TV Viewing and Direct Adult Modeling." Paper presented at American Psychological Association, New Orleans, La., 1974.

Singer, J. *The Child's World or Make-believe*. New York: Academic Press, Inc., 1973.

Slobin, D.I. "The Acquisition of Russian as a Native Language." In F. Smith and G.A. Miller, *The Genesis of Language*. Cambridge, Ma.: M.I.T. Press, 1966.

Smilansky, S. *The Effects of Sociodramatic Play on Disadvantaged Pre-School Children*. New York: John Wiley & Sons, Inc., 1968.

Stern, V. "Cognitive Aspects of Young Children's Symbolic Play." Final Report, Research Division, Bank Street College of Education, 1974.

Sutton-Smith, B. "Play, Games and Controls." In J.P. Scott (ed.) *Social Control*. Chicago: University of Chicago Press, 1970.

Sutton-Smith, B. "A Syntax for Play and Games." In R.E. Herron and B. Sutton-Smith, *Child's Play*. New York: John Wiley & Sons, Inc., 1971.

Sutton-Smith, B. "Boundaries." In R.E. Herron and B. Sutton-Smith, *Child's Play*. New York: John Wiley & Sons, Inc., 1971.

Sutton-Smith, B. "The Playful Modes of Knowing." In G. Engstron (ed.), *Play: The Child Strives Toward Self-Realization*. Washington, D.C.: National Association for the Education of Young Children, 1971.

Sutton-Smith, B., and J.M. Roberts. "The Cross-Cultural and Psychological Study of Games." In G. Luschew (ed.) *The Cross-cultural Analysis of Games*. Champaign, Ill.: Stipes, 1970.

Updegraff, R. and E.K. Herbst. "An Experimental Study of the Social Behavior Stimulated in Young Children by Certain Play Materials." *Journal of Genetic Psychology*, 1933, 42: 372–391.

Valentine, C.W. *The Psychology of Early Childhood*. London: Methuen & Co., Ltd., 1942.

Vygotsky, L.S. *Thought and Language*. Cambridge, Mass.: The MIT Press, 1962.

Vygotsky, L.S. "Play and Its Role in the Mental Development of the Child." *Soviet Psychology*, 1967, 5: 6–18.

Werner, H., and B. Kaplan. *Symbol Formation*. New York: John Wiley & Sons, Inc., 1963.

White, R.W. "Motivation Reconsidered: The Concept of Competence." *Psychological Review*, 1959, 66: 297–333.

Whiting, J.W. , and I.L. Child. *Child Training and Personality*. New Haven, Conn.: Yale University Press, 1953.

Wolfgang, C. "An Exploration of the Relationship Between the Cognitive Area of Reading and Selected Developmental Aspects of Children's Play." *Psychology In the Schools.* (July 1974) 11: (3) 338–343.

Yura, M., and M. Galaso. "Adlerian Usage of Children's Play." *Journal of Individual Psychology*, 1974, 30: 194–201.

# Section

# III

# Curriculum Models for Developing Language/Reading Programs for Young Children

This section has been designed to introduce you to the components of effective early language/reading programs. In Chapter 5, you will be presented with an analysis of various program models that have been used in the education of young children. Chapters 6 through 9 include an investigation of research related to practical suggestions for using language experiences to extend the young child's speaking, listening, writing, and reading abilities as well as a review of current children's literature. Chapter 10 fully explains why and how parents can successfuly participate in your program.

# 5

# Preschool Curriculum Models of Teaching Language/Reading to the Young Child

*Figure 29.* Much of the existing preschool curricula places the young child in an environment that encourages individual exploration. (Photo by Linda Lungren)

One of the results of the intensive search in the 1950–60s for more thorough methods of conducting the educational enterprise was the development of schools and curricula specifically designed for the very young child. Such curricula were based on a variety of philosophical theories that emphasized the ways that young children learn to organize information. These curricula integrated the disciplines of linguistics, philosophy, history, biology, psychology, political science, sociology, economics, and anthropology. As a result of this integration, the embryonic discipline of early childhood education has emerged.

Much of the existing preschool curricula places the young child in a "discovery" learning environment that encourages individual exploration. The discovery method as well as other learning programs have been built upon theories that are primarily devoid of systematic testing. In an attempt to rectify the lack of continuous evaluation of early learning curriculum models, we encourage you to ask the following evaluative question as you study each of the models that we will present in this chapter:

> Does this model of early learning provide alternatives which enable me as a teacher
>
> to be sufficiently responsive to the human variability of each child in my classroom?

## The Normative-Developmental Model

### Aims and Objectives

The normative-developmental curriculum model is designed to enrich the experiential readiness of each child. It has been the model most commonly used in Head Start programs. Specific program objectives include the following:
1. The development of each child's positive self-image.
2. The development of each child's ability to work and play cooperatively.
3. The development of each child's language skills.
4. The development of self-expression through art and music.
5. The development of perceptual-motor coordination.
6. The development of each child's awareness of self within the environment.

### Curriculum Components

All components of this model are designed to encourage social/emotional development. The works of Freud (1913), Gesell (1940), and Erikson (1963) characterize the philosophical parameters of this model; the works of these researchers suggest the concept of developmental stages of maturation. These theorists believe that the adult life of each person is greatly influenced by his early life experiences.

After Gesell (1940) and several of his colleagues collected samples of children's motor, social, and intellectual behaviors, they determined chronologically normative stages of development for young children. These norms were then plotted on a growth and development chart and used to categorize children as "slow" or "fast" developers. This maturational point of view was similar to Froebel's (1967) concept of "unfolding" and closely related to the mind-set of the early romantic educators who believed that learning is an intensely involved process. The romantic point of view suggests that responsibility for learning belongs primarily to each student and education is a natural growing process between the student and a stimulating environment.

The curricular focus of this model was to provide quality learning experiences for young children. Because student development was a long process, it was believed that short-term outcomes were of lesser importance. Concrete activities included prereading and science experiments, art and musical experiences, and sociodramatic play.

> The major goals in using sociodramatic play as a teaching device are to develop the concentration and attention skills of the child; to help him integrate scattered experiences; and to enable him to consider possibilities in his mind as well as with his hands, that is, to engage in "make-believe" rather than depend wholly on toys. . . Through sociodramatic play, the child develops his ability to use symbols and broadens his comprehension of the relationships among things and events in his environment.
>
> (Silverman, 1969, pp. 14–15)

*Figure 30.* Educators have found it important to design activities which encourage interaction among students. (Photo by Linda Lungren)

Activities of this type were designed to encourage interaction among students. Student experiences were sequenced to encourage children to adjust to an environment other than their homes and to interact with other children within the newly formulated environment. Adjustment to these two factors was the prime concern of every teacher who taught in this type of program.

A classroom espousing this curriculum might look similar to the one illustrated in Figure 31.

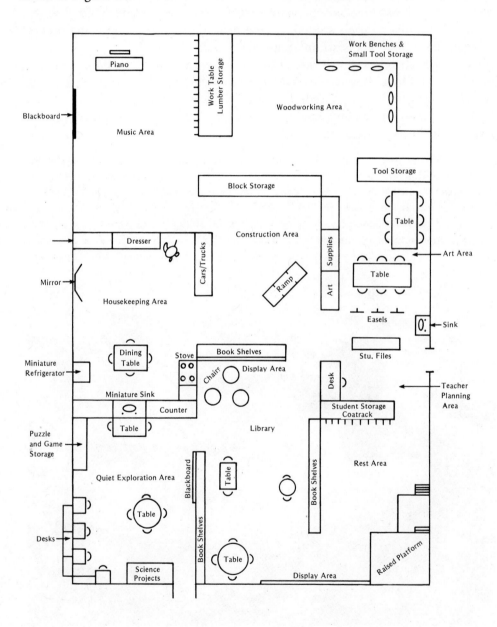

*Figure 31.* Normative-Development Model

A classroom of this type is designed to encourage interactions that help each child in his developmental process. Its emphasis can best be characterized by the following statement:

The statement that individuals live in a world means, in the concrete, that they live in a series of situations. And when it is said that they live in these situations, the meaning of the word "in" is different from its meaning when it is said the pennies are "in" a can. It means, once more, that interaction is going on between an individual and objects and other persons. The conceptions of situation and of interaction are inseparable from each other. An experience is always what it is because of a transaction taking place between an individual and what, at the time, constitutes his environment, whether the latter consists of persons with whom he is talking about some topic or event, the talked-about being also a part of the situation; or the toys with which he is playing; the book he is reading (in which his environing conditions at the time may be England or ancient Greece or an imaginary region); or the materials of an experiment he is performing. The environment, in other words, is whatever conditions interact with the personal needs, desires, purposes, capacities to create the experience . . . Even when a person builds a castle in the air, he is interacting with the objects which he constructs in fancy.

(Dewey, 1938, pp. 43–44)

*Figure 32.* Reading stories to young children can provide verbal interaction between students and teacher. (Photo by Linda Lungren)

## The Verbal Discourse and Cognitive Development Model

### Aims and Objectives

The verbal discourse and cognitive development curriculum model is designed to accomplish all of the goals that have been delineated in the normative-developmental model.

### Curriculum Components

The composition of this classroom and the components of the curriculum are similar to the normative-developmental model. The primary difference between these two models is the *role of the teacher*. The teacher's role in the verbal discourse and cognitive development model is much *more directive* than in the normative-developmental model.

The teacher of the verbal discourse and cognitive development model engages in continuous verbal interaction with the children. The day begins with a shared communication "planning session," which is generally followed by a group game and a review of the day's schedule of events. The schedule of events generally includes the following types of activities:

1. Manipulation of file cut-outs.
2. Listening to stories read by the teacher.
3. Sorting and classifying games.
4. Counting and coloring.
5. Verbal discussion of classroom-related events.

These activities adhere closely to the cognitive development program of Piaget (1962, 1964), which stresses the development of the following:

1. Language.
2. Physical knowledge (stoves are hot).
3. Social knowledge (chairs are to sit on; the farmer has a certain task).
4. Logical knowledge (classification, seriation, number, space, and time).
5. Knowledge related to the representation of the symbol system.

Piaget (1962, 1964) suggests that cognitive developmental changes are related to biological developmental processes. Whereas curriculum may be planned to foster this development, each of the following four stages of cognitive growth, as explained earlier in Chapter 2, emerges logically and inevitably from the preceding one.

1. **Sensory Motor Stage.** The sensory motor stage is the preverbal stage that occurs between birth and approximately two years of age. It is during this stage that the child discovers many of the properties of objects through his eyes, hands, ears, mouth, and muscular action. Throughout this stage the child experiences his environment through perceptual and motor behaviors.

Adults in the environment can be helpful in providing many experiences that include language interaction with the child. It is important not to anticipate behavioral results that are unreasonable expectations for the young child; for example, the young child is unable to recognize and memorize the characteristics of newly presented materials. Attempts by adults to engage the child of this age in meaningless memorization activities are equally as useless as asking a beginning reader to learn to memorize nonsense syllables.

**2. Preoperational Stage.** During the preoperational stage of development the child begins to group and categorize materials. This stage commonly occurs between the ages of two and seven years. During this stage of development the child should be encouraged in the following learning experiences: imitation, forming objects from clay, pouring or transferring various quantities of liquids and solids into different sized containers, drawing representations of experiences, identifying experiences and objects through pictures, stacking, building, binding, stretching objects, tearing, cutting, pasting, coloring, and fastening. Such activities aid the child in understanding transformations and relationships.

**3. Concrete Operational Stage.** During the concrete operational stage, which occurs between the ages of seven and eleven, the child engages in concrete

*Figure 33.* The child should be engaged in activities that provide experiences in grouping, classification, seriation, and conservation of number and space. An entymology project can provide such an experience for an advanced student. (Photo by Linda Lungren)

thinking operations with objects and events. During this stage of development the child should be engaged in activities that provide experiences in grouping, classification, seriation, and conservation of number and space.

**4. Formal Operational Stage.** It is during the formal operational stage, which spans from age eleven to adulthood, that the child engages in abstract hypothetical thinking.

Throughout these stages of cognitive development the child adapts to new stimuli through the processes of *accommodation* and *assimilation*. When the child encounters something new to his existing knowledge structure, he *accommodates* the new by modifying and reorganizing the existing structures. The child has been able to *assimilate* the new when the alteration has been so internalized that he can handle additional experiences with ease.

A program based on these theories of Piaget can be more clearly implemented by examining the processes involved in *logical thinking*. Some of these processes are *concept formation*, *the generalizing process*, and *hypothesizing and predicting*.

*Concept formation* is the mental process that refers to more than one object/experience or the relationship between objects/experiences. Concept formation (mental conception) denotes process, whereas concept denotes product. In language, a *term*, a word, often illustrates a concept.

*Concept* may be defined as a word or phrase that identifies either singular or multiple objects, events, or ideas. When presented with a group of similar objects, events, or ideas, there is a need to determine similarities so that they may be classified/labeled. A concept may be more or less *inclusive*. *Animal* is more inclusive than *mammal*; *mammal* is more inclusive than *cat*; *cat* is more inclusive than *Persian Cat*.

L. S. Vygotsky, a psychologist who has given much study to the processes involved in concept formation, suggests

> When the process of concept formation is seen in all its complexity, it appears as a movement of thought within the pyramid of concepts, constantly alternating between two directions, from the particular to the general and from the general to the particular.
>
> (Vygotsky, 1960, pp. 80–81)

This movement of thought may be explained by studying the complexity of transition from *perception* (awareness) to *conception*. Piaget suggests that as one moves from perception to conception

1. There exists a reduction in the amount of material redundancy.
2. One develops a greater tolerance for irrelevant information, therefore not allowing it to cause response interference.
3. There is increase in the spatial and temporal separation over which the total information contained in the stimulus field can be integrated.

(Piaget, 1962, p. 12)

In its simplest form, concept formation consists of the following three processes:

1. Differentiating properties/elements or objects/events. This involves the subdividing of global wholes into specific criteria.
2. Grouping or integrating related elements. At this point a careful analysis of common properties must be made because commonalities provide pattern detection.
3. Labeling or categorizing elements. This process also involves decision making regarding the inclusion or exclusion of new elements in categories.

(Lapp et al., 1975, p. 175–176)

After the students have collected and organized all existing topical information, they can begin to make generalizations from the data.

> However timid we may be, there must be interpolation. Experiments only give us a certain number of isolated points. They must be connected by a continuous line, and this is a true generalization.... The curve thus traced will pass between and near the points observed; it will not pass through the points themselves. Thus, we are restricted to generalizing our experiment, we correct it. . . . Detached facts cannot therefore satisfy us and that is why our science must be ordered, or better still, generalized.
> (Poincaré, 1952, pp. 142–43)

On the basis of these generalizations, students are able to begin the processes of hypothesizing and predicting.

> The facts observed will never be repeated. All that can be affirmed is that under analogous circumstances an analogous fact will be produced. To predict we must therefore invoke the aid of analogy.
> (Poincaré, 1952, p. 142)

According to Piaget, one's ability to *hypothesize* and *predict* suggests a transition between the concrete and formal operational stages of thinking. As the child transcends time and space parameters through symbolic/verbal representations, he realizes the hypothetical consequences of a proposal and he is able to suggest alternate solutions by hypothesizing about effects of each possible solution. The ability to hypothesize the possible antecedent consequences of an action is often referred to as *antecedent/consequence thinking*.

As the teacher engages the child of the verbal discourse and cognitive development model in activities that support the development of cognitive strategies, she is viewed as the classroom manager in a discovery learning environment. In a classroom of this type, young children "make their discoveries through what they already know: they match the unfamiliar against a thoroughly incorporated body of fact. . . . Novelty arises out of variations of the familiar." (Pribram, 1964, p. 107)

In the same way that the normative-development model makes use of blocks, clay, paint, dolls, trucks, sand, water, puzzles, and pictures, the verbal discourse and cognitive development model adheres to the implementation of discovery through planned experiences that have been designed to foster the development of verbal and cognitive competencies. For example, one could play a game with the child that involves grouping same/different objects, or the child could be involved in sociodramatic play, which, as Smilansky suggests, "helps the child crystallize his experiences and facilitates both his emotional and intellectual adjustment to the environment." (1968, p. 72)

*Figure 34.* A game could be played with the child which involves grouping same/different objects. (Photo by Linda Lungren)

As presented in Chapter 4, Smilansky (1968) suggests that sociodramatic play involves the following:

1. Imitative role-play.
2. Make-believe in regard to objects.
3. Make-believe in regard to actions and situations.
4. Persistence (ten minutes of play).
5. Interaction (two or more children).
6. Verbal communication related to the play episode.

(1968, p. 98)

Sociodramatic play is part of the curriculum of both the normative development and the verbal discourse and cognitive development models. In the verbal discourse and cognitive development model, the teacher is encouraged to mediate the interaction by participating as a question-asking member of the activity. "If, for example, the teacher does not use make-believe in regard to objects, the teacher acting as a nurse will suggest to her, 'Mrs. Ohajon, here is the medicine' (while pretending to hand her something). 'Give it to your baby twice a day.'" (Smilansky, 1968, p. 102). The teacher-student interactions are carefully designed and sequenced by the teacher to encourage student development of "skills involving the ability to organize thoughts, to reflect upon situations, to comprehend the meaning of events, and to structure behavior so as to be able to choose among alternatives." (Blank and Solomon, 1968, p. 380)

The following example of verbal discourse between students and teacher illustrates an attempt to implement theories of cognitive development.

> The teacher is reading a story to a classroom of four-year-olds. The sounds of approaching footsteps and voices in the hall can be heard from the classroom:
>
> Mr. Cunningham:   Is someone coming to visit our classroom?
> Denny: I think so.
> Jimmy: I don't know.
> Mr. Cunningham:   Denny, why do you think someone is coming?
> Denny: I hear footsteps and voices.
> Mr. Cunningham:   Denny, could the footsteps and voices be going somewhere else?
> Denny: Yes.
> Mr. Cunningham:   Jimmy, why are you unsure?
> Jimmy:   Because no one has knocked on our door.
> Mr. Cunningham:   Where could the footsteps and voices be going if they aren't coming here?
> Shannon:   They could be visiting one of the other classrooms in the building.

Through the use of question-asking techniques, Mr. Cunningham poses a problem, "Is someone coming to visit our classroom?" which requires the children to synthesize data, hypothesize, and provide support for each hypothesis. The teacher, in this situation, exemplifies the curricula focus of this model, which places emphasis on *learning* and the *transferability* of what has been learned.

## The Sensory/Perceptual/Cognitive Model

### Aims and Objectives

The sensory/perceptual/cognitive curriculum model is designed to aid the child in the following:

1. Determining likenesses and differences between sounds, colors, textures, and weights.
2. Classifying similar objects, sounds, textures.
3. Ordering objects according to ascending size, pitch, or weight.
4. Caring for self.
5. Caring for others in one's environment.
6. Caring for the animals and plants in one's environment.
7. Counting.
8. Writing.
9. Learning letter sounds.
10. Developing the ability to focus one's attention.

### Curriculum Components

The foregoing objectives are derived from Maria Montessori's theories of learning, which provide the theoretical underpinnings of the sensory/perceptual/cognitive model. Unlike the two preceding curriculum models, no specific attention is given to the extension of language, art, or music skills in this model. While classroom art and music activities may be available to an individual they are not the core of this curriculum.

Montessori concurred with Piaget in her beliefs that cognitive development evolves through stages and that the child needs to interact with his environment as he develops the ability to order and classify concrete and abstract concepts.

As seen in Figure 35, a classroom derived from this model would contain low shelves and attractive, uncluttered materials that would be easily accessible to children. The room contains small chairs and low tables but the floor space is open and, for the most part, unencumbered by furniture. Children have personal rugs (stored orderly in one corner of the room) where they can work individually with the many classroom materials.

All parts of the classroom are accessible to children because

> Scientific observation has established that education is not what the teacher gives; education is a natural process spontaneously carried out by the human individual, and is acquired not by listening to words but by experiences upon the environment.
> (Montessori, 1963A, p. 3)

The environment and the teacher who prepares the environment are critical to the success of this model.

> The environment must be a living one, directed by a higher intelligence, arranged by an adult who is prepared for his mission. It is in this that our conception differs both from that of the world in which the adult does everything for the child and from that of a passive environment in which the adult abandons the child to himself. . . . This means that it is not enough to set the child among objects in proportion to his size and strength; the adult who is to help him must have learned how to do so.
> (Montessori, 1963B, p. 224)

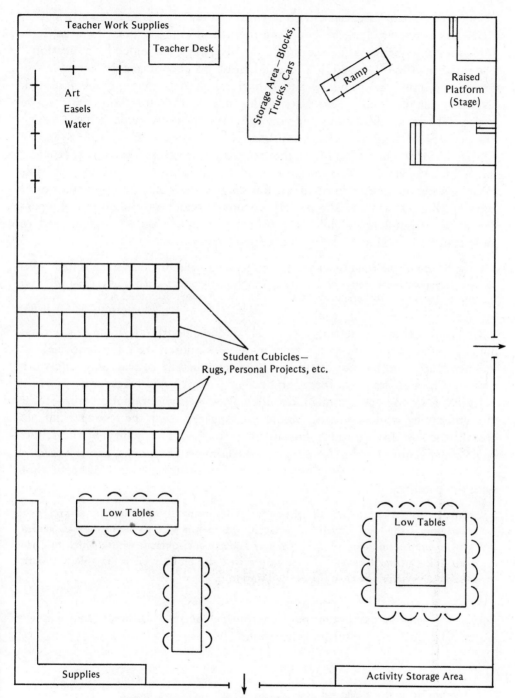

*Figure 35.* Sensory/Perceptual/Cognitive Model

The teacher of the sensory/perceptual/cognitive model must prepare an environment that encourages freedom, structure, order, reality, a love of nature, sensory and perceptual refinement, community, and an understanding of beauty and atmosphere.

Freedom is the essential environmental element because it is only within a free environment that the child can reveal and explore himself. "Real freedom is a consequence of development. . .of latent guides, aided by education." (Montessori, 1964A, p. 205) The child must be encouraged to act independently and must be provided the behavioral models that can be imitated. "No one can be free unless he is independent: therefore, the first, active manifestations of the child's individual liberty must be guided that through this activity he may arrive at independence. . . ." (Montessori, 1964B, p. 95)

The development of self-discipline is also an attribute that the teacher of this model encourages. "To obtain discipline. . .it is not necessary for the adult to be a guide or mentor in conduct, but to give the child the opportunities of work." (Montessori, 1963A, p. 79) In conjunction with freedom, independence, and discipline, a child in this program must also be encouraged to understand and exhibit socially acceptable behavior.

> The liberty of the child should have as its limit the collective interest; as its form, what we universally consider good breeding. We must, therefore, check in the child whatever offends or annoys others, or whatever tends toward rough or ill-bred acts.
>
> (Montessori, 1964B, p. 93)

Children within this setting often work independently after the teacher has demonstrated proper use of a certain material. Children are free to move about independently and are not restrained by a set schedule of rest, play, and work periods. Children are never forced to become part of a group activity.

Children in this environment do not engage in sociodramatic play because the underlying philosophy of Montessori suggests that the young child has great difficulty distinguishing fantasy from reality. The reality of the school environment must be closely related to the home environment, and the teacher within the sensory/perceptual/cognitive model must maintain close affiliation with the parents.

> Man is. . . a social product, and the social environment of individuals in the process of education is the home. Scientific pedagogy will seek in vain to better the new generation if it does not succeed in influencing also the environment within which this new generation grows! I believe. . . we have solved the problem of being able to modify directly the environment of the new generation.
>
> (Montessori, 1964B, p. 64)

Thus, the sensory/perceptual/cognitive model acts as an agent that has the potential of influencing future generations.

### The Verbal-Behavioral Model

#### Aims and Objectives

The verbal-behavioral model is designed to aid preschool children in developing competency in the following areas:

1. Basic arithmetic skills.
   a. Recognizing numbers.
   b. Counting.
   c. Grouping similar objects.
   d. Understanding polar sets (big-little; up-down).
2. Language skills.
   a. Syntax.
   b. Semantics.
   c. Understanding and using affirmative and nonaffirmative statements.
   d. Understanding and performing if–then deductions.
   e. Naming basic colors.
3. Reading skills.
   a. Letter recognition.
   b. Phonics.
   c. Ability to read basic sight words (is, are, was, I, am).

### Curriculum Components

The foregoing objectives are derived from the Bereiter-Engelmann theory of learning that provides the theoretical parameters of the verbal-behavioral model. Kohlberg suggests that proponents of this model "assume that what is most important in the development of the child is his learning of cognitive and moral knowledge and rules of the culture and that education's business is the teaching of such information and rules to the child through direct instruction." (1968, p. 105)

The curriculum is structured to accomplish specified goals. Activities are primarily teacher-induced and directed. Correct responses of the children are rewarded and reinforced with verbal compliments, cookies, candies, and hand-shakes. Child-child and child-material interactions are given less attention in this model because a prime goal of language development (standard English) is believed to be more easily and effectively obtained through teacher-student interactions than through child-child or child-materials interactions.

This model can be viewed as an attempt at social intervention because it was originally designed for a "culturally deprived" population. It was intended that teacher-student interactions would be the means of providing the child an appropriate language model.

In response to this model, many educators have asked: "A language model appropriate for whom?" "Who has a dialect?" "Who is disadvantaged?" Although the theories of a behavioral model are well intended and believed by many to be appropriate for some successful learning situations, they may not be appropriate as a language development model because the correctness of an utterance is not sufficient evidence of comprehension of a concept.

Teachers within the verbal–behavioral model focus their attention on observable, measurable events and on the objective environment. This focus is an outgrowth of the Stimulus-Response (S–R) Theory of education. An objective analysis of behavior is one of the commonalities of modern versions of S–R Theory.

The emphasis within the S–R Theory has varied among psychologists. Some theorists might inquire, "What is the stimulus?" whereas others may be more concerned with the reinforcement that follows the response. Skinner (1968, 1972) might ask, "What was the reinforcer?" because he believes that the behavior one exhibits is dependent upon the current reward contingencies. Teachers who implement this model should synthesize the findings of all existing research insights, paying close attention to the stimulus and the reward.

The attempts by Bereiter, Engelmann, and other behavioral learning theorists to condition behavioral responses are referred to as *behavior modification*. The study of behavior modification has been given much attention since the 1950s as a comprehensive theory to explain human information processing. Its appeal has been encouraged by educational technologists because of its direct application and intended ability to alter undesirable behavioral problems.

The teacher who wishes to implement the verbal–behavioral model needs to fully understand the underlying theories of behavior modification so as to determine, "when to do what, for which behaviors, and with what resources, . . . [for] knowing how to monitor and test treatment effectiveness continuously is the challenging aspect of behavior modification." (Kanfer, 1973, p. 4)

In attempting to understand the parametric constructs of behavior modification, you will need a basic understanding of *classical* and *operant conditioning*.

### Classical and Operant Conditioning

In addressing the question, "How does learning occur?", educators and psychologists have presented a series of possible answers. Theorists who subscribe to the verbal behavioral model of early learning have accepted, extended, and adapted a psychological theory of behavior modification that relies heavily upon the processes of classical and operant conditioning.

*Classical conditioning* is contingent on the simultaneous presentation of two stimuli to which the response is gradually elicited by only one of the stimuli. This form of conditioning was first explored by psychologist Pavlov (1960) with his canine experiments.

Pavlov sounded a tuning fork and the dogs did not salivate; next, he showed food to them, and still they did not salivate; so he paired the two stimuli, the tuning fork and the food. After multiple experiences of listening to the tuning fork and then immediately seeing the food, the dogs began to salivate at the sound of the tuning fork.

You may wonder if the proponents of the verbal-behavioral model believe that similar conditioning is possible with humans. An example of an adaptation of the Pavlov experiment to humans is demonstrated in the experiment completed with the eye blink reflex of humans. An individual, in this experiment, was asked to watch a light, the brightness of which was continuously increased. The individual exhibited no reaction to the light brightness increase. The individual was then hit in the eye with a puff of air. That caused the individual to respond with a blink. The two stimuli, light brightness increases and a puff of air, were then presented simultaneously, and the individual reacted by blinking. After several identical encounters, the individual blinked as soon as the light brightness increased. Because the changing light alone now caused the eye to blink, learning was believed to have occurred.

*Operant conditioning* differs from classical conditioning in the use of proper reinforcement. The use of proper reinforcements can be more thoroughly understood by examining a Skinnerian experiment. Skinner placed a white rat into a 12-foot square box. One side of the box was placed next to a lever that was connected to an automatic recording device and to a magazine filled with pellets of rat food. When the lever was pressed, a pellet of rat food was released. When the rat was hungry, he would sniff the air and pan the sides of the box, eventually hitting the lever that released the food. Once the rat realized that the pressing of the lever provided the food, he began to press the lever at a rate of speed commensurate with his eating speed. Thus, it was concluded that the rat had learned.

As suggested by Bereiter and Engelmann, the teacher in the verbal-behavioral model can use operant conditioning techniques when cookies, candies, handshakes, and congratulatory responses are given for correct replies. Patterns of reinforcement should be consistent. Only those behaviors that are to be strengthened should be reinforced; those to be eliminated should be ignored.

Activities designed to implement this theory include drill and one word short sentence responses from the child. Concrete manipulative experiences are not essential to this model; objects are shown by the teacher only when they are needed to clarify a concept. Curriculum sequence is determined by the complexity of the concept being presented. All of the children experience similar curriculum; variations among children occur only with regard to the amount of material being covered.

Bereiter and Engelmann suggest that positive teacher-student interactions are as possible through direct instruction as they are through play-oriented activities. They also suggest that once the child begins to experience academic success he will begin to develop positive self-esteem.

## What Model Is Best for Your Classroom?

Within this chapter we have discussed the philosophical, psychological, and curricular constructs of four models of early childhood education. It is hoped that these models have not been oversimplified. Educational models do not happen by accident. As you realize, they are the result of gradual reformations of a long-standing set of beliefs. They are also the result of a continued interchange between the school personnel and the demands of the society. Of major importance to the success of any educational model is the degree to which it intends "to preserve the spirit of the age" or to which it attempts "to prepare for and shape the future."

*Figure 36.* You, the teacher, must select a teaching model that is most clearly aligned with your educational beliefs. (Photo by Linda Lungren)

Your task as a classroom teacher will be to determine the model that is most closely aligned with your educational beliefs. Regardless of the model you select, you, the teacher, will be the essential element for its success.

## BIBLIOGRAPHY

Bereiter, C. and Engelmann, S. *Teaching Disadvantaged Children In The Preschool.* Englewood Cliffs, N.J.: Prentice-Hall, Inc., 1966.

Blank, M. and F. Solomon. "A Tutoring Language Program to Develop Abstract Thinking in Socially Disadvantaged Preschool Children." *Child Development,* (1968), 39:380.

Dewey, J. *Experience and Education.* New York: Macmillan Publishing Co., Inc., 1938.

Erikson, E. H. *Childhood and Society*, 2nd ed. New York: W. W. Norton & Company, Inc., 1963.

Freud, S. *Totem and Taboo.* Vienna: Hugo Heller, 1913. Copyright, 1950 by Routledge and Kegan, and published in New York by W. W. Norton & Company, Inc., 1962.

Froebel, F. "The Young Child," in *Friedrich Froebel, A Selection From His Writings.* Edited by I. M. Lalley. Cambridge, England: Cambridge University Press, 1967.

Gesell, A. L. *The First Five Years of Life.* New York: Harper & Row, Publishers, 1940.

Ginsberg, H., and S. Opper. *Piaget's Theory of Intellectual Development.* Englewood Cliffs, N.J.: Prentice-Hall, Inc., 1969.

Inhelder, B., and J. Piaget. *The Early Growth of Logic in the Child: Classification and Seriation.* New York: W. W. Norton & Company, Inc., 1969.

Kanfer, F. H. "Behavior Modification—An Overview." In C. E. Thoresen (ed.), *Behavioral Modification in Education, The Seventy-Second Yearbook of the National Society for the Study of Education.* Chicago: University of Chicago Press, 1973.

Kohlberg, L. "Early Education: A Cognitive-Developmental View." *Child Development*, 39 (1968).

Lapp, D. "Behavioral Objectives Writing Skills Test." *Journal of Education*, (February 1972) 154: 13–24.

Lapp, D. *The Use of Behavioral Objectives in Education.* Newark, Delaware: The International Reading Association, 1972.

Lapp, D., H. Bender, S. Ellenwood, and M. John. *Teaching and Learning: Philosophical, Psychological, Curricular Applications.* New York: Macmillan Publishing Co., Inc., 1975.

Lavatelli, C. S. *Piaget's Theory Applied To An Early Childhood Curriculum.* Boston: American Science and Engineering, 1971.

Lilly, I. (ed.) *Friedrich Froebel, A Selection From His Writings.* Cambridge, England: Cambridge University Press, 1967.

Montessori, M. *Education for a New World.* Wheaton, Ill.: Theosophical Press, 1963A.

Montessori, M. *The Secret of Childhood.* Calcutta: Orient Longmons, Ltd., 1963B.

Montessori, M. *To Educate the Human Potential.* Wheaton, Ill.: Theosophical Press, 1963C.

Montessori, M. *The Absorbent Mind.* Wheaton, Ill.: Theosophical Press, 1964A.

Montessori, M. *The Montessori Method.* New York: Schocken Books, Inc., 1964B.

Montessori, M. *Reconstruction in Education.* Wheaton, Ill.: Theosophical Press, 1964C.

Montessori, M. *Spontaneous Activity in Education.* New York: Schocken Books, Inc., 1965.

Pavlov, I. P. *Conditional Reflexes; An Investigation of the Physiological Activity of the Cerebral Cortex.* Translated and edited by G. V. Anrep. New York: Dover Publications, Inc., 1960.

Piaget, J. *Language and Thought of the Child.* New York: International Universities Press, 1955.

Piaget, J. *Plays, Dreams, and Imitation in Childhood.* New York: W. W. Norton & Company, Inc., 1962.

Piaget, J. *The Origins of Intelligence In Children.* New York: International Universities Press, 1962.

Piaget, J. "Development and Learning." In R.E. Ripple and V.N. Rockcastle (eds.), *Piaget Rediscovered*. Ithaca, N.Y.: Cornell University Press, 1964.

Poincaré, H. *Science and Hypothesis*. New York: Dover Publications, Inc., 1952.

Pribram, K. H. "Neurological Notes in the Art of Educating." In *Theories of Learning and Instruction*, National Society for the Study of Education. Chicago: University of Chicago Press, 1964.

Rousseau, J. J. *Emile, Julie, and Other Writings*. New York: Barron's Educational Series, Inc., 1964.

Schwebel, M, and J. Raph. *Piaget In The Classroom*. New York: Basic Books, Inc., Publishers, 1973.

Sears, P.S., and E.M. Dowley. "Research on Teaching in the Nursery School." In N.C. Gage (ed.), *Handbook of Research on Teaching*. Chicago: Rand McNally & Company, 1965.

Silverman, C. (ed.) "Ypsilanti Preschool Curriculum Demonstration Project." Ypsilanti, Michigan Public Schools. (October 1969), pp. 14–15.

Skinner, B. F. *The Technology of Teaching*. New York: Appleton-Century-Crofts, 1968.

Skinner, B. F. *Beyond Freedom and Dignity*. New York: Alfred A. Knopf, Inc., 1972.

Smilansky, S. *The Effects of Sociodramatic Play on Disadvantaged Children*. New York: John Wiley & Sons, Inc., 1968.

Sonquist, H. D., and C. K. Kamii. "Applying Some Piagetian Concepts in the Classroom for the Disadvantaged." In D.P. Weikart (ed.), *Preschool Intervention: A Preliminary Report of the Perry Preschool Project*. Ann Arbor, Mich.: Campus Publishers, 1967.

Vygotsky. L. S. *Thought and Language*. Cambridge, Mass.: The M.I.T. Press, 1960.

Weikart, D. P. "Preschool Programs: Preliminary Findings." *Journal of Special Education* (1967), 1: 163–181.

# 6

# Language Experiences of Speaking, Listening, Reading, Writing: The Wonderful World of Words

*Figure 37.* The context of a daily experience such as picture painting can provide the beginning experience that the young child needs to understand color names. (Photo by Linda Lungren)

*Curious. Inquisitive.* These are terms that are continuously used to describe the behaviors of the preschool child. Teachers of young children often capitalize on these behaviors as a primary means of helping children to explore their environment through manipulative activities that develop language and reading abilities.

The young child's preschool environment should be rich with blocks, clay, paint, sand, water, paper, animals, and games. Written words, phrases, and sentences are easily and naturally related to these everyday experiences. The *context* of a daily experience such as picture painting can provide the beginning experience that the young child needs to understand color names (red, green, yellow).

The teacher's challenge of "Let's find how many of our first names begin with the letter *L*," or "Let's list on the board all of the things in our room that begin with the letter *B*," can provide opportunities for exploring ideas and their orthographic representations. Repeated daily experiences with these kinds of activities provide children with consistent exposures to ideas, materials, and experiences that can be expressed in words, sentences, and stories.

The ideas expressed in this chapter will enable you, as a teacher of young children, to provide the informal experience that children need as they begin to explore the wonderful world of spoken and written discourse.

## Early Experiences with Spoken and Written Language Discourse

An introductory language/reading program should be one that integrates the communication processes of speaking, listening, reading, and writing in an attempt to accomplish the following goals:

1. Enhance student interest in the various forms of language.
2. Emphasize the relationships between spoken and written discourse.
3. Illustrate the parameters of written discourse (travels through time, places, and the thoughts of others).
4. Emphasize the dimensions of the printed page (left-to-right, top-to-bottom).
5. Identify names of letters and letters as part of words.
6. Identify the parameters of the "word" in isolation and in context.
7. Illustrate contextual changes because of punctuation and capitalization.
8. Enhance spoken and written comprehension.

The accomplishment of these goals is, of course, dependent on the child's auditory and visual ability. The Appendix of this text contains the names of language/reading readiness tests that measure these and other areas of development.

The preceding goals can be accomplished by using the experiences that young children bring with them as they begin their schooling. Every opportunity should be made to add printed words to their conceptual realities; for example, you may want to follow some of these simple suggestions:

*Figure 38.* Every opportunity should be made to add printed words to experiences. (Photo by Linda Lungren)

1. Label classroom furniture and space.

2. Label individual child's materials.

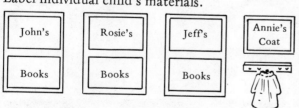

3. Discuss children's art work and add a caption they believe is appropriate (Figure 39).

4. Prepare lists of directions for completing classroom tasks or experiments (Figure 41).

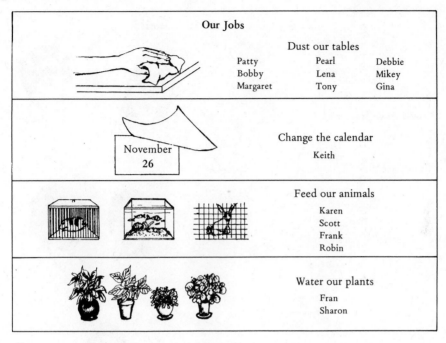

*Figure 41.*

5. Prepare labeled maps and diagrams of the school, community, or field trips (Figure 42).

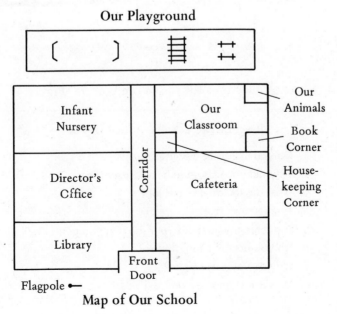

*Figure 42.*

6. Develop lists of children's feelings as they relate to books, pictures, weather, seasons, holidays (Figure 43).

**How I feel when I listen to stories**

*Amelia Bedelia Stories*

Happy

*Mystery Stories*

Scared

*Biographies*

Thoughtful

*Figure 43.*

7. Prepare lists of questions for classroom visitors (Figure 44).

---

**Questions to ask the Police Officer**

1. Do you like to be a police officer?
2. Why did you choose to be a police officer?
3. What do you do on your job?
4. Are you ever scared?
5. Are there things about your job that you don't like?
6. Do you ride on a motorcycle?
7. Why do you carry a gun?
8. How can I become a police officer?

---

*Figure 44.*

8. Prepare parent letters, invitations, and other appropriate seasonal or social messages (Figure 45).

Dear Parent,

Please come to our Thanksgiving Party on Wednesday, November 23 at 10:30 in our room.

The Squirrels

*Figure 45.*

## The Language Experience Method

One effective method for integrating listening, speaking, writing, and reading experiences is the language experience method. It capitalizes on the language skills that the child has acquired and the interests that the child has already developed. This method stresses the relationships among thought, spoken language, and written language. Lee and Allen (1963) described their view of the language experience method in the following twelve steps:

1. What a child thinks about he can talk about.
2. What he can talk about can be expressed in painting, writing, or some other form.
3. Anything he writes can be read.
4. He can read what he writes and what other people write.
5. As he represents his speech sounds with symbols, he uses the same symbols (letters) over and over.
6. Each letter in the alphabet stands for one or more sounds that he makes when he talks.
7. Every word begins with a sound he can write down.
8. Most words have an ending sound.
9. Many words have something in between.
10. Some words are used over and over in our language and some words are not used very often.
11. What he has to say and write is as important to him as what other people have written for him to read.
12. Most of the words he uses are the same ones which are used by other people who write for him to read.

One of greatest advantages of the language experience method is its spontaneity. Language experience is not meant to preclude training in phonics analysis, structural analysis, or contextual analysis but, rather, is meant to coexist with other language/reading instructional methods as a natural extension of the listening and language skills that children have already acquired. Language experience activities are interesting to the student because they capitalize on the student's real-life interests. The student uses ideas he or she already knows as building blocks toward mastery of the printed symbol.

In an area where language versatility is the goal that teachers seek for their students, it seems highly sensible to begin with the ingredient that each child brings to school—his own *language*. Because an understanding of oral language is vital to the development of a reading vocabulary, the language experience method is especially effective. You can use the objects, ideas, and occasions that surround your students as stepping stones to an understanding of sound/symbol correspondences. As we mentioned before, items and places within the classroom can be labeled. Concepts that are familiar to the children can be explored as sight words:

The Fonz is cool.      Candy loves french fries.
Mom works at the hospital.      Jay won my best marble.

Events that figure prominently in the children's lives can first be illustrated, then verbalized, next written down, and finally read:

Thanksgiving is only five      Today our teacher told us
days away, and I can't wait!      about Martin Luther King.

*Figure 46.* You can use the objects, ideas, and occasions that surround your students as stepping stones to understanding. (Photo by Linda Lungren)

*Figure 47.* A class trip to the animal zoo means hundreds of possible new words for your class to share. (Photo by Linda Lungren)

Every new activity that your children experience can generate new instructional material. For instance, a class trip to a farm may mean hundreds of possible new words for your class to share. Children may want to write down all the names of the animals they saw. They may want to illustrate a poster with these names:

## What I Saw On The Farm

Philip — horse

Michael — cow

Clems — bird

Tomas — aquirrel

Lulu — duck

Benjie — pig

Eileen — sheep

Bridie — bird

Maureen — swan

Kevin — horse

Donna — goat

Bob — bird

Sharon — turkey

Harry — lizard

Yael — cow

Jonathan — pig

Andrew — bird

The language experience method allows you to use the bounty of spoken words available to the child to develop language/reading skills through interaction with his environment. Because the child is not just learning reading skills in isolation, and because the approach capitalizes on the interests of the child as the basis for instruction, the child is more likely to see reading as a useful tool, not a boring school subject. Language experience accentuates the worth of knowing how to read and the enjoyment of whole language processes.

### *Language Experience in Prereading Programs*

The language experience method for developing the language/reading skills of the young child can be implemented in many different ways. It can be implemented in a structured, yet informal, way in a preschool, kindergarten, or primary-level program. The following design (Hoover, 1975) has been used in a successful program for kindergartens who exhibit an interest in learning to read.

### *Procedures for Implementing the Language Experience Methods in Preschool Programs*

On Monday mornings each child was asked to tell his teacher a "news bulletin" in preparation for a weekly "News of the Weekend" that was scheduled at the end of the morning. After telling his news bulletin, each child was asked to draw a picture that would illustrate his news. For the children who could print, the teacher printed each of the words on separate index cards. For example,

#### Larry's News Bulletin

As his news bulletin, Larry told Ms. Kurmis, "I went to my grandmother's house." Ms. Kurmis asked him if he would like to draw a picture on the art paper she provided for him. He chose to draw a picture of his grandmother's house. While he was drawing the picture, his teacher printed each word on a card.

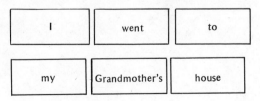

She asked him to print these words under his drawing. After he finished printing the words, she practiced reading the sentence with him.

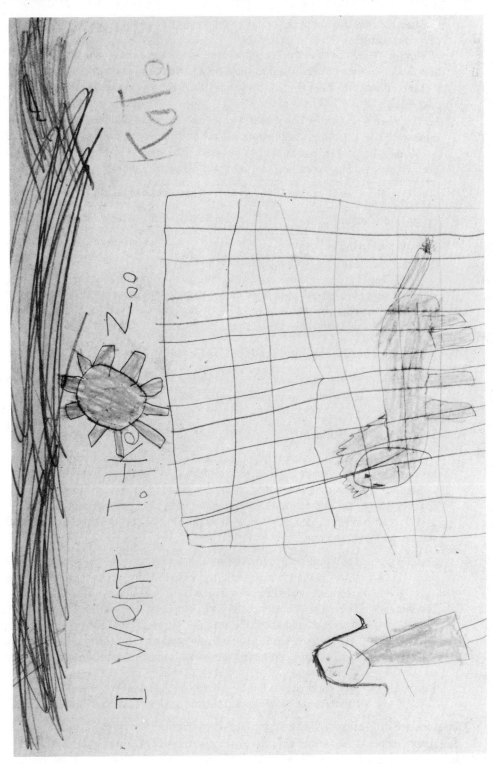

She gave him the index cards and told him they were the beginning of his deck of reading cards.

During "News of the Weekend," when Larry's turn came, Ms. Kurmis asked him to read his news bulletin and to show his drawing to the class.

Kate added the following words to her illustration: "I went to the zoo" (see page 141).

The next week, after Larry told Ms. Kurmis his news bulletin, "I went to the museum," she asked him to illustrate his bulletin. When he finished, she told him he already had three words that were needed to write his news bulletin in his deck of words. She asked him to find them. Together, they pulled out the cards

| I | | went | and· | | to | . Then, she wrote the following word

on an index card: | the | . She asked him to print the sentence under his

drawing: (see page 143).

Again, he "read" his story at "News of the Weekend."

As his reading deck increased, Ms. Kurmis used his set of cards to play reading games. The games served as a practice for reading and as an opportunity for Ms. Kurmis to increase the words in his deck. If he won the game, he was allowed to ask for two new words, any words that he chose. These new words became part of

his reading deck. He chose the words | monster | and | motorcycle | .

By the end of the school year, his reading deck was quite extensive, and, through the practice of the games, he was able to read every word in his deck.

## Sharon's News Bulletin

Because Sharon did not print yet, her teacher printed her news bulletin under her drawing, but still made her a deck of cards.

She practiced reading her words during the course of the year in the same way as Larry did. At the end of the year, Sharon began to print her own words.

This approach provides children with opportunities to develop their language skills in an integrated way:

Speaking:     The children had to assemble their thoughts in order to tell their story to their teacher. During "News of the Weekend," the children were encouraged to discuss each other's stories.

Listening:     The children listened to each other's stories during "News of the Weekend" and asked the writer questions about his stories.

Writing:     The children wrote (copied) their words from their deck of reading cards. These cards were also used to create spontaneous stories by the children.

Reading:     The children read their stories to their teachers and to the other children. They were also encouraged to read each other's stories.

**Classroom Simulation of the Language Experience Method.** Implementing the language experience approach in your classroom is a very difficult task. In the next few pages we will present a classroom simulation of Mr. Cunningham's attempts to implement a language experience approach for a class trip to the science museum.

The language experience method allows you to use the bounty of spoken words available to the child to develop language/reading skills through interaction with his environment. Because the child is not just learning reading skills in isolation, and because the approach capitalizes on the interests of the child as the basis for instruction, the child is more likely to see reading as a useful tool, not a boring school subject. Language experience accentuates the worth of knowing how to read and the enjoyment of whole language processes.

### *Language Experience in Prereading Programs*

The language experience method for developing the language/reading skills of the young child can be implemented in many different ways. It can be implemented in a structured, yet informal, way in a preschool, kindergarten, or primary-level program. The following design (Hoover, 1975) has been used in a successful program for kindergartens who exhibit an interest in learning to read.

### *Procedures for Implementing the Language Experience Methods in Preschool Programs*

On Monday mornings each child was asked to tell his teacher a "news bulletin" in preparation for a weekly "News of the Weekend" that was scheduled at the end of the morning. After telling his news bulletin, each child was asked to draw a picture that would illustrate his news. For the children who could print, the teacher printed each of the words on separate index cards. For example,

### Larry's News Bulletin

As his news bulletin, Larry told Ms. Kurmis, "I went to my grandmother's house." Ms. Kurmis asked him if he would like to draw a picture on the art paper she provided for him. He chose to draw a picture of his grandmother's house. While he was drawing the picture, his teacher printed each word on a card.

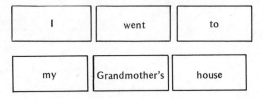

She asked him to print these words under his drawing. After he finished printing the words, she practiced reading the sentence with him.

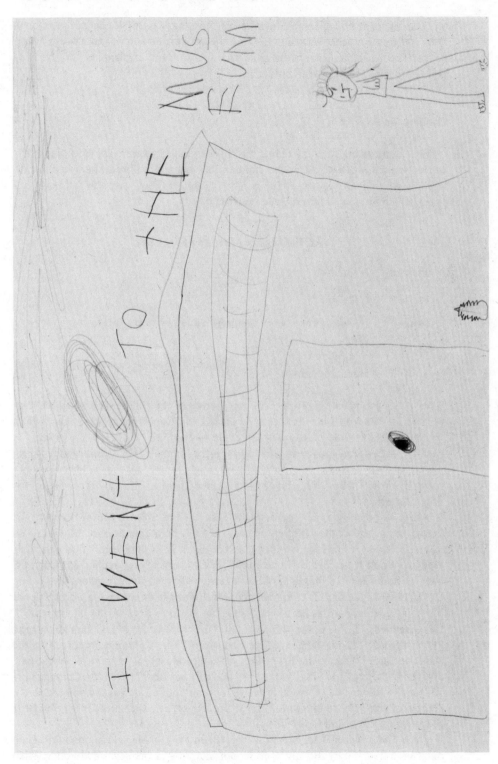

Mr. Cunningham was planning to take his morning class of kindergarteners on a field trip to the Science Museum. Because the anticipated trip was two weeks away, he decided to capitalize on the children's involvement in planning for the trip, taking the trip, and evaluating their trip.

### Planning for the Trip

Mr. Cunningham began by telling the children that they were going to take a trip to the Science Museum. After the children 'hooted and hollered,' he asked if they knew what they would see at the Science Museum. They gave the following answers, which Mr. Cunningham listed on chart paper:

### At The Science Museum I Might See:

Shannon:  Animals.

Jimmy:  Planets.

Denise:  I've been there, and I saw how babies are born.

Dennis:  Rocks.

Erin:  How food grows.

After Mr. Cunningham listed the initial responses of the children, he asked the class to read the list with him. As they read the list, Mr. Cunningham asked the children to elaborate on some of the items that he had initially listed on the chart. For example, after the class read Shannon's entry, animals, Mr. Cunningham asked, "What specific animals do you think we might see?" As the children guessed, gorillas, birds, snakes, Mr. Cunningham added these additional responses to the original chart.

After completing the What I Might See At The Science Museum chart, Mr. Cunningham asked the children if they knew where the Science Museum was located. They did not know so he asked them how they could find out. Eric replied, "Look it up in the phone book." "Good suggestion," replied Mr. Cunningham, as he placed the phone book on a table and asked for two volunteers to find the address. Linda and Eric volunteered. Mr. Cunningham wrote the words Science Museum on the board as he asked, "How can we look it up in the phone book?" Linda replied, "Look under the first letter of the word." Mr. Cunningham said, "Which word?" Linda replied, "The first word." Mr. Cunningham turned to the class and said, "What is the first word in Science Museum?" Lynne excitedly said, "Science" "Good, and what is the first letter in Science?" asked Mr. Cunningham. "S," replied Jay. "We've found it, we've found it," said Linda as she pointed to the address of the Science Museum. "It's at 966 Riverview, and the telephone number is 395-1592. Come and look," she said.

After the children had looked at the telephone number and address, Mr. Cunningham asked if they thought their school was close to the Science Museum. When the children didn't know, Mr. Cunningham asked them how they could find out. They gave the following responses which Mr. Cunningham wrote on the board:

Sharon:    Call up the Science Museum and ask them.

Susan:    Go to the office and ask Ms. Melanson (the principal).

Gary:    Look it up on a map.

After further discussion with the children, everyone agreed that although all of the responses were correct, the one that caused the least amount of inconvenience to others was to look it up on a map. "Should we use a world map, a state map, or a city map?" asked Mr. Cunningham. Together they discussed the various types of maps and decided that the city map was the most appropriate.

Mr. Cunningham asked Mary to locate 966 Riverview on the map. While she did so, Mr. Cunningham explained how locations are made. Next, he asked Mary how far away the school was from the Science Museum. "I need to know what street our school is on," responded Mary. "Who knows?" asked Mr. Cunningham. "It's on Manet Road," responded Tommy. Mr. Cunningham asked Tommy to locate Manet Road on the map (see Figure 48).

After the locations had been charted and the approximate distance calculated, Mr. Cunningham and the children wrote a letter to the Science Museum requesting information about class field trips. Mr. Cunningham also volunteered to call the Science Museum to confirm a visiting time. Next, the children discussed possible transportation. They decided to take the bus. Mr. Cunningham volunteered to secure bus schedules.

As the children and Mr. Cunningham talked, he listed every possible word, phrase, and sentence stated by the children regarding the trip. He read books to them about the possible animals, planets, plants, and rocks they might see at the museum. They drew pictures of their forthcoming experiences. Mr. Cunningham helped label the pictures. When the bus schedules arrived, they charted their route and discussed the money needed and possible means of securing the money. They discussed and listed the acceptable behavior for the trip. Soon it was the day of the trip.

## Taking the Trip

Before the class left for the bus shanty, Mr. Cunningham asked them to think about the following questions:

1. What do I like about the trip?
2. What is the best thing I am seeing at the Science Museum?

## Evaluating the Trip

When the class returned to school, Mr. Cunningham asked each child to draw one picture that showed what he liked best about his trip and one picture that showed what he had liked best at the Science Museum. Each child shared his pictures with the class and Mr. Cunningham helped with labels for each. They then bound the labeled pictures together into a class book.

Mr. Cunningham then asked the children if at the Science Museum they had seen what they thought they were going to see. As the children responded, Mr.

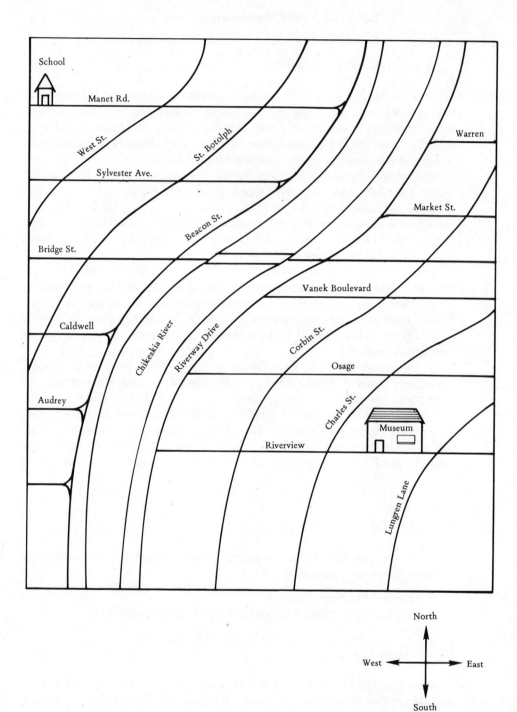

*Figure 48.*

Cunningham charted their responses and then together they compared what they had seen with what they had originally believed they might see.

They discussed the term <u>Science Museum,</u> and why that was an appropriate name for the place they had visited. They also discussed other names that might have been appropriate. Together, they composed a class letter to the Museum workers, thanking them for the experience. Mr. Cunningham wrote the letter on chart paper as each child copied it onto his own piece of paper. Together they prepared envelopes in which they could mail their letters. As they prepared the envelope, they decided to invite a postal worker to their classroom to tell them what happens to their letters once they are stamped and dropped into the mail slot.

If you refer back to the goals of this text you will see that through the life learning experience in which Mr. Cunningham and his children were engaged it was possible to accomplish these goals as well as the development of many content-area-related reading skills, such as reading transportation schedules and discussing scientific topics.

## BIBLIOGRAPHY

Allen, R. Van. *Report of the Reading Study Project*, Monograph No. 1, San Diego, California: Department of Education, San Diego County, 1961.

Allen, R. Van. *Language Experience in Communication*. Boston: Houghton Mifflin Co., 1976.

Hall, M. *Reading as a Language Experience*. Columbus, Ohio: Merrill, 1975.

Hoover, C. "Language Experience with Kindergarteners." Notes from a conversation. April, 1975.

Lee, D. and Allen, R. Van. *Learning to Read Through Experience*. New York: Appleton-Century Crofts, 1963.

# 7

# Oral Language: Developing the Listening and Speaking Abilities of Young Children

*Figure 49*. Developing the Oral Language Abilities of Young Children. (Photo by Linda Lungren)

Most children come to preschool with oral language. As we explained in Chapter 3, language acquisition is a developmental process. Children become more proficient in each aspect of language (phonology, morphology, syntax, and semantics) as they mature. In your teaching of young children, it is extremely important to understand the developmental stages of language maturation in order to provide appropriate instruction for every one of your students.

## Listening Skills

Experiments to help us better understand the listening process have been carried on for half a century. Sara Lundsteen's concise definition of listening is practical and useful for classroom teachers. She defines listening as "the process by which spoken language is converted to meaning in the mind." The results of many studies have suggested that phases of listening may be measured in controlled testing situations.

Although definitions of what listening is continues to be debated and effective teaching practices have been documented, listening activities still are only infrequently included in classroom curricula. The schools' neglect to offer formal instruction in listening skills can be attributed to the relationship between listening and reading. Some educators have believed that reading and listening skills tap the same thought processes although each of these processes is complex. Because they believed that reading and listening are similar, they have argued that listening skills can be developed "naturally," but reading instruction requires formal instruction. Therefore, they have suggested that reading instruction can be substituted for listening instruction. Devine (1978), however, argues that the two processes frequently occur in dissimilar situations and they require different amounts of time for completing the communication processes. He further argues that even though the higher levels of both skills share a similar thinking base, it must be concluded that relevant instruction will occur only when we begin to think of "the two as different communciation processes."

Listening is a means of learning. As students, we spend a great deal of time listening. Wilt (1959) found that the elementary school children spent about two and one-half hours of a five-hour school day in listening activities. This was nearly twice as much time as their teachers had estimated that children spend in listening.

Brown (1954) suggested that the terms *listening* and *learning* are both limited in definition, and that the gerund *auding*, based on the neologic verb *to aud*, more accurately describes the skill with which classroom teachers are concerned. "Auding is to the ears what reading is to the eyes." If reading is the gross process of viewing, recognizing, and interpreting written symbols, auding may be defined as the gross process of listening to, recognizing, and interpreting spoken symbols.

In an attempt to contrast reading and auding, Russell and Russell (1959) devised the following formula:

Seeing is to Hearing

as

Observing is to Listening

as

Reading is to Auding

*Figure 39.* A Happy Circus Clown

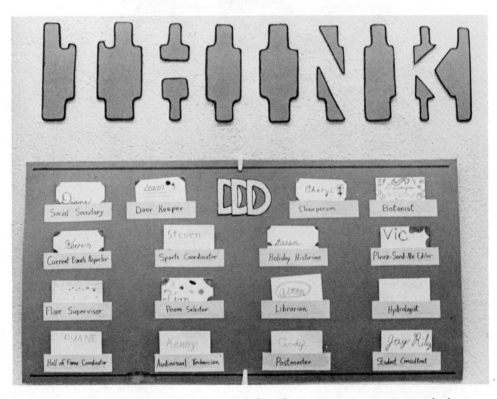

*Figure 40.* Designing an attractive job board encourages interaction with the printed word and teaches students a sense of responsibility. Photo by Linda Lungren)

# Oral Language: Developing the Listening and Speaking Abilities of Young Children

*Figure 49.* Developing the Oral Language Abilities of Young Children. (Photo by Linda Lungren)

Most children come to preschool with oral language. As we explained in Chapter 3, language acquisition is a developmental process. Children become more proficient in each aspect of language (phonology, morphology, syntax, and semantics) as they mature. In your teaching of young children, it is extremely important to understand the developmental stages of language maturation in order to provide appropriate instruction for every one of your students.

149

## Listening Skills

Experiments to help us better understand the listening process have been carried on for half a century. Sara Lundsteen's concise definition of listening is practical and useful for classroom teachers. She defines listening as "the process by which spoken language is converted to meaning in the mind." The results of many studies have suggested that phases of listening may be measured in controlled testing situations.

Although definitions of what listening is continues to be debated and effective teaching practices have been documented, listening activities still are only infrequently included in classroom curricula. The schools' neglect to offer formal instruction in listening skills can be attributed to the relationship between listening and reading. Some educators have believed that reading and listening skills tap the same thought processes although each of these processes is complex. Because they believed that reading and listening are similar, they have argued that listening skills can be developed "naturally," but reading instruction requires formal instruction. Therefore, they have suggested that reading instruction can be substituted for listening instruction. Devine (1978), however, argues that the two processes frequently occur in dissimilar situations and they require different amounts of time for completing the communication processes. He further argues that even though the higher levels of both skills share a similar thinking base, it must be concluded that relevant instruction will occur only when we begin to think of "the two as different communication processes."

Listening is a means of learning. As students, we spend a great deal of time listening. Wilt (1959) found that the elementary school children spent about two and one-half hours of a five-hour school day in listening activities. This was nearly twice as much time as their teachers had estimated that children spend in listening.

Brown (1954) suggested that the terms *listening* and *learning* are both limited in definition, and that the gerund *auding*, based on the neologic verb *to aud*, more accurately describes the skill with which classroom teachers are concerned. "Auding is to the ears what reading is to the eyes." If reading is the gross process of viewing, recognizing, and interpreting written symbols, auding may be defined as the gross process of listening to, recognizing, and interpreting spoken symbols.

In an attempt to contrast reading and auding, Russell and Russell (1959) devised the following formula:

Seeing is to Hearing

as

Observing is to Listening

as

Reading is to Auding

Children hear the siren of an ambulance, the chirp of a cricket, and the honk of a horn. They listen either passively or actively to these sounds and to their favorite song or television program. Their degree of listening depends on their interest. But as they listen attentively to a parent for instruction, to a teacher for directions, to get facts from a classmate's report or to understand both sides of a debate, they may be said to be *auding*, for they are listening to verbal symbols with comprehension and interpretation.

Different levels of listening may really be signifying our different levels of involvement and concentration. Anderson and Lapp (1979) illustrate the following degrees of listening:

1. Hearing sounds of words but not reacting to the ideas expressed: a mother knows that Daryl is speaking.
2. Intermittent listening: turning the speaker on and off; hearing only one idea in a lecture but ignoring the rationale for the idea.
3. Half listening: following the discussion only well enough to find an opportunity to express your own idea; disregarding the ideas of others but listening to the conversation to find a place to tell how you handled a situation.
4. Listening passively with little observable response: the child knows the teacher is telling him once again how to walk in the hall.
5. Narrow listening in which the main significance is lost as the listener selects details that are familiar or agreeable to him: a good Democrat listening to a candidate from another party.
6. Listening and forming associations with related items from one's own experiences: a first-grade child hears the beginning sound of *Sally, says* and *said*, and relates it to the letter *s*.
7. Listening to a report to get main ideas and details or follow directions: listening to the reader and descriptions of a new spelling game.
8. Listening critically: a listener notices the emotional appeal of words in a radio advertisement.
9. Appreciative and creative listening with genuine mental and emotional responses: a child listens to the teacher read *Miracle of Maple Hill* and shares the excitement of sugar making.

## Developing Good Habits in Listening

Many bad habits develop in the language art of listening. We are all aware of the processes involved in avoiding difficult or unpleasant listening. Every parent knows the "Surely, he is not talking about me!" attitude of the child who is being corrected. Emotions often interfere with listening to ideas. "Who is she to be saying that?" "They will never convince me that those horrible sounds are music!" and "How would he know, he's never been a father!" are emotional statements that may limit reception.

Some individuals have a habit of seeking distraction even when they could be interested in the speaker or topic. In your classroom you will be able to detect a wide variation of student responses to a distraction because it will command the attention of some, and it will be totally ignored by others.

A good listener not only thinks with the speaker, but he flexibly anticipates the speaker's direction of thought, objectively evaluating the verbal evidence

*Figure 50.* A good listener not only thinks with the speaker but he flexibly anticipates the speaker's direction of thought. (Photo by Jonathan Sutton)

offered in terms of the speaker's purpose while mentally viewing the facts represented by the speaker. Many people who have difficulty listening find that taking notes during a presentation aids their attention. Giannangelo and Frazer (1975) suggest that notetaking and other aids which strengthen listening skills can be taught. As teachers it is important to provide activities which will extend the listening skills of students. Too often the language art of listening is forgotten.

When a child asks a question and concerns himself with an answer, he is truly engaged in attentive listening. You will find times like that to be some of your most teachable moments. You can set the stage for careful listening by aiding children in preparing questions to ask a visitor or the principal or people who can be interviewed on a field trip in the community.

Be sure the listening experience being provided within your classroom is worth the child's time and effort. The sharing period in your classroom may better extend both the language and listening skills of your students if you ask each speaker to think of his audience and how he wants them to respond. The time spent in sharing should involve more than merely free conversational exchange. The school curriculum must have purpose and direction since it is too crowded to allow it to be usurped by exchanges appropriate for recess. You may provide direction to this exchange by encouraging a discussion of some of the following:

1. Seasonal changes noted on the way to and from school
2. Pleasant experiences which have happened at home or school
3. Important happenings of a trip
4. Characteristics of favorite trips

5. Kindnesses demonstrated toward us or by us to others
6. Local or school news
7. Articles we have made or collected
8. Jokes or riddles
9. Facts about birds, rocks, music, coins, insects, hobbies, history
10. New words

The sharing period is much more effective if children plan in advance. We are not suggesting that you eliminate spontaneity, but rather that you provide a framework for spontaneity. The most flexible classroom is the one that is well planned. Planning must come before flexibility.

As a teacher you will be responsible for the quality of the material shared in literature. If children are to listen to material being read, it should be material that provides enrichment. The beauty of words can be shared through well-read poetry that is appropriate to the child's interests. Stories that add stature to the child's value concepts should be discussed.

Your attitude toward listening will certainly influence your students. Teaching is as much listening as telling. We discover interests and needs through listening. The following suggestions from Nichols and Stevens (1957) may aid you in providing a positive example for listening.

1. Take time to listen. When someone is troubled or needs to talk, give him the time if at all possible. It will help clarify communication between you.
2. Be attentive. Let tirades flow uninterrupted. Try to indicate that you want to understand.
3. Employ three kinds of verbal reactions only—"Hmmm" or "Oh" or "I see." Remain silent, nodding to show understanding. If the talker is unreasonable, restate what he said, putting it in the form of a question.
4. Never probe for additional facts. There is a difference between willingness to listen and curiosity. Your purpose in therapeutic listening is seldom to obtain information.
5. Avoid evaluating what has been said. Avoid moral judgments and the temptation to advise. The talker is clarifying his problem through talking and then must define alternative solutions.
6. Never lose faith in the ability of the speaker to solve his own problems. The speaker is really talking things over with himself as he talks with you.

You may want to discuss with your students the responsibility of the listener. All children are able to understand the need for courtesy. "You listen to me and I will listen to you." You may also want to provide children with standards for listening by discussing situations where listening is important: You are a waiter taking an order; you are to go to the principal's office with a message and you are asked to return with an answer; you are to interview a famous person; you are to report on a news broadcast. Anderson and Lapp (1979) suggest that these types of exercises may lend to the following inventory of listening habits:

1. Do I give the speaker my attention?
2. Do I think with the speaker?

    3. Can I select the main idea?
    4. Can I recall things in order?
    5. Can I follow directions?
    6. Can I retell what I hear?

Through classroom simulations and discussions, children learn that a good listener is polite, gets the facts, listens thoughtfully, listens for a reason, and intelligently uses the information heard.

### Instruction in Listening Skills

To begin your initial listening instruction program, try this sample activity. Ask your class to cease all talk and movement until the classroom is completely silent. Ask the children to close their eyes and listen to as many sounds as they can (the clock ticking, the teacher talking in the next room, birds singing outside the window). Ask the children to remember as many different sounds as they can. This will reinforce their attention and memory skills. After a short while, ask the children to describe the things they heard. Ask them to be specific in descriptions. Put a list of the sounds that the children described on the board, and discuss ways that they could listen more effectively.

A more complex listening activity is "following directions." Divide the class into teams of three, and explain to the children that the purpose of this activity is to see how well each group listens to directions. Give each group a different set of directions (prepared in advance), ranging in difficulty from "Write your middle initial on a piece of paper and bring it to me," to "Untie your shoelaces, subtract nine from fifteen on your paper and erase the nine, count the number of erasers on the blackboard, and find a book that has the letter 'p' in its title."

Another strategy for improving your students' listening skills is to ask students to listen to passages that you read aloud. Make sure that your students understand what to listen for before you begin reading. Familiarize them with their purpose in listening so they can develop their skills of discrimination. For example, if you were reading Horton Hears a Who by Dr. Seuss to your class, you might first ask them to listen for the different types of animals that tried to stop Horton from saving his little friends. Then, at the conclusion of the story, you could ask the class to recall these animals and match their names with the ways in which they attempted to stop Horton from his mission.

People rarely listen for the sake of listening. They need a purpose. Ask your students to fixate on an object in your room, and read a worthwhile story to them. You'll be surprised how attentive they can be.

The following two lessons may provide you with examples of how to plan experiences which extend the listening skills of your students.

### Strategy Development: Listening

Age Level: 6, 7

Construction: Develop a series of simple sentences utilizing vocabulary that is familiar to the children.

Procedure: Dictate a few short, simple sentences to the group, reinforcing the idea of beginning capital letter, space between words, and ending punctuation. You can also give a simple set of sentences to partners so that they may enjoy dictating sentences to each other and checking for these three points.

### Strategy Development: Listening

Age Level: 7, 8

Construction: Record one side of a pretend telephone conversation between two animals. Use an interesting voice and some comical lines. Be sure to leave long pauses between each passage.

Procedure: After the children listen to the tape once, give out ditto sheets on which is written one side of the dialogue; include blank lines for the missing part. Have the children read along silently as you play the tape again. Give each child a partner and instruct them to write the missing words and make their own recording of the entire conversation.

Listening is the language art that is often taken for granted because most children come to school with no hearing impairment. Remember to develop and extend your student's listening skills because they provide a base for the other language arts.

## Speaking Skills

The perennial problem that plagues all educators of young children is that of deciding whether to emphasize "correct" communication or "effective" communication. As explained in Chapter 3, many theorists such as Lennenberg (1970) emphasize the innate aspects of language acquisition, whereas others such as Skinner (1972) stress behavioral reinforcement as a prime factor in language development. Yet, others such as Piaget (1962) focus on the child's interactions within his environment as an essential factor in establishing concepts that will later be communicated through language.

As you review these theories you may continue to wonder, "What type of language patterns should I stress in my classroom?" In making this decision, it is important to evaluate the extent to which correct communication encourages effective communication. Although knowledge of the rules of syntax may provide a general understanding of the syntax of written communication, knowledge of the rules in itself will not help children to communicate effectively. We must also examine the role of cultural backgrounds in determining whether to stress correct or effective communication.

*Figure 51.* The basic structures of language are learned by the age of five or six. (Photo by Linda Lungren)

Wanat (1971) has cautioned that "group differences have generally been ignored in research on language development." Thus, dialect differences, possible ethnic differences in capacities and strategies for processing information, differences in thinking style, and emotionally related factors are not adequately taken into consideration. According to Wanat (1971) none of the theories reviewed gives an adequate explanation of the way a child acquires his language. Each of the theories is wrong in that each unjustifiably claims to provide a complete explanation. Yet, each of the theories is valuable in that each provides part of the information we need to understand language (Wanat, 1971, p. 147).

While there is definitely a need for continued research involving larger sample populations with greater sociological and motivational contexts, classroom teachers are being called upon daily to make decisions regarding language programs for their students. Therefore, it is important to remember that existing theories offer much of the information that is needed to understand the language base of the communication process.

The basic structures of language are learned by the age of five or six. Along with these basic structures come language "habits," which are determined by age, socioeconomic group, and geographical region. Once acquired, these language habits are difficult to change. Most children come to school with language and the desire to communicate, but the communication process can break down *if* the teacher's inflexible teaching practices insist on "correct" language and fail to take into account discrepancies in the child's pronunciation, lexicon, phrasing, and construction. The dichotomy between correct language (the language of the school) and effective language (the language of the child) can become broadened and can lead to student failure (Loban, 1976) if teachers refuse to recognize the existence of language habits.

## Establishing Patterns of Correct Public Usage

Children come to school with private language, the language of the home, and varying degrees of public language, the language of the school. Correct public usage is concerned with proper form. The agreement of verb and subject in number and tense, the form of the pronoun in various positions in the sentence, and word order in sentences are some of the situations that present learning problems of proper form. The child who says, "I done my work." is using the wrong verb form. Another who says, "Him and me are friends." is using the incorrect form of the pronoun. Children use these forms because they hear them at home, on television, and in the playground.

In an attempt to facilitate continued language growth among students it is important for teachers to provide positive experiences; for example, if a young child says, "I busted it!" you can reply, "I see that you *broke* it. Delicate things *break* easily. *Broken* things are hard to repair, but let's try." Children will learn various dialects of language when you use them in nonthreatening verbal interactions. As you react in this manner, you are encouraging the child to enjoy his private language while extending his public language. His language is the verbal expression of his thoughts and feelings. If his language is rejected, he is rejected.

Speech patterns of children are extended through situations which provide them with opportunities to talk. During a child's early years the content of "talk" will focus on self, home, and family. At first you will need to accept the child's own word groupings if they are in communication units.

Anderson and Lapp (1979) suggest the following language forms that should be given careful attention as you attempt to extend public language skills.

1. A transition from all "baby-talk" and "cute" expressions.
2. The acceptable uses in speech and writing of *I, me, him, her, she, they,* and *them.*
3. The appropriate uses of *is, are, was,* and *were* with respect to number and tense.
4. Standard past tenses of common irregular verbs such as *say, gave, brought, took, stuck.*

5. Elimination of the double negative: "We don't have no apples."
6. Elimination of analogical forms: *ain't, hisn, hern, ourn, hisself, theirselves.*
7. Appropriate use of possessive pronouns: *my, mine, his, hers, theirs, ours.*
8. Mastery of the distinction between *its* (possessive pronoun) and *it's* (it is, the contraction). (This applies only to written English.)
9. Elimination of this *here* and that *there.*
10. Approved use of personal pronouns in compound construction: as subject (Mary and I), as object (Mary and me), as object of preposition (to Mary and me).
11. Attention to number agreement with the phrases *there is, there are, there was, there were.*
12. Elimination of *learn* for *teach, leave* for *let.*
13. Avoidance of pleonastic subjects: *my brother he; my mother she; that fellow he.*
14. Sensing the distinction between *good* as adjective and *well* as adverb (for example, "He spoke well.").

The English language is a constantly changing language. The meaning difference between *shall* and *will* that is still taught in language books has for all practical purposes disappeared in usage.

Teachers often ask, "At what age should I begin to stress usage practice?" Unfortunately, few studies have been conducted that examine this question. Those which do exist are surveys of city courses of study and textbooks. This means that teacher judgement, as much as any other factor, has influenced the standards of usage practice. Many textbooks ignore such practice. Therefore, when one of your students is having difficulty, you will need to devise appropriate instruction. The following suggestions may provide you with needed insights:

1. Discuss with your students the need for both public and private language. Classroom simulations of conversational interactions may be effective illustrations. Work together as a group remembering that one's feelings may be easily offended.

2. Observe the language patterns of your students as a group and as individuals.

3. Select common patterns of error to share with your students.

4. Concentrate on a few errors at a time.

5. Illustrate correct word usage.

6. Suggest the correct usage after the child, in error, has completed his thought. Children cannot learn to improve language until they feel free to use language. Language modification will occur only after the child feels accepted by the group and sufficiently self-confident so that correction will not silence him.

7. Follow a period of oral expression with a short drill period in which the child hears the correct form repeated several times.

8. Play games in which the correct form is frequently used.

Much time and patience may be required to modify incorrect usage patterns. Once the incorrect pattern has been identified, oral paractice should be stressed until the established form sounds correct to the learner. Writing practice should be incorporated as a means of practicing the new pattern. Your attitude will influence the attitudes of your children toward classroom language modification. The spirit in which corrections are made is perhaps the most important factor in the child's language development.

### Extending the Language Patterns of All Students

Because most American classrooms contain populations which are multi-ethnic and culturally diverse you may, as a teacher, be required to provide language experiences for the bilingual child.

> "By the time the native child reaches the age of seven, his cultural and language patterns have been set, and his parents are required by law to send him to school. Until this time he is likely to speak only his own local dialect of Indian, Aleut, or Eskimo or, if his parents have had some formal schooling, he may speak a kind of halting English.
>
> He now enters a completely foreign setting—a Western classroom. His teacher is likely to be a Caucasian who knows little or nothing about his cultural background. He is taught to read the Dick and Jane series. Many things confuse him: Dick and Jane are two gussuk (Eskimo term for "white person," derived from the Russian Cossack) children who play together. Yet, he knows that boys and girls do not play together and do not share toys. They have a dog named Spot who comes indoors and does not work. They have a father who leaves for some mysterious place called "office" each day and never brings any food home with him. He drives a machine called an automobile on a hard-covered road called a street which has a policeman on each corner. These policemen always smile, wear funny clothing, and spend their time helping children to cross the street. Why do these children need this help? Dick and Jane's mother spends a lot of time in the kitchen cooking a strange food called "cookies" on a stove which has no flame in it, but the most bewildering part is yet to come. One day they drive out to the country, which is a place where Dick and Jane's grandparents are kept. They do not live with the family and they are so glad to see Dick and Jane that one is certain that they have been ostrasized from the rest of the family for some terrible reason. The old people live on something called a "farm" which is a place where many strange animals are kept: a peculiar beast called a "cow," some odd-looking birds called "chickens," and a "horse" which looks like a deformed moose. . . .
>
> So it is not surprising that 60 per cent of the native youngsters never reach the eighth grade." (Bilingual Schooling in the United States, 1972)

The non-native English speaker encounters some difficulty in speaking and reading English because he is exposed to a life-style and language which is unlike his own. Therefore, as you plan learning experiences to extend his English language skills it is important to consider the following elements of the child's world: (1) culture, (2) self-image, (3) language.

**Culture.** Many teachers and students experience problems of cultural interference.

"Too many teachers are inadequately prepared to understand or accept these dissimilar cultural values. Teachers come from homes where the drive for success and achievement has been internalized early, where "work for work's sake" is rewarded, and where time and energy are spent building for the future. Many children come to the classroom with a set of values and background of experiences radically different from that of the average American child. To teach these children successfully, the teacher must be cognizant of these differences and must above all else seek to understand without disparagement those ideas, values, and practices different from his own." (Zintz, 1975)

**Self-Image.** An important characteristic of a good teacher is the ability to accept every child without prejudice or preconception. Children are very aware of their teacher's and peers' acceptance of them. When you are working with a bilingual child, you need to accept the language of the child because it is the language of his home. When a child, who has a foreign accent or an American dialect other than the teacher, is ridiculed or made to feel foolish, his self-concept is often damaged. Trust and confidence between a teacher and child must precede linguistic corrections.

**Language.** The following four linguistic categories will need specific attention when you are working with your bilingual children.

1. Experiential background
   The ability to share one's conceptual knowledge becomes increasingly possible as the child gains multiple experiences in English. A child from a city may find it quite difficult to read about the Kansas wheat fields because he has never experienced such a phenomenon.

2. Auditory discrimination
   Children from language backgrounds other than English will possess a phonemic system that differs considerably from the English phonemic system; e.g., Spanish-speaking children often have difficulty discriminating between minimal pairs in English.

| pin | hit | ship | bit |
|-----|-----|------|-----|
| pen | heat | sheep | beet |

3. Lexicon
   As you work with bilingual children it is important to remember two important facts about vocabulary extension. First, the child may have an English word for a phenomenon that is culturally determined. This meaning may not be shared by native English speakers. Second, there are many words in other languages

that sound like English words but have different meanings. These words are called false cognates. Some examples in Spanish are:

salvar        to save a life, not to save money

libreria       bookstore, not library

chanza        joke, not chance

4. Syntax

Since the syntactic structures of many languages differ from English, it is very important to provide the bilingual child with time and practice as he attempts to acquire a second syntactic structure. You may find that your bilingual children experience difficulty with one of the following

a. Reversed/inverted word order:

The house white.

(La casa blanca)

I don't know where is the boat.

(No se donde esta el bote)

b. Grammatical elements:

| | |
|---|---|
| Copula confusion: | Today she working downtown. |
| Pluralization: | His foots are sore. |
| Comparison: | He is more big. |
| Possession: | The pen of Jose is red. |

These sources of possible confusion for the child can be the basis of your instruction. With time, practice, and competent teachers, all children can learn to communicate in both their native language and in English.

## The Young Student

Your function as a teacher is to accustom children to variations of speech while encouraging the child's own standards of language within your classroom. Some methods of providing this instruction, all of which have their basis in an opportunity for student oral expression, are presented next.

### Ideas for Developing Listening/Speaking Skills

#### Puppetry

Puppetry is a stimulating exercise for promoting oral language. By making a puppet and using it as a device for oral communication, children can expand their creativity as both speakers and artists. For instance, the following activity uses puppetry for oral language development.

Purpose:     Learning to interpret information orally.

Materials:   Picture book with large pictures and hand or stick puppet for each
             child.

Procedure:   1. While looking at the pictures in a wordless book with the children,
                describe the happenings on each page.
             2. Pass out one puppet to each child. Puppets represent storybook
                characters.
             3. The children using the puppets create a dialogue that the char-
                acters on each page may have spoken during the story. Show them
                the picture before beginning each dialogue, and ask, "What do you
                think the characters might be saying in this situation?"
             4. Allow the children to switch puppets and try different roles. Films
                and how-to books are available to enable you to use puppetry in
                your classroom.

### Using Puppets in Reading Development

#### Films

| Title | Time | Publisher |
|---|---|---|
| Stories | 14 minutes | Coronet |
| Puppets | 15 minutes | ACI Productions |
| Puppets You Can Make | 16 minutes | Coronet |

#### How to Books

#### Using Puppets

| Title | Author | Age Range | Publisher & Date |
|---|---|---|---|
| Puppet Party | Goldie Taub Charnoff | Preschool | Scholastic Book Services, |
| Making Puppets Come Alive | Larry Engler & Carol Fijian | Toddler | Taplinger Pub. Co. |
| How to Make Puppets and Teach Puppetry | Margaret Bevesford | Primary | Taplinger Pub. Co. |
| Making Easy Puppets | Shari Lewis | Primary | E. P. Dutton & Co. |

### Creative Dramatics

Children must be allowed to express themselves as individuals, and creative
dramatics provides an appropriate forum. The following example will

demonstrate the ways in which creative dramatics can enhance oral language development.

| | |
|---|---|
| <u>Purpose:</u> | Encouraging language development by creating situations that require verbalizations. |
| <u>Materials:</u> | One package of objects per group of three or four children (suggested objects: baseball cap, apron, ball, blocks) |
| <u>Procedure:</u> | 1. Distribute the packages to each group of children and let them examine the objects. Discuss possible uses of the objects. |
| | 2. Explain that they are to create a situation (develop a small "script") using all of their objects. |
| | 3. Have the children perform their plays. |

### Reader's Theater

Reader's Theater uses the oral language traditions of drama to give practice in reading aloud. No scenery, costumes, or actions are necessary. Imagination plays a large role in the activity's success. The audience must imagine all the settings and actions, and the readers must project the story line through their verbal interpretations of scripts.

Reader's Theater is a fairly recent approach that teachers have been using to arouse more enthusiasm in their students for reading. It is a technique in which the student listens to lines being read, but must envision for himself the scenery, actions, costumes, and other effects.

Unlike a traditional theatrical production, all the characters in Reader's Theater hold copies of the script while they speak. They do not attempt to become the character, but to give the audience an idea of the character, and let the audience use its imagination to complete the picture. For the same reason, no action or other effects are allowed to interfere with the audience's personal perceptions, which can often be more exciting than a more formal production.

For a number of reasons this kind of reading task works well for many students. First, it does not require them to portray a character physically, (a threatening assignment for some students). The student is simply required to read the part and interpret it orally. Second, this type of reading can involve less able readers, because they may participate in the preparation of the script and can assume roles that require less reading. Third, students who are part of the audience must visualize what is being said, thereby sharpening their listening abilities.

Although a basic familiarity with the material will give the student more confidence, it is not necessary to memorize lines and rehearse for perfection. Reader's Theater is designed to be experimental in form and not to limit the audience's personal impression. Students may want to use music or other audio-visual aids and should feel free to be creative in this respect.

Reader's Theater can integrate a wide range of activities and can be effective in team-teaching formats. A group of students may research the life of a famous person or a well-known historical event and write Reader's Theater scripts from the information they find. In this way they use their research, writing, and comprehension skills, and turn out a more creative result than a research report. Students can also benefit from the practice of rewriting literature into a play. This activity requires them to pick out the most significant events and reinterpret them for dramatic production. Participants should remember, though, that the best stories for adaptation are those that include a great deal of dialogue and few actions that are vital to an understanding of the scene.

A teacher guiding students in a Reader's Theater production should take care to emphasize that the students are interpreters. Young children especially may want to play act, but they should be led to an understanding that their impact should be on the ears and minds rather than on the eyes of their audience.

The stage for a Reader's Theater production is a specified section of your classroom. The characters may be placed on the stage in a variety of ways. They may be sitting or standing, all together or scattered about. Scene changes or actions can be narrated. Entrances and exits may be played by small movements such as standing up or sitting down, turning front or back, stepping forward or backward, or by any other appropriate method. Just remember that no important action should actually be portrayed so that the audience will supply their actions mentally.

On the following pages you will find some sample Reader's Theater scripts to help you begin your program.

## THE GIVING TREE

**Shel Silverstein**

(Elementary 3–6)

NARRATOR 1
NARRATOR 2
TREE
BOY

NARRATOR 1: Once there was a tree ... and she loved the little boy. And everyday the boy would come and he would gather her leaves and make them into crowns and play King of the Forest.
NARRATOR 2: He would climb her trunk and swing from her branches and eat apples.
NARRATOR 1: And they would play hide and seek.
NARRATOR 2: And when he was tired he would sleep in her shade. And the boy loved the tree very much.

NARRATOR 1: And the tree was happy.

NARRATOR 2: But time went by and the boy grew older.

NARRATOR 1: And the tree was often alone. Then one day the boy came to the tree and the tree said,

TREE: Come boy, come and climb up my trunk and swing from my branches and eat apples and play in my shade and be happy.

BOY: I am too big to climb and play. I want to buy things and have fun. I want some money. Can you give me some money?

TREE: I'm sorry, but I have no money. I have only leaves and apples. Take my apples, Boy, and sell them in the city. Then you will have money and you will be happy.

NARRATOR 2: And so the boy climbed up the tree and gathered her apples and carried them away.

NARRATOR 1: And the tree was happy.

NARRATOR 2: But the boy stayed away for a long time. And the tree was sad. And then one day the boy came back and the tree shook with joy and she said,

TREE: Come boy, climb up my trunk and swing from my branches and be happy.

BOY: I am too busy to climb trees. I want a house to keep me warm. I want a wife and I want children and so I need a house. Can you give me a house?

TREE: I have no house. The forest is my house, but you may cut off my branches and build a house. Then you will be happy.

NARRATOR 1: And so the boy cut off her branches and carried them away to build his house.

NARRATOR 2: And the tree was happy.

NARRATOR 1: But the boy stayed away for a long time and when he came back, the tree was so happy she could hardly speak.

TREE: Come, boy,

NARRATOR 1: She whispered,

TREE: Come and play

BOY: I am too old and sad to play. I want a boat that will take me far away from here. Can you give me a boat?

TREE: Cut down my trunk and make a boat. Then you can sail away and be happy.

NARRATOR 2: And so the boy cut down her trunk and made a boat and sailed away.

NARRATOR 1: And the tree was happy ... but not really.

NARRATOR 2: And after a long time the boy came back again.

TREE: I am sorry boy, but I have nothing left to give you—my apples are gone.

BOY: My teeth are too weak for apples.

TREE: My branches are gone. You cannot swing on them.

BOY: I am too old to swing on branches.

TREE: My trunk is gone. You cannot climb ...

BOY: I am too tired to climb.

TREE: I am sorry (sigh). I wish that I could give you something but I have nothing left. I am just an old stump and I am sorry.

BOY: I don't need very much now. Just a quiet place to sit and rest. I am very tired.

TREE: Well,

NARRATOR 1: Said the tree, straightening herself up as much as she could.

TREE: Well, an old stump *is* good for sitting and resting. Come, boy, sit down.
Sit down and rest.
NARRATOR 2:  And the boy did.
NARRATOR 1:  And the tree was happy.

## POOR OLD LADY

1:  Poor old lady, she swallowed a fly.
I don't know why she swallowed a fly.
2:  Poor old lady, I think she'll die.

3:  Poor old lady, she swallowed a spider.
It squirmed and wriggled and turned inside her.
1:  She swallowed the spider to catch the fly.
I don't know why she swallowed a fly.
2:  Poor old lady, I think she'll die.

4:  Poor old lady, she swallowed a bird.
How absurd!  She swallowed a bird.
3:  She swallowed the bird to catch the spider.
1:  She swallowed the spider to catch the fly,
I don't know why she swallowed a fly.
2:  Poor old lady, I think she'll die.

5:  Poor old lady, she swallowed a cat.
Think of that!  She swallowed a cat.
4:  She swallowed the cat to catch the bird.
3:  She swallowed the bird to catch the spider,
1:  She swallowed the spider to catch the fly,
I don't know why she swallowed the fly.
2:  Poor old lady, I think she'll die.

6:  Poor old lady, she swallowed a dog.
She went the whole hog when she swallowed the dog.
5:  She swallowed the dog to catch the cat.
4:  She swallowed the cat to catch the bird.
3:  She swallowed the bird to catch the spider,
1:  She swallowed the spider to catch the fly,
I don't know why she swallowed the fly.
2:  Poor old lady, I think she'll die.

7:  Poor old lady, she swallowed a cow.
I don't know how she swallowed the cow.
6:  She swallowed the cow to catch the dog,
5:  She swallowed the dog to catch the cat,
4:  She swallowed the cat to catch the bird,
3:  She swallowed the bird to catch the spider,
1:  She swallowed the spider to catch the fly.
I don't know why she swallowed a fly.
2:  Poor old lady, I think she'll die.

8:  Poor old lady, she swallowed a horse.
All:  She died, of course.

The following books may enhance your Reader's Theater program:

## Reader's Theater & Creative Dramatics

| | | | |
|---|---|---|---|
| You Can Put on a Show | Lewy Olfson | Toddler | Sterling Pub. Co., Inc. |
| Costumes for You to Make | Susan Purdy | Preschool | J. B. Lippincott Company |
| Found Theater | Carolyn R. Fellman 315 S. Aurora St. Ithaca, N.Y. 14850 | For Teachers | |
| Do You Move As I Do? | Helen Borten | Primary | Abelard-Schuman, 1963 |
| The Marcel Marceau Alphabet Book | George Mendoza | Infant to Preschool | Doubleday & Company 1970 |

### Choral Reading

Choral reading provides children with experience in speaking the lyrics of poems. Using children's interest in reciting rhymes can develop memory, "refined" speech habits, and interpretive skills. Children can begin to appreciate poetry through verbally sharing their experience with others. They may also begin to form personal preferences about different poets's styles. A choral reading activity may be conducted by asking children to recite a poem in unison, as a dialogue in which each part is read by a different group or individual, and/or as a dramatization in which the children determine the oral reading expression of a poem that they find most pleasing by listening to different presentations. The following procedures can be used to implement a choral reading activity.

Purpose:   Providing experience in listening, reading, and speaking words.

Materials:   One copy of a lyric poem for each child. Record or tape recording of the same poem.

Procedure:   1. Read the poem to the children in an exciting manner, and then play the recording of it for them.
2. Distribute copies of the lyrics, and practice saying the poem with the children as they try to follow the words. While the children are learning the lyrics it may be helpful to write the words on the chalkboard and point to each word as it is spoken.
3. Have them say the poem along with the recording.
4. Let pairs of children speak their "own" lyric, both with the recording and without.

The following activities are provided to aid you in implementing the many topics discussed throughout this chapter.

## Suggested Activities

### Listening Skills

1. Repeat a familiar nursery rhyme or read a story with rhyming sentences. Stop at predictable times and have the children supply the missing rhyming word.

2. Read a short story such as Where Have You Been? by Margaret Wise Brown. Give the children something specific to listen to as you read. Examples:

   Listen and see if you can remember how many different animals are in this story.

   or

   How many times did you hear the word "little" in this story?

3. Read a short story such as The King With the Terrible Temper. Divide the class into groups and assign each group a certain sound that must be made on cue as you read along.

### Speaking Skills

1. Have children participate in small plays or skits. The scripts that they read from can serve as effective role models.

2. Start choral reading groups in the classroom.

### Creative Dramatics

1. Use book reports. After children have read a favorite book or have enjoyed a book that was read to them, have them dress up as the main character and tell the class something about themselves (learned through the book). If you wish, you may attempt to have the rest of the class guess who the character is.

### Listening

1. Clap and tap a pattern of sounds. Have the children listen and repeat the pattern.

2. Teacher: repeat word pairs. Have children listen for:
   a. rhyming words (hat, cat): if they rhyme, have the children put their hands on their head

      or

   b. words beginning with same letter (bag, bed)

      or

   c. words ending with the same letter (flag, tug)

      or

   d. words that go together (saw, wood; baby, crib).

# BIBLIOGRAPHY

Anderson, P. S. and D. Lapp, *Language Skills in Elementary Education*. New York: Macmillan, 1979.

*Bilingual Schooling in the United States*. Washington, D.C.: Office of Education, 1972.

Brown, D. "Auding as the Primary Language Ability." Unpublished dissertation, Stanford University, 1954.

Carroll, J. "Language Development." In Aslow, A. B. and F. L. Weaver (ed.) *Child Language*. Englewood Cliffs, N.J.: Prentice Hall, Inc., 1971.

Devine, T. "Listening: What Do We Know After Fifty Years of Research and Theorizing?" *Journal of Reading*, 1978.

Giannangelo, D. M. and B. M. Frazer, "Listening: A Critical Skill That Must Be Taught." *Kappa Delta Research*. 12: No. 2 (December, 1975) pp. 42–43.

Lennenberg, E. H. "On Explaining Language." In Gunderson, D. V. (ed.) *Language and Reading—An Interdisciplinary Approach*. Washington, D.C.: Center for Applied Linguistics, 1970.

Loban, W. *The Language of Elementary School Children*. Champaign, Ill., NCTE, 1976.

Lundsteen, S. *Listening—Its Impact on Reading and the Other Language Arts*. Urbana, Illinois: NCTE/ERIC, 1971.

Nichols, R. G. and Stevens, L. A. *Are You Listening?* New York: McGraw-Hill, 1957.

Piaget, J. *Plays, Dreams and Imitation in Childhood*. New York: Norton, 1962.

Russell, D. and E. F. Russell. *Listening Aids Through the Grades*. New York: Bureau of Publications, Teachers College, Columbia University, 1959.

Skinner, B. F. *Beyond Freedom and Dignity*. New York: Knopf, 1972.

Wanat, S. F. "Language Acquisition: Basic Issues." *The Reading Teacher*, 25 (November, 1971), pp. 142–147.

Wilt, M. *Creativity in the Elementary School*. New York: Appleton-Century-Crofts, 1959.

Zintz, M. V. *The Reading Process*. 2nd edition. Dubuque, Iowa. Wm. C. Brown, 1975.

# Developing the Writing
# Abilities of Young Children

*Figure 52.* Children begin their interest in writing at a very early age. (Photo by Linda Lungren)

At first consideration, it might seem logical and correct to you that children be taught to read before they are encouraged to write. Prevailing teaching methods in the past have stressed reading over writing as an initial skill priority because educators believed it was necessary to first read and understand words before one could put them down on paper. Interestingly enough, recent research into the nature of the developmental writing process (Chomsky, 1976) has indicated that children are able to invent spellings for words and write *before* they can read.

> Indeed, the spelling activity precedes reading by its very nature. It's a more concrete task. It requires translating from pronunciation to print when the word is already known. Reading is more abstract, in that it requires, as part of translating from print to pronunciation, identifying the word. This added component of reading, identifying the word, is out of reach of many children who are able to spell, sometimes for months, before they move onto reading. (pp. 12–24)

The basic premise behind the belief in early student writing is the theory that the experience the child receives from experimenting with the written language will benefit him greatly when the time comes to learn the rules of written language.

To understand the system that children use to master the writing process we have to understand their acquisition of spoken language. We know from the work of Piaget that acquisition of knowledge is a matter of reconstruction, in which the child actively creates his own "foundation" and then adds to that framework. In the case of a child's acquisition of writing skills, children's linguistic competence and cognitive abilities help them to design foundations to be built upon. When children begin their formal instruction in writing, they do not begin with empty slates because language has been an integral part of their preschool experiences. This assumption can be supported by the fact that some children learn to write before they go to school. Children have begun their interest in writing by the time they ask questions about printed material, such as, "What does that sign say?"

## Research in Early Writing

Research was undertaken in 1976 by Emilia Ferreiro into children's abilities in establishing correspondences between parts of written sentences and parts of corresponding oral utterances. The children included in this study were a group of four-, five-, and six-year-old children in Buenos Aires, Argentina. The children came from two different groups: highly literate, middle-class families and low-income, working-class families. The children were asked to tell the following:

1. If all the words spoken by the adult were actually written on their papers, and in what order they appeared.

2. If divisions and spaces between words were necessary.

3. If it is possible for additional information to be a part of the written language on their paper.

Ferreiro found that young children ignore traditional rules of writing. He also found that children have no objections to sentences written without spaces between words because he believes young children think this practice closely reflects spoken sentences, and he found that many children expect only "reality" words to be written on their paper. He concluded this because the children tended to exclude all articles that consisted of less than three letters. He found that children do not think articles are words until about age seven.

Ferreiro also found children who were able to see the whole utterance on their paper but were unable to segment the utterance into parts. For example, a child might agree that a sentence says, "The bear eats honey," but would not agree that the word *bear* actually appears on the page as part of the sentence. Some children saw whole sentences in each word.

Children take a big step forward in their experimentation with written language when they begin to see articles and verbs in print. When this happens, they are beginning to recognize the important connection between sound and symbol, and they are starting to give meaning to "non-concrete" words. By allowing children to make these initial mistakes with written language, children can discover the relationship between the printed and spoken word. From their own experiments with written language, they can develop the linguistic skills necessary for *reinventing* writing and adapting to the conventional rules of a communal writing system.

## Writing in the Early Years

The language experience method will present opportunities to you for encouraging children to write. Although the language experience simulation presented in a previous chapter involved kindergarten-aged children, it is possible to engage older children in similar activities. When older children are engaged in a program of this type, it is possible to "get a writing program started."

The story in Figure 53 was prepared by Eric, an eight-year-old boy after a visit to the circus. You can take advantage of an experience such as this by discussing his experience with him. After the discussion, he spent many hours writing and illustrating his story.

As you noticed by reading Eric's story, young children are capable of expressing their ideas in writing. As the young writer relates personal experiences and ideas or shares his thoughts about a picture or an object, you can ask

*Figure 53.*

One day Elephant was walking sadly in the forest,
a Monkey came and said hello, Hi! said Elephant,
You look sad said Monkey, I am said Elephant,
Let's go to the pond said Monkey. O.K. said
Elephant

P.1

Hi! Mr. Frog. Hi! Monkey, ribit! ribit!, Elephant looks sad. ribit! ribit! He is sad said Monkey. Let's go see Owlford owl, he is smart and wise. ribit! ribit! So they went to owlfords tree.

Hi! owlford. Elephant is sad. ribit! ribit!!
Did anyone ask why Elephant was sad? no! said Monkey
and Mr. Frog. Ask him, Elephant why are you sad?
ribit! ribit! I can't find my mommy said Elephant.
Where do you think she is said owlford? Home said
Elephant. Did you look? No. Lets all go and look said owlford. said
ok. They said.

Hi! Dorthy Door, Hi! said Dorthy Door
Did you see Elephants mom? No! said Dorthy
Door. Did you ask the **stork**? No! So Elephant
-Monkey- Mr. Frog and owlford went to stonk quar-
ters.

questions and make suggestions about words, ideas, or manner of presentation. The child could also do as Eric did; he can draw the picture story first, *then* write the story of each picture.

If the child has difficulty providing a title for his story you might ask the class to listen to the story and ask them to suggest story titles. Then the author can select the title he likes best. After the selection has been made, write the title for all to see. When writing is a pleasant, shared experience children will want to dictate stories that you write and all the children read.

As the teacher writes the story, she can provide a model of acceptable format by pointing out where she begins and ends each sentence. "I'll put the first word here, then go to the right. This is the end of the sentence, so I will put a period here." A "book" of such stories can be covered and placed on the reading table so that children can share the stories they have written.

Writing experiences can be a class-wide experience, the efforts of a small group, or an individual working alone or with the teacher. Writing experiences are more productive when they follow a discussion period where children "think together" and express themselves freely. When students work in groups of three or four all members seem to work rapidly and successfully because the teacher is able to circulate among the groups supplying needed words or correct spellings, stimulating thinking, and building curiosity.

When working with young children it is more productive to have all groups working on one topic, such as "Thanksgiving." During the discussion period, words that relate to the topic might be listed on the chalkboard.

| | |
|---|---|
| turkey | family |
| Pilgrims | American |
| Indians | Massachusetts |
| pumpkin pie | thankful |

These words can then become part of the student's dictated or written composition.

As children observe your model of writing they need to be helped to understand that good writing involves selecting, eliminating, arranging words, proofreading, correcting errors, and rewriting. Any writer's first efforts usually contain misspelled words, incomplete sentences, and meager attempts at punctuation and capitalization. First attempts are often corrected as you and the child read the story together. With your assistance children are then able to supply appropriate periods, questions marks, and capitals.

As the child becomes a more proficient writer he will be able to correct his first rough draft. Once the child has gained confidence that his writing is interesting, he should be encouraged to find his own errors. *Encouragement* must precede *corrections* if the end goal is to be a child who writes well and enjoys writing. The following activities are presented to aid you in encouraging the development of such writers.

## ACTIVITIES FOR MOTIVATING WRITING

- <u>Goal</u>: To develop visual motor skills (prewriting)

  <u>Age Level</u>: 4, 5

  <u>Construction</u>: Make several different strips of patterned shapes. The following is an example:

  | ◯ | △ | ◯ | △ | ◯ | △ |
  |---|---|---|---|---|---|
  | red | blue | red | blue | red | blue |

  <u>Utilization</u>: Direct the children to trace each shape without lifting the pencil, beginning with the first red circle on the left and moving to the figure on the right. When they have finished tracing each shape, they can continue to draw shapes to complete the pattern to the end of the strip. They can also color their shapes to match the pattern.

- <u>Goal</u>: To reinforce the relationship between speech and writing

  <u>Age Level</u>: 4, 5

  <u>Construction</u>: Discuss the concept of "helping others" by showing pictures of various situations in which one person is doing a job to help another person. As the children relate what is happening in each picture, tape it up, and write a sentence beneath it.

  <u>Utilization</u>: Have each child draw a picture of a situation in which he/she is helping someone at home or in the neighborhood. As the child explains his finished picture to you, write the sentence along the bottom, and then have each child share his/her product with the group.

- Goal: To reinforce sound/symbol relationships (prewriting)

  <u>Age Level</u>: 4, 5

  <u>Construction</u>: Make several very large tracing patterns for the letter <u>t</u>. Obtain old newspaper to be used as stuffing and magazines that can be cut up.

  <u>Utilization</u>: Have each child trace and cut out two letter t's from heavy graph paper. Glue three quarters of the perimeter tightly leaving an open edge through which the child can insert crumpled newspaper stuffing. Glue together final edges. The child can then look through magazines for pictures of objects that begin with the letter <u>t</u> and can glue them on his life-sized letter.

- <u>Goal</u>: To reinforce sound/symbol relationships

  <u>Age Level</u>: 5, 6

Construction: Prepare bound leaflets consisting of twenty-seven blank pages. On the top of each page, put one letter of the alphabet, and on the front cover put the title "My Picture Diary."

Utilization: As the children participate in activities acquainting them with the alphabet, have them find two pictures of objects that begin with that sound, and paste them on the appropriate page. Some children may be able to label both pictures with some help. After a period of time, each child will have a complete picture dictionary.

● Goal: To enhance imaginative thinking

Age Level: 5, 6

Construction: Obtain a red marker and chart paper. Paste a red circle and the word red at the top of the paper.

Utilization: Ask the children what the word red brings to mind. List all responses as given. Encourage every child to give at least one response and challenge them to help you fill the sheet with red words. When this activity is completed, read the entire list aloud and display it in the classroom. Give the children a sheet on which they can trace the word red with a red crayon and have them draw three of the items listed.

● Goal: To illustrate story composition

Age Level: 5, 6

Construction: Obtain large, lined chart paper and a magic marker. With the paper in full view of all the students, write a catchy story title.

Utilization: Direct your questioning to encourage the students to cooperatively create a story as you write it on paper. Write the story beginning on sheet 1, the middle on sheet 2, and the story conclusion on sheet 3. Tape the story on the board in correct sequence, and divide the children into three groups. Assign each group to draw a picture of the beginning, middle, or end of the story. Display the pictures accordingly.

● Goal: To reinforce sequencing skills for composition

Age Level: 5, 6

Construction: Obtain simple (wordless) comic sequences from the newspaper. Mount each frame on a piece of oak tag. On the back of each put a letter of the alphabet in correct sequence in order to make the sequence self-correcting (comic is correctly ordered when letters are in correct sequence).

Utilization: Direct a small group, partners, or individuals to arrange the comic story in correct order. When completed, have the child tell the story as he/she sees it.

● Goal: To develop skill in compositon

Age Level: 5, 6

Construction: Prepare a sheet of paper with three large boxes. Above the first box write morning; the second, afternoon; the third, night.

Utilization: Instruct the children to draw a picture of something they do in the morning, something they do in the afternoon, and something they do at night. As each child describes each of his/her pictures, write a sentence below it. Cut the paper into three sections and fasten at the top with a paper fastener to make a flip book. Have each child tell his story as he flips his pictures.

- Goal: To develop sentence sense

  Age Level: 6, 7

  Construction: Utilizing the reading vocabulary with which the children are familiar, make up strips of words that can be rearranged to form a sentence. Make a dotted line between words so the strip can be cut apart.

  Utilization: Children should cut up the strip and place the words in logical order to form a sentence. Children can then copy the correct sentence on paper with the appropriate capital letter and ending punctuation.

- Goal: To encourage sentence construction

  Age Level: 6, 7

  Construction  Collect magazines that have many action pictures (nature or sports types would be best).

  Utilization: Children should cut out pictures and glue each on white paper. Have each student write two sentences about his/her picture.

- Goal: To develop the ability to write descriptive sentences

  Age Level: 6, 7

  Construction: Write a series of simple sentences on strips of paper.

  Utilization: Introduce one sentence at a time and encourage students to help you make the sentence more interesting. For example: "The ball rolled" can be expanded to "The smooth red ball rolled slowly down the bumpy country road." Pose leading questions in order to guide the students in expanding many simple sentences.

- Goal. To develop sentence writing skills

  Age Level: 7, 8

  Construction: Instruct the children to draw a self-portrait. Next to the picture, place the word bubble (similar to those in comic strips).

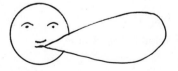

In the bubble, write the beginning of a sentence. For example: "When it is raining, I . . . ." or "My greatest wish is to . . . ."

Utilization: Instruct each student to complete the sentence in his word bubble. The bubble for each child's self-portrait can be changed often. The same procedure can be used with endings of sentences, as the children fill in appropriate beginnings.

- Goal: To develop writing skills

  Age Level: 7, 8

  Construction: Read to the children sets of three sentences that describe a particular object. Follow each set with, "What am I?"

  Utilization: Instruct the children to write three clues about themselves, followed by "Who am I?" Write each riddle on a ditto master and make a booklet of riddles for each child to read and guess. When all the children have had enough time to guess, read and verify the correct response for each.

- Goal: To encourage imaginative composition

  Age Level: 7, 8

  Construction: Make a pile of cards that contain a list of inanimate objects such as chair, doorbell, telephone, mirror.

  Utilization: Direct each child to choose one of these objects and to draw it. Then ask each student to think about what it would be like to be that particular object. If the object could talk, what would it tell us about its feelings? Instruct children to write or tape record their response. Write the responses next to each object in a display or have children draw their objects on ditto masters with accompanying dialogue for distribution as a class book.

## 6 Steps to a Successful Writing Program

In addition to utilizing these activities the following six-step sequence may aid you in providing a successful writing program.

### 1. Motivation

The first step in a successful writing program is to motivate children to write or help them to recognize that they have something to express in writing. The following activities may be helpful as motivators.

A. Tell a story using these facts.

    1. I am a firefighter named Ann. One day there was a big fire. Tell what happened.

2. I am a raindrop. The skies are beginning to clear. Tell how you feel.
3. I am a puppy named Spotty. I love to tease my masters. Tell how this got me into trouble.

B. Picture Stimulators.

The use of pictures as stimulators is an excellent way to motivate a child to write. A picture of a monkey is glued to an idea card. Below it are some stimulating questions: Have you been to the zoo? Why is the monkey so funny? On the back of the card are words the child might wish to use when writing or telling a story.

| zoo | joke | cage |
|------|---------|----------|
| animal | trip | swinging |
| trick | hanging | climbing |

C. Personal Stories.

Encourage your children to draw and label their own stories. A book may be made by compiling the stories of several students or the work of one. Topics may include: Our Pets, Our Favorite Shows, I Like . . ., I'm Happy When . . . .

D. Classroom Diary.

At first the children may dictate a report on "what we did today." Later they can write their own story. This may be a rotating activity. One group may be sharing orally for the day or week, another working on a project, and a third keeping a diary.

E. Titles.

Children are very eager to dictate or write stories once the title or topic has been generated.

| Vacation! Vacation! | Help! |
|---------------------|--------------|
| Loneliness | Our House |
| Fun for a Day | Grandmother |

F. Beginnings.

Getting started is often difficult. These first lines reproduced on writing paper will often help.

1. Dear _____, Please _____.

2. Once there was an alligator _____.

3. I can _____. I have _____. I am_____.

## 2. *Vocabulary Development*

The second step in a successful writing program is to provide writers with words they need.

### A. Seasonal Words.

Seasonal words will be needed yearly, therefore it may be efficient for you to construct the words that will be used to describe each season.

Autumn
  A. Thanksgiving
     pumpkin
     turkey
  B. Halloween
     witches
     bats

### B. Words That Describe Our World.

Prepare packets of word cards that will be used often in writing. These might include packets using the following topics:

1. Our Week
   Sunday, Monday, Tuesday, Wednesday, Thursday, Friday, Saturday.

2. Our Months
   January, February, March April, May, June, July, August, September, October, November, December.

3. Animal Sounds

| | |
|---|---|
| neigh | oink oink |
| moo | mew mew |
| baa baa | bow wow |
| quack | cluck |

4. Our Weather

| | |
|---|---|
| foggy | cold |
| dreary | hot |
| drizzly | humid |
| sunny | cloudy |

5. Our Senses

| | |
|---|---|
| taste | lick |
| touch | feel |
| sight | look |
| hear | listen |
| smell | sniff |

### 3. Current Forms

The third step is to provide correct language forms.

Correct language usage should be presented as aids for expression rather than as interference to creativity. Practice with proper forms will be an aid to any young writer. You can design wall charts that illustrate forms of usage.

Punctuation
I am so tired.
Gosh! It was great.
Are you ready?

Capital Letters
All proper names start with capital letters: Ohio, Mary, Halloween.

Sentences begin with capital letters.

See the dog.
Where were you?

### 4. Writing Practice

The fourth step is to provide practice.

Children need to experiment with writing if they are to become proficient writers. As with any other language art, children will evidence varying degrees of ability in writing. Continued teacher guidance is needed as writing skills are practiced. Beginning writing experiences are often more successful when children work together in a group setting. Working on a group composition helps to establish security among members of the class and gives the teacher an opportunity to help students with spelling and usage. The activities presented throughout this chapter are designed to aid you in providing writing practice situations.

### 5. Sharing

The sharing of one's story is the fifth very important step of writing. Stories may be shared through a class book, bulletin board, daily readings, class or school newspaper, and folders sent to parents.

## 6. *Extending Composition Skills*

The sixth step is to lavish your students with praise.

Praise each child's writing. "Your ending is wonderful." "I like the way you used the word _____." "Marvelous!, Marvelous! Your beginning really excites me." Once the child's self confidence as a writer is secure you can suggest corrections.

Sager (1976) suggests a four-part program in "Reading, Writing, and Rating Stories" which encourages children to improve the clarity and style of their writing. Children are provided with stories that they are taught to rate according to vocabulary, elaboration, organization, and structure. They are given the criteria for rating each factor, and in the process of assigning values to the stories in their lessons, they develop an understanding of the need for *rewriting* in the achievement of a good written product. Sager found through her research that when children return to their own compositions they apply the same judgements they used in the lessons; they rework and rewrite their own stories.

## Writing? Are Children Interested?

In many classrooms, *writing* experiences have become a laborious chore used to fill dreary Friday afternoon space. The results of such programs were reflected in the December 8, 1975 cover story of *Newsweek* entitled, "Why Johnny Can't Write." This article reflected the following findings, which were based on the 1976 comparative study conducted by the National Assessment of Educational Progress.

### HIGHLIGHTS OF RESULTS*

- For a majority of students, first-draft expressive writing is unstructured and lacking in coherence.

- The tendency to integrate feelings and organize them into coherent expressions develops between the ages of 9 and 13; although there is some progress in this area between ages 13 and 17, it is not nearly as great as the progress made between 9 and 13.

- The proportions of good expressive papers written by females, by students whose parents have post-high school education and by students who live in relatively affluent communities are greater than the proportions for males, blacks, children of the poorly educated and children who live in relatively impoverished areas. This is so

*Expressive Writing*, National Assessment of Educational Progress. Writing Report No. 05-W-02: Denver, Colorado, 1976.

even when mechanical and dialect considerations are discounted. The difference between the performance of the low-achieving groups and the nation increases at each successive age level.

● The capacity to enter into an imaginary situation with a controlled and consistent point of view grows steadily with age. Nevertheless, at age 17, almost half the students remain unable to do this competently.

As we reflect on these findings and begin to plan programs that will evidence continuous growth in children's writing skills, it is important to remember that:

> Creative expression should never be confused with the teaching of the techniques of writing. These are two distinct procedures. It should always be remembered that creation is a flowing of ideas. Given a stimulus, ideas come pouring from the mind like water from a fountain. It is all too easy to stop this creative flow. Rules for punctuation, spelling, grammar, and handwriting will stop it. Emphasis on rules is sure to stifle creative thinking. (Lenski, 1949, p. 102)

As children write, it is important that the teacher maintain a balance between the emphasis placed on the *process* and the *product*.

Children share their ideas, fantasies, experiences, and dreams through their writings. You should not make a distinction between creative and noncreative forms of writing because, unless the child is engaged in the direct copying of another's manuscript, he is engaging in the creative process of sharing his thoughts through a written language mode. Naturally, for these expressions to be successfully shared, they must adhere to conventional forms of punctuation. Realizing this, many of you may be wondering, how is it possible to teach a writer to maintain this delicate balance?

As we have observed writing programs in many schools, it seems that those that appear to be the most successful adhere to the following two principles that we have been continually addressing throughout this chapter.

1. Children must have models of 'good writing.'
2. Children must be encouraged to write about *something.*

Let's examine each of these principles more closely.

### 1. *Children Must Have Models of 'Good Writing'*

If we expect children to communicate their thoughts and feelings in written form, they must understand the mechanics of the task. Very few published books, articles, poems, and cartoons are the author's first attempt. Children should be reminded that although the finished product of one's writing may be fun to share, it is often a time-consuming task to get it to that publishable state.

Teach children *to write* and *to edit.* Too often we encourage them *to write,* but we avoid the *editing* process because of fear that we will inhibit creativity. All successful writers edit their materials. You may be able to provide successful writing models by:

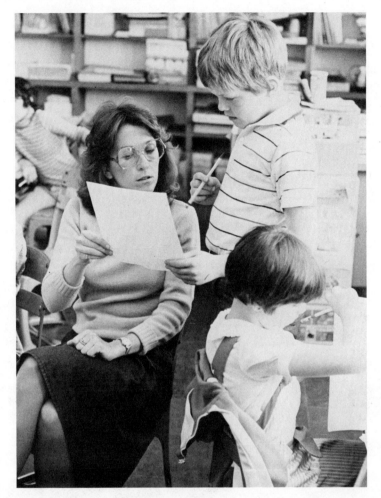

*Figure 54.* As children write it is important for the teacher to maintain a balance between the emphasis placed on the process and product. (Photo by Linda Lungren)

A. Preparing an environment that is rich with samples of 'good writing.'
   1. Newspapers and magazine clippings.
   2. Poems.
   3. Books.
   4. Children's essays.
B. Discussing the elements that contribute to a good piece of writing.
   1. Well thought through topics.
   2. Good organization.
   3. Correct punctuation and use of language.
C. Providing the stimulus for writing.
   1. A letter requesting information.
   2. A pen pal letter.

3. A greeting note or thank you card.
4. An invitation.
5. A poem or creative essay.

D. Encouraging children to get their thoughts down on paper. This is their first (rough) draft. "Get it said!"

E. Helping children to edit their writing by providing scissors and scotch tape. Cut and tape similar ideas to ensure good organization. Check punctuation, spelling, and language flow.

*Figure 55.* A trip to the library and an explanation of library facilities can encourage student interest in writing. (Photo by Linda Lungren)

As the children edit their own manuscripts, they should be encouraged to ask themselves the following questions:

1. Could I have said it better?
2. Will everyone be able to understand my message?
3. Have I left out some important information?
4. Does each sentence begin with a capital letter and end with the appropriate punctuation?

5. Have I spelled all of the words correctly?
6. Are all of the sentences in a paragraph related?
7. Are the paragraphs correctly sequenced?
8. Are the paragraphs indented?

## 2. *Children Must Be Encouraged to Write About Something*

Too often the arduous task of determining "what to write about" is left to the discretion of the child. When this happens, the child quickly assures us that he has nothing to write about. As with almost any endeavor, it is more effectively accomplished if a problem-solving approach is used. The children need a purpose for writing.

*Figure 56.* Children need a purpose for writing—a stimulation for thought. (Photo by Linda Lungren)

In the earlier classroom simulation in Chapter 6 of this text, we observed Mr. Cunningham recording in writing many of the children's ideas as they prepared for a field trip. The ideas were spontaneous because they were related to a field trip. He often asked children to copy what he had written. He was engaging children in a combined speaking, listening, reading, and writing program.

Once children have mastered the skill of transcribing their orthography, the process of writing becomes simpler and throughout the day they can be encouraged to write:

a. Their reactions to something they've just read (newspaper, magazine, book) or heard (radio, TV, class story).

b. Haiku poetry or cinquains.

## HAIKU POEMS

### My Birthday

It is my birthday.  (5 syllables)
I am only five years old.  (7 syllables)
My name is Shannon.  (5 syllables)

### The Game

I like to play ball.  (5 syllables)
I am very good at it (7 syllables)
I am a pitcher.  (5 syllables)

Haiku poems consist of three lines. Line one has five syllables, line two has seven syllables, and line three has five syllables.

## CINQUAINS

### Rain

Rain beat against my window
Thunder invaded the sky
Silence was violated
Sleep destroyed
Awake!

This pattern of cinquain contains five lines, the first of which contains five words, and each following line contains one less word.

### Snow

Cold, Fluffy
Falling, Freezing, Melting
Shivers, Chills, Excitement, Anticipation
Cottonballs

This second form of cinquain contains five lines, each of which has a purpose.

Line 1—state a one word title.
Line 2—state two words that describe the title.
Line 3—state three words that express action.
Line 4—state four words that express feeling.
Line 5—state one word for the title.

c. A greeting or letter.
d. An essay.
e. Captions for student-drawn pictures.
f. Songs.
g. Stories or plays with dialogue.

After these pieces of writing have been edited by the student (with the teacher's help), they should be available for reading by other students and parents. Be sure to praise children for what they have written.

As you begin your combined reading and writing program with a young child, it is essential to remember that each child "has three major avenues for his ideas: he can tell them orally, act them out, or paint a picture. This is where the teacher starts." (Anderson and Lapp, 1979, p. 327) Once you have begun, you will become similar to Mr. Cunningham as you naturally form one topic of exploration after another.

## Teaching Punctuation

The common punctuations marks of our language include:

| | |
|---|---|
| ; semicolon | - . . . - paired dashes |
| : colon | ( . . .) paired parentheses |
| – linking dash | [ . . .] paired brackets |
| - linking hyphen | " . . ." paired quotation marks |
| . period | ' apostrophe |
| ? question mark | . omission period in abbreviations |
| ! exclamation mark | – omission dash |
| , separating comma | . . . triple periods |
| , . . . , paired commas | . . . . quadruple periods |

This type of punctuation was used in the King James Edition of the Bible which was designed and punctuated for oral reading. As readers, we are well aware of the importance of punctuation in written communication since the misplacement of punctuation may result in a loss of meaning.

### *Period*

The use of punctuation in the very earliest grades is introduced with the *period* at the end of a sentence, after initials, and after an abbreviation in titles of persons and things.

*Figure 57.* As you begin your combined reading and writing program with a young child it is essential to remember that each child can tell them orally, act them out, or paint a picture. (Photo by Linda Lungren)

This is my desk.

S. A. Ryan.

Dr. Coryea.

"This little dot is called a period," explains the teacher. It tells us to stop because this is the end of a sentence.

### Question Mark

When teaching punctuation help your children understand that a question mark appears:

1. Following a direct question: <u>Did you bring the ball?</u>
2. Following a direct question within the sentence: <u>Did you bring the ball and bat?</u>" asked Denny or Denny asked, "<u>Did you bring the bat and ball?</u>"

## Comma

In an attempt to provide a model of the appropriate use of a comma, design a chart which contains the following examples.

1. To separate the date and day of the year: July 21, 1990.
2. To separate the city and state: Warren, Ohio.
3. After a letter salutation: Dear Harry,
4. After the close of a letter: your sister, Margaret.
5. To set off a direct quotation: "I'm hungry," shouted Linda.
6. After introductory clauses: While they were traveling, a tire blew.
7. Between parts of a compound sentence joined by a short conjunction: Mr. De Leo took Patty, and Bernie went in Ms. Melanson's car.
8. Before and after a parenthetical expression: You told your brother, I suppose, about the surprise party.
9. Before and after appositives: The principal, Ms. Baxter, talked to the parents.
10. Before and after a nonrestrictive clause: That child, who is tardy, is in the fourth grade.
11. To separate a series of words: Lynne, Bess, Susan, and Eleanor are sisters.

## Colon

Charts are helpful when teaching punctuation because the correct model is always available to the child.

1. After a business letter greeting: Dear Dr. Roser:
2. Before a long series: Mary asked Harold to buy: oranges, grapes, bananas, cherries, apples, and pears.
3. To separate the hour and minutes: 11:28 A.M.
4. To illustrate an example: All proper names begin with capitals: Mildred, Thomas.

## Apostrophe

Correct placement of the apostrophe aids children in spelling.

1. S is used to indicate possession: Gertrude's coat, boys' coats.
2. To emphasize omitted letters: isn't (is not), o'er (over).
3. To illustrate the omission of a number from a date: Class of '88.
4. To show letter and figure plurals: C's, 6's.

## Quotation Marks

Quotation marks are often forgotten by writers, therefore, a model of correct usage will be helpful to your students.

1. She screamed, "Get me a cape!"
2. "Get me a cape!" she screamed.

## Semi-colon

Conjunctions may join words or groups of words. When a conjunction is preceded by a comma (when joining two clauses), a semicolon may be used instead of the comma and conjunction.

Brian was happy, but Kelly was sad may be written Brian was happy; Kelly was sad.

## Hyphen

The hyphen is an orthographic feature rather than a punctuation mark. Most writers avoid the use of the hyphen except at the end of a line. In order to avoid overuse children should be discouraged from using the hyphen.

## Capitals

Capitals are used:
1. To begin a sentence: I like to sing.
2. To illustrate the names of months and holidays: July, Thanksgiving.
3. To name streets and schools: Riverview St., Parker School.
4. To illustrate the first and important words in a title: The Happy Dog and Cat.
5. To name people, pets, and initials: Eric Michael, Collie, E.M.
6. To name countries, cities, rivers, and mountains. American, Kalamazoo, Lake Erie, Rockies.
7. To state greetings and salutation: Dear Jim, Your sister, Margaret.
8. To make reference to God: God, Buddha, Yahweh.

Anderson and Lapp (1979) illustrate how punctuation marks come alive for children through dramatization.

A question mark with a face and legs, a comma with a smiling face and wearing a hat, and a chubby little period are placed on a bulletin board, each with a caption telling one thing they do. These characters—Chubby Little Period, Jolly Question Mark, Mr. and Mrs. Comma, and Tall Exclamation Point—are introduced via the bulletin board. Each figure with its rule and title is shown. Other rules of punctuation are added as introduced.

The teacher describes how these "punctuation characters" are used:

I have the little people made up into plywood puppets. They are kept on hand in the schoolroom at all times. We use them to point up discussion of punctuation in many ways—in language class, social studies, written work, spelling. For example: in oral reading, we talk about "Chubby Little Period" being at the end of a sentence to tell us that we stop here for a short time before going on. "Mr. Comma" helps us by telling us this is the place to pause when we are reading a sentence.

I use this lesson in teaching how to begin and end sentences. In this lesson I also introduce the good English habit. Use a question mark "Jolly Question Mark" after each sentence that asks a question.

Using the wooden "Chubby Little Period," I say:

> Chubby Little Period
> Runs and sits.
> The end of the sentence
> Is always his place.

A sentence is written on the board. Using the puppet, I then demonstrate the period's place. (p. 231)

After the children in your class have dictated stories, work together, as a group, adding the correct punctuation. Children can also gain practice in punctuation by adding the correct punctuation to a piece of literature from which you have removed all markings.

## Teaching Letter Writing

When teaching letter writing emphasize *correct format* and *organization of thought* as the two essential elements for effective communication.

### *Format*

An illustration of the correct form of a letter should be one of your classroom charts. Children model what they see. The sample letter should contain lines for the date, salutation, body of the letter, and closing.

Beginning practice in letter writing may take the form of student dictation which is transcribed on the chalkboard by the teacher. Children can then practice penmanship, punctuation, and letter format by copying the completed letter. Once the children have mastered penmanship and letter format they should be encouraged to write individual letters to ill classmates, relatives, the janitor or any other appropriate recipient. Design a classroom mailbox and encourage children to write notes to each other. All notes must contain the proper letter format.

If children are to become effective adult communicators they must be provided with practice throughout the early years. Addresses of pen pals may be secured through the *Christian Science Monitor* in Boston, Mass.; the *Junior Red Cross* in Washington, D.C.; *The International Friendship League*, 40 Mt. Vernon St., Boston, Mass. and the *Parker Pen Company* in Janesville, Wisc.

Children should be guided in selecting the appropriate tone of a letter. Sample letters may be written with the children illustrating the differences in tone of a letter which expresses appreciation to an author for a well written book and one which asks an author for more information on a topic. Sample letters could be bound and labeled "Letter Forms." Children could then refer to this collection whenever they wish to prepare a letter.

### Organization

Communication is more effective if the ideas of the writer are well organized. Encourage young letter writers to make a brief outline of the information they wish to convey in a dictated or written letter.

You might start your discussion with the following statement, "Let's write a letter to Denise who is in the hospital. Let's tell her how we are and find out how she feels. Our letter should sound just like a verbal visit."

1. Tell about school happenings.
   a. Our projects
   b. Our plants
   c. Our activities
2. Tell about ourselves.
   a. Shannon has a new dog.
   b. Paul has a new sister.
   c. Bob is in Florida.
   d. Janet broke her glasses.
   e. Cheryl and Tommy are on the All-Star Team.
3. Ask about Denise.
   a. We miss her.
   b. We hope she feels better.
   c. We wonder what it is like to be in the hospital.

After the letter has been organized, dictated, or written, encourage children to evaluate and edit by asking:

1. Does the letter sound like a verbal visit?
2. Is the letter written in public language?
3. Is our punctuation correct?
4. Would you enjoy receiving this letter?
5. Does it convey the thoughts intended?
6. Does it provide the receiver with appropriate information?

## Teaching Handwriting

Basic to all of the forms of communications we have discussed throughout this chapter is good handwriting which includes *uniformity of letter size, shape, spacing, and conformity to a standard.*

The young child often lacks the muscular coordination needed for writing. Big muscle and nerve centers develop before the small muscles of the fingers. Dominant handedness may be observable at the age of three but not fully developed until eight. Farsightedness is normal in young children; when practicing handwriting avoid long periods which require close work with small details.

Prerequisites to writing must include work with clay, finger paint, or other materials that require finger coordination. Large muscle coordination can be developed by having the child form chalkboard letters about three inches high. Use your own discretion in providing lined or unlined writing paper. Halpin (1976) suggests that the kind of paper used at the primary level has no effect on the later quality of handwriting. Many schools order standard writing equipment. However, the child should be allowed to use the instrument which offers him comfort and writing ease. Never emphasize speed or copy work which forces constant refocusing of the eye.

Young children are eager to make marks on paper. These marks are often the child's beginning attempts at written communication. Drawing or scribbling with chalk or crayons also encourages small muscle development. During the preschool years, children should work with many manipulatives such as toy letters. Through manipulation and tracing they can develop an awareness of the letter pattern.

Oral expression must precede written expression. As children express themselves the teacher should transcribe their expressions to provide a written model of their thoughts. Listening to songs, poems, and stories also provides children with language samples that may later be part of their written vocabularies.

A beginning writing lesson designed for kindergarten or first grade children might include instruction in the following areas:

1. Holding the pencil
2. Positioning the paper
3. Writing of letters in words. Sample charts of correct letter formation should be displayed in the classroom.

If the children are of preschool age or have not completely developed large muscle motor control, they might be encouraged to write on the chalkboard. Reserve a section of the chalkboard for writing practice during free time. When making the transition from chalkboard to paper, provide the child with a model of the letters. Letters should be presented in words. Queen, Quiet, Quit, Quilt. Children enjoy writing a word which has meaning more than the writing of isolated letters. Be careful to plan small amounts of writing instruction since young children often tire after writing after six to ten minutes. Young children who are writing on oversize easel paper may have better letter formation if they stand while writing. Be careful not to discourage the left-handed writer. Be sure that in your instruction you provide a model of pencil and paper positioning for the left-handed child.

Don't rush children! As in all of the language arts, children who are learning to write pass through stages of development. The rate of time to mastery will develop at individual rates. If a child cannot make the appropriate strokes without tedious, time-consuming muscular drive he is not ready for this task. Continue his work with manipulation until he evidences the needed muscular development.

Many published handwriting kits, which have been designed on the basis of sound research, are available to the classroom teacher.

## BIBLIOGRAPHY

Ackov, E. N. and K. N. Greff. "Handwriting: Copying vs. Tracing as the Most Effective Type of Practice." *Journal of Educational Research* (September, 1976), 668-669.

Anderson, P., and D. Lapp. *Language Arts in the Elementary School*. 3rd ed. New York: Macmillan Publishing Co., Inc. 1979.

Chomsky, C. "Creativity and Innovation in Child Language." *Journal of Education* (May 1976), 158:12-24.

Enstron, E. A. "Those Questions on Handwriting." *Elementary School Journal* (March 1969), 327-333.

*Expressive Writing*. National Assessment of Educational Progress, Writing Report No. 05-W-02: Denver, Colorado, 1976.

Ferreiro, E. "What is Written in a Written Sentence? A Developmental Answer." *Journal of Education*, vol. 160, No. 4, (Fall, 1978).

Flesh, R. "How To Make Sense." New York: Harper, 1954.

Groff, P. "Can Pupils Read What Teachers Write?" *Elementary School Journal* 76, No. 1 (1975), 32-39.

Halpin, G. "Special Paper for Beginning Handwriting: An Unjustified Practice?" *Journal of Educational Research*. (September 1976), 668-669.

Lenski, L. "Helping Children To Create." *Childhood Education* 26 (November 1949), 101-105.

MacDonald, R. "Grading Student Writing: A Plan for Change." *College Compositional Communication*. (May 1975), 154-158.

Sager, C. "Improving the Quality of Written Composition Through Pupil Use of a Rating Scale." *Language Arts* (October 1975), 52:1021-23.

Sealy, L., N. Sealy, and M. Millmore. *Children's Writing*. Newark, Delaware: International Reading Association, 1979.

Torrance, P. E. *Guiding Creative Talent*. Englewood Cliffs, New Jersey: Prentice-Hall, 1962.

Torrance, P.E. "Expressive Writing." Writing Report No. 05-W-02. Denver, Colorado, 1976.

9

# Children's Literature

*Figure 58.* Children of all ages have common as well as individual needs. Books can open new worlds of beauty with pictures of nature and unknown places. (Photo by Linda Lungren)

## The Importance of Teaching Literature to Young Children

Children of all ages have individual needs. They need to know everything about everything, and a need to see beauty and to learn to appreciate it. They require physical care, love, a sense of belonging, a changing environment, and an environment that includes daily routines.

Books can serve to help meet these needs. An intuitive teacher or parent recognizes early the needs and interests of each child and chooses books accordingly. Books can open new worlds of beauty with descriptions and with pictures of unknown places. They can describe the love that exists between parent and child, grandparents, and friends. Children can never learn too early that if they want to find answers to questions or problems, they can often discover their answers on the pages of a book.

A preschool teacher once told the story of her first student; she was fascinated by the question, "When is tomorrow?" She would ask this question over and over again. Her teacher, tiring of giving the absurd answers, "Tomorrow is the day after today" or "Tomorrow is tomorrow," took the child to the library to find an answer and, sure enough, there was a book with the title, *When is Tomorrow*?

Literature can help children to find an appreciation for life that they may be unable to experience in any other way. Reading about other people who have experienced problems similar to their own problems will help children to become confident in their ability to cope with problems and confident in their own judgment. Every child needs to simultaneously feel that he is unique *and* that he belongs to a larger body, the human race. Through literature, the child can see that other people have feelings just like his own: love, envy, joy, jealousy, courage, and cowardice. By examining characters in books, children can learn that there are honorable solutions to all sorts of problems. Every emotion, even jealousy and envy are human emotions; they do not have to be destructive emotions. Children can learn to accept jealousy and envy, and they can learn to deal with these emotions by learning about the ways in which other children have dealt with these emotions. Literature, carefully selected and taught, can help children to learn to control their own behavior, to become masters of their own destiny.

Children have a right to their literary heritage. They have a right to learn about folklore, to learn about Mother Goose and Johnny Tremaine and Tom Sawyer and Cinderella. In learning the intricate plots of "The Three Little Pigs," "Little Red Riding Hood," and "Snow White" children become able to deal with many themes that they will experience in their later reading: innocence can outwit evil, beauty is ephemeral.

## Understanding Young Children

In selecting books for children, it is important to keep in mind their needs, desires, and interests in order to foster a lifelong love for books. In doing this, you will be giving them the greatest gift you could possibly give.

It is important to review your knowledge about the natural growth processes of young children before you begin to select books for them. Remember to think about children's language development and personality development as you start to select and make recommendations for their reading.

### Language Development

A child's development is marked by an amazing growth of language. When you stop to think how long it takes an adult to become fluent in a foreign language, it is truly phenomenal to think that a small child can learn to communicate more than adequately in a year or two.

Children develop their language skills by being exposed to rich language environments. It has been found that when families provide books and magazines, experiences with museums, zoos, parks, and answers to children's questions, language develops rapidly and fully.

Books can help to increase the spontaneous vocalization of preschool children. In a study by Cazden (1976), the children of mothers who expanded their childrens' sentences such as "car blue" to "That's right, the car is blue," did not increase their language skills as much as those children to whom stories were read and discussed. Cazden commented:

> Reading to an individual child may be a potent form of language stimulattion for two reasons: first, the physical contact with the child, and second, such reading seems inevitably to stimulate interpolated conversation about the pictures which both adult and child are attending to. (p. 12)

Our earlier discussion of language acquisition and development in Chapter 3 stressed the importance of understanding the natural, organic ways in which young children learn their native language. The words that other human beings speak to children greatly enhance their language development. These words may be the natural result of the interaction of parent and child during a reading episode. Children often ask for explanations, descriptions, and summaries during reading episodes. Parents and teachers must be ready to provide rich samples of natural language to young children in order to help them acquire all of the elements of their native language. At the end of this chapter, we will offer some suggestions for the most productive ways for you to read to your children.

### Personality Development

Books can assist in the positive development of a child's personality. Characters described in fiction as well as nonfiction can serve as role models and as a source for understanding one's self.

Although it is an awesome task, parents and schools have a responsibility to instruct children in society's customs, traditions, and values. Although the question of what values schools should teach has been the source of great debate, books can help to instill values to young children by showing the requisites for growing up in a particular culture.

At the present time, there is no single theory of personality development that adequately explains how personality is formed. Literary experiences may indeed help to shape personality, to mold values, and to develop behaviors in young children. Children need to be exposed to many different forms of literature with many different kinds of characters in order to help them to explore arrays of behaviors and solutions to problems.

You, as the teacher of the young child, have a grave responsibility to contribute to the creation of full, rich, and healthy personality in each child. One way in which you can ensure that you are helping each child is to provide each of your students with a rich and varied literature program in which values are freely discussed. The task is a difficult one, but a childhood without literary experiences may be like a childhood without sunshine.

## Contemporary Issues in Children's Literature

### Sex Stereotyping

In recent years, sex stereotyping has become an important issue in the selection of appropriate literature for young children. In Jenning's (1975) study, she found that preschool girls found male roles in stories far more acceptable to them than boys found female roles in the stories that were read to them. Murphy (1975) studied the roles of females in preschool literature and found a majority of the roles to be consistent with negative stereotypical models. Hillman (1976) compared the roles of female characters in children's literature of the 1970s with children's literature of the 1930s and found little change in the roles assigned to women.

The results of these studies suggest that children should be exposed to carefully selected literature that acknowledges female and male roles can be interchangeable. The literature that you select for your children should have some of the following elements:
1. females in many different roles
2. males in many different roles
3. females *and* males in compassionate, empathetic situations

The following list may help you in selecting non-sexist literature for your students:

T = Toddler
P = Preschool
S = School Age (Grades 1–3)
J = Intermediate (Grades 4–6)

| Author | Title | Age Range | Publisher and Date |
|---|---|---|---|
| C. W. Anderson | *A Pony for Linda* | P | Macmillan, 1951 |
| Stan & Jan Berenstein | *He Bear, She Bear* | P–S | Random House, 1974 |
| Miriam Cohen | *Will I Have a Friend?* | P | Collier, 1967 |
| E. P. Dutton | *Girls Can Be Anything* | P–S | E. P. Dutton, 1973 |
| Margrit Eichler | *Martin's Father* | P–S | Lollipop Power, 1971 |
| Joan Fassler | *Howie Helps Himself* | P | Albert Whitman, 1975 |
| Paula Goldsmith | *Did you Ever?* | T or P–S | Lollipop Power, 1971 |
| Stewart and Polly Anne Graff | *Helen Keller: Toward the Light* | P | Garrard, 1965 |
| Sandy Grant | *Hey, Look At Me!* | T or P–S | Bradbury Press, 1973 |
| Phyllis Hollander | *American Women in Sports* | P–S | Grosset & Dunlap, 1972 |
| Gabriel Lisowski | *Miss Piggy* | I, T or P–S | Grosset & Dunlap, 1972 |
| Sharon Lorree | *The Sunshine Family and The Pony* | P–S | Seabury Press, 1972 |
| Margaret Mahy | *Ultra-Violet Catastrophe* | P | Parent's Magazine Press, 1975 |
| Eve Merriam | *Mommies At Work* | T or P–S | Alfred A. Knopf, 1955 |
| Rosemary Mirard, Ed. | *Womenfolk and Fairy Tales* | P | Houghton Mifflin, 1975 |
| Harlow Rockwell | *My Doctor* | P–S | Macmillan, 1973 |
| Norma Simon | *I Was so Mad!* | P | Albert Whitman, 1974 |
| Bernard Waber | *Ira Sleeps Over* | P–S or P | Houghton, 1972 |
| Ilon Wikland | *I Can Help Too!* | P–S | Random House, 1974 |

## *Racial and Cultural Stereotyping*

In recent years, it has also been noted that many children's literature selections contain negative racial and cultural stereotypes. As the teacher of young children, you must guard against this because children's racial/cultural identity may be affected by the literature that they read. Racial/cultural identity is closely related to self concept, one of the most important ingredients in successful learning.

As you select your children's literature, be sure to select books that portray all races in all different types of situations, behaviors, and jobs.

It was lunchtime when they arrived at the Great Square. There some of the city children were eating bean-curd sweets and buying sugared fruits on long sticks.

Mei Li wanted candy too, but even more she wanted a firecracker. She spent her second penny on firecrackers. She was too frightened to shoot them off herself, so she gave them to San Yu and ran away with her fingers in her ears.

Handforth, Thomas. *Mei Li*. New York: Doubleday, 1938, 12.

The following list may help you as you select multi-ethnic literature for your children:

| Author | Title | Age Range | Publisher and Date |
| --- | --- | --- | --- |
| Arnold Adoff | *Black Is Brown Is Tan* | P | Harper and Row, 1973 |
| Betty Baker | *Three Fools and a Horse* | P | Macmillan, 1975 |
| Anne Norris Baldwin | *Sunflowers for Tina* | P | Four Winds, 1970 |
| Hetty B. Beatty | *Little Owl Indian* | P | Houghton, 1951 |
| June Behrens | *Soo-Ling Finds A Way* | P | Goden Gate Jr. books, 1965 |
| Marc and Evelyn Bernheim | *The Drums Speak* | P | Harcourt, 1971 |
| Charles Bible | *Jennifer's New Chair* | T or P–S | Holt, 1978 |
| Margaret Boone-Jones | *Martin Luther Kind, Jr., A Picture Story* | P–S or P | Childrens, 1969 |
| Jeanette P. Brown | *Ronnie's Wish* | P–S or P | Friendship Press, 1954 |
| Peter Buckley | *I Am From Puerto Rico* | P | Simon, 1971 |
| Nardi R. Campion | *Casa Means Home* | P | Holt, 1970 |
| Lucille Clifton | *Don't You Remember?* | P–S | Dutton and Co., 1973 |
| Ruth Franchere | *Cesar Chavez* | P | Crowell, 1970 |
| Aline Glasgow | *A Pair of Shoes* | P | Dial, 1971 |
| Sally Glendinning | *Jimmy and Joe Catch an Elephant* | P | Garrard, 1969 |
| Sally Glendinning | *Jimmy and Joe Catch a Ghost* | P | Garrard, 1969 |
| Eloise Greenfield | *Bubbles* | P–S | Drum and Spear Press, 1972 |
| Ernest Gregg | *And the Sun God Said: That's Hip* | P | Harper, 1972 |
| Sidonie M. Gruenberg | *Favorite Stories Old and New* | P–S or P | Doubleday, 1955 |
| Ruth Jaynes | *Friends, Friends, Friends* | P | Bowmar, 1967 |
| Jacob Lawrence | *Harriet and the Promised Land* | P | Simon and Schuster, 1968 |
| Lucy Sprague Michell | *Here and Now Story Book* | T, P–S or P | Dutton, 1948 |
| Virginia Ormsby | *Twenty-One Children Plus Ten* | P–S | Lippincott, 1971 |
| Deborah Ray, illustrator | *Abdul Abul-Bul Amir and Ivan Skavinsky Skavor* | T, P–S, or P | Macrae Smith, 1969 |
| Alma K. Reck and Helen H. Fichter | *First Book of Festivals Around the World* | P and T | Watts, 1957 |
| Kenneth Rudeen | *Jackie Robinson* | P | Crowell, 1971 |
| Byrd Baylor | *Amigo* | P–S or P | Macmillan, 1963 |

| Mark Taylor | *A Time for Flowers* | P | Golden Gate Jr. Books, 1967 |
| Junichi Yoda | *The Rolling Rice Ball* | P | Parent's Magazine, 1969 |

## Censorship

It is difficult to talk about children's literature without discussing the issue of censorship. There are some educators who believe anything the least bit grim or tragic has no place in children's literature; they think it should be removed from children's classrooms. There are other educators who would censor nothing in children's books, insisting that children should face reality as early as possible.

Children need broad exposure to books, and it seems no more valid to rob them of reading material that may provide sadness than to rob them of happy endings. Certainly, real life contains some of each. Books are removed from classrooms for various reasons, some of which are valid, some not.

Deciding what content is appropriate or inappropriate is a weighty responsibility; no one person alone can make that decision. One criterion that seems reasonable is the book's general orientation. Is the book basically uplifting? There are those who believe that children can cope with any amount of violence, extreme poverty, and tragedy as long as the book ends on a hopeful note. They argue that with a positive ending children have generally not learned hopelessness, pessimism, and cynicism. Some educators will argue that whatever children must endure personally, they must be always given the hope that things will get better.

## Death

Several studies have shown that children have fixed perceptions about death. Yet death has been virtually ignored in children's literature until recent years. Frequently, the perceptions that children have about death are unrelated to what we know about it. Literature can be an excellent means for helping children to explore their feelings and beliefs about death by comparing their own perceptions with characters in the literature that is read to them.

The following titles may help you as you select appropriate materials about death for your children: *The Tenth Good Thing About Barney* by Judith Viorst, *Growing Time* by Sandol S. Warburt, *The Dead Bird* by Margaret Wise Brown, and *Annie and the Old One* by Miska Miles.

## Violence in Children's Literature and Violence on Television

A great deal of criticism has been directed at television, some of it with good reason, some of it without support. Some parents and educators ask why they

## V·LONG AFTERNOON

AT LAST the river voyage was ended and the Boones were crossing the
Mississippi, the Father of Waters, into the little easy-going town of St.
Louis. Boone was treading on the same spot where the great La Salle had built
the first fort so long ago. He, too, had been a wilderness explorer of the farthest
reaches, with his head full of great visions for a French empire of the Mississippi.
And even before La Salle, at a point farther down the river, on a moonless night
they had dropped into the dark waters the worn body of another seeker of far
horizons, the Spaniard De Soto.

[86]

Daugherty, James. *Daniel Boone*. New York: The Viking Press, 1939, p. 86.

should worry about violence in children's books when children are confronted with violence the minute they turn on the television. Children watch a great deal of television from the early years throughout adolescence. This should also be the time of their greatest reading development, and it has been found that good readers watch less television than poor readers. These statistics do not necessarily mean that the fact of watching television dulls reading ability, but it may mean that children who spend five or six hours a day in front of the television have little time left for reading. They may come to expect all reading to be as fast moving and vivid as television and may become bored with books more easily.

It should be remembered that many fine programs are made for children: the impact of a television show can be enormous, both positively and negatively. Therefore, adult supervision, discussion, and participation are vital for proper viewing.

## Reading To Young Children

There are many educators who will encourage you to read to young children in order to improve their language development, but few educators will tell you *how* to read to young children. Sir Allan Bullock's report, "A Language for Life" (1975) briefly discusses the *how to* of reading to young children when he states: "The best way to prepare the young child for reading is to hold him on your lap and read aloud to him stories he likes—over and over again." (p. 28)

In a study by Flood (1977), he found that the most effective way to read to young children was to follow these four steps during a reading episode:

1. Prepare children for the story by asking warm-up questions, e.g., before reading *The Story of Ferdinand*, you may want to ask children some of the following questions:
   a. Have you ever seen a bull?
   b. What are bulls like?
   c. Are bulls scary?
   d. Did you like to smell beautiful flowers?
   e. Sometimes animals are tame and sometimes they are wild. How would you expect a bull to be?

   Then introduce the story, e.g.,
   "We are going to read a story about a tame bull who loves to smell flowers. His name is Ferdinand."

2. Verbally interact with the child during the reading. Ask and answer many different kinds of questions, e.g.,
   a. Why was Ferdinand's mother worried about him?
   b. Why did the men choose Ferdinand to go to the bull fight in Madrid?

3. Reinforce your student during the reading episode, e.g., If one of your children says: "Ferdinand was a nice bull. He didn't want to be picked for the bull fight." you might say: "That's right. You're paying very close attention to the story."

4. Finish the episode by asking children to evaluate the story, e.g., you may want to ask some of the following questions:
   a. Did you like the story?
   b. Do you think Ferdinand is happy now?
   c. Did you like Ferdinand?

In addition to these four steps, there are a few simple rules to follow when you are reading to your students.

1. Read to one child or to a very small group. Try not to read to a group larger than 5 to 7 students. If the group is too large, some children will not be able to see the book.

2. Prepare before you begin to read to children.

3. Show the book to the children as you read so they can see the pictures and the words on each page.

4. Pause periodically to ask questions in order to make sure that the children are comprehending the story.

*Figure A.* Try not to read to a group larger than 5 to 7 students. (Photo by Linda Lungren)

PART FOUR

*ATTILA*

On a summer night in the year 408 a flaming red comet appeared over Europe striking terror into the hearts of all who saw it; a menacing omen, a flaming red comet shaped like a tremendous eagle with a sword in its talons.

In that year, when the walls of Rome were cracking before the onslaught of the Goths led by King Alaric; when the Vandals were invading Hispania led by King Gunderic; when Roman Britain was fighting a losing war against the terrible barbarian pirates, the Saxons—on a summer night of that year was Attila born.

And on that night did pity, tenderness, and love die forever in the heart of Bendeguz. The thousands who had heard his reckless challenge and had witnessed the dreadful punishment could and did shed tears of pity for him. The eyes of Bendeguz were dry, his face a cold mask, for the heart within him had turned to stone. He did not see the hand of Honor held out to him with pity and love. He did not feel the restraining hand of Damos as he made his way, once more to the now cold and dark altar.

Seredy, Kate, *The White Stag*. New York: Viking Press, 1937, pp. 66–67.

## Books To Read To Young Children

The following list may help you in selecting titles to read to your young children. These titles have been divided into three categories: 1. Mother Goose and Nursery Rhymes, 2. Counting Books, and 3. Picture Books.

### MOTHER GOOSE AND NURSERY RHYMES

Briggs, Raymond. *The Mother Goose Treasury*. New York: Coward, McCann & Geoghegan, Inc., 1966.

Domanska, Janina. *I Saw a Ship A-Sailing*. New York: Macmillan Publishing Co., Inc., 1972.

Emberley, Ed. *London Bridge Is Falling Down*. Boston: Little, Brown and Company, 1967.

Galdone, Paul. *The House that Jack Built*. New York: McGraw-Hill Book Company, 1966.

Lines, Kathleen. *Lavender's Blue*, illustrated by Harold Jones. Franklin Watts, 1964.

Reed, Philip, *Mother Goose and Nursery Rhymes*. New York: Atheneum Publishers, 1963.

Spier, Peter. *To Market, to Market*. New York: Doubleday & Company, Inc. 1967.

Watson, Clyde. *Father Fox's Pennyrhymes*, illustrated by Wendy Watson. Cromwell, 1971.

### COUNTING BOOKS

Allen, Robert. *Numbers*, photographs by Mottke Weissman. Platt and Munk, 1968.

Carle, Eric, *1, 2, 3 to the Zoo*. William Collins & World Publishing Co., Inc., 1968.

### PICTURE BOOKS

Chaimatz, Bill. *The Cat's Whiskers*. New York: Macmillan Publishing Co., Inc., 1960.

Frasconi, Antonio. *See Again, Say Again*. New York: Harcourt Brace Jovanovich, Inc., 1964.

Hoban, Russell. *Bedtime for Francis*, illustrated by Garth Williams. New York: Harper and Row Publishers, 1960.

Holl, Adelaide. *The Rain Puddle*, illustrated by Roger Duvoisin. New York: Lothrop, Lee & Shepart Company, 1965.

Kunhardt, Dorothy. *Pat the Bunny*. New York: Golden Press, 1962.

Lamouise, Albert. *The Red Balloon*. New York: Doubleday, 1956.

Lobel, Arnold. *Frog and Toad Are Friends*. New York: Harper and Row Publishers, 1970.

Seuss, R., Pseud. (Theodore S. Geisel). *The Cat in the Hat*. New York: Random House, Inc., 1957.

Williams, Garth. *Baby's First Book*. Golden Press, 1955.

## Teaching Stories

In the early years of the child's life, the emphasis in children's literature should be on verse, fable, narratives, and folklore. From these types of writings children learn the different ways in which stories begin and end, the differences between real and "flat" characters, and the ways in which authors can make their characters happy or sad.

Young children can be taught some very important aspects of the narrative by asking them some of the following literary questions. We will base the list of literary questions on the story *Sylvester and the Magic Pebble* by William Steig.

### Plot

1. What happened in the story?
2. What happened first in the story?
3. What happened after Sylvester found the pebble?

### Characterization

1. Can you describe Sylvester? What did he look like? Is he old or young?
2. What does Sylvester want? What does Sylvester think is important in this story?
3. Does Sylvester change his attitudes during the story?

### Setting

1. Where does the story take place?
2. How does the forest affect what happens in the story?
3. Is there a struggle between the forest and Sylvester and his parents?

### Tone and Mood

1. What words in the story tell you the tone of the story?
2. Can you tell if this is a true story from the words that the writer uses?
3. Is this a funny story? A sad story? How can you tell?

### Type of Story Pattern

1. Who tells Sylvester's story? How would the story be different if someone else told it?
2. Is there a lesson in this story?
3. Is this story like any other story that you have read?

### *Lesson Plan*

If you decided to read *The Story of Ferdinand* by Leaf and Boyd to your students, you may want to use one of the following lesson plans.

Grade Level:     Primary:

Objective:       to have children recall the plot of the story

Procedure:       1. Following the procedures explained in the section "How to
                    Read Stories to Young Children" read the story to the
                    children.
                 2. After you have completed reading the story and answering
                    your questions, tell them that you are going to prepare a
                    language experience chart with them about the events of the
                    story.
                 3. On a large sheet of oak tag paper, plot the story sequentially
                    for the children. Elicit the story from the children by asking
                    them: "What happened next."

Your chart may look like this illustration:

---

## The Story of Ferdinand

Todd:        Ferdinand was a little bull in Spain.

Alex:        He liked to sit and smell flowers.

Nitaya:      He grew up to be strong and brave.

Jane:        All the other bulls wanted to be picked to fight in the bull ring.

Thomas:      But not Ferdinand.

Wolfgang:    Five men came to pick the fiercest bull.

John:        All the bulls made noises so they would be picked.

Thomas:      But not Ferdinand.

Lisa:        Then Ferdinand sat on a bee and the bee stung him.

Ben:         He screamed and kicked the ground and looked very fierce.

Rebecca:     So the men picked him to fight in Madrid.

Todd:        They took him in a parade to the bull ring.

Alex:        Everyone was dressed up and waiting for Ferdinand.

Gary:        But Ferdinand wouldn't fight. He smelled the ladies flowers.

Wolfgang:    They had to take him home.

Anita:       He lived happily ever after.

Evaluation:        After the children have retold the story and you have charted it, you may ask them to read the chart and then tell the story to a child who was not in the group when you read the story.

You may also want to use the following language experience suggestions when you are teaching.

### Sylvester and the Magic Pebble

1. Pretend you've found a magic pebble—what would you wish for?

   (Examples: Gina would wish for a puppy, and Debbie Sam would wish she could be Batman)

2. How would you feel if you turned into a rock and had to stay outside all year?

   or

   If you had to stay outside all year, which season would be your favorite? Why?

   (Examples: Wolfgang loves to be outside in the fall. All of the leaves are pretty. Andrea said, "The winter is cold but I love the snow.")

3. Have each child draw a picture·about the story. Then record the child's description on his picture.

The following activities focus on *Where the Wild Things Are*.

1. Have each child draw a "wild thing." Label the picture. Have the child tell you something about it and write it down.

2. Make a chart called How We Will Tame the Wild Things. Let each child tell how he or she would do it.

   (Examples: Sharon said that she would tie them up. Keith said that he would give them some cookies.)

3. Make a "wild thing" village using blocks and clay (for the animals). Label the animals and buildings.

4. What would you do in your room if you were sent to bed without supper? Make a story chart about it.

   (Examples: Kevin plays with his airplane.
   Philip reads a book.
   Clemens would be hungry.)

## Teaching Poetry

Young children ought to be exposed to verse very early in their schooling. Even young children can learn about some of the basic elements of poetry by asking them some of the following directed questions:

### Rhythm and Melody

1. Can you name the rhyming words in the following couplet?

   Listen my children and you shall hear
   of the midnight ride of Paul Revere.

2. Can you hear the melody of the sea in Amy Lowell's "Sea Shells"?

### Plot/Story

1. Can you retell the story in the ballad "Barbara Allen"?

### Appreciation For Events You Have Experienced

1. Have you ever experienced shopping for shoes? How is your experience the same or different than the speaker in "Choosing Shoes" by Efrida Wolfe?

### Understanding Symbolism and Imagery

1. What do the clouds represent in "Boats Sail on the Rivers" by Christina Rossetti?

### Sensitivity to Writing Styles

1. Have you ever used words to make a joke?
2. Have you ever used words to say the opposite of what you really mean?

### *Lesson Plan*

If you decided to read the poem below to your children, you may want to use the following lesson plan.

## Downside Up
### by jp

Darrell and Dwayne and Don
  rolled up the hill in pairs

To gaze into the river top
  and pluck lilies from the sky.

They ran from the pond
  to return the silver trout
    to their earthen homes.

They sat on the sky
  and munched on the green leaves
    of the twinkling stars.

They laughed of their fear
  and cried of their bravery

They dreamed of their yesterday
  and remembered their tomorrow

Summer joy in snug down-parkas
  Winter fun in cotton plaid smocks
    Autumnal spring in drenched parasols

They saw a world downside up
  And smiled and frowned
    for a moment and forever.

Grade Level:     Primary-Intermediate

Objective:       1. to have children understand the writing style of the speaker of
                    the poem
                 2. to have children understand that the speaker is saying the
                    opposite of what is real in the world
                 3. to have children discuss the use of symbols

Procedure:       1. After you have introduced the concept of symbols by explain-
                    ing that a symbol stands for something else, e.g., a country's
                    flag stands for that country, you might ask children if they can
                    name any symbols that they understand, e.g. Does anyone
                    know what the eagle stands for on the dollar bill?
                 2. Then read the poem to the children asking them to pay close
                    attention to the writing style of the poem.
                 3. Ask them to paraphrase the poem and to tell what it means.
                 4. Reread the poem with the children explaining to them that the
                    author is using his words to describe the opposite of what we
                    know is true, e.g., you cannot roll uphill; you can only roll
                    downhill.
                 5. Ask the children why the author uses his words to describe the
                    opposite of what he is saying.
                 6. Ask the children if they think the author is using his words as
                    symbols for something else. What is the author trying to say?

Evaluation:      Ask the children to write their own poem using opposites to explain their feelings. Start them off with some of the following:

a. I am laughing in sorrow.
b. Larry's bathing suit was lined with icicles.
c. The Thanksgiving dinner we complained about was this year's.

## Creating an Environment for Reading Children's Literature

*Figure 59.* Whether in the classroom, the library, or the home, an environment that is conducive to learning must be inviting. (Photo by Linda Lungren):

Whether in the classroom, the library, the home, or any other community facility, an environment that is conducive to learning must be inviting. Without this primary requirement, the best of materials will often go unused. In fact, it is often best to let children create their own environment by way of posters, bulletin boards, or other artwork that they have created. In the classroom, a well-defined space can be sectioned off, perhaps covered with a piece of carpeting, or each child may be assigned his own personal reading area, if space permits. The important thing is to have the designated space as a reading corner set off from the rest of the classroom. Pillows, chair cushions, beach chairs, or anything comfortable may be added to make the reading corner a comfortable place to be.

A good supply of books, of course, should be readily available. Many classrooms have their own supply of outside reading books. If they are placed strategically about the reading corner, with their covers showing, many children will be tempted to pick them up and read them during unassigned times. The school library will probably be a major source of books for your children, and they should be encouraged to patronize it. Many school libraries are expanding their services before and after school hours. The most important part of the learning environment, however, is adult supervision: the teacher in the classroom, the librarian in the library or media center, and the parent at home. Enthusiasm for learning is highly infectious, and a teacher, librarian, or parent who enjoys reading, who makes books readily available to children, and who knows how to engage in stimulating discussions about what has been read, will help foster an atmosphere of curiosity for books.

## Sources for Children's Literature

Each year approximately four thousand new books are published for young children. Although it would be extremely difficult for you to read even a portion of this list every year, it is extremely important for you to stay up-to-date in the field of children's literature so that you can recommend the best books for each of your students. One way to do this is to read the following reference books on children's literature:

1. Adell, Judity, and Hilary Dole Klein. *A Guide To Non-Sexist Children's Books*, Academy Press Limited (Chicago, 1976).
2. Cardozo, Peter, and Ted Menten. *The Whole Kids Catalog*, Bantam Books (New York, 1975).
3. Children's Book Council, *Children's Books: Awards and Prizes*, The Children's Book Council, Inc. (New York, 1975).
4. *Children's Catalog.* New York: The H. W. Wilson Company.
5. *Children Literature Review*, Volume 1 (Block and Riley, 1976) and Volume II (Riley, 1976).
6. Boston University School of Education, *Journal of Education*, "High Interest Books" Trustees of Boston University, vol. 160, number 1, 1978 supplement, February 1978.

## CHILDREN'S BOOK AWARDS

Several book awards are presented each year. Books that have received these awards are usually worth having in your library. Some of these awards are:

John Newberry Medal—annual award presented to the "author of the most distinguished contribution to American literature for children."

National Book Award, Children's Book Category—the "book considered to be the most distinguished juvenile book of the preceding year written by an American author and published in the United States."

Laura Ingalls Wilder award—"to an author or illustrator whose books, published in the United States, have over a period of years made a substantial and lasting contribution to literature for children."

Hans Christian Anderson Prize—(the first international children's book award) "Given every 2 years, recognizes the winner's entire body of work for children."

Caldecott Medal—annual award presented to the "artist of the most distinguished American picture book for children."

### Caldecott Award Winners

The following books have received the Caldecott Award:

| Year | Title | Author | Publisher |
|------|-------|--------|-----------|
| 1938 | *Animals of the Bible* | Helen Dean Fish | Lippincott |
| 1939 | *Mei Li* | Thomas Handforth | Doubleday |
| 1940 | *Abraham Lincoln* | Ingri & Edgar Parin d'Aulaire | Doubleday |
| 1941 | *They were Strong and Good* | Robert Lawson | Viking |
| 1942 | *Make Way for Ducklings* | Robert McCloskey | Viking |
| 1943 | *The Little House* | Virginia Lee Burton | Houghton |
| 1944 | *Many Moons* | James Thurber | Harcourt |
| 1945 | *Prayer for a Child* | Rachel Field | Macmillan |
| 1946 | *The Rooster Crows* | "Mother Goose"—Traditional | Macmillan |
| 1947 | *The Little Island* | Golden MacDonald | Doubleday |
| 1948 | *White Snow, Bright Snow* | Alvin Tresselt | Lothrop |
| 1949 | *The Big Snow* | Berta & Elmer Hader | Macmillan |
| 1950 | *Song of the Swallows* | Leo Politi | Scribner |
| 1951 | *The Egg Tree* | Katherine Milhous | Scribner |
| 1952 | *Finder's Keepers* | Will Lipkind and Nicholas Mordvinoff | Harcourt |
| 1953 | *The Biggest Bear* | Kynd Ward | Houghton |
| 1954 | *Madeline's Rescue* | Ludwig Bemelmans | Viking |
| 1955 | *Cinderella, or the Little Glass Slipper* | Charles Perrault | Scribner |
| 1956 | *Frog Went A-Courtin* | John Langstoff, Ed. | Harcourt |
| 1957 | *A Tree is Nice* | Janice May Udry | Harper |
| 1958 | *Time of Wonder* | Robert McCloskey | Viking |
| 1959 | *Chanticleer and the Fox* | Adapted from Chaucer | Crowell |
| 1960 | *Nine Days to Christmas* | Maria Hall Ets and Aurora Labastida | Viking |
| 1961 | *Baboushka and the Three Kings* | Ruth Robbins | Parnassus |
| 1962 | *Once a Mouse* | Marcia Brown | Scribner |

| 1963 | *The Snowy Day* | Ezra Jack Keats | Viking |
| 1964 | *Where the Wild Things Are* | Maurice Sendak | Harper |
| 1965 | *May I Bring a Friend?* | Beatrice Schenk de Regiers | Atheneum |
| 1966 | *Always Room for One More* | Sorche Nie Leodhas | Holt |
| 1967 | *Sam, Bangs, and Moonshine* | Evaline Ness | Holt |
| 1968 | *Drummer Hoff* | Barbara Emberley | Prentice |
| 1969 | *The Fool of the World and The Flying Ship* | Arthur Ransome | Farrar |
| 1970 | *Sylvester and the Magic Pebble* | William Steig | Windmill/Simon Schuster |
| 1971 | *A Story — A Story* | Gail E. Haley | Atheneum |
| 1972 | *One Fine Day* | Nonny Hagrogian | Macmillan |
| 1973 | *The Funny Little Woman* | Arlene Mosel | Dutton |
| 1974 | *Duffy and the Devil* | Harve Zemach | Farrar |
| 1975 | *Arrow to the Sun* | Gerald McDermott | Viking |
| 1976 | *Why Mosquitoes Buzz in People's Ears* | Vema Aardema | Dial Press |
| 1977 | *Ashanti to Zulu—African Traditions* | Margaret Musgrove | Dial Press |
| 1978 | *Noah's Ark* | Peter Spier, illustrator | Doubleday |
| 1979 | *The Girl Who Loved Wild Horses* | Paul Goble | Bradbury |

## HIGH INTEREST/EASY VOCABULARY BOOKS

You may find the following list useful for recommending books to children who are not reading at their grade level:

| Berthe Amoss | *By the Sea* | T, P-S, or P | Parents, 1969 |
| Beverly Cleary | *Socks* | P | Morrow, 1973 |
| Eleanor Clymer | *The Eggman and Me* | P | Dutton, 1972 |
| Ethel Collier | *Who Goes There In My Garden?* | P | Scott, 1969 |
| Leonard Kessler | *On Your Mark, Get Set, Go!* | P-S or P | Harper, 1972 |
| Arnold Lobel | *Frog and Toad Together* | P-S or P | Harper, 1971 |
| Julian May | *Horses—How They Came to Be* | P | Holiday, 1968 |
| Emilie McLeod | *The Bear's Bicycle* | P-S or P | Atlantic Monthly Press, 1975 |
| Sheena Morey | *Old MacDonald's Farm* | P-S or P | Follett, 1966 |
| Peggy Parish | *Too Many Rabbits* | P | Macmillan, 1974 |
| Bernard Waber | *Nobody Is Perfick* | P-S or P | Houghton, 1971 |

## Developing Appreciation for Literature Through Art, Cooking, Music, Movement, and Drama

There are many ways to develop your literature program. One way is to integrate literature into all of your daily activities. The following suggestions may help you to integrate literature into your art, cooking, music, movement, and drama program.

## Art

Stimulating stories containing vivid imagery help children respond creatively to their readings. The material automatically derives deep meaning as the child becomes actively involved in interpreting the book. For example, a collage can be created as a demonstration of artistic expression about the child's feelings in response to a book.

Example:

1. Read an exciting story to a group of children.
2. Discuss their interpretations and reactions to the story.
3. Provide them with poster board and a variety of materials (yarn, paint, clay, buttons).
4. Encourage them to portray a part of the story by arranging (and eventually gluing) the materials on the poster board.

## Cooking

Children enjoy sharing their creations with others. Preparing a simple dish that applies to some aspects of a story produces both an interest in reading and a delight in cooking. Following recipes will develop reading, measuring, and social interaction skillls.

Example:

1. After reading a story, present the children with a simple recipe for cookie dough.
2. Once the ingredients have been combined, have the children form characters from the story on a cookie sheet with the dough.
3. Bake enough cookies to share with another class and allow the "bakers" to tell the story to the other class as they enjoy eating the cookies.

## Music

Literature and music appreciation can be used simultaneously to develop interest in reading. Children can view a picture book and enjoy listening to the recorded song that accompanies it. An exciting activity incorporating both music and literature might include having the children draw the illustrations to a favorite song.

Example:

1. Allow each child to select a short song or one or two stanzas of a song.
2. Provide each child with four or five blank pages to begin making their illustrations, along with drawing tools (crayons, chalk).
3. Encourage the children to read each line of the song carefully so they know exactly what it means before they begin to draw.

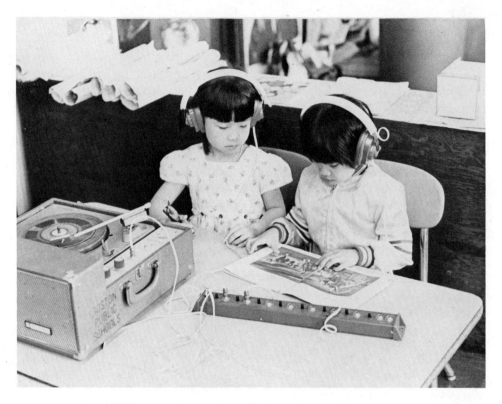

*Figure 60.* Children can view a picture-book and enjoy listening to the recorded song that accompanies it. (Photo by Linda Lungren)

### Movement

Children may be encouraged to react to tempos through movement. Dramatic actions to poetry help a child coordinate his or her thinking processes with movement while developing a sense of rhythm. For instance, children can react to nursery rhymes such as "Three Blind Mice" or "Hickory Dickory Dock" by tiptoeing, swinging, and jumping.

### Drama

Young children frequently identify with adult roles by acting them out. This form of creative play can intensify a child's experiences in reading by providing a close identification with story characters. Children should be free to perform their own character interpretations.

Example:

1. Read a short story (without much character dialogue).
2. Allow the "actors" to select costumes and props for their play.
3. Permit them to be creative and spontaneous in their dialogue and actions while acting out the story that has just been read.

# BIBLIOGRAPHY

Brown, M. *Once A Mouse*. New York: Charles Scribner's Sons, 1961, p. 21.

Bullock, A. "A Language for Life." Report of the Government of the United Kingdom, 1975.

Cazden, C. *Child Language and Education*. New York: Holt, Rinehart and Winston, 1976.

Daugherty, J. *Daniel Boone*. New York: The Viking Press, 1939, p. 86.

Durkin, D. *Teaching Them To Read*. Boston: Allyn & Bacon Co., Inc., 1974.

Flood, J. "Parental Styles in Reading Episodes With Young Children." *The Reading Teacher*, Volume 30 (May 1977).

Haley, G. E. *A Story-A Story*. New York: Atheneum, 1970, p. 31.

Handforth, T. *Mei Li*. New York: Doubleday, 1938, p. 12.

Hillman, J. S. "Occupational Roles in Children's Literature," *Elementary School Journal* (September 1976), p. 1-4.

Jennings, S. "Effects of Sex Typing in Children's Stories on Preference and Recall," *Child Development* (March 1975), p. 220-223.

Leaf, M. and J. Boyd. *The Story of Ferdinand*. New York: The Viking Press, 1936.

Murphy, C. "Sex Stereotyping in Literature During Early Childhood," *Counseling and Values* (April 1975), p. 186-191.

Sendak, M. *Where The Wild Things Are*. New York: Harper & Row, 1969.

Seredy, Kate. *The White Stag*. New York: The Viking Press, 1937, p. 66-67.

Steig, William. *Sylvester and the Magic Pebble*. New York: Simon and Schuster, 1969, p. 2.

Templin, M. *Certain Language Skills in Children*. Minneapolis: University of Minnesota Press, 1957.

# 10

# Involving Parents

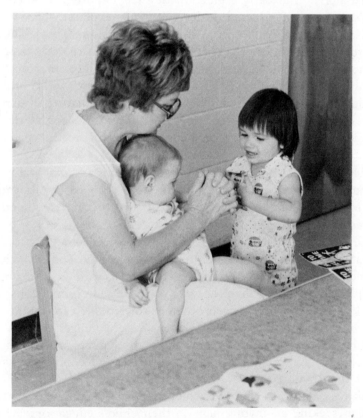

*Figure 61.* The recognition of parents as important teachers of their own children is not a new idea. As their child's first and most important teacher, parents must give their children the necessary language background. (Photo by Linda Lungren)

The recognition of parents as important teachers of their own children is not a new idea. The importance of parental participation in early childhood education is emphasized in the writings of many educators. In fact nursery schools were originally designed by Rachel and Margaret McMillan as extensions of the child's home environment. Teaching the mothers of their students to be the teachers of the children was an early idea of the McMillan sisters. The first nursery schools in the United States were essentially parent cooperatives. This concept was also part of kindergartens since the first kindergarten in this country, established by Mrs. Carl Schurz, was designed for her own children.

Whereas private schools have always seemed to value the skills of parents, public schools have historically excluded parents from any significant participation in the education of their children. In many school districts, the activities of PTO and PTA groups have been limited to social gatherings and fund raising. The attitude of "professionalism" among teachers evolved in such a way that parents were viewed as too untrained and inexperienced to be directly involved in educating their children.

In the past few years, several events succeeded in renewing interest in the role of parents in the early education of their children. Much of the early educational research conducted during the 1960s explored the ways in which children learn and the conditions under which they learn best. The results of this research indicated that the traditional attitude of the school towards the participation of parent in education was not as beneficial as previously thought. As a result of two different studies, Benjamin Bloom (1954) and Jane McVickers Hunt (1961) concluded that the quality and nature of early learning experiences have a lasting effect on the child's intellectual development. Because of these findings, they urge educators to realize that parents are the primary and essential teachers of their children.

Attitudes toward the concept of day care programs and parental involvement in the education of their young children were changed significantly by the Women's Movement of the 1960s and 1970s. Until recently, women who used the services of day care centers had no voice in the care the center provided for their children. Mothers of children in day care centers were often criticized as "unfit" parents for leaving their children during the day. Today, with more and more women working outside the home, attitudes toward day care are changing. More people are becoming involved with day care centers and this involvement is helping to upgrade the unpopular opinions toward day care centers.

The "conscious consumerism" movement has encouraged parents to become more involved in every area of their child's life. Parents are no longer passive consumers; they are becoming directly involved and concerned with factors that affect their children's lives. They voice objections to such things as flammable pajamas, unsafe toys, and violence on television. What then is more natural than seeking an involvement in their child's education. As taxpayers they are demanding a cooperative partnership in their children's education. As teachers it is important to recognize the value and importance of including parents in the educational process of their children.

### Parents and Reading

Most parents if asked "What is the most important thing you would like your child to learn in school?" would respond ". . . learn to read. . . ." What many parents do not realize is that they have an important role to play in their child's progress in reading.

Parents frequently view talking and listening to young children as unimportant to a child's education. However, before a child can be a successful reader, he must have fully developed language concepts. Children learn language from hearing it and speaking it. Concepts are developed through experience. As their child's first and most important teacher, parents must provide an environment which fosters the development of language.

Parents can also encourage an interest in reading by letting children know that reading is important. This can be done in several ways. Modeling is an effective, nonverbal communication device; young children delight in mimicking adults. What parent has not encountered a young child speaking to a stuffed animal or another child, using a vaguely familiar tone of voice and vocabulary. When children see adults reading, they will begin to pick up books and try to read them.

Taking children to the library and buying books as gifts for them are two ways of saying that books (and reading) are important in their lives. Reading should be seen as entertainment as well as a tool to help children answer questions. The parent should be a companion to the child in the world of books, not an impartial observer standing on the sidelines, directing and demanding, but never sharing.

The importance of reading to children every day should not be underestimated. Reading to an infant is not too soon to begin. Although infants may not understand what is read to them, they can enjoy the inflections of a parent's voice. Flood's (1977) study, explained in Chapter 9, demonstrated components of the parent/child reading episode correlated significantly with the prereading score:

1. Total number of words spoken by the child.
2. Number of questions answered by the child.
3. Number of questions asked by the child.
4. Warm-up, preparatory questions asked by the parents.
5. Post-story evaluative questions asked by the parents.
6. Positive reinforcement by the parent.

These components seem to suggest that the reading episode between parent and child or between teacher and child is most effective when the following four steps are followed:

1. Preparation for reading. Warm-up questions are profitable for the child. For example: "This is a story about two children who went to the zoo. Remember when we went to the zoo? What animal did you like?" Such questions help to both settle the children in preparation for the story and stimulate their interest in their story.

2. Active involvement. It appears important that children be made part of the process. They need to be given opportunities to speak and to ask and answer questions. This verbal  interaction between child and parent enhances the overall effect of the episode.

3. Positive reinforcement. The data suggest that positive reinforcement during the episode is an effective component of the process. It is always encouraging to note that this reinforcement is performing a useful function.

4. Evaluation. The cycle is complete by post-story evaluation and questioning. These questions help the child to learn to assess, evaluate, and integrate, for example, "Did you like the story?" or "Was the zookeeper sad when the children left?"

Children need to be involved in the story from its beginning until its end. It is not the book that is teaching them to read; it is the interaction with the parent that extends ideas, helps them to question their  own understanding, and relates their experiences to the ideas presented in the book.

The following list, from *How Can I Help My Child Get Ready to Read?* by Norma Rogers, summarizes some parental *do*'s and *don't*'s  about teaching young children to read. The most important thing to remember is that reading is fun; relax and enjoy it.

### Parental Do's and Don't's

| Do's | Don't's |
|---|---|
| Do love and enjoy your children. | Don't show worry or anxiety about your children. |
| Do help them to feel that they are wanted and loved and that they are an important part of family life. | Don't be too critical of them. |
| Do encourage them to be self-reliant (zip a coat, dress, brush teeth). | Don't remove every frustration; they must learn to cope with some. |
| Do teach them to listen attentively and follow simple directions. | Don't overemphasize learning tasks such as reading. |
| Do talk to your children from birth, softly, gently, and lovingly, but don't use baby talk. | Children must not feel pressured by tense, worried,  and over anxious parents. |
| Do answer their questions, simply and directly. | Don't compare them with other brothers and sisters or friends. |
| Do teach an awareness of things around them (wind, noise, weather, people). | Don't have unrealistic expectations for them. |

Rogers, Norma. *How Can I Help My Child Get Ready to Read?* Newark, Delaware: International Reading Association, 1972.

Do's

Do help them to express themselves
well orally. Give them the correct
name for things.

Do read to your children regularly and
help them to love books and to develop
a desire to learn to read.

Do build up their background of experiences through conversations, books,
games, pictures, trips, and so on.

Do consult a specialist if you suspect
that any serious physical, emotional, or
mental problems exist.

## Materials

Many materials exist that encourage the participation of parents in helping
their children to learn to read. The following references may help in recommending sources of materials for your students' parents:

1. "Helping Your Children Discover"—available from the New Hampshire Right to Read,
   Department of Education, Division of Instruction, 64 North Main Street, Concord,
   New Hampshire 03301. Price, fifty cents. The phamphlet is designed to guide conversations between parents and children toward thinking processes rather than "yes" and
   "no" answers.

2. "Tips for Parents"—available from the Dallas Independent School District, 3700 Ross
   Avenue, Dallas, Texas 75204. Price, $10.41 (includes booklet and all related materials).
   This contains specific reading-related activities for parents to do at home with their
   children.

3. "You can Encourage Your Child to Read"—available from International Reading Association, 800 Barksdale Road, P.O. Box 8139, Newark, Delaware 19711. Price, no charge
   for a single copy; $3 for 100 copies.

4. "Children's Reading: What Parents Can Do To Help"—available from Publications, 206
   Whitten Hall, University of Missouri, Columbia, Missouri 65201. Price, fifty cents (order
   no. UED47). Specific tips are given to parents for working on their child's reading at
   home. For example, parents are given suggestions for types of comprehension questions
   to ask their child after he or she has finished reading.

5. "Recipes for Reading" or "Receta Para Leer"—available in either English or Spanish from
   the National Urban Coalition, 1201 Connecticut Avenue, N.W., Washington, D.C. 20036.
   Price, $1.65 per copy; $1.25 for orders of 100 or more copies. It includes suggestions for
   parents on possible activities that their children can do with their hands.

The following list of "Books To Read Aloud" from the Columbus, Ohio
Public Schools Division of Instruction, is only a beginning. Parents will enjoy
adding their child's favorites.

## Books to Read Aloud

### 5, 6, and 7 Years

Aardema, Velma *Why Mosquitoes Buzz in Peoples Ears.* New York: Dial, 1976.

Asbjornsen, P. S., and J. E. Moa. *The Three Billy Goats Gruff.* New York: Harcourt, Brace Jovanovich, Inc., 1957.

Bemelmans, Ludwig, *Madeline's Rescue.* New York: The Viking Press, Inc., 1953.

Burningham, John. *Mr. Grumpy's Outing.* New York: Holt, Rinehart and Winston, 1971.

Burton, Virginia Lee. *The Little House.* Boston: Houghton Mifflin Company, 1942.

Duvoisin, Roger. *Petunia.* New York: Alfred A Knopf, Inc., 1950.

Emberly, Ed. *Klippity Klop.* Boston, Little, Brown and Company, 1974.

Freeman, Don. *Dandelion.* New York: The Viking Press, Inc., 1964.

Galdone, Paul. *Little Red Hen.* New York: Seabury, 1973.

Goble, Paul. *The Girl Who Loved Wild Horses.* New York: Bradbury, 1979.

Hoban, Russell. *A Baby Sister for Francis.* New York: Harper & Row, Publishers, 1964.

Hogrogian, Nonny. *One Fine Day.* New York: Collier Books, 1971.

Hutchins, Pat. *Rosie's Walk.* New York: Macmillan Publishing Co., Inc., 1968.

Keats, Ezra J. *Snow Day.* New York: The Viking Press, Inc., 1962.

Krauss, Ruth. *The Carrot Seed.* New York: Harper & Row, Publishers, 1945.

Lionni, Leo. *Swimming.* New York: Pantheon Books, Inc., 1963.

Lobel, Arnold. *Frog and Toad Together.* New York: Harper & Row, Publishers, 1972.

McCloskey, Robert. *Blueberries for Sal.* New York: The Viking Press, Inc., 1948.

Musgrove, Margaret. *Ashanti to Zulu — African Traditions.* New York: Dial 1978.

Potter, Beatrix. *The Tale of Peter Rabbit.* New York: Warne, 1904.

Sandra, Maurice. *Where the Wild Things Are.* New York: Harper & Row, Publishers, 1963.

Seuss, Dr. *The 506 Hats of Bartholomew Cubbins.* Eau Claire, Wis.: Hale, 1938.

Stalg, William. *Sylvester and the Magic Pebble.* New York: Simon & Schuster, Inc., 1969.

Waber, Bernard. *Lyle, Lyle, Crocodile.* Boston: Houghton Mifflin Company, 1955.

Watson, Clyde. *Father Fox's Pennyrhymes.* New York: Crowell, 1971.

Wildsmith, Brian. *Brian Wildsmith's Mother Goose.* New York: Franklin Watts, 1963.

Zemach, Harve. *Duffy and the Devil.* New York: Farrah, 1974.

Zion, Gene. *Happy and Dirty Doc.* New York: Harper & Row Publishers, 1956.

## *Materials to Help Parents Understand Their Teaching Role*

Parents may often ask you to suggest materials that may help them to teach their children. While it is useful to suggest children's literature titles to parents, sometimes it is equally useful to recommend books and films that will help parents to understand their children as learners and themselves as teachers.

# Booklists

The following list is a collection of books that parents may enjoy reading in their efforts to understand their role as a teacher.

Axline, Virginia. *Dibs in Search of Self.*

Becker, Wesley. *Parents Are Teachers.*

Braselton, Barry. *Toddlers and Parents.*

Chess, Stelle. *How to Help Your Child Get the Most Out of School.*

Cohen, Dorothy. *The Learning Child.*

Curtis, Jean. *A Parent's Guide to Nursery Schools.*

Gordon, Thomas. *Parent Effectiveness Training.*

Hoover, Mary B. *The Responsive Parent: Meeting the Realities of Parenthood.*

Larrick, Nancy. *A Parent's Guide to Children's Reading.*

Neisser, Edith. *A Primer for Parents of Preschoolers.*

Sims, Mary. *A Child's Eye Flow: Piaget for Young Parents and Teachers.*

# Films

The following films may be helpful for parents in understanding their children and their role as their child's most important teacher. These four films are available from Perennial Education, P.O. Box 215, Northfield, Illinois, 60093.

1. Everyday Parenting

   28½ minutes

   A sensory game for a bus ride; color size and shape discrimination at the grocery store; talking together on a park bench; math concepts with the cans; experimenting with bathtub boats, and roleplaying in a "dress-up" sequence.

2. The Working Mother

   28½ minutes

   Sorting and matching in the laundromat; a counting experience while walking in the city; making a telephone; exploring nature on a family picnic; writing a "book" based on a paper airplane experience; helping a working mom with cooking; creating a rhythm band.

3. Fun with Dad

   28½ minutes

   Thinking games for waiting in the clinic; comparing footprints at the beach; sick-at-home activities; play dough, macaroni jewelry and printing; parent/infant interaction: growing a flower garden; dealing with the fear of water.

4. Grandmother and Leslie

   28½ minutes

   Word game for a long car ride; sorting the groceries; imaginative shadow play between a father and son; home math experiences; infant/sibling/grandmother interrelationships; language development through storytelling and puppetry.

The next three films are available from New York University Film Library, 26 Washington Place, New York, New York 10003.

### 1. Mothers and Toddlers

18 minutes

Focus is on the mother rather than the child. The film is set in an inner city (Chicago) high rise project. Some rooms have been set aside for mothers and toddlers. Here a modest program is shown in which a parent-oriented view is dominant. We see parents moving toward greater awareness of themselves and we see children as they work out play problems with the help of adults.

### 2. Let Your Child Help You

11 minutes

A charming film that was made to enable parents to participate in the educational program with a basis for their behavior. Deals with the simple activities that are part of the home; dishwashing, setting the table, preparing food. A bit dated, but useful.

### 3. Your Children and You

31 minutes

Deals in simple language and fine photography with the needs of parents and children. Everyday activities such as eating habits, weaning, discipline, sibling rivalry, and the arrival of a new baby are treated in practical and helpful ways.

The next four films and the addresses where they can be secured are listed below:

### 1. Crossroads at 4

Informative film on the early identification of amblyopia or lazy-eye blindness. Especially interesting for parents and workers with preschool children.

National Society for the
 Prevention of Blindness
79 Madison Avenue
New York, NY 10010

### 3. Right from the Start

22 minutes

A film on immunization and the young child. This is a most useful film for parents and workers in a preschool setting.

Public Affairs Commission
22 East 38th Street
New York, NY 10016

2. <u>Parents Are Teachers Too</u>

22 minutes

Useful film for parents, aides, and
teachers. Gives a good view of
parents as original teachers of the
child. Home visits are conducted by
school personnel. Relatedness of
school through the home visitor is
stressed.

Modern Talking Pictures
1212 Avenue of the Americas
New York, NY 10036

4. <u>One Day's Poison</u>

20 minutes

Useful film related to the problem of
children and poisoning. Setting is the
Poison Control Center and the Toronto
Sick Children's Hospital.

Syracuse University Films
Collendale Campus
1455 East Colvin Street
Syracuse, NY 13210

## Strategies for Involving Parents

Before we can begin to discuss the most effective ways of involving parents
in the child's education, you might want to ask *why* they should be involved.
Simply stated, parents are the *primary models* for their children's behavior.
It is reasonable to assume that if parents are concerned with educational
matters and are involved with these matters, their children will also be concerned and involved in educational endeavors.

Much of the research that has been conducted with the Head Start programs
concluded that children who participated in programs that involved their
parents in the classroom sustained their gains better than did children whose
parents were not involved. This may be because participating parents learn
techniques and methods that they can take home with them and use in their
parenting role. Concepts such as the importance of a child's self-image, the use
of positive reinforcement as a reward, and recognition of the individuality of
each child were carried back to the home by parents who were involved in
these programs.

Including parents in your classroom program develops understanding between parents and teachers. As parents become more familiar with school
policies, goals, and objectives, they usually become much more cooperative
with the school, and they become more comfortable in discussing their child's
real and potential problems.

### Enlisting Aid

If you are going to involve parents in your classroom programs, the beginning of the school year is very important. If you are contemplating the use of
parents in your classroom, it is important to understand that one of your
primary responsibilities is to learn as much as possible about the community

where you teach. Many teachers live in communities other than where they are employed and, as a result, are not familiar with the goals of the people in their school community. Attending community meetings and visiting the homes of the children you teach can help you appraise community ideals.

Any teacher who wants to begin a parental involvement program in his classroom should be fully aware of his own goals and objectives for using parents. It is difficult to advise a parental volunteer if you are unsure of the outcome that you desire. Planning on your part is essential. You must feel comfortable with the idea of working with parents. Only you can decide the number of parents with whom you can work. It is usually a good idea to begin modestly and to increase the number of parents who are involved in your program as you become more familiar with the procedures that are critical for effective parental involvement.

In order to work successfully with parents, a teacher must recognize parents as experienced teachers and diagnosticians of their own children. A wise teacher will use this parental expertise.

### Initial Contact

The recruiting of parents must be handled with care. Initial contact with parents is absolutely important. If you decide to begin a parent volunteer program, and if you want to explain your program to parents, a meeting at the beginning of the school year may be a good idea. This meeting should be very informal. Refreshments should be served and "drawing cards" should be used to lure parents to your meeting. Media projects that include children's works (what parent can resist a meeting in which his child is featured in something) can be used as drawing cards. It is important for you to try to predict problems that may prevent parents from attending your meeting. Your foresight may forestall problems before they happen. Examples follow.

1. Problem:   If there is no sitter available, how can a parent attend your school meeting?

    Possible Solutions:   a. Provide a room with adult supervision so that parents may bring children with them and leave them in this room.
    b. Allow parents to bring their children to the meeting with them.

2. Problem:   Transportation.

    Possible Solutions:   a. Suggest that friends come together.
    b. Arrange for a van or minibus to pick up interested parents in predetermined pickup points.

3. Problem:   Language other than English is spoken at home.

    Possible Solutions:   a. Send messages in the language of the home.
    b. Arrange to have translators at the meeting.

In addition to the meeting at which you explain your parent involvement program, you may also want to establish visiting days in your classroom. Parents who might be frightened at the thought of actually doing something in a classroom might be less reluctant to visit you to observe your program. If you set aside one day each week to welcome parents, you may find parents regularly visiting your classroom. The advantage of an all-day visiting period is that the likelihood of having many parents there at one specific time is reduced. If you do expect to have parent visitors, it might be wise to have the children engage in some independent activities so that you will be free to spend some time with each visitor. It may also be wise for you to plan some simple, nonacademic activities in addition to the usual academic routine, so parents might be convinced that they may be of help if the thought of academics frightens them.

"Proceed slowly" should be your dictum as you prepare to obtain some commitment from parents. You might tell parents how much they are needed in your program. Let each parent know what you expect. It is often helpful to ask parents to do an activity in which they have expertise (a hobby, cooking, carpentry, their job). The territory will then be familiar for the parent, and the whole situation will be less threatening. You may wish to offer specific choices of activities to the parent.

> Example: "Mr. Jones, would you be able to come in one day next week and either read a story to a small group of children or help Gilda and Jake with the multiplication tables?"

There is no quicker way to lose parents than to ask them for help in the one area they dreaded as children. Offering them choices gives them options for selecting activities that will be comfortable for them. Of prime importance is to let them know that their contribution is fully appreciated. It is important to be flexible and not to extract a weekly obligation. The thought of long-term involvement may be too threatening in the early stages.

You need to devise some compelling reasons to ensure that parents come back to your classroom. Special days such as hobby day, pet shows, tea parties, special breakfasts, and birthdays are good ways to lure parents to school. Encouraging friends to come and to visit together often lessens the anxiety that parents feel when they have to visit classrooms by themselves.

### Activities for Effective Parent Involvement

You will find that most of the parents with whom you will work have a wide range of abilities. You might ask each parent to do something that is acceptable to him or her.

> Example:
> 1. Chaperoning field trips.
> 2. Supervising an art project.
> 3. Simple table games.
> 4. Supervising a cooking session (perhaps using the parent's "specialty" recipe).
> 5. Correcting paper work.
> 6. Hanging a bulletin board.

Some of these activities do not require special skills, but parental help is really needed. The success and confidence developed during this first effort will be the ingredients needed for future participation.

As your parental involvement program progresses, it is important to let parents know what is expected of them. For example, every parent should know the following:

1. What to do if the children are not cooperative.

2. About the materials: Where are they kept? Is it expected that they be put away? Are scraps to be saved or thrown away? Is there a certain way to store materials?

3. How long to continue each activity.

4. How to keep a record of the activity if record keeping is necessary.

As the teacher, you should be careful to elicit feedback from parents (how did everything go?). Be sure that parents are enjoying their tasks and remember to assign a variety of jobs to the parents so they will not become bored. It is important to remember to include parents who do not speak English in your program. Children can learn new words or new signs from adults who speak other languages. There are many activities in which a gesture or a smile works beautifully, for example, passing out supplies or helping with a cooking lesson requires little or no English.

### Ways Volunteers Can Participate*

Often, teachers ask, "What type of tasks are appropriate for the parent volunteers? The following list suggests a few of the many ways that parents may facilitate classroom activities. The following list of suggestions is presented by Miller and Wilmhurst (1975):

#### Nonteaching Activities

Make name tags for volunteers and children.
Make teaching aids such as flannel board stories, puppets.
Keep activity cards up to date and replenishing supplies.
See that art supplies are clean and in order.
Rotate exhibits on the science table.
Repair small toys.
Take charge of one bulletin board.
Volunteer coordinator.
Keep one cupboard in order.
Wash paint aprons on a regular basis.
Keep a vegetable or flower garden at school.
Librarian: Keep room supplied with theme books.
Newsletter chairman.
Keep class supplied with wood and nails.
Babysit to free parents to volunteer.
Telephone chairman.
Keep records.
Make and process dittos.

Keep housekeeping corner supplied with dramatic play possibilities.
Wash dress-up cloths.
Chaperone field trips.
Keep cooking supplies in order.
Community resources coordinator.
Room hostess.
Parent bulletin board.
Coffee chairman for parent center.
Book club chairman.

## Teaching Activities

Tutoring.
Supervise learning center or assist teacher in these areas:

| | | |
|---|---|---|
| Art | Singing | Dramatics |
| Cooking | Musical instruments | Physical education |
| Sensory motor activities | Science table | Dancing |
| Math activities | Handwriting | Creative writing |
| Reading worksheets | Social planning | |
| Language arts | Carpentry | |

*Reprinted from Miller, B.L., and A. L. Wilmhurst, *Parents and Volunteers In the Classroom: A Handbook for Teachers.* San Francisco: R&E Research Associates, Inc., 1975, pp. 47–48.

## How to Keep a Parent Involved

Getting parents to volunteer may be a difficult task, but your work does not stop once the initial contact and initial visits are completed. To have the continued support of parents, you and your colleagues must attempt to make them feel comfortable. There are a number of ways in which this can be done.

1. A must is a *Volunteers' Corner*. This can be a tiny spot, but it is very important because it provides a feeling of belonging for the volunteering parent. It is a place where parents can hang up their coats, flip through magazines, and look over notices that may be hanging on your Parent Bulletin Board. Different parents coming into the room can use the bulletin board to share notices such as babysitting and lost and found articles with other parents. You can also use this board to advertise your needs, such as "Empty egg cartons needed for class art project," or "Our class will be going to the Science Museum on Tuesday, March 27. If you are interested in accompanying us, please sign this sheet." The bulletin board can also be used to post articles of interest from the local newspaper, reports on current research in education, notices of community events, and listings of community resources.

If a volunteers' corner is not feasible in a crowded classroom, or if it would be too disturbing, another alternative is a *Parent Room*. An empty classroom can serve this purpose for all of the volunteers in the school building. It can be simply equipped—a few chairs, a coffee pot, a discarded school table. Parents could use the room in numerous ways: to browse through educational magazines and other publications; to leave a note on the bulletin board; to wait for children on a rainy day; to work on materials for a classroom teacher.

Teachers could also use this room. It could become a place to leave a stack of handouts that you would like parents to see or to leave book lists of age/grade appropriate material for children to read at home.

Whether one chooses a *Volunteers' Corner* or a *Parent Room*, its possible uses are unlimited. This might be the single most important factor in encouraging parents to "keep coming back." As their feeling of belonging develops, so does a feeling of responsibility and importance. If parents regard their job as important, they will want to coninue to participate in your program, and they will feel good about it.

2. Immediate feedback. Whenever possible, the teacher should always try to talk to a parent before he or she leaves the classroom for the day. It is important to know whether parents have felt good about what went on—was the group too small; too large? Were there any discipline problems?

3. Positive reinforcement is something we all need. Parents should be told again and again how much they have helped and how much they are appreciated. This can be done in several ways, complimenting a parent's work as well done is one way. Other appropriate ways are to write thank you notes, or to hang thank you posters made by the children, or to host a thank you party.

4. A quick and ready smile can do more than anything else to build confidence and convey a feeling of being welcome.

5. Be ready for some failure. No matter how carefully a teacher selects an activity for a parent to do, unexpected things may arise. Some parents may not be able to relate well to a group of children or may not be able to explain directions so that children will be able to understand, for example, Ms. Intili is in the corner with a small group of children trying to develop some creative writing stories. You notice that her themes are much too sophisticated for your first graders and that she seems to be doing all of the "creative" thinking and writing. At the end of her stay, you should thank her for spending so much of her time in your classroom. You may then want to suggest some creative thinking/writing topics that are appropriate to the age group for next time and explain to her some techniques for getting the *children* to do the writing.

### Parent Involvement Outside of the Classroom

No matter how hard you work, there are still going to be parents who cannot or will not come to your classroom to work. These parents can and should be able to offer assistance outside of the classroom. Some of the following activities can be completed outside of the classroom:

1. Collecting and contributing materials for art projects.
2. Making games and materials at home.
3. Repairing small toys.
4. Collecting old books for a class library.
5. Babysitting to free other parents to volunteer.
6. Supplying old clothes for the dramatic play corner.
7. Arranging visits to their places of employment.

A classroom newsletter that children take home with them on a regular basis is an excellent way to keep all of your parents involved with your classroom activities. A newsletter can contain general announcements of field trips and funtime plans, school events, new information learned that week in class, and possible follow-up activities to do at home ("The children in 3J spent the week busily learning their multiplication tables. Here are some games you might like to try."), notices of meetings, summaries of educational articles that may be of interest to parents, advertisements for "Help Wanted" in the classroom, phone numbers of other children in the class, lists of books to read to children, and thank you's to parents who have already volunteered in your classroom, for example,

> ALL OF US ARE ENJOYING THE BEAN SPROUTS ON OUR SALADS. A SPECIAL THANK YOU TO MR. GILL FOR COMING IN AND SHOWING US HOW TO GROW THEM.

Not only will these public thank you's please the people whom they acknowledge, but they may serve to interest some new volunteers.

A column in a local newspaper for parent questions and answers is an excellent vehicle for reaching and involving parents. If using the local paper is out of the question, a column in your newsletter devoted to parental questions may encourage involvement and communication. This "Question Box" column should answer parents' questions succinctly, yet should not talk down to its readers. Examples follow.

1. My three-year-old son loves toy games. He takes every opportunity to play with them. In fact, even when he does not have the actual toy, he'll use anything around (sticks, pencils, crayons, even just his finger) to substitute and will run through the house making "firing" noises. I am very much against this. I abhor guns and I feel that by allowing this behavior in my son, I am indirectly condoning them. On the other hand, I am afraid that I would in some way be hampering his emotional development by prohibiting this play. How would you suggest I handle this?

2. My four-year-old daughter attends a preschool where the teacher spends time having the children recognize letters of the alphabet and discriminate between them. At our conference I asked her why she was doing this, and she explained that she was training them in visual discrimination. Shouldn't she be concentrating more on fundamentals such as classification ("pick out the one that does not belong") and recognizing geometric shapes before jumping into actual reading? I am concerned that she may be skipping an important step. Is she?

3. We are the parents of an impressionable seven-year-old son. We are concerned with the violent and stereotyped content of most commercial television programs. In an effort to counteract this, we have tried to restrict our son's viewing of such shows as "The Six Million Dollar Man" and "Spiderman." This has become a problem because our child feels left out when his peers talk about these shows. He becomes extremely upset and cannot understand why he cannot watch the programs that "all the other kids watch." Are we being unreasonable in our concern?

4. My daughter has a constant companion—her imaginary friend, Susie. Beth is an only child and, when she was younger, I thoroughly understood her need for "pretend." However, she is now six and I do think that she has carried this far enough. "Susie" goes everywhere with us and, frankly, I am beginning to wonder if Beth has deeper psychological problems. She seems normal in every other way. Do other six-year-olds go through this?

5. Sally, our four-year-old, has always been a picky eater, but her "latest" has us perplexed as to what to do. She totally refuses to eat any vegetable no matter what the variety or method of preparation. We have tried coaxing and threatening; nothing seems to work. We are afraid that she is not getting all of her vitamins. She's such a slight child. What can we do?

6. My daughter has just begun third grade. When she comes home from school, I always ask her how her day has gone and if she has any homework to do. Her response is always that she does all of her work in school. I arranged a conference with her teacher and when I brought up the homework situation she became evasive. Still not satisfied, I talked to the principal and was told that this was the teacher's first year and that classroom methods vary with teachers. To me this is also evasive. Do you think I should pursue this further (and risk possible bad feelings against my child from the teacher) or should I just keep my thoughts to myself?

7. My five-year-old daughter seems preoccupied with nakedness. On a recent visit to a museum, she seemed fascinated with the paintings of naked figures and with the naked sculptures. She has even drawn some pretty explicit pictures. How does one handle this embarrassing situation?

8. My child's preschool class has been working on numeral recognition. Billie's teacher says he is having a bit of trouble with this task and that we should practice with him at home. We've been doing this without too much success. My concern is that this will affect Billie's math skills later. After all, if he cannot recognize "2" and "3", how will he be able to add them later? What do you suggest we do? We don't want to cause pressure for Billie; yet, we want to do what is right.

Other ideas for involving parents outside of the classroom include the following:

1. Periodically send home Parent Tips. These could explain topics in greater detail than the newsletter. For instance, a Parent Tip might be devoted to a special theme (such as beginning reading) and would begin by explaining the theory or philosophy underlying the skill. It would include some activities that parents can do to reinforce this skill at home.

2. You may wish to have each child keep an individual notebook in which you write some personal specifics such as, "Emma learned these three new words today. Ask her to read them to you." Parents can use the notebook to write back to the teacher. The lines of communication are open and the parent is involved.

## Parents and Television

It has been estimated that students graduating from high school will have spent 50 per cent more hours watching TV than they will have spent in school and that at the present rate, people in their lifetimes will have spent more time watching television than doing anything else except sleeping. Television effects virtually everyone in this country, especially children who probably learn more than any other age group. Children see many life-styles and cultures, sometimes shown accurately, sometimes inaccurately. Over and over again, they see violence as an easy solution to problems, materialism as a way to true happiness. Their perceptions of the world are shaped and reshaped by television.

Television viewing begins at a very early age. The habits fostered by early and excessive viewing take their toll. Many homes have replaced reading with TV viewing. Some parents no longer read to their children at bedtime, having opted instead for the electronic babysitter. The rapid and commonplace violent solutions to most problems shown in television programs, followed without a pause by the next program, leaves no time for critical thought, assimilation of valid ideas, or evaluations of events/actions presented in the program.

Television is powerful. Studies have shown that TV can influence children's social behavior and attitudes (Gerbner, 1972; Barcus, 1972; Bandura, 1965; Leifer and Roberts, 1972; Paulson, McDonald, and Whittemore, 1972; Friedrich and Stein, 1972). There is no doubt that television is here to stay. Therefore parents must be made aware of the ways in which they can use television with their children so that its influence is positive. Several researchers have already demonstrated that parents are important in shaping their children's attitudes toward television. Lyle and Hoffman (1972) report, "Mothers who watch television at least three hours per day are likely to have children who watch a great deal of television." Unfortunately, researchers have found that only one third of parents state that they have definite viewing rules (Lyle and Hoffman, 1972). Parents need to understand the extent to which existing TV content can be used for both entertainment and socialization. Parents need to be active in limiting and guiding their young child's exposure to TV. They need to be active in cultivating program preferences, and they need to comment on specific content as it is shown. They also need to react when their children act out something that they have seen on TV. It is their responsibility to help their children discern the reality and relevance of what they are seeing.

The first year evaluation, which was conducted on the "Sesame Street" program in the United States, indicated that children who had learned the most had watched more and have had mothers *who watched with them* and talked about the program's content (Ball and Bogatz, 1971).

There are organizations and committees dedicated to encouraging diversity in children's programming. Perhaps one of the best known is Action of Children's Television (ACT), located in Newton, Massachusetts. It publishes and distributes many materials that parents and teachers can use when educating children about TV. A copy of one of ACT's notices to parents is presented on page 245.

The National PTA has also organized a special television project that publishes the *Program Review Guide*. It is designed to assist parents in selecting programs for family viewing and in encouraging children (and adults) to develop their own analytic television skills.

As teachers, you have to be knowledgeable about the use and abuse of television, and you should be able to convey this knowledge to parents. A useful self-assessment exercise is to prepare a lesson plan for a children's television program that parents could use with their children. 1. As you do this, talk about the value of a parent previewing a show whenever possible, 2. Discuss interactions between child and parent that might occur during the program and 3. Suggest follow-up activities that can be completed after the program has been completed. As you become better equipped to do this, you will be better able to guide your parents.

No discussion of television would be complete without the mention of "Sesame Street" and "Electric Company." There is scarcely a child born today who has not heard about these shows.

### "Sesame Street"

"Sesame Street," a children's program, which was designed with joint funding from the Carnegie and Ford Foundations and the United States Office of Education, presents early language/reading instruction through rhythm, puppetry, songs, stories, and direct instruction. Although reactions to programs of this type are often controversial, there exists a significant body of literature suggesting that educational television in general, and the Children's Television Workshop in particular, are beneficial for children. In an evaluation of "Sesame Street," Ball and Bogatz (1971) stated the following:

> The facts are that the show was seen to have a marked effect, not only in the areas of rote learning of basic skills, such as counting, and in simple contiguity association learning, as in learning the names of letters and numbers, but also in higher areas of cognitive activity, such as sorting and classifying pictorial representations. (p. 7)

Frequent viewing of "Sesame Street" seemed to be a better predictor of performance at post-test than was age. In this study, post-test frequency of viewing matched the present data. Ball and Bogatz maintain that the implication of this finding is that "we should think of beginning with younger than four-year-old children and perhaps raise our expectations of what these young children can learn." According to them:

> The children who watched the most learned the most, and skills that received the most attention in the program were the best learned by the children. The goals of the program directly related to reading included recognizing, naming, and matching capital and lower-case letters, recognizing and matching letters in words, recognizing initial sounds and reading words. . . . The results from "Sesame Street" point up the importance of being specific about educational goals and directing the educational program toward these goals. (p. 18)

Further investigation was conducted by Blanton (1972), who explored the origins and specific goals of educational television.

# treat TV with T.L.C.*

## T ALK ABOUT TV WITH YOUR CHILD!

TALK ABOUT PROGRAMS THAT
DELIGHT YOUR CHILD

TALK ABOUT PROGRAMS THAT
UPSET YOUR CHILD

TALK ABOUT THE DIFFERENCES
BETWEEN MAKE BELIEVE & REAL LIFE

TALK ABOUT WAYS TV CHARACTERS
COULD SOLVE PROBLEMS WITHOUT VIOLENCE

TALK ABOUT VIOLENCE & HOW IT HURTS

TALK ABOUT TV FOODS THAT
CAN CAUSE CAVITIES

TALK ABOUT TV TOYS THAT
MAY BREAK TOO SOON

## L OOK AT TV WITH YOUR CHILD!

LOOK OUT FOR TV BEHAVIOR YOUR
CHILD MIGHT IMITATE

LOOK FOR TV CHARACTERS WHO
CARE ABOUT OTHERS

LOOK FOR WOMEN WHO ARE COMPETENT
IN A VARIETY OF JOBS

LOOK FOR PEOPLE FROM A VARIETY
OF CULTURAL & ETHNIC GROUPS

LOOK FOR HEALTHY SNACKS IN THE
KITCHEN INSTEAD OF ON TV

LOOK FOR IDEAS FOR WHAT TO DO
WHEN YOU SWITCH OFF THE SET...

READ A BOOK... DRAW A PICTURE
... PLAY A GAME

## C HOOSE TV PROGRAMS WITH YOUR CHILD!

CHOOSE THE NUMBER OF PROGRAMS
YOUR CHILD CAN WATCH

CHOOSE TO TURN THE SET OFF WHEN THE
PROGRAM IS OVER

CHOOSE TO TURN ON PUBLIC TELEVISION

CHOOSE TO IMPROVE CHILDREN'S TV BY WRITING
A LETTER TO A LOCAL STATION... TO A TELEVISION
NETWORK... TO AN ADVERTISER...
TO ACTION FOR CHILDREN'S TEVEVISION

* TENDER
LOVING
CARE

ACTION FOR
CHILDREN'S TELEVISION
46 AUSTIN ST. NEWTONVILLE
MASS., 02160

## Blanton's Educational Television Prereading Objectives*

### Letters

1. <u>Matching</u>: Given a printed letter, the child can select the identical letter from a set of printed letters.
2. <u>Recognition</u>: Given the verbal label for a letter, the child can select the appropriate letter from a set of printed letters.
3. <u>Labeling</u>: Given a printed letter the child can provide the verbal sound.
4. <u>Letter sounds</u>:
   a. For sustaining consonants (f, l, m, n, r, s, v), given the printed letter, the child can produce the letter's corresponding sound.
   b. Given a set of words presented orally, all beginning with the same letter sound, the child can select from a set of words another word with the same initial letter sound.
5. <u>Recitation of the alphabet</u>: The child can recite the alphabet.

### Words

1. <u>Matching</u>: Given a printed word, the child can select an identical word from a set of printed words.
2. <u>Boundaries of a word</u>: Given a printed sentence, the child can correctly point to each word in the sentence.
3. <u>Temporal-sequence/spatial-sequence correspondence</u>: (Words and sentences are read from left to right.)
   a. Given a printed word, the child can point to the first and last letter.
   b. Given a printed sentence, the child can point to the first and last word.
4. <u>Decoding</u>: Given the first five words on the reading vocabulary list (ran, set, big, mop, fun), the child can decode other related words generated by substitutions of a new initial consonant. (Example: given the word ran, the child can decode man and can.)
5. <u>Word recognition</u>: For any of the words on the <u>Sesame Street</u> word list, the child can recognize the given word when it is presented in a variety of contexts.
6. <u>Reading</u>: The child can read each of the 20 words on the <u>Sesame Street</u> word list.

Blanton concludes that:

> the *Sesame Street* series has been accepted by the public and by many educators with some enthusiasm. The effectiveness of the series has been questioned, sometimes with more passion than objectivity. The educational community would be well advised to withhold judgment of the effectiveness of the series until additional evidence is offered.

### *The "Electric Company"*

The "Electric Company" was designed to address the language/reading skill development of children ranging in age from seven to ten. The curricular em-

---

*From "How Effective is Sesame Street?" by William Blanton in the ERIC/CRIER column in the May 1972 issue of *The Reading Teacher*, p. 807. Reprinted by permission.

phasis of this program was explored by Roser (1974), who found that the following areas were given special attention:

1. The left-to-right sequence of print corresponds to the temporal sequence of speech.
2. Written symbols stand for speech sounds. They "track" the stream of speech.
3. The relationship between written symbols and speech sounds is sufficiently reliable to produce successful decoding most of the time.
4. Reading is facilitated by learning a set of strategies for figuring out sound-symbol relationships (p. 684).

The effectiveness of the curriculum was studied by Ball and Bogatz (1973). They used a pretest and post-test design. Half of the classes (a total of 100 classes) viewed "Electric Company" in school; the other half was encouraged by the teacher to watch it at home. The results seemed to show that the classes that viewed "Electric Company" had significantly larger adjusted gain scores on the total than did the nonviewing classes. Although most teachers generally liked the program, students' attitudes toward school and toward reading were not affected.

In summary, television cannot and should not be ignored as a vehicle of potential in children's learning. Even though there are those who are concerned only with reading via print, the world of television (and it is here to stay) should be utilized, making it possible for children to respond more easily to print with greater understanding.

## ACTIVITIES FOR PARENTS AND CHILDREN

### Activities for Parents to Help Their Children with Language/Reading

The following activities may be helpful for parents as they assume their role as their child's most important teacher. The activities that are presented in the next few pages include ideas for parents to use as they participate in the classroom program *and* for parents to use at home. All the activities include suggested age levels.

### *0 to 1 Years of Age*

#### 1. Let There Be Light

Goal: Development of visual awareness

Age level: 0–1

Construction and Utilization: Infants love to look at bright, different colored lights at holidays or any other time. Push the crib or bassinet where the child can get a good view.

## 2. Learning to Speak

Goal: Language development

Age level: 0–1

Construction and Utilization: When the child begins to try out different sounds, repeat the sound after him. Try to understand what he is trying to say, and tell him the appropriate word. Talk normally and naturally, as a child can sense boredom in your voice. Baby talk and slurring words will only confuse the child. It can also be helpful to hold up or point to the object while you are teaching a new word.

## 3. Interesting Sights to See

Goal: Development of visual skills

Age level: 0–1

Construction and Utilization: Attach a piece of string or elastic across the child's crib. Attach brightly colored and different-textured objects such as aluminum foil, old necklaces, stuffed animals. Let the infant watch them move and try to reach for them.

## 4. Ring the Bell

Goal: Listening, Cause-Effect Relationships

Age level: 0–1

Construction: Attach a rattle or bell to a piece of rope or elastic string across the crib. Tie a piece of string to the noisemaker, making the string long enough for the child to reach.

Utilization: Demonstrate for the child how to pull the string to ring the bell or shake the rattle.

## 5. Touching Textures

Goal: Development of sense of touch

Age level: 0–1

Construction and Utilization: Give the infant a variety of different textured materials to hold and touch. These can include a soft blanket, old towels, foil, sandpaper, a rubber ball, Also, give the child soft objects to explore with his mouth.

## 6. Sucking and Grasping

Goal: Development of reflexes

Age level: 0–1

Construction and Utilization: Infants are born with very few reflexes, but two of the most obvious ones are sucking and grasping. An infant will have plenty of practice sucking during feeding times, but the grasping reflex can be exercised during waking hours. Give the infant various objects to grasp such as a finger, a soft rattle, or a piece of yarn. Use objects of different textures, but don't let the infant put harmful things in its mouth. Let the child try to pull himself up while grasping onto your fingers.

### 7. What's the Noise?

Goal: Listening development

Age level: 0–1

Construction and Utilization: Gently shake a rattle or noisemaker about twelve to fifteen inches from the infant's ear. Encourage him to turn his head in the direction of the sound. Repeat the activity from other directions and with the other ear.

### 8. Busy Box

Goal: Visual, auditory, and motor development

Age level: 0–1

Construction: Build a simple busy box to place in the crib or playpen. Cover a piece of wood with cloth and glue or nail in various objects the child can manipulate. This could include knobs to turn, bells to ring, a sponge to squeeze, or a light switch to turn.

Utilization: Demonstrate for the child how to move all the objects and he will enjoy opening, closing, and turning them for hours.

### 9. Listening for Words

Goal: Speech development

Age level: 0–1

Construction and Utilization: Repetition of familiar words and names of objects can aid in the child's development of speech. Frequently call him by name and the child will recognize that as a sound that belongs to him. When giving him a favorite blanket or toy, always say "blanket." In time, the child will connect particular sounds with objects.

## *1 to 2 Years of Age*

### 1. Sounds All Around

Goal: Language development

Age level: 1–2

Construction and Utilization: At this age, it is crucial for future language development to talk with a child and to encourage him to speak. Have him repeat words after you, ask for things rather than just point, and make any kind of sounds. Listening to music on records or a radio can also aid the development of language.

## 2. Counting and Moving Songs

Goal: Language development and body awareness

Age level: 1–2

Construction and Utilization: Children love to sing and to be sung to. Counting songs such as "Ten Little Indians," "This Little Piggy Went to Market," and "This Old Man" can be valuable learning vehicles. Also, songs involving parts of the body such as "Thumbkin," "Pat-a-Cake," and "The Eensy Weensy Spider" can be useful.

## 3. Matching Pots and Pans

Goal: Understanding relative size

Age level: 1–2

Construction and Utilization: Give the child an assortment of pots, pans, and lids. Demonstrate for the child how to find the lid that fits the right size pan. The child then tries to match the lid with each pan.

## 4. A Real Puzzler

Goal: Visual discrimination

Age level: 1–2

Construction and Utilization: Simple puzzles are an excellent way to teach a child that a whole is made up of individual parts, and to focus on how shapes fit together. Start with two or three piece puzzles or make your own by gluing a colorful picture onto cardboard, and then cutting it into pieces.

## *2 to 3 Years of Age*

## 1. Find My Mate

Goal: Matching

Age level: 2–3

Construction: Collect pairs of many different objects. For example, two blocks, two crayons, two straws, two spoons. Place one of each object on a table, and put the other half of each pair in a bag or pillow case.

Utilization: Let the children handle the objects. Then give each child a particular object and let him find the mate in the bag, just by touching.

## 2. What Do I Do With This?

Goal: Language development

Age level: 2–3

Construction and Utilization: Collect a group of familiar objects such as a bar of soap, comb, toothbrush, spoon, cup, towel, crayon. Pick up one object at a time and ask the child to show you how he would use it. Ask him to say the name of the object, and if he doesn't know, tell him and have him repeat it.

## 3. Where's the Ball?

Goal: Development of memory

Age level: 2–3

Construction: Acquire several boxes or cannisters of graduated sizes that can fit inside each other. Choose a small, colorful ball, or another small toy.

Utilization: While the child is watching closely, put the ball inside the smallest cannister and cover it with the lid. Place that cannister inside the larger one, and give it to the child. The child should be able to remember where the ball was placed. Repeat the activity, using three cannisters, the smaller ones going inside the larger one.

## 4. The How-To Book

Goal: Fine motor development and vocabulary

Age level: 2–3

Construction: Have a clever parent make a simple book that can give children practice in buttoning, snapping, zippering, and buckling. Cover pieces of cardboard with material onto which you have sewn buttons and buttonholes, a zipper, and snaps.

Utilization: Demonstrate for the child how to manipulate the buttons and snaps. Have him repeat the name of the materials while he is doing it. "I am buttoning. I am zipping the zipper. I am snapping together the snaps."

## 5. Picture to Object

Goal: Matching, vocabulary development

Age level: 2–3

Construction: Cut out large colorful pictures from magazines, showing objects that would be familiar to the child. For example, pictures of a spoon, ball, basket, apple, or plate would all be appropriate. Glue the pictures to a piece of cardboard. Then collect real objects that are shown in the pictures, and spread the pictures and the objects in front of the child.

Utilization: Let the child attempt to match the picture with the correct object.

## 6. What Do I Look Like?

Goal: Self-Concept; Body image; vocabulary

Age level: 2-3

Construction and Utilization: Most mirrors in a home are located at an adult's eye level, which would be above a child's head. Body image and awareness are important in the development of a positive self-concept. A child with a good self-concept is eager to try new things and takes pride in his accomplishments, both of which are important characteristics for future success in school. Stand with your child in front of a full-length mirror, and identify various parts of the body. Call attention to color, number of arms and legs, and the different shapes. Then call out the name of a body part and have the child point to it. While the child takes a bath, say, "Wash your leg, wash your toes, wash your neck," and so on.

## 7. Make Your Own Puppet

Goal: Language development

Age level:  2-3

Construction: Make hand puppets for you and your child, using old socks or paper bags. The bottom of the paper bag is used as the head of the puppet. Help your child color and paste various objects such as buttons and yarn onto the bag. If socks are used these objects can either be sewn or pasted on.

Utilization: Act out everyday situations using the puppets. For example, two children playing, a parent scolding his child, or a child frightened by a monster.

## 8. Follow the Leader

Goal:  Recall, sequencing

Age level: 2-3

Construction and Utilization: While you are sitting at a table or walking around the house or outdoors, have your child  imitate certain actions. This can include blinking one eye, touching your toes, clapping to a certain rhythm, touching three different objects, making noises with your tongue. Try doing two, three, then four actions in a row to see if he can remember.

## 9. Magic Lines and Shapes

Goal:  Fine motor matching

Age level: 2-3

Construction and Utilization: Give the child a large magic marker or crayon and blank sheets of paper. Tell him you are going to play a game in which he draws exactly what you draw, and then you will copy him. Make simple lines going in one direction, or circles, or squares. Then have him draw a line or shape with you copying it.

## 10. Muffin Classifying

Goal: Classifying objects

Age level: 2–3

Construction: Collect many small objects such as buttons, pennies, nuts and bolts, small macaroni noodles. Several muffin tins will also be needed.

Utilization: Demonstrate for the child how to put similar objects into the same section of the muffin tin.

## *3 to 4 Years of Age*

## 1. Do It Yourself Twister

Goal: Reinforcing shapes and colors

Age level: 3–4

Construction: On large squares of cardboard, draw a square, circle, or rectangle. Paint or color in each shape, using a different color for each card.

Utilization: Place the cardboard squares on the floor. With a small group of children, the parent or teacher gives each child a particular direction. For example, "John, put your foot on the red square." "Jane, put your hand on the blue rectangle." Players must keep touching the original block even after they are given a new direction. Whoever falls down first loses the game.

## 2. The Box Game

Goal: Understanding position words

Age level: 3–4

Construction: Acquire a large box that was formerly used for storage or for a new appliance.

Utilization: Working with a small group of children, have them take turns following your directions. For example, "Sit inside of the box." "Put your leg inside the box." "Put the box over you." Increase the complexity of the directions as the children become more proficient.

## 3. Draw Yourself

Goal: Body image and awareness

Age level: 3–4

Construction and Utilization: Have children lie on a large piece of brown wrapping paper or shelf paper. Trace around the child's body and show the child how to color in clothing, color of hair and eyes, and so on.

## 4. The Circle Game

Goal: Following directions, understanding direction words

Age level: 3–4

Construction and Utilization: With a large piece of yarn or rope, make a circle in a large area of the room. A small group of children should stand around the outside of the circle. Call out simple directions such as "Put your coat in the circle," "put your thumb in the circle," "shake your hand over the circle." Students follow the directions given to the best of their ability.

## 5. Traveling Around

Goal: Language experience

Age level: 3–4

Construction and utilization: Take your child to as many different places as possible, using all types of transportation. Visits utilizing buses, trains, cars can include stores, zoos, museums, and parks. Urge your child to talk about the new things he has seen and perhaps help him to draw simple pictures about them.

## 6. Is It Larger Than a Bread Box?

Goal: Understanding size and inflectional endings

Age level: 3–4

Construction: Play a game in which your child must find an object according to its size. For example, "Bring me something that is smaller than a car and larger than a baseball bat," or "Bring me something that is smaller than a dog and larger than a button." Decrease the difference in size as the child becomes more efficient.

## 7. Sounds From the Environment

Goal: Development of listening skills

Age level: 3–4

Construction and Utilization: Take your child for a walk in the woods or to a quiet place in the country. Both of you should close your eyes and just listen for one minute. Then list each of the sounds you both heard during that time. Repeat the same activity in the middle of a busy city. Discuss reasons for the differences in the kinds of sounds heard in both places.

### *4 to 5 Years of Age*

## 1. Touchy-Feely Book

Goal: Word recognition, sight words

Age level: 4–5

Construction: Assist a small group of children in making their own book about different textures. Help them cut small pieces from materials of different textures—corduroy, sheep's wool, a Brillo pad. Glue a different texture to each page. Have the children dictate a label for each texture, such as "rough, smooth, soft, scratchy." Staple the pages together or make a cardboard cover.

Utilization: Have the children "read" each page to you by touching the material on each page. They can then present it to the rest of the class.

## 2. Finding the Opposite

Goal: Understanding opposites

Age level: 4–5

Construction: Cut from magazines pictures showing opposites. For example, hot and cold, wet and dry, smile and frown, happy and sad. Paste the pictures onto a piece of cardboard.

Utilization: Spread the pictures in front of a small group of children. Choose one picture and have them locate its opposite or encourage the children to ask each other to develop a match.

## 3. Bag a Sound

Goal: Reinforcing beginning consonant sounds

Age level: 4–5

Construction: Give each child in a small group a large paper bag. Assign each child a consonant sound with which they are somewhat familiar. On the front of the bag, help children draw or paste a magazine picture of an object that begins with that sound.

Utilization: Each child must go around the room and put small objects that begin with his consonant sound into the bag. Whoever can collect the most objects in ten minutes wins the game. For example—"B"—bat, ball, block, button.

## 4. Copy My Design

Goal: Visual discrimination

Age level: 4–5

Construction and Utilization: Using tinker toys, colored blocks of different shapes, or pieces of paper cut into shapes, make a simple design. This could be a simple geometric shape, a face or house. Help your child to copy your design using duplicate blocks or tinker toys.

## 5. What Do You Remember?

Goal: Development of memory

Age level: 4–5

Construction: Cut out several colorful, detailed pictures from a magazine. Paste them onto pieces of cardboard.

Utilization: Working with one child or a small group of children, hold up the picture for one minute. Then let the children tell you as many details as they can about the picture. Ask questions about the picture, such as "How many cars were in the picture? Did the people look happy or sad? What was the dog doing in the picture?"

### 6. You Finish the Rhyme

Goal: Memory, rhyming words

Age level: 4–5

Construction and Utilization: After children are familiar with several nursery rhymes, try reading them and leave out a word at the end of the sentence. For example, "Little Miss Muffett sat on a _____." The same activity can be used with rhyming riddles: "When I'm in the park, I can hear a dog _____." Children must then supply the missing word.

### 7. Spelling on the Refrigerator

Goal: Letter recognition and reading word patterns

Age level: 4–5

Construction and Utilization: Purchase a commercial letter set in which the plastic letters have magnets on the back. Place them on the refrigerator door at the child's eye level. Have the child spell his own name and name individual letters on the door. Try showing him word patterns such as "can, man, tan" if he is familiar with letter sounds.

### 8. Flashing Letters

Goal: Letter recognition and learning consonant sounds

Age level: 4–5

Construction: Help your child to make flashcards on individual pieces of cardboard. The child can help you look through magazines to cut out pictures of objects that begin with particular consonant sounds. Paste the picture above the upper- and lower-case letters on each card.

Utilization: According to the child's level, go through the flashcards one by one, having the child identify the name of the letter and, if ready, another word that begins with that sound.

### 9. "Sesame Street"

Goal: Letter and sound recognition

Age level: 4–5

Construction and Utilization: Watch "Sesame Street" with your child and reinforce throughout the day the letter names and sounds learned on the program.

## 10. What's Making That Sound?

Goal: Development of listening skills

Age level: 4–5

Construction: Record on a tape recorder various sounds that could be heard around the house—a vacuum cleaner, toilet flushing, water faucet dripping, a cartoon on television. Then draw pictures on separate 5 x 7-inch cards of each of the objects making the sounds.

Utilization: The child listens to the noises on the tape recorder and chooses the card showing the object that could make that sound.

## 11. Tongue Twisters

Goal: Memory of the spoken word

Age level: 4–5

Construction and Utilization: While traveling or doing simple chores around the house, have the child try various tongue twisters. Increase them in length as the child becomes more proficient. For example: "She sells sea shells down by the sea shore." "Peter Piper picked a peck of pickled peppers." Ask your child what is the sound heard most often at the beginning of each word.

## *5 to 6 Years of Age*

### 1. Labelling the Classroom

Goal: Word recognition, sight words

Age level: 5–6

Construction: On 3 x 5-inch index cards, write the names of various objects in the classroom, for example, table, chair, calendar, flag, closet.

Utilization: Give each child in a small group a few cards, and have them walk around and attach the label to the correct object. At first, they may need help reading the words, but if the activity is repeated every-day, the children will become proficient in recognizing the words without assistance.

### 2. Getting Into Groups

Goal: Individualizing

Age level: 5–6

Construction and Utilization: Parents can be a big help in working individually with students. Schedule two parent volunteers per day. For a half-hour period, one parent can play a reading board game with a small group, another can help a group with worksheets or workbooks; and the teacher can instruct a third group. If one group finishes early, the parent can be given a book to read to them. A short workshop can be given in the beginning of the year, together with the school reading teacher. In this workshop, parent volunteers can learn about the goals and philosophy of your reading program, teaching techniques, and how to construct reading games.

### 3. Letter Back Rub

Goal: Letter recognition and beginning consonant sounds

Age level: 5–6

Construction and Utilization: Working with a small group of children, take turns tracing an upper-case letter on their backs. The child must guess the letter and, if ready, say a word that begins with that letter.

### 4. Parents' Show and Tell

Goal: Understanding and recall

Age level: 5–6

Construction and Utilization: Encourage parents to bring into the classroom any kind of hobby or interesting pet. This could include turtles, a snake, chickens, weaving, or even a new baby. After the presentation, the teacher or parent can ask the children questions requiring inferences, cause-effect, and critical thinking. The class can also draw pictures to describe what they have learned.

### 5. Story Time on a Record

Goal: Recall, listening skills

Age level: 5–6

Construction: The school or public library has many long-playing records that tell a story. Borrow a record and using earphones set it up for a small group.

Utilization: Listen to the record with the group and afterwards ask questions about the story. For example, "Who was your favorite character? How would you end the story? What was the most scary part of the story for you?"

### 6. Hopscotch

Goal: Letter recognition

Age level: 5–6

Construction: Using colored chalk, draw a hopscotch board on your driveway or sidewalk. In each square, write a letter.

Utilization: Rules for hopscotch are followed. When a player lands on a particular square, he must say the name of the letter. The same activity can be done using short vowel words.

### 7. A Search for Shapes

Goal: Recognizing shapes

Age level: 5–6

Construction and Utilization: Choose a particular shape and have your child dictate to you the names of all the objects inside your house of that shape. For example, rectangle—doors, windows, cabinets, fish tank. As a follow-up activity, cut these shapes from construction paper. Have your child paste them to another piece of paper, adding crayon to make a picture.

### 8. Search for Words

Goal: Word recognition

Age level: 5–6

Construction and Utilization: Once your child begins to recognize and decode simple words and sight words, have him look through the newspaper. Give him a raisin or a gold star for every word he can identify on a page, particularly in the advertisements.

### 9. Movies and Puppet Shows

Goal: Recall, understanding

Age level: 5–6

Construction: Take your child to puppet shows and local movies that are sponsored by the library or summer art programs.

Utilization: When your child arrives home, have him sit down and dictate to you what went on in the show or movie. Write the descriptive sentences on separate pages, and have your child illustrate them.

### 10. Which Comes Next?

Goal: Sequencing, ordering

Age level: 5–6

Construction: Acquire three to five objects of different lengths. They could be pieces of yarn, straws, rope, or building blocks. Have the child put them in order from shortest to longest. Increase the number of objects as the child becomes more proficient.

### 11. Which Has More

Goal: Understanding concepts of more and less

Age level: 5–6

Construction: Acquire several piles of small objects such as blocks, buttons, pennies. Divide one pile at a time into two smaller parts, with one part obviously larger than the other.

Utilization: Point to the two piles of pennies, for example, and ask "Which has more?" "Which has less?" "Which would you rather have?" "Which is bigger?" If the child can master this activity, try it using three piles. Also try spreading the objects out in straight lines.

## 6 to 7 Years of Age

### 1. A Story About <u>You</u>

<u>Goal</u>: Reinforcing vocabulary and spelling

<u>Age level</u>: 6-7

<u>Construction</u>: Design three or four ditto masters to determine personal information about the child. For example, My name is _____. I live at _____. I have _____brothers and sisters. My favorite toy is _____. Leave room for students to illustrate each answer.

<u>Utilization</u>: Parents help students in writing the requested information. The students can draw a picture of themselves, their home, and family. The parent then staples the pages together to make a book.

### 2. Human Letters

<u>Goal</u>: Word recognition and spelling

<u>Age level</u>: 6-7

<u>Construction</u>: Cut 30 to 35 pieces of 9 x 11-inch cardboard or oaktag. On each card, print a letter, including three each of A, E, I, O, and U. Punch two holes at the top of each card and tie a loop string to them. The cards will be worn around each child's neck.

<u>Utilization</u>: A group of five or six students each chooses a card. The group should decide which words they can spell using those letters. The members of the group should then stand in front of the class with their letters forming a word. They can act out the meaning of the word. The rest of the class must guess the word. Group members should make up as many words as possible using those letters, and then they can choose different ones.

### 3. What's Your Favorite Color?

<u>Goal</u>: Understanding bar graphs

<u>Age level</u>: 6-7

<u>Construction</u>: Give each student in a small group (three or four students) a sheet of graph paper with large squares. In each square at the bottom of the page, the students should make a small dot, using different colors of crayon.

<u>Utilization</u>: Each student in the group must walk around the classroom and ask each of the other students in the class what is his/her favorite color. If a student says "red," the questionner colors in the square above the red dot. After each student has given an answer, the student, should write a short summary of the results. For example, "The most popular color in our class is green."

### 4. A Picture Story

<u>Goal</u>: Understanding sentence structure and sequencing

<u>Age level</u>: 6-7

Construction: Acquire several small, inexpensive cameras and have a parent take a small group of students on a short field trip on the school grounds. After the students have been instructed on how to use the camera, have each take twelve pictures to tell a story. The pictures can be of animals, objects, other students.

Utilization: After the pictures have been developed, students should paste them in the correct sequence on a sheet of paper. Underneath each picture, the students should write a sentence which tells 'what's happening in the story.'

## 5. Growing Your Own Plant

Goal: Sequencing

Age level: 6-7

Construction and Utilization: Have the parent assist small groups of students in planting a bean seed. The students should make careful records of the plant's growth by drawing pictures of the various stages. When the plants are full grown, draw the various stages of growth on individual cards. Students must put the cards in the correct sequence of growth.

## 6. Obey My Command

Goal: Word recognition

Age level: 6-7

Construction: On 3 x 5-inch index cards, write simple commands such as "Touch your toes," "Smile," "Do a somersault."

Utilization: The child picks a card from the pile and obeys the command. At first he may need assistance reading the words, but with additional practice he will recognize them as sight words.

## 7. Crazy Sentences

Goal: Word recognition, understanding what is read

Age level: 6-7

Construction: Assist your child in locating and cutting random phrases from magazine stories and advertisements.

Utilization: Paste the phrases on another sheet of paper and then have the child illustrate it. For example, "Your hair will be as soft as . . . a ripe banana."

## 8. Cooking and Reading

Goal: Understanding and acting upon what is read.

Age level: 6-7

Construction: Help your child in choosing and reading a book involving food. Good examples are *Cranberry Thanksgiving, Johnny Appleseed, Blueberries for Sal.*

Utilization: Look through a cookbook and choose a recipe that calls for one of the foods mentioned in the book. Then follow the recipe together, and serve the results to the rest of the family.

## 7 to 8 Years of Age

Parents can be helpful as resource people in conducting units of study. The following activities were designed around the study of the Plains Indians.

### 1. Tip the Chips

Goal: Reinforcement of sight words

Age level: 7-8

Construction: Acquire a large wooden bowl and ten small wooden or heavy cardboard circles. A piece of cloth or other material should be placed under the bowl to deaden the noise. Write sight words on one side of each of the chips.

Utilization: Circles are placed with the words face down in the bowl. Students take turns banging the bowl once on the table, trying to flip the circles over. The object of the game is to turn over as many circles as possible. The student must read the words on all the chips he has turned over. Whoever turns over the most chips wins.

### 2. Indian Word Puzzle

Goal: Forming compound words

Age level: 7-8

Construction: Make puzzle pieces so that when two are combined they form a compound word. Select compound words from reading selections, and separate the words on the puzzle pieces.

Utilization: The student matches the appropriate pieces to form compound words.

### 3. Words from Different Cultures

Goal: Understanding vocabulary from context

Age level: 7-8

Construction: The parent can select Indian words such as teepee, papoose, buffalo meat from reading selections and have students write down the words we use in our culture to describe the objects. Teepee-house. Papoose-baby. Buffalo meat-cattle meat.

### 4. Magnet Madness

Goal: Practice in decoding words

Age level: 7-8

Construction and Utilization: Give your child a list of names of objects, some that are metals and some that are not. The child should read through the list and check off those objects that he thinks a magnet will pick up. Then let him prove his answers; provide a magnet and a sample of each object.

## 5. Secret Codes

Goal: Word recognition and spelling

Age level: 7–8

Construction: Sit down with your child and devise a secret code. This could be a simple reversal of the alphabet, such as 26 = A; 2 = Y, or something more complex. Then, write secret messages to each other and hide them around the house. For example, in the bathroom write, "Brush your teeth," or near the telephone, "Jane called."

## 6. Password

Goal: Word recognition, vocabulary

Age level: 7–8

Construction: The commercial password game can be used to give practice in decoding words and increasing vocabulary. One member must give clues to the other team members, giving a one-word definition. The number of points that can be won decreases according to how many clues are given. Whoever guesses the word first gets that number of points.

## 7. A Neighborhood Play

Goal: Recall and understanding

Age level: 7–8

Construction and Utilization: Assist several neighborhood children in staging their own play for their parents. Children can be taken to the library to choose the work or play they would like to produce. Read through the story with them, making sure everyone understands the plot, setting, and characters. The parent can then assist them in writing dialogue and assigning parts, including Director and Stage Manager. After acquiring props, scenery, and costumes and after many rehearsals you can enact the play.

## 8. Family Charades

Goal: Memory, understanding what is read

Age level: 7–8

Construction: Make up a list of books your seven-year-old and other members of the family have read. Write the name of each book on small pieces of paper and put them in a paper bag.

Utilization: In turn, each member of the family draws a name of a book from the bag. He then must act out the main idea of the book using pantomime actions. Motions should be determined before the game to indicate whether the guesses are close or if they said half the title. Whoever guesses the name of the book gets to draw the next title.

## 9. Dioramas and Displays

Goal: Understanding what is read, recall

Age level: 7–8

Construction and Utilization: Help your child choose a favorite book and discuss the setting, main events, and idea of the story. Then help your child plan a diorama or three-dimensional display. Collect materials to show scenery, characters, and appropriate props, and glue them into a shoe box or onto heavy cardboard. The diorama can then be displayed at home or at school.

## *8 to 9 Years of Age*

## 1. A School Newspaper

Goal: Reinforcing vocabulary, spelling, sentence structure

Age level: 8–9

Construction and Utilization: A parent can help a group of students write and produce a monthly school newspaper. Students can ask other teachers and students for school news and write their own stories and poems. The parent can type the stories and news on ditto masters and distribute them throughout the class and the school.

## 2. Reading at the Grocery Store

Goal: Reinforcing word parts

Age level: 8–9

Construction and Utilization: Have a parent take a small group of students to the grocery store. Each student has a pad and pencil in hand and is given a particular assignment. This could be writing down the name of all the products that have the same vowel sound or the same consonant blend. The first person to write a list of ten items wins. Courtesy in the grocery store, such as no running or pushing, should be stressed.

## 3. Back In My Day. . . .

Goal: Understanding oral histories, recall

Age level: 8–9

Construction: Invite a parent or grandfather from the community to describe to the class what it was like to live in the town many years ago. He or she should include the activities kids did for fun, how they listened to radio instead of watching TV, or modes of transportation before cars and planes were invented.

Utilization: Students listen to the presentation and illustrate on a piece of large drawing paper different aspects of the life described. The paper should be divided into six to nine sections, and a short description should be written under each picture.

### 4. It's a Carnival!

<u>Goal</u>:  Reinforcing vocabulary and spelling

<u>Age level</u>:  8-9

<u>Construction and Utilization</u>: Help children organize a neighborhood carnival. This can include advertising—making up signs and contacting the local newspaper, and setting up games such as bingo, spin the spinner, and card games. The children can also follow simple recipes to sell baked goods.

### 5. Scrabble

<u>Goal</u>:  Understanding word structures and spelling

<u>Age level</u>:  8-9

<u>Construction and Utilization</u>: Scrabble is an excellent game to improve spelling and an understanding of inflectional endings. Children's scrabble games are also available.

### 6. A New Twist Monopoly

<u>Goal</u>:  Reinforcing vowel and consonant diagraphs

<u>Age level</u>:  8-9

<u>Construction</u>: Make up a small deck of cards with a word containing a vowel or consonant diagraph on each. These are to be used with the commercial Monopoly.

<u>Utilization</u>: When a player lands on another player's property, he must not only pay the rent, but draw a card from the new pile as well. If he cannot read the word correctly, he must pay an additional few dollars.

### 7. Your Own Magazine Subscription

<u>Goal</u>:  Comprehending what is read

<u>Age level</u>:  8-9

<u>Construction and Utilization</u>: There are many excellent children's magazines available, such as <u>Ranger Rick</u> or <u>Highlights for Children</u>. Read over the stories with your child, asking him questions about the story characters, outcome, and events. Children love to have their own magazine subscription and to receive mail every month.

### 8. Reading the Newspaper Together

<u>Goal</u>:  Understanding what is read

<u>Age level</u>:  8-9

<u>Construction and Utilization</u>: Choose a particular newspaper column in the daily newspaper with your child that you both agree to read everyday. This could be in the sports section, horoscope, movies and entertainment, or weather. After both of you have read the column, ask your child questions about what he has read. Then give him a chance to ask <u>you</u> questions.

## 9. Knock, Knock Jokes

<u>Goal</u>: Understanding word structures–prefixes

<u>Age level</u>: 8–9

<u>Construction and Utilization</u>: Choose a particular prefix and take turns telling each other Knock, Knock Jokes. For example, for the prefix "un": "Knock, Knock." "Who's there?" "Un." "Un who?" "Unwanted." Try to think of as many words beginning with that prefix as possible.

# BIBLIOGRAPHY

Ball, S., and G. A. Bogatz. *The First Year of Sesame Street: An Evaluation.* Princeton, N.J.: Educational Testing Service, 1970.

Ball, S., and G. A. Bogztz. "Research on Sesame Street: Some Implications for Compensatory Education." Paper presented at the Second Annual Blumberg Symposium in Early Childhood Education. John's Hopkins Press, 1971.

Ball, S., and G. A. Bogatz. *Reading With Television: An Evaluation.* Princeton, N.J.: Educational Television Service, 1973.

Bandura, A. "Influence of Models Reinforcement Contingencies of the Acquisition of Imitative Responses," *Journal of Personality and Social Psychology*, Vol. 1, pp. 539–595, 1965.

Barcus, F. E. *Network Programming and Advertising in the Saturday Children's Hours: A June and November Comparison.* Boston: Action for Children's Televison, 1972.

Blanton, W. "How Effective is Sesame Street?" *Reading Teacher.* May 1972, p. 807.

Bloom, B. "The Thought Processes of Students in Discussion." In S. J. French, *Accent on Teaching.* New York: Harper and Row Publishers, 1954.

Dentsch, T. "Caution: TV Could Be Hazardous to Children's Health," *The Massachusetts Teacher*, April 1978, pp. 20–21.

Flood, J. "Parental Styles in Reading Episodes With Young Children" *The Reading Teacher*, May, 1977.

Friedrich, L. K., and A. H. Stein. *Agressive and Prosocial Television Programs and the Natural Behavior of Preschool Children* 1972.

Gerbner, G. "Violence in Television Drama: Trends and Symbolic Functions." In G. A. Comstock and E. A. Rubinstein, (ed.) *Television and Social Behavior*, Volume 1, Washington, D.C.: United States Government Printing Office, 1972.

Hunt, J. McV. *Intelligence and Experience.* New York: The Ronald Press Company, 1961.

Leifer, A. D., and D. F. Roberts. "Children's Responses to Television Violence." In E. A. Rubinstein and G. A. Comstock, (ed.) *Television and Social Behavior*, Vol. 2, Washington, D.C.: United States Government Printing Office, 1972.

Lyle, J., and H. R. Hoffman. "Children's Use of Televison and Other Media." In E. A. Rubinstein, G. A. Comstock, and J. P. Murray, ed. *Television and Social Behavior*, Volume 4, Washington, D.C.: United States Government Printing Office, 1972.

Miller, B. L., and A. L. Wilmhurst. *Parents and Volunteers In the Classroom: A Handbook for Teachers.* San Francisco: R & E Research Associates, Inc., 1975.

Morgan, E. L. "TV and Reading: Are They Compatible?" *The Massachusetts Teacher,* (January 1978) p. 24.

Paulson, F. D., D. L. McDonald and S. L. Whittemore. *An Evaluation of Sesame Street Programming Designed to Teach Cooperative Behavior.* Mommouth, Oregon, 1972.

Rogers, N. *How I Can Help My Child Get Ready to Read.* Newark, Delaware: International Reading Association, 1972.

Roser, N. L. "Electric Company Critique: Can Great Be Good Enough?" *The Reading Teacher,* Vol. 17, No. 7 (April 1974), pp. 680–684.

Shorr, J. "Basic Skills of TV Viewing," *Today's Education,* (April–May 1978) pp. 70–73.

*TV Program Review Guide,* National PTA TV Action Center, Chicago, Illinois.

# Section

# IV

# For Those Who Are Ready: The Reading Process

# 11

# Historical Perspectives on the Teaching
# of Reading to Young Children

The teaching of reading is an extremely important venture in the United States today. Educators hold many different views on the issues that are involved in the teaching of reading to young children. Some of their differences of opinion are rooted in historical events. Two of these important issues have a rich history that we will explore throughout this chapter:

1. When should a young child be instructed in reading?
2. What is the best way to teach young children to read?

## When Should a Young Child Be Instructed in Reading?

The answer to this question is extremely complex. Most Americans who reflect on this issue might say, "In first grade." This answer probably reflects their own school experience where they equated first grade with learning to read. This phenomenon is the result of the plethora of research that deemed six as the magical age for beginning to learn to read.

A review of the early literature shows that concerned educators who suggested that reading should not be introduced until at least six or eight years of age may have been reacting more against the regimented, unnatural methods used to teach reading than to the child's curiosity about the printed word.

> The child makes endless questionings about the names of things, as every mother knows. He is concerned also about the printed notices, signs, titles, visiting cards, etc., that come in his way, and should be told what these "say" when he makes inquiry. It is surprising how large a stock of printed or written words a child will gradually come to recognize in this way. (Huey, 1908, p. 313)

*Figure 62.* Written words, phrases, and sentences are easily and naturally related to everyday experiences. (Photo by Linda Lungren)

During the 1920s and 1930s, educational literature was filled with statements by those who suggested that any attempts to teach reading were to be postponed until after six years of age.

> It seems safe to state that, by postponing the teaching of reading until children reach a mental age of six and a half years, teachers can greatly decrease the chances of failure and discouragement and can correspondingly increase their efficiency. (Morphett and Washburne, 1931, p. 503)

> Nowadays each first-grade teacher in Winnetka has a chart showing when each of her children will be mentally six-and-a-half, and is careful to avoid any effort to get a child to read before he has reached this stage of mental growth. (Washburne, 1936, p. 127)

The rationale for such statements might be found by examining the writings of many psychologists (Hall, 1904; Terman, 1925; Gesell, 1928), who strongly believed that the child's readiness for reading occurred in stages affected only by heredity and that little could be done to alter these developments.

> The most general formulation of all the facts of development that we yet possess is contained in the law of recapitulation. This law declares that the individual, in his development, passes through stages similar to which the race has passed, and in the same order. (Hall, 1904, p. 8)

Also characteristic of this time were attempts by many (Thorndike 1917; Dickson, 1923; Holmes, 1927; Reed, 1927; Thurstone, 1935) to measure all dimensions of the child's behavior and to conclude that children who were failing first grade were having reading difficulties. This awareness caused other educators to speculate that reading success might be dependent upon more than genetic development. These insights led to early reading research that resulted in statements that suggested reading success was not totally dependent on children's genetic endowments or chronological maturation.

> The optimum time of beginning reading is not entirely dependent upon the nature of the child himself, but it is in a large measure determined by the nature of the reading program. (Gates and Bond, 1936, p. 684)

> Reading is begun by very different materials, methods, and general procedures, some of which a pupil can master at the mental age of five with reasonable ease, others of which would give him difficulty at the mental age of seven. (Gates, 1937, p. 508)

> The study emphasizes the importance of recognizing and adjusting to individual limitations and needs . . . rather than merely changing the time of beginning. It appears that readiness for reading is something to develop rather than merely to wait for. (Gates and Bond, 1936, p. 648)

## Why Reading Was Not Taught Until Six Years of Age

Until 1931, beginning school at about age six and learning how to read were considered synonymous. The accepted practice was to expect children of beginning school age to be capable of learning to read and to instruct them accordingly. This practice had few detractors (with the exception of Huey [1908]), until the "scientific" movement toward educational measurement and assessment in the late 1920s spawned a new concern for evaluation of children's achievement. The new measurement and assessment techniques used by investigators such as Holmes (1927) and Reed (1927) demonstrated the fact that large numbers of children were failing first grade because they failed to learn how to read. These same investigators, who failed to take into account such factors as instructional approaches, reading materials, class size, and teacher preparation, concluded from their research that children entering first grade were not ready to learn to read. As a result of the popularity of these findings, readiness programs began to emerge throughout the country.

## Determining Readiness for Reading

Because exactness of measurement was in vogue, the public was not interested in vague notions of stages of development. Psychologists and educators had to design a system to assess the exact age when reading instruction should begin. It was natural for group intelligence tests to become an intermediary in the assessment because intelligence quotient (IQ) testing had recently become available to the educational community. The IQ tests provided teachers with a concrete, numerical statistic of the mental age of each child. These group intelligence tests became the instrument for pinpointing the moment when a child was able to learn to read. The formula for determining mental age was the following:

$$\text{Mental Age} = \frac{\text{Intelligence Quotient} \times \text{Chronological Age}}{100}$$

High correlation between reading achievement and intelligence was found in many studies conducted in the 1920s. The criteria for reading readiness programs during the next thirty years were based upon findings by Arthur (1925), Morphett and Washburne (1931), and other researchers who stated that a mental age of six to six and a half was the proper mental age at which to begin reading instructions. In retrospect, a study such as Morphett and Washburne's seems less than a definitive statement on reading readiness, especially when we consider that their study was conducted on children using one method of instruction in one school system in Winnetka, Illinois.

We have already established the fact that in the past too much emphasis was placed upon standardized readiness testing scores and not enough attention was given to the individual needs of each child. More recently, theories of reading readiness have taken individual differences into account in determining the aspects of reading instruction that may be beneficial to the child. Ausubel (1959) states that readiness is "the adequacy of existing capacity in relation to the demands of a given learning task." His definition suggests that the "when" of reading instruction depends upon the child, the instruction, and the specific components of what is being taught. As an example, let us design a hypothetical, chronologically age-grouped class of beginning readers. Some of the young children in the class may be "ready" to learn the letters of their first names. Other members of the same class may be ready to learn to read the following sentence:

The hat is red.

This second group of children has already learned to decode these few words and have committed them to their sight vocabulary. But as the teachers of this class, you should not infer that the children in the second group are more intelligent than the children in the first group. Their readiness preparation is simply at a different stage of development than that of those in the first group.

Differences of this sort are a function of each child's unique growth patterns and external environment.

A brief analysis of practices in other countries of the world reinforces the belief that there is no single age at which all children should be taught to read. Contrary to the American practice of beginning reading instruction at age six, many other countries begin formal instruction at age five or earlier. Two examples of this initial instruction are the United Kingdom, where children generally begin reading at five years of age and, in some programs, at age four, and Israel, where formal instruction in reading often begins at age four. Readiness is different for every child.

## Early Childhood Education Programs with Reading Instruction

Many myths surround the issue of how worthwhile early reading is for a young child. Much research has been conducted to evaluate the effect of reading instruction at a young age. In order to determine whether early reading is a help or a hindrance to the young child, let us review several of these research studies and reports on early reading programs.

Perhaps the most prominent study of the phenomenon of early reading was conducted for six years by Durkin in Oakland, California and New York City in 1966. In her results, she reported that some children read before they entered first grade and before they received formal reading instruction. She concluded that early reading was not necessarily a function of socioeconomic status, ethnicity, or intelligence. Furthermore, she found that early readers achieved higher reading scores than their nonearly reading counterparts during their entire elementary school careers.

However, in her latest research, reported in "A Six-Year Study of Children Who Were Taught to Read in School at the Age of 4" (*Reading Research Quarterly*, vol. 10, 1974–75), Durkin did not reach the same conclusion. In this study, conducted in Illinois, she found that early readers who had been trained in a special two-year preschool language arts/reading program scored significantly higher than their nonearly reading classmates on standardized reading tests in grades one and two, but the differences between the two groups were not statistically significant in grades three and four. "One very likely explanation for the reversal," she maintains, "is that the characteristics of a family that fostered preschool reading ability would continue to foster achievement, with or without an instructional program in school."

Several other researchers in the last few years have investigated the effects of early reading, but few have investigated its causes. Despite the fact that some educators and researchers (Durkin, 1966, 1970, 1974), have acknowledged the existence of early reading, there has been little systematic research into these important questions: What factors in the home contribute to the success of early reading? Is there an environment that is conducive to early reading? What is the role of the parent-child relationship in early reading?

These questions remain seriously underinvestigated, but folk wisdom abounds. Some parents and some educators have favorite anecdotes about young children who have learned to read "on their own." Durkin (1966, 1972) asserts that young children do not learn to read by themselves. Through interviewing, she discovered that parents of early readers had spent a great deal of time conversing with their young children, that it was characteristic of early readers to ask many questions, and that parents had taken time to answer these questions. Among her early readers, Durkin found "What is that word?" to be a very common question.

*Figure 63.* Children simply do not learn to read spontaneously. A great deal of time is spent preparing children for reading. (Photo by Linda Lungren)

Children simply do not learn to read spontaneously. At the risk of belaboring the obvious, it is important to once again stress that parents of successful early readers spend a great deal of time preparing their children for reading. The "code" has to be "broken" for a child before he or she can start to read on his or her own.

Despite research problems in design and analysis, investigation into early reading has produced the expected results: early reading generally produces successful readers. McKee, Brzienski, and Harrison (1966) found that kindergarteners who were taught to read in the Denver public schools were able to sustain their early achievement "when the reading program in subsequent years capitalized upon their early starts."

Shapiro and Willford (1969) reported that children who were taught the Initial Teaching Alphabet (ITA) approach to reading in kindergarten performed better at the end of the second grade than did children who were not taught to read until the first grade, using the same approach. Gray and Klaus (1970) found excellent results at the end of the first grade for high-risk children who had participated in intervention programs; however, they found no continued growth after first grade. Unfortunately, this study did not take into account the instruction that each child had received after first grade.

King and Freisen (1972) found that early readers who were selected in kindergarten outperformed nonearly readers at the end of first grade. However, intelligence was not taken into consideration; the mean intelligence score was eleven points higher for early readers than for nonearly readers (115 to 104).

Beck (1973) found that early readers had significantly higher intelligence scores than nonearly readers. Adjusting for intelligence, she found that children who started to read in kindergarten outperformed their nonearly reading classmates in grades one through five. The selection process for early readers in this study was unique: teachers selected them as being "ready" to read. She suggests that her results should be interpreted cautiously because of her unusually small sample, which dwindled to only eight early readers by fifth grade.

Although there are some flaws in the design and analysis of these studies, it can be concluded that early readers score higher than their nonearly reading counterparts in many cases. However, objections to early reading still seem to occur in many parts of the country. It might be useful to list traditional objections and to analyze their validity in light of current research findings.

### Criticisms of Early Reading

1. Criticism: Early reading hurts young children's vision.

   Rebuttal: There is little evidence to support this claim. In fact, it may be argued that a child's vision is ready for reading because many children are writing by four or five years of age.

2. Criticism: No parents can teach reading.

   Rebuttal: Parents may not have formal reading courses, but there are many activities they can do with their children at home.

3. Criticism: Children who learn to read early will not like school; they will be bored.

   Rebuttal: Children will be bored with reading only if they have to begin again. However, with personalized programs that give individual attention to each child, there seems no logical or inherent reason for boredom.

4. Criticism: Young children should play, not work.

   Rebuttal: Reading can be a playful, enjoyable activity for young children. If children have as much reading activity as they seem to want, then the concern about introducing academics too early seems unwarranted.

## Early Intervention

### *Need for Early Intervention*

The wise remark, "Get them while they're young" seems entirely appropriate in this context. Early programs are often quite successful. In a time when medicine is moving out of the area of remedial care into prevention of disease, the field of education would do well to take note. There is a greater need for early programs of instruction in reading and other areas now than ever before in the history of education. High-risk, potentially handicapped children need to be identified when they are young so that appropriate measures can be taken to deal with their problems before they fall far behind their peers.

## Why Intervene Early in a Child's Life?

Researchers who favor early intervention often assert that the causes of reading failure can be found in germinal stages in a child's first few years of life (Hallgren, 1950; DeHirsch, et al., 1966; Ingram, 1970; Owens, et al., 1968; Silver, 1971).

Based on these and other research findings, educators have supported a concept of timely intervention, arguing that very young children are often more sensitive and receptive to remediation than older children. Caldwell (1969) stated, "There is some evidence to suggest that the child may be more sensitive to environmental stimulation (for example, remedial intervention) during that period in which maturation of the brain is evolving and when behavior is less differentiated" (p 220).

In the last few years, a broader knowledge base regarding the general development of language ability in children has also developed. The research indicates that basic language ability develops between birth and the age of five or six (Menyuk, 1963). Such evidence suggests that amelioration of reading difficulties in elementary school children might be best accomplished through intervention during the preschool years.

J. McV. Hunt (1961) in *Intelligence and Experience* presented a well-developed rationale for early intervention programs. During the past decade programs such as Head Start have been developed as a result of Hunt's theories of cognitive development in young children. Based on continuous evaluation data, these early intervention programs have been modified in an attempt to further their effectiveness. Program modifications have included 1) starting intervention earlier and incorporating parent involvement as an integral part of the intervention (Parent and Child Centers; Home Start); 2) extending the intervention support into the primary grades (Follow Through); 3) coordinating services to children and their families over an extended period of time

(Child and Family Resource Centers); and 4) supporting the development of innovative educational programs (Planned Variation).

## The Acquisition of Reading

There are many researchers who support the belief that there is a critical period for the *beginning* of reading instruction. The value of this theory lies in the belief that reading instruction should begin at an early age; it is based on the belief that initial reading instruction should take place between four and six years of age. This time span has been pinpointed as the critical period because the child has acquired most of the rules of English syntax but has not advanced to the "concrete operations" stage, wherein the repetitive drills involved in reading may be interruptive. Kohlberg (1968) has stated:

> Learning the mechanics of reading and writing need not depend heavily upon the development of new levels of cognitive structure (categories of relation), although it may depend on the development of perceptual structure . . . Compared with cognitive-structural transformations required for development of spoken language at age two or five, the cognitive-structural requirements in tying together spoken and written signs seems modest . . . Because reading and writing (especially reading) are relatively low-level sensorimotor skills, there is nothing in the cognitive structure of the reading task which involves any high challenge to the older child. In contrast, the identification of letters and words . . . may be challenging fun for younger children. (pp. 103–108)

Teachers who have experienced failure in instructing a particular four, five, or six-year old to read may disagree with Kohlberg's conclusions. However, Kohlberg's other point is clear: learning to speak is, in principle, a less difficult task than translating the spoken form to a written form of language. Almost all children learn to speak, but many children experience great difficulty when trying to read. The fact that reading has been traditionally taught when the child is six to eight years old may explain some of this difficulty. The problem may be that there is a mismatch between the child's cognitive development and beginning reading instruction. Therefore, we agree with those who propose beginning reading instruction at an earlier age, particularly if researchers discover there is a gap in cognitive development at the age of four to five.

Many researchers already have reported a major change in cognitive behavior at five or six, the age at which American children enter school. White (1975) states, "four contemporary points of view concerning cognitive development have held the five to seven period to be important, each on its own evidence and in its own terms" (p. 210).

Among the psychologists whose efforts related directly to this research is Eleanor Gibson. Her work on the nature of visual form perception is summarized in Gibson and Levin's *Psychology of Reading* (1975). By using novel letter-like forms, Gibson's research has provided insights into the development of perceptual processes. Gibson, et al. (1962) showed that letter-like forms remained perceptually invariant under specific transformations (for example, a change in perspective) but not under other transformations (rotation or reversal). There were fairly dramatic changes in the degree of perceptual invariance around the ages of four to five; four-year-olds accepted rotations and reversals as equivalent to a standard about half of the time; at five years of age, these confusions occurred only about one fifth of the time. The results of this research indicate that young children are able to abstract distinguishing features and separate them from the context of a visual perceptual task.

Between the ages of five and seven, factors such as the child's level of intellectual functioning and/or language improved organizational abilities, and changes in attention (duration and fixation) signal another major change in skill performance. This would seem to indicate again that earlier years are the optimal ones for beginning reading instruction, the time before the child makes adjustments that affect his or her interest in the beginning reading process. Here, the best proposal seems to come from Gates (1937) and Calfee and Hoover (1973) when they suggest that instruction should match the needs of the child.

## What Is the Best Way to Teach Young Children to Read?

The second question raised at the beginning of this chapter, "What is the best way to teach young children to read?", also demands a complicated answer. The best place to begin in helping you to find your own answer is with an overview of the approaches and methods that have been used in the teaching of reading in the United States.

## Approaches and Methods of Teaching Reading

### Historical Overview

The teaching of reading during the colonial period in the United States was essentially a system that used an alphabetic spelling system as its base. There was instruction in single-letter recognition, followed by combined letter-sound correspondences ( ab, ac), parts of words such as tab, and finally the whole word table). The reading process included intensive instruction in pitch, stress, enunciation, gesticulation, memorization, and recitation; it was almost a totally oral process. Only a limited number of persons were actually taught to read, and reading instruction was an extremely simplified process that was directed toward a single purpose, the reading of prayer books and religious books. The *Hornbook* and the *New England Primers* were among the earliest readers in the United States; most children learned their alphabet from these books.

The *whole-word* method of teaching reading was introduced by Horace Mann in the early 1800s. Not only did he stress memorizing entire words before analyzing letters and letter patterns, but he stressed silent reading and emphasized reading comprehension. At about this time, the *McGuffey Eclectic Reader*, which emphasized a controlled repetition of words, was introduced.

*Figure 64.* Approaches and Methods of Teaching Reading. (Photo by Linda Lungren)

Stories, parables, moral lessons, and patriotic selections were used as instructional devices in an attempt to develop "good" citizens. Although these stories were often uninteresting, the *McGuffey Readers* were a definite improvement over the existing texts of the time. They used an organizational scheme in which sentence length and vocabulary were controlled to match students' developmental levels. A selection from the primer reader of the *McGuffey Eclectic Readers* (1881, 1879) is presented on page 282).

During the latter half of the nineteenth century, attempts were made to organize reading instruction into meaningful sequential steps. The following timeline illustrates the history of reading instruction in the United States.

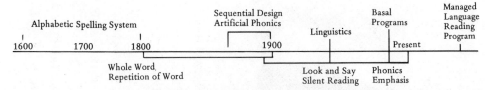

Essentially, the history of reading instruction in the United States is a record of shifts in emphasis from a sequential approach to the teaching of reading to a spontaneous approach to the teaching of reading or vice versa. The primary strengths and weaknesses of each approach are:

|  | Sequential Reading Approach | Spontaneous Reading Approach |
|---|---|---|
| Strength: | Prepare materials that are logically ordered | Personalized curriculum emphasizing the integration of the language arts |
| Weakness: | Lack of personalization | Lack of prepared materials |

## LESSON XXII.

grāss        thеy        cŏme        ŏff        bärn

shāde        hŏt

cows̱        our

ẹ        ou

The day is hot.
The cows are in the shade of the big tree.
They feed on the new grass.
Our cows do not run off.
At night they come to the barn.

## LESSON XXI.

whạt        nīght

owl          dāy

ăn           bŭt

wĕll         bĭḡ

eȳe̱s̱        bĕst

ạ        ow        wh

What bird is this?
It is an owl.
What big eyes it has!
Yes, but it can not see well by day.
The owl can see best at night.
Nat Pond has a pet owl.

In recent years, however, educators have been attempting to maximize reading instruction by combining the best of both approaches into a managed language/reading method.

In the next few pages you will be introduced to several different methods (each method exemplifies one approach emphasis) and to the managed language/reading method.

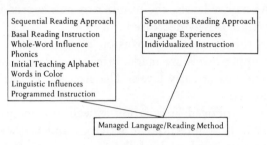

Sequential Reading Approach

Basal Reading Instruction
Whole-Word Influence
Phonics
Initial Teaching Alphabet
Words in Color
Linguistic Influences
Programmed Instruction

Spontaneous Reading Approach

Language Experiences
Individualized Instruction

Managed Language/Reading Method

## Sequential Reading Approach

The philosophy that spawned the sequential approach to reading was based upon certain beliefs about the ways in which children acquire knowledge. Forerunners of this approach were the Puritans who made the first attempts to logically organize printed material to meet their students' capabilities. This approach is consistent with Bruner's theory that "knowledge is a model we construct to give meanings and structure to regularities of experience" and Piaget's theory "intelligence is sequentially related to age". The sequential reading approach today means charting out a continuum of skills that the child needs to master in order to read accurately, and then determining the skills that should logically precede other skills. This theory assumes that the child is capable of some intellectual functions before he is capable of other functions. In this theory lies the sequential reading approach's sense of structure and logical organization. Basal readers and programmed materials that emphasize a sequential reading approach have been designed upon this premise.

The basal method fits into the sequential reading approach category because it assumes that learning to read necessitates acquiring major skills (which can each be broken down into many subskills). Furthermore, because these skills vary in complexity, they should be introduced to the reader in a logical, prescribed order. These skills and subskills need to be integrated into the instructional program in such a way that the reader can begin to interrelate them. When this succeeds, reading becomes a whole, meaningful process.

Traditionally, basals have been developed for use in the elementary grades. Most basal programs include texts with reading levels that range from the readiness level through the sixth grade, although there are some basal systems that include the junior high grades and above. For schools that favor a non-graded approach, basals exist to fit whatever system the school uses to designate different learning levels. The materials of a basal program commonly include supplemental materials such as workbooks, worksheets, films and filmstrips, records, and supplementary readers as well as the texts for each grade level. Also provided with each text in the basal program is a teacher's manual. This manual consists of the program's basic philosophy, a series of lesson plans for the basal's stories, unit tests, lists of the supplementary materials included, and other related information.

A salient feature of such a program is its method of introducing new words. Basal programs present a carefully controlled vocabulary. At the early stages, small numbers of words are introduced, and they are repeated over and over for reinforcement. At higher levels, the number of new words is slowly increased, and the repetitions are slowly decreased.

In addition to the controlled expansion of vocabulary, other adjustments from primary to upper levels are made. Print size is larger and spacing between letters is more generous at early levels. The size and frequency of illustrations are likewise controlled.

New words are introduced in isolation as well as in context. Silent and oral reading follow as well as interpretive activities and further skill development such as word recognition and study skills.

For all this careful sequencing, there are many people who believe that basals are far from ideal. Their criticisms include such issues as boring content, speech patterns that do not match the children's lack of creativity, inflexible groupings, lack of provision for individual learning styles, sex, stereotyping, and others.

It should be noted that there are many different basal programs available, all with different emphasis, and that more recent basal series have attempted to accommodate the language diversity found in classrooms. Teachers should also remember that a basal program is just what its name suggests: the base of a reading program. A creative teacher can and should personalize her program to fit her students' needs.

### Whole-Word Influence

The whole-word approach is one method of instruction that appears in most basal readers. Because many common English words are phonetically irregular, it is sometimes more productive to teach the children to identify these words immediatly by sight rather than by letter-sound analysis. For this reason, the approach is sometimes referred to as the "look-and-say" method. This approach is also helpful in teaching homographs and homophones. Homographs are two words that look alike but have different meanings and pronunciations, such as:

> Read me a story, please.
>            and
> Yesterday I read a new story.

Homophones are two words that sound alike but are spelled differently and have different meanings, such as:

> What a strange tale!
> Look at that cat's tail.

The whole-word approach is heavily dependent upon a child's visual discrimination ability, his ability to recognize differences between letters and words. The child is exposed to the word several times, and it becomes part of his basic sight vocabulary.

## *The Influence of Phonics*

By the late 1800s, when educators began to see that letter-sound relationships could help in identifying unfamiliar words, the phonics influence in reading instruction became popular. Phonics instruction is still considered an important part of many reading programs, but it cannot be used as the sole method of instruction. There are many inconsistencies in words, and many English words are borrowed from other languages and do not follow English rules.

## *Initial Teaching Alphabet*

Over the years people have attempted to develop programs that would eliminate inconsistencies. One of these is the Initial Teaching Alphabet (ITA), an augmented alphabet. Because the English alphabet has only twenty-six letters to represent forty-four sounds, ITA attempts to establish a one-to-one correspondence of sounds and letters so that each letter the student looks at stands for one sound and one sound only.

ITA need not be used in one specific method of reading instruction but can be integrated into a number of different programs. Criticisms of this approach are that children who learn it sometimes have difficulty making the transition to reading traditional orthography and many children have problems learning to spell.

The ITA is presented below:

| æ | b | c | d | ɛɛ |
|---|---|---|---|---|
| face | bed | cat | dog | key |

| f | g | h | ɩe | j | k |
|---|---|---|---|---|---|
| feet | leg | hat | fly | jug | key |

| l | m | n | œ | p | ɼ |
|---|---|---|---|---|---|
| letter | man | nest | over | pen | girl |

| r | s | t | ʋe | v | w |
|---|---|---|---|---|---|
| red | spoon | tree | use | voice | window |

| y | z | ƨ | wh | ʤ |
|---|---|---|---|---|
| yes | zebra | daisy | when | chair |

| ʧh | ᚦh | ʃh | ʒ | ŋ |
|---|---|---|---|---|
| three | the | shop | television | ring |

| ɑ | au | a | e | i | o |
|---|---|---|---|---|---|
| father | ball | cap | egg | milk | box |

| u | ω | ⍵ | ɑu | ɑi |
|---|---|---|---|---|
| up | book | spoon | out | oil |

### Words in Color

Words in color is a second method believed to help alleviate the confusion of phonic analysis. In this method, traditional letter configurations remain, and the special feature is the use of colors to represent English speech sounds. A single letter or combination of letters representing one English speech sound is presented on a chart with a corresponding color. For example, long $\bar{a}$ sounds are coded a shade of green, long $\bar{e}$ sound blue. Color codes are presented for thirty-nine sounds.

As with the Initial Teaching Alphabet, children can become dependent upon these learning aids, and their early reading selections may be limited. A second criticism is that there is always the potential of visual discrimination difficulties in some similar color hues.

### Linguistic Influences

This approach to basal reading instruction is fairly new. Because linguistics is the scientific study of language, a linguistic-based reading program emphasizes the following: investigation of the sounds used in language, the words that result from combinations of sounds, the meanings attached to these sounds, and the structuring of words with meaningful units.

Some series that feature a linguistic base are Blomfield-Barnhart's *Let's Read*, *Merrill Linguistic Readers*, and the *Palo Alto Linguistic Program*. A typical example of the early levels of these programs is the following:

> I see Tam, the ram.
> I see Tat, the ram.
> I see Tam and Tat, the rams.

The idea is that the children master specific consonant and vowel combinations and then expand their knowledge by forming as many words from these regular combinations as possible.

There is some disagreement over the use of pictures in linguistic-based materials. Some authors believe that they provide too much of the wrong kind of decoding assistance.

One important criticism directed at linguistic-based series, as well as at basal readers in general, is that the sentence patterns are unnatural and the content boring. This criticism is acknowledged to be true at lower levels, but usually disappears at the more advanced levels where wider vocabulary knowledge allows for more freedom in writing texts.

A positive aspect of this approach is its flexibility. Linguistic programs have been used in regular basal series, paperback series, and programmed formats. The following example is taken from the *Palo Alto Reading Program*:

| **Ham for Nat** | **Ham for Dan** |
|---|---|
| Dad had a tin can. | A bit of ham is in a tin can. |
| The can had bits of ham in it. | It's for Dan. |
| The ham is for Nat. | |
| Dad had to fit the bits of ham | Dan looks into the can. |
| into Nat's tin pan. | Rags looks at Dan. |
| | He sits and wags for the ham. |
| Nat ran to look. | |
| He had a bit of ham. | Ham fat is bad for Rags. |
| | The ham in the can is Dan's. |

From the *Palo Alto Reading Program: Sequential Steps in Reading*, Book 1 by Theodore E. Glim. Copyrighted © 1968 by Harcourt Brace Jovanovich, Inc. Reprinted by permission of the publisher.

## *Programmed Instruction*

Programmed instruction is a second type of sequential reading approach. This method emphasizes the organization of a block of information for logical, sequential learning. A specific segment of information to be mastered is divided into small, manageable units, to be approached in one of two ways, linear or branched.

In a branched arrangement, the learner is allowed to bypass certain units that may repeat something he already knows. With a linear arrangement, however, each student must pass through each unit. Thus, the individualization of this type of arrangement is simply speed of learning.

A definite asset of programmed instruction is its instant feedback. The learner knows immediately whether his answer is correct. If it is not, he is corrected before he is allowed to move on. Programmed instruction may take the form of a series of workbooks, or it may be computer-based, but the sequential organization and the immediate feedback are always present.

The following is an example of a child using programmed instruction.*

Eric Michaels entered his nongraded school and took his seat at a learning carrel. He keypunched his name onto the empty computer spaces.

Good morning—The punching of his name alerted the computer to the fact that Eric was ready to begin study of the program his teachers had earlier prepared for him.

As the first frame appeared, . . .

---

1. Programmed instruction is a learning experience in which a program replaces a tutor. The student is led through the program by a sequence of learning sets which are structured to teach the student a desired skill.

   _____ _____ is a learning experience that replaces a tutor.

---

Eric remembered that earlier in the week Ms. Roser, one of his instructors, had mentioned that Eric was interested in computers and he might enjoy learning about programmed instruction. Eric keypunched the words <u>programmed instruction</u> and smiled as frame two appeared.

---

2. Good work, please continue.
   The program, which may be presented to the student in the form of a teaching machine or a programmed textbook, consists of statements, facts, and questions to which a student is asked to respond. The response may be made by filling in short answers or selecting an answer from multiple choices. Correct program responses are made available for the student to compare with his own. Frame one of this program asked you to respond by
   
   A. filling in a short answer.
   B. selecting from multiple choices.
   _____ C. leaving the space blank.

---

Eric hesitated and then punched A. and B.  Frame three appeared

---

3. Very good thinking, please continue.
   In programmed instruction, large subject areas are divided into smaller thought sequences called frames. Material presented in one frame is related to material presented in preceding frames. Material contained in a frame is brief, with generally one question being asked about the material. In many programs, the ability of the student to answer the questions is a prerequisite for proceeding to the next frame. The above discussion of a programmed instruction frame is in itself a _____ .

---

While very interesting to Eric, this was somewhat difficult. He read the frame again and keypunched the word <u>frame</u>.  Immediately frame four appeared.

*From Lapp, D., et al. *Teaching and Learning: Philosophical, Psychological, Curricular Applications.* New York: Macmillan, 1975, pp. 95-101.

## Spontaneous Reading Approach

Like the sequential reading approach, the spontaneous reading approach is sequentially organized according to levels of cognitive development. A major difference between the two, however, is that the spontaneous reading approach is highly dependent upon student interest. These personalized methods usually take the form of either the language experience approach or individualized instruction.

### Language Experience

The language experience approach, explained and illustrated in previous chapters, attempts to integrate listening, reading, and writing skills development with the already existing language of the child. It is designed to build upon the language skills that a child already possesses. The aim of this approach can be seen in Allen's (1961) often quoted statement:

What I can think about, I can talk about.

What I say I can write.

What I write I can read.

I can read what I write and what other people write for me to read.

The basic procedure is that instead of learning to read from ready-made materials, the children tell their own story as the teacher records and repeats it. The story and its individual words and sentences are reread a number of times, and skill development exercises are derived from the words in the story.

*Figure 65.* The language experience approach attempts to integrate listening, reading, and writing skills development with the already existing language of the child. The teacher should try to involve everyday experiences in language instruction. (Photo by Linda Lungren)

### Individualized Instruction

The individualized instruction method has as its aim the substitution of student-selected material for basals, which cannot provide for the wide interest range in a class. Each student sets his own pace and sequence for reading instruction. Simply outlined, the program is set up in the following manner:

> The teacher must know the reading abilities of her students and have access to a wide variety of books to accommodate each student's interests and instructional levels. Additional materials such as workbooks and exercise packets must also be available to supplement the books and provide skill-building activities.
>
> Conferences are scheduled with a few students each day, and blocks of time are set aside for special assistance. Careful record-keeping is vital in the absence of a skills sequence. A potential problem, especially at the start, is classroom management. Some advantages, however, are the absence of comparisons, the higher interest levels resulting from self-selection and the self-pacing aspects of this type of instruction.

## Managed Language/Reading Method

The managed language/reading method attempts to combine the best features of the sequential and spontaneous approaches. Individualization is emphasized, but content is logically, sequentially organized. It is like the language experience method because stories in these new systems are designed to reflect the language of real children in real-life situations.

Because of the emphasis on individualization, these new systems include easy-to-manage record-keeping systems and provide for diagnosis, prescription, and evaluation for each child. Some publishers that feature this combined system are Ginn, Macmillan, Economy, and Laidlaw. The following description of a management system has been taken from Ginn's *Reading 720*.

> The management system for an instructional program is neither the content of that program nor the teaching method by which content is presented to pupils. Rather, it represents a kind of framework or pattern by means of which content and teaching methods can be organized to assure that some specific outcomes occur. Usually, the desired effects of managing instruction are as follows: (1) that pupils are systematically taught at least a core set of specified educational objectives, with the exception of those pupils who have previously become proficient in certain of these objectives, (2) that evidence is generated to show whether pupils learn these objectives at a level of proficiency prespecified as desirable, (3) that provision is made for systematic reinstruction of pupils on any of the objectives for which they have failed to demonstrate proficiency, and (4) that teaching pupils to acceptable proficiency on this set of core objectives is accomplished in the minimum reasonable time.
>
> When the core strands of Reading 720 are taught in the management mode, the foregoing outcomes can be realized. Using a management system, the teacher may select from the rich pool of hundreds of objectives, those specific ones that represent the core skills of Reading 720, drawn from the comprehension, vocabulary, and decoding strands. The teacher may then build lesson plans emphasizing, or even restricted to, these core objectives and teach those children known to need them. Additional Reading 720 components allow the teacher to evaluate with precision the proficiency of pupils on the core objectives. Other Reading 720 resources can then be used to reteach missed objectives

to just those pupils who need reinstruction. Because managed instruction focuses so tightly on core essentials and attempts to limit instruction within the core strands to that demonstrably required, whether initial or reteaching, it moves pupils with maximum efficiency toward attainment of the desired outcomes.

Implementing a management system in teaching Reading 720 aids the teacher in the following ways:

in helping to select what pupils are to learn

in systematic planning for and provision of supplementary instruction

in individualizing instruction according to pupil needs

in establishing an instructional pace that is efficient yet accomplishes desired goals

The components of a successfully managed language/reading system are integrated into the existing basal program. The following example and materials, taken from Ginn's *Reading 720*, emphasize such integration.

## COMPONENTS OF READING 720
## MANAGEMENT SYSTEM

A management system is integrated or built into Reading 720. All the directions needed for managing core skills instruction are found in this Teacher's Edition. Instructions will be found placed sequentially, as needed, throughout the various sections of the lesson plans and in the manuals accompanying the various components that are essential to managing instruction in Reading 720. All such manuals are supplied with these components when purchased separately, and are also reproduced in this section of the Teacher's Edition.

The following are necessary for managing the instruction of the core skills. These items are also available as separate components.

### Activities in Part 4 of the lesson plan

Activities in Part 4 of each plan are designed to introduce and give practice reinforcement of objectives taught in unit.

### Unit Criterion Exercises

The Unit Criterion Exercises may be used to assess pupil proficiency on the specified core skills of a unit. Pupils scoring at or above Suggested Criterion Score (SCS) are assumed to have attained acceptable proficiency on the tested objective. The rationale for establishing the SCS is described in the Criterion Exercise manual.

### Criterion Exercise Record Sheets (CERS)

The CERS are forms for recording and organizing groups of pupils' Unit Criterion Exercise scores and referencing them to specific supplemental instruction or enrichment resources. The CERS for each unit are found on pages 265–267.
unit are found on pages 265–267.

### Booster Activities

Paper-and-pencil instructional activities are designed to give practice or reinforcement to pupils scoring below Suggested Criterion Score on any of the objectives tested in a Unit Criterion Exercise. All the Booster Activities for Level 5 are found on page 271–280 and the manual of directions for their use is on pages 268–270. Instructions for selecting the proper Booster Activity are found in the manual. It is important to note that Booster Activities "boost" marginally performing pupils to an acceptable level. When pupils score *very* low on an objective, especially if they get none of the items right, they need reteaching. After reteaching has been accomplished, the Booster or the other practice activities may be given.

Reading Achievement Card

The Reading Achievement Card is a chart for recording and organizing all of an individual pupil's criterion exercise scores for one level. This component is reproduced in this Teacher's Edition. It is also found on the last two pages of each Unit Criterion Exercise booklet, and, in addition, is available separately printed on tag board.

## Reading 720
## Reading Achievement Card
## Level 2

Pupil's Name_____

School_____

_____

**Key:** Total = Number of Items; SCS = Suggested Criterion Score; PS = Pupil's Score

**Directions:** Record in the appropriate box the pupil's score on each part of the Criterion Exercise. At the end of a level, sign and date the card.

### Unit 1
DECODING
initial consonants
/b/b, /l/l, /r/r, /h/h

| Total | SCS | PS |
|-------|-----|-----|
| 12 | 10 | |

Notes:_____
_____
_____

VOCABULARY
Word Recognition

| Total | SCS | PS |
|-------|-----|-----|
| 8 | 6 | |

_____
_____

### Unit 2
DECODING
initial consonant / ĭ /j

| Total | SCS | PS |
|-------|-----|-----|
| 4 | 3 | |

Notes:_____
_____
_____

VOCABULARY
Word Recognition

| Total | SCS | PS |
|-------|-----|-----|
| 10 | 8 | |

_____
_____

### Unit 3
DECODING
initial consonant /k/c

| Total | SCS | PS |
|-------|-----|-----|
| 4 | 3 | |

Notes:_____
_____
_____

VOCABULARY
Word Recognition

| Total | SCS | PS |
|-------|-----|-----|
| 12 | 10 | |

_____
_____

### Unit 4
DECODING
initial consonants
/f/f, /y/y, /n/n

| Total | SCS | PS |
|-------|-----|-----|
| 9 | 7 | |

Notes:_____
_____
_____

VOCABULARY
Word Recognition

| Total | SCS | PS |
|-------|-----|-----|
| 10 | 8 | |

_____
_____

Several other reading 720 components are optionally usable with management mode instruction and, except for the Informal Reading Inventory, do not appear in this Teacher's Edition. Each has its own manual or other directions describing its use. These components include the following:

### Initial Placement Test

The Initial Placement Test aids in determining the level in which to start pupils new to Reading 720.

### Informal Reading Inventory

The Informal Reading Inventory helps in making initial individual placement decisions or in post-instruction diagnosis as a supplement to the Unit Criterion Exercises.

### Unit Decoding Pretests

The Pretests are an aid in determining which decoding skills pupils already know before they start a unit.

### Level Mastery Tests

Level Mastery Tests may be used for surveying pupil achievement on an entire level, or for providing a cumulative, final check on pupil proficiency on the level's objectives.

### Reading Progress Card

The Reading Progress Card serves as a device for recording cumulative reading achievement test and other data for all thirteen levels. It is available in file-folder format.

A class work sheet is also available. This is a smaller sample of the sheet:

## CLASS WORK SHEET

Teacher's Name
School                                                                    Date
City                                                                      Grade

| PUPIL'S NAME | IPT Level | Initial Assigned Levels | Assigned Level After 2 Weeks | COMMENTS |
|---|---|---|---|---|
| 1. | | | | |
| 2. | | | | |
| 3. | | | | |
| 4. | | | | |
| 5. | | | | |
| 6. | | | | |
| 7. | | | | |
| 8. | | | | |
| 9. | | | | |
| 10. | | | | |
| 11. | | | | |
| 12. | | | | |
| 13. | | | | |
| 14. | | | | |
| 15. | | | | |
| 16. | | | | |
| 17. | | | | |
| 18. | | | | |
| 19. | | | | |
| 20. | | | | |

## What Method You Should Use

Although no method is effective for every child, the managed language/
reading method is a good way to begin. Ultimately you will have to decide
what works best for you and for each of your students. It will be a constant
challenge for you, but its rewards will be numerous. You will be performing
society's most noble task: educating its young.

## BIBLIOGRAPHY

Allen, R. Van. *Report of the Reading Study Project,* Monograph L1, San Diego, California:
Department of Education, San Diego County, 1961.

Arthur, C. "A Quantitative Study of the Results of Grouping First Grade Children According to Mental Age." *Journal of Educational Research* (October 1925), 12:173–185.

Ausubel, D. P. "Viewpoints from Related Disciplines: Human Growth and Development."
*Teachers College Record* (February 1959) 60:245–54.

Beck. I. L. *A Longitudinal Study of the Reading Achievement Effects of Formal Reading
Instruction in the Kindergarten: A Summative and Formative Evaluation.* Ph. D. dissertation, University of Pittsburgh, 1973.

Bloom, B. S. *Stability and Change In Human Characteristics.* New York: John Wiley and
Sons, 1964.

Bruner, J. *The Process of Education.* Cambridge, MA: Harvard University Press, 1960.

Caldwell, B. M. "The Usefulness of the Critical Period Hypothesis in the Study of Filistive
Behavior." In Endler, N. D., Boulter, L. R., and Osser, H. (Ed.) *Contemporary Issues in
Developmental Psychology.*

Calfee, R., and K. Hoover. "Policy and Practice in Early Education Research." Paper presented at the California Council for Educational Research, November 1973, Los Angeles,
California.

DeHirsch, K., J. J. Jansky, and W. S. Langford. *Predicting Reading Failure.* New York:
Harper & Row, Publishers, 1966.

Dickson, V. E. *Mental Tests and the Classroom Teacher.* New York: World Book Co., 1923.

Durkin, D. *Children Who Read Early: Two Longitudinal Studies.* New York: Bureau of
Publications, Teachers College Press, Columbia University, 1966.

Durkin, D. "A Language Arts Program for Pre-First Grade Children: Two-Year Achievement
Report." *Reading Research Quarterly,* (Summer 1970), 5:534–565.

Durkin, D. Teaching Them to Read. Boston: Allyn & Bacon, Inc., 1974.

Durkin, D. *Teaching Young Children to Read.* Boston: Allyn & Bacon, Inc., 1972.

Durkin, D. "A Six-Year Study of Children Who Were Taught to Read in School at the Age
of Four." *Reading Research Quarterly,* vol 10, 1974–75.

Durkin, D. "A Fifteen-Year Report on the Achievement of Early Readers," *Elementary
School Journal* 65 (1964): 76–80.

Educational Policies Commission. *Universal Opportunity for Early Childhood Education.* Washington, D.C.: National Education Association, 1966.

Gates, A. I. "The Necessary Mental Age for Beginning Reading." *Elementary School Journal,* (1937), 37:497–508.

Gates, A. "The Role of Personality Maladjustment in Reading Disability." In Matchez, G. (Ed.) *Reading Problems.* New York: Basic Books, Inc., Publishers, 1968.

Gates, A. and G. L. Bond. "Reading Readiness: A Study of Factors Determining Success and Failure in Beginning Reading." *Teachers College Record,* (May 1936), 37:679–85.

Gesell, A. L. *The Mental Growth of the Preschool Child.* New York: The Macmillan Co., 1928.

Gibson, E., and H. Levin. *Psychology of Reading.* Cambridge, Massachusetts: MIT Press, 1975.

Gibson, E. J., and J. J. Gibson, A. D. Pick, and H. A. Osser. "A Developmental Study of the Discrimination of Letter-Like Forms." *Journal of Comparative and Physiological Psychology,* (1962), 55:897–906.

Gray, W. S., and R. Klaus. "The Early Training Project: A Seventh-Year Report." *Child Development* (December 1970), 41:900–24.

Gray, Wm. S. "Reading," *Child Development and the Curriculum.* Chapter IX. Thirty-eighth Yearbook of the National Society for the Study of Education, Part I. Bloomington, Illinois: Public School Publishing Company, 1939.

Hallgren, B. "Specific Dyslexia: A Clinical and Genetic Study." *Acta Psychiatrica et Neurologis* (1950), 65:1–287.

Hall, G. S. *The Psychology of Adolescence.* New York: D. Appleton and Co., 1904.

Holmes, M. C. "Investigation of Reading Readiness of First Grade Entrants." *Childhood Education* (January 1927), 3:215–21.

Huey, E. B. *The Psychology and Pedagogy of Reading.* New York: Macmillan Publishing Co., Inc., 1908.

Hunt, J. M. *Intelligence and Experience.* New York: The Ronald Press Company, 1961.

Ingram, T. T. S. "The Nature of Dyslexia." In Young, F. A. and D. B. Lindsley (Ed.) *Early Experience and Visual Information Processing in Perceptual and Reading Disorders.* Washington, D.C.: National Academy of Sciences, 1970.

King, E. M., and D. T. Friesen. "Children Who Read in Kindergarten." *Alberta Journal of Educational Research* (September 1972), 18:147–61.

Kohlberg, L. "Early Education: A Cognitive-Developmental View." *Child Development* (December 1968), 39:1013–62.

Lapp, D., and J. Flood. *Teaching Reading To Every Child.* New York: Macmillan Publishing Co., Inc., 1978.

Lenneberg, E. H. *Biological Foundations of Language.* New York: John Wiley & Sons, Inc., 1967.

McKee, D., J. Brzinski, and L. Harrison. "The Effectiveness of Teaching Reading in Kindergarten." Cooperative Research Project No. 5-1371. Denver Public Schools and Colorado State Department of Education, 1966.

Menyuk, P. "Syntactic Structures in the Language of Children." *Journal of Child Development* (1963), 34:407–22.

Morphett, M., and C. Washburne. "When Should Children Begin to Read?" *Elementary School Journal* (March 1931), 31:496–503.

Owens, F., P. Adams, and T. Forrest. "Learning Disabilities in Children: Sibling Studies." *Bulletin of the Orton Society* (1968), 18:33–62.

Reed, M. M. *An Investigation of Practices in First Grade Admission and Promotion.* New York: Bureau of Publications, Teachers College Press, Columbia University, 1927.

Shapiro, B., and R. Willford. "ITA. Kindergarten or First Grade?" *Reading Teacher,* (January 1969).

Silver, L. B. "Familial Patterns in Children with Neurologically Based Learning Disabilities." *Journal of Learning Disabilities* !(1971), 4:349–58.

Terman, L. M. *Genetic Studies of Genius.* Vol. I. Stanford, California: Stanford University Press, 1925.

Thorndike, E. L. "Reading as Reasoning: A Study of Mistakes in Paragraph Reading," *Journal of Educational Psychology,* 8, 1917, pp. 323–332.

Thurstone, L. L. *The Victors of Mind.* Chicago: University of Chicago Press, 1935.

Washburne, C. "Ripeness," *Progressive Education.* XIII (February 1936), pp. 125–130.

White, B. *First Three Years.* Englewood Cliffs, N.J.: Prentice-Hall, Inc., 1975.

# 12

# Understanding and Implementing Word Analysis Strategies: Phonics, Sight Words, Structural Analysis, and Contextual Analysis

*Figure 66.* By using a child's own world experiences, he will understand more easily that reading is not a mysterious message-decoding process but merely his spoken language written down. (Photo by Linda Lungren)

**Understanding Word Analysis**

One of the difficulties of teaching young children is the wide range of pre-reading skills that they bring to school with them. Some children may come to school already familiar with the reading process, but there are many who appear to have no prereading skills and no concept of what reading is. These children are sometimes viewed as behind even though their education has barely begun.

There is one prereading skill, however, that nearly all children possess well before beginning school, the skill of oral language. By using a child's own world experiences and spoken language as a starting point, a major stumbling block can be eliminated. The child will understand more easily that reading is not a mysterious message-decoding process, but merely his spoken language written down. Beginning with the child's own speaking vocabulary does away with the question of whether his is understanding the meaning of the words he is reading.

In many areas the language arts have become compartmentalized: reading skills are seen as distinct from writing, speaking, and listening skills, when, in reality, they are all closely related. Although understanding a spoken word in no way assures that a child can read, write, or even vocalize it, the comprehension indicates that some kind of language ability exists.

This listening vocabulary is, in fact, crucial to language development. It is the first vocabulary that a child develops, and by the age of four, he can usually discriminate between most sounds in the English language. Long before he utters his first intelligible word, he has been hearing and differentiating between sounds and associating them with concepts. He has stored up a great deal of information, despite the fact that he cannot express it. This tendency to comprehend more language than one can express, either in speech or writing, is one that continues throughout life. Our listening capacity, then, represents our broadest vocabulary.

The second strongest language skill is the speaking vocabulary. In children, this ability develops soon after the listening vocabulary. Children's speech is based upon what they hear, and by age four, most children display fairly broad listening and speaking vocabularies, as well as considerable understanding of the structure of the English language. Their grammar may not be entirely correct, for example, you might hear, "I goed to the circus," instead of "I went." The marvel of this error is the fact that somehow the child has learned that "ed" endings signify past actions. This is no small accomplishment and exceptions to the rule can be clarified easily.

In sum, what we want to do as teachers is not to teach reading as a completely new language in itself but to show children a new facet of the language they already know: the written symbols. Because reading involves two kinds of perceptual abilities, visual and auditory, this chapter will introduce the process of beginning reading instruction by examining the visual and auditory skills that lead to the ability to read. You will find considerable background information in this chapter as well as many implementation strategies to aid you in teaching beginning reading.

### Visual Perception

By the age of four the normal child is able to perceive visual objects and to discriminate between fine details.

### Shape Discrimination

The ability to discriminate between shapes is considered a helpful forerunner to the more complex task of discriminating between letters.

If you begin by teaching children to name some basic shapes such as the square, rectangle, triangle, and circle, they can then learn to classify articles by shape and note differences in sizes and colors. Extend this activity by examining objects in the classroom and determining their basic shapes. Obvious examples are blackboards, clocks, or windows. In other activities, you may ask children to pick out two matching shapes from a series or to find the shape that is different in a series. These activities can be graduated in difficulty, so that powers of discrimination can become finer.

Examples: find the shapes that match:

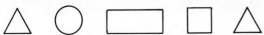

Now find the shape that is different:

Once these activities can be performed with ease, the child is ready for the finer distinctions of discriminating letters. Similar activities may be used in matching and differentiating between letters.

The Gibson study of 1974, (in Gibson and Levin, 1975) which explored how children identify abstract visual symbols, concluded that their approach is to find sets of distinctive features and to group the figures accordingly. There are four distinctive features that the child notices:

1. Straight-Line Segments. E F H I L and T represent letters that consist of this kind of visual symbol.
2. Curved Segments. C and O are examples of curved segmental visual symbols.
3. Symmetries. M W and X are examples of symmetries.
4. Discontinuities. B D J and R are examples of discontinuities.

These are the basic features that children attend to in trying to identify a letter. Problems can arise when the child perceives only part of the letter or only one feature in the letter. For example, one child presented with the letter G might see only the curved segment of the letter and perceive the letter as C, whereas another child would see the straight-line segment as well as the curved

*Figure 67.* Letter identification can often be enhanced by prior work in shape discrimination. (Photo by Linda Lungren)

segment and perceive the letter correctly. The following developmental plan is an example of letter discrimination training that will help to avoid potential problems.

STEP 1: Have children look at single letters.

d    a    c    w

STEP 2: Ask children to tell you whether the letters in the pairs are the same or different.

1. cd       2. db       3. da       4. dd

STEP 3. Now show the children sets of letters and ask them to find two sets that are the same.

ab          ad          ab          bc

STEP 4: Now have the children look at sets of words, and ask them to tell you whether they are the same or different.

| mat    hat |          | rat    tar |          | but    but |

When children can successfully complete these tasks, be sure to explain that one word can be written in four or more different ways. From this point you may want to try the following exercise:

STEP 5: Show children sets of words such as the following. Ask them to tell you if they are the same or different.

Hat                    HAT                    hat                    *hat*

**Letter-Name Knowledge.** Is it really important to know the names of the letters in order to learn to read? Is it a better idea to teach children the letter sounds first and then the letter names? What is the best way to teach letter names?

These are some of the questions arising today from teachers as well as researchers in education. Although many people in education consider mastery of letter names to be a sign that a child is ready to learn to read, there are also those who contend that teaching letter names apart from the letter sounds makes little difference in the child's ability to read (Jenkins, Bausel, and Jenkins, 1972; Silberberg, Silberberg, and Iverson, 1972). Even if it is true that knowing letter names does not necessarily help, certainly it cannot hurt, as long as the training does not induce frustration. There are a number of ways to teach letter names that make the learning fun and colorful. You might want to try various kinds of board games or materials that enable the student to handle the specific letters, such as felt letters on a felt board, sandpaper letters, or magnetic letters on a magnetic board.

### Auditory Perception

Certain sounds in the English language are more difficult to pronounce than others, and some children are unable to produce these sounds before the third grade. This does not mean that these children do not perceive the sounds correctly; by the age of four most children can perceive almost all the sounds in their environment.

Asking a child to discriminate between letter sounds may prove a frustrating experience for student and teacher if the child has not first developed his auditory perception skills with easier sounds. A good way to begin is to have a child identify rhyming words or matching beginning and ending sounds in words. Gaining confidence in exercises such as these will make the task of discriminating between letter sounds seem easier.

### Auditory Discrimination

Given minimal pairs of sounds, young children can usually tell the differences between them. Try rhyming phonograms, such as *rat, sat; man, fan,* and so on. Then try words with different medial vowels, such as *pin* and *pen,* or *but* and *bit.* They should also be able to match sounds. For instance, *bat* begins with a *b* sound. Which of these words begins with the same sound?

    hat                  wet                  back                  pat

Because the child already has a substantial understanding of the English language, including phonology, syntax, and vocabulary, we are not really start-

*Figure 68.* There are a number of ways to teach letter names which make the learning fun. (Photo by Linda Lungren)

ing from scratch in teaching letter-sound correspondence. Often the child knows the letters of the alphabet and can tell them apart. Establishing the letter-sound correspondence is extending this knowledge one step further. For children who are having difficulty with the letters of the alphabet or with letter-sound correspondence, this game is both fun and easy to direct. Assign each member of the class a different letter each day. For example, "Brian, you be *R* today, Katie, you be *S*," and so on. See how quickly the class can get to the front of the room, assembled in the right order, and then pronounce their individual letter sounds. If you have a stopwatch, this might lend added excitement, as children love trying to "beat the clock." Another approach is to have the children sit in a circle and take turns making the letter sounds. As each sound is made the other children imitate the sound. The more they vocalize new sounds, the more likely they are to internalize them.

### *Letter-Sound Correspondence (Grapheme-Phoneme Correspondence)*

The following charts contain lists of consonant and vowel correspondence in various parts of words. They contain most of the sounds in the English language, and therefore can be helpful in teaching students word analysis skills. You may want to use the charts as checklists. When the children can exhibit a thorough familiarity with all the sounds and their uses, they have probably become confident decoders of words.

## CONSONANT CORRESPONDENCE IN VARIOUS POSITIONS

Letter-Sound (Grapheme-Phoneme) Relationships

| Phoneme | Grapheme | Phoneme In Initial Position | Phoneme In Medial Position | Phoneme In Final Position |
|---------|----------|-----------------------------|----------------------------|---------------------------|
| /b/ | b | bake<br>baby | cabin | tub |
| /k/ | c | cat | become | tick |
|  | k | kite | making | work |
|  | ck |  | tracking | back |
|  | x |  | complexion |  |
|  | ch | charisma | anchor<br>echo | monarch |
|  | qu | queen | racquet | bisque |
|  | cc |  | account |  |
| /s/ | s | suit | insert | porous |
|  | ss |  | massive<br>possessive | miss<br>possess |
|  | c | cite | pencil<br>glacier | face |
|  | st |  | gristle<br>listen<br>fasten |  |
|  | ps | pseudonym |  |  |
|  | sc | scissors | Pisces<br>visceral |  |
| /č/ | ch | cherry | lecher | such |
|  | t |  | picture<br>nature<br>virtue |  |
| /d/ | d | dish | body | hard |
|  | dd |  | middle | odd |
| /f/ | f | fish | safer | knife |
|  | ff |  | raffle | muff |
|  | ph | phonograph<br>phrase | telephone<br>cephalic | graph |
|  | gh |  |  | tough |
| /g/ | g | good | rigor | bag |
|  | gh | ghetto<br>ghost |  | ugh |
|  | gg |  | trigger | egg |
|  | gu | guest | beguile<br>unguent | rogue |

| Phoneme | Grapheme | Phoneme In Initial Position | Phoneme In Medial Position | Phoneme In Final Position |
|---------|----------|------------------|------------------|------------------|
| /h/ | h | horse | behead | |
| | wh | who | | |
| /l/ | l | long | bailer | stale |
| | ll | | falling | doll |
| /m/ | m | moon | hamper | game |
| | mb | | tombstone | dumb |
| | mm | | drummer | |
| /n/ | n | nest | diner | pin |
| | nn | | thinner | |
| | gn | gnat | | |
| | kn | knight | | |
| /ŋ/ | ng | | stinger | song |
| | n | | think | |
| /p/ | p | point | viper | hip |
| | pp | | hopping | |
| /r/ | r | rat | boring | tear |
| | rr | | merry | |
| | wr | write | | |
| | rh | rhyme | hemorrhage | |
| /š/ | sh | shadow | crashing | dish |
| | s | sure | | |
| | ci | | precious | |
| | ce | | ocean | |
| | ss | | obsession | |
| | | | assure | |
| | ch | chic | machine | |
| | | chevron | | |
| | ti | | motion | |
| /t/ | t | test | water | cat |
| | tt | | letter | putt |
| | pt | | | receipt |
| | bt | | debtor | debt |
| /θ/ | th | thin | either | wreath |
| | | | lethal | |
| /ð/ | th | then | ether | bathe |
| /v/ | v | violet | hover | dove |
| /w/ | w | will | throwing | how |
| | ui | | sanguine | |
| /ks/ | x | | toxic | box |
| | cc | | accent | |
| /j/ | y | yarn | lawyer | day |

| Phoneme | Grapheme | Phoneme In Initial Position | Phoneme In Medial Position | Phoneme In Final Position |
|---------|----------|------------------|------------------|------------------|
| /z/ | z | zipper | razor | blaze |
| | s | | visit | logs |
| | | | amuser | |
| | zz | | drizzle | fizz |
| | | | nozzle | |
| | x | xanthippe | | |
| | | xylophone | | |
| /ž/ | z | | azure | |
| | su | | treasure | |
| | si | | allusion | |
| | ss | | fissure | |
| | g | genre | | decoupage |
| /gz/ | x | xeroxes | exhibit | |
| | | | exert | |
| | | | exact | |
| | gs | | | digs |

## VOWEL CORRESPONDENCES

| Sound Label | Vowel | Letter Label | Example |
|-------------|-------|--------------|---------|
| Unglided or short | /a/ | a | an |
| | | au | laugh |
| Glided or long | /ey/ | a.e | pane, bake |
| | | ai | rain |
| | | ea | steak |
| | | ei | feign |
| | | ay | tray |
| | | ey | obey |
| | | ua | guaze |
| Unglided or short | /e/ | e | pen |
| | | ea | lead |
| | | eo | jeopardy |
| | | ei | heifer |
| | | ai | stair |
| | | ie | friendly |
| Glided or long | /iy/ | e.e | mete |
| | | e | he |
| | | ea | heat |
| | | ee | tree |
| | | ei | conceive |
| | | ie | believe |
| Unglided or short | /i/ | i | hit |
| | | ui | guild |

| Sound Label | Vowel | Letter Label | Example |
|---|---|---|---|
| | | y | gym |
| | | u | business |
| Glided or long | /ay/ | i.e. | write |
| | | uy | buyers |
| | | ie | tries |
| | | ai | aisle |
| | | ia | trial |
| | | y | spy |
| | | i | find |
| | | ei | sleigh |
| | | igh | night |
| Unglided or short | /o/ | o | not, fought, thought |
| Glided or long | /ow/ | o.e | shone |
| | | oa | goat |
| | | ow | snow |
| | | o | no |
| | | ew | sewing |
| | | ough | dough, through |
| | | oo | floor |
| | | eau | beau, bureau |
| | | oe | hoe, doe |
| | | jo, yo | fjord |
| Unglided or short | /ə/ | u | nut |
| | | oo | flood |
| | | ou | enough, curious, pretentious |
| | | ough | rough |
| | | o | hover, cover, come |
| Glided or long | /yuw/ | u.e | yule |
| | | eau | beauty |
| | | ew | dew |
| | | ieu | lieu, lieutenant |
| Unglided or short | /u/ | oo | good |
| | | u | putt |
| | | ew | grew |
| | | ui | fruit |
| Unglided or short | /o/ | a | walk |
| | | au | maul |
| | | o | frog |
| | | aw | saw |
| Unglided or dipthong | /aw/ | ow | down |
| | | ou | cloud |
| Glided or dipthong | /oy/ | oy | boy |
| | | oi | loin |
| | | ai | stair |
| Note: an unglided | /ar/, /er/ | ar, ea | art, pear |
| or short vowel | /ir/, /or/ | ea, oa | tear, boar |

| Sound Label | Vowel | Letter Label | Example |
|---|---|---|---|
| followed by -r is some-<br>times referred to as an<br>r-controlled vowel | /ur/, /yur/<br>/ər/ | oo, u.e<br>e<br>i | poor, cure<br>her<br>sir |

Reprinted with permission from Lapp, D. & Flood, J. *Teaching Reading to Every Child.* New York: Macmillan Publishing Company, 1978.

Sometimes, a little word that the child may already have learned may cause problems when a similar looking word is introduced at the same time. *From* may be confused with *form* or *for*. *On* may be confused with *or* or *in*, *of* confused with *off*, and so on. Try reading the following passage as quickly as possible:

> All the inmates of the inn wanted to go to Innsbruck in April, so they went. Instead of getting off the train in Innsbruck, they wanted to wait and see Salzburg. When they saw that Salzburg was snowy, they each ate lettuce hearts there, then came back here to earn money to eat there more often.

Children's books tend to contain many of these "little" words. If a child is having trouble, exercises that emphasize differences between the forms and meanings of these little words may help. Following is a sample exercise:

> Directions: Find the correct word from the following list, and fill in the blanks. The teacher may read the exercise orally.
>
> Mary knew that _____ she looked _____ the kitchen _____ top _____ the counter, she would find _____ lunch _____ .
>
> in    on    if    her    there    of

Following is a list of "little" words that may be commonly confused.

| inn | ache | to | it | of | for | each | here |
|---|---|---|---|---|---|---|---|
| in | ate | too | in | off | from | eat | her |
| on | ace | toe | is | oft | form | ear | hear |
| and | atom | tow | if | often | foam | earn | heart |

A significant part of the ability to discriminate between words is decoding for meaning, attaching the printed symbols to mental concepts. A primary decoding strategy is phonics skills, which supply the child with a vital tool to unlock the message of new words. On the following pages you will find an explanation of the content of phonics and its application to reading.

## Phonics Strategies

### The Sound System of English

Phonetics is the study of speech sounds in their most subtle physiological and acoustical variations. From this large body of knowledge, educators have derived the system of phonics, which includes the most common English sounds and the most often used letters or groups of letters to record these sounds. Phonics is taught to children because it systematically presents the most common sounds with which they will come into contact.

### The Origin of Phonics Instruction

Before the 1890s children were drilled on only the letters of the alphabet; that is, naming the letters. Even when drills in phonics were later introduced, the two exercises were unrelated. A typical phonics drill would look like this:

| da | de | | ma | me | | ra | re |
|----|----|--|----|----|--|----|----|
| fa | fi | | na | ne | | sa | si |
| la | li | | pa | pi | | ta | ti |

In 1890 Rebecca Pollard introduced her synthetic phonics method to the schools. The following steps were suggested.

1. Articulation drills in single letters before reading instruction began.
2. Drills for each consonant; each consonant had the sound of a syllable: /bə/, /kə/, /də/, /fə/, /gə/, /lə/, /mə/, /nə/, /pə/, /rə/, /sə/, /tə/.
3. Drills on phonograms (word families): man, fan, can, pan, ran, tan; sick, tick, click, trick, flick, stick.
4. Drills on diacritical markings in sentences: The lamb slept on the grass at night.
5. Drills on phrases in sentences: The cat/sat/on the mat/ and meowed.

*Figure 69.* The introduction of the syllable is considered a good starting point in teaching phonics. (Photo by Linda Lungren);

### Syllable Generalizations

The introduction of the syllable is considered a good starting point in teaching phonics. Many children, according to the Gibson and Levin studies (1975), attempt to syllabicate almost automatically when decoding. Although specific syllable boundaries may be difficult to determine, it is fairly easy to detect the number of syllables in a word by saying it aloud. Instructing children to clap their hands for each part of a word you say may be a useful exercise to introduce the idea that a syllable is a part of a word. Syllable boundaries can usually be detected by the presence of a vowel, and the phonological features within a syllable are a vowel and a consonant(s).

The following are six generalizations about syllables that may be helpful in planning your program.

1. All syllables have a vowel sound: book - let, try.
2. When a second vowel appears in a word, the final e does not add another sound: cake.
3. When two consonants exist between two vowels, a division takes place between the consonants: pen - cil.
4. When a consonant exists between two vowels, a division takes place between the first vowel and the consonant: a - wake.
5. If the single consonant preceded and followed by vowels is x, the x and the preceding vowel are in the same syllable: ax - is.
6. When a word ends in le, and it is preceded by a consonant, the consonant and le make up a new syllable: Han - dle, cas - tle.

### Stress Rules

The following stress rules are helpful in planning your phonics program:

1. If a root has two syllables, the first is usually stressed: father, cattle, answer.
2. If a root has two syllables and the second syllable contains a long vowel, the syllable with the long vowel is stressed: decide, between.
3. If the first vowel in a multisyllabic root is a short vowel and it precedes two consonants, the first syllable is stressed: restaurant, interest, atmosphere.
4. If the first vowel in a multisyllabic root is a schwa and it precedes two consonants, the syllable that contains the long vowel is stressed: alliance.
5. If the final syllable contains le, it is not stressed: miserable, humble, missile.

Before we begin discussing consonant and vowel sounds, let us examine the following chart containing the full range of English phonemes with a transcription key, using the symbols of the International Phonetic Alphabet. This key may be helpful in assisting children in decoding words they cannot pronounce. For example, seeing the word *pleasure*, a child might say /pli • sur/ instead of /plEžr/.

## English Phonemes With Key For Pronunciation

### Consonants

| Phoneme Symbol | Key Word (target underlined) | Transcription of Key Word |
|---|---|---|
| /p/ | pin | /pIn/ |
| /b/ | bin | /bIn/ |
| /t/ | tile | /tal/ |
| /d/ | dime | /daIm/ |
| /k/ | cope | /kop/ |
| /g/ | goat | /govt/ |
| /c/ | church | /čɜ̌č/ |
| /j/ | judge | /yʌd₃/ |
| /f/ | find | /faInd/ |
| /v/ | vine | /vaIn/ |
| /θ/ | thin | /θIn/ |
| /ð/ | that | /ðæt/ |
| /s/ | sin | /sIn/ |
| /z/ | zip | /zIp/ |
| /s/ | shoot | /šut/ |
| /z/ | treasure | /trezɤ/ |
| /l/ | lid | /lId/ |
| /r/ | rid | /rId/ |
| /m/ | mean | /min/ |
| /n/ | neat | /nit/ |
| /n/ | sing | /sIn/ |
| /w/ | wit | /wIts/ |
| /y/ | yelp | /j lp/ |

### Vowels

| Phoneme Symbol | Key Word (target underlined) | Transcription of Key Word |
|---|---|---|
| /i/ | seat | /sit/ |
| /I/ | sit | /sIt/ |
| /e/ | gait | /geIt/ |
| /E/ | get | /get/ |
| /æ/ | rat | /ræt/ |
| /a/ | top | /tap/ |
| /o/ | coat | /kovt/ |
| /U/ | put | /pvt/ |
| /u/ | root | /rut/ |
| /ʌ/ | but | /bʌt/ |
| /ol/ | toy | /toI/ |
| /aU/ | cow | /Kav/ |
| /al/ | kite | /kaIt/ |

## Consonants

The phonetic principles that regulate the articulation of consonants in English are important to understand. Some consonants have only one sound, whereas others have a number of sounds. Here and on the following pages we will present a series of rules concerning consonant sounds.

We will begin with the least confusing consonants. Each of the consonants listed here has only one possible sound when used at the beginning of a word.

| | | | |
|---|---|---|---|
| b boy | j joy | n nut | t turn |
| d day | k kind | p pen | v vase |
| f fat | l lend | r run | w wish |
| h hold | m man | s see | z zinc |

The consonants c, g, q, and x do not appear on the list. C and g each has a hard and a soft sound in the initial positions:

| | | |
|---|---|---|
| c | can (hard) | city (soft) |
| g | gate (hard) | ginger (soft) |

The consonant q, as we know, never appears in English without the vowel u following it. The qu combination has two sounds: qu as the /k/ sound, as in antique, quay, and quahog; qu as the /kw/ sound, as in quest, quick, quaff, quorum, and others.

Like c and q, x makes sounds that are often represented by other letters: x as the /z/ sound, as in xylophone or xylem, x as the /ks/ sound, as in fox or tax, and x as the /gz/ sound, as in example or exhausted.

The letters w and y are unusual because they can act as both consonants and vowels. They are consonants only when used as the first letter in a syllable, as in these words:

| | | | |
|---|---|---|---|
| year | yes | yeast | yank |
| way | water | winter | want |

## Consonant Clusters or Blends

The appearance of two or more consonants together in a word is referred to as a consonant blend when they each retain their individual sounds. Here are some samples of initial position consonant blends:

| | | | |
|---|---|---|---|
| bleak | dwindle | plea | sprain |
| brown | flight | pray | strain |
| crown | glee | skate | tray |
| dream | grade | spot | twins |

Following are some examples of consonant blends in the final position:

| | | | |
|---|---|---|---|
| fir<u>st</u> | wa<u>nt</u> | tu<u>ft</u> | we<u>lt</u> |
| ta<u>sk</u> | le<u>nd</u> | pa<u>lm</u> | he<u>lp</u> |
| wi<u>sp</u> | ca<u>mp</u> | shri<u>nk</u> | o<u>ld</u> |

### Consonant Digraphs

Not all two-consonant combinations form consonant blends. To be considered a blend, both consonant sounds must be heard. If only one of the sounds is heard, as in *gh*oul, *kn*ow, or *gh*astly, or if the two letters together produce a sound unlike either of the individual sounds, such as in *ch*air, cou*gh*, *ph*ysical, or *sh*in, the combination is called a consonat digraph.

The *th* digraph should be noted separately because it has two different sounds, voiced and voiceless:

> Voiced:  they, that, bathe
> Voiceless: thanks, through, math

### Three-consonant Combinations

Three-consonant combinations may consist of a blend alone, such as *spl*ash, in which all three consonants are sounded, or of a digraph and a blend, such as in *phr*ase, in which the first two consonants form a digraph, or a sound different from either *p* or *h* separately, but are then blended with a sounded consonant, in this case, *r*.

Here are some additional terms you may find in reading about phonics:

> **Voiced consonants:**  Consonants that cause the vocal chords to vibrate when their sounds are articulated are voiced consonants. They are:
>
> /b/, /d/, /g/, /j/, /l/, /m/, /n/, /r/, /v/, /w/, /th/ (<u>th</u>ough) and /z/.
>
> **Voiceless consonants:** Consonants that do not cause the vocal chords to vibrate when their sounds are articulated are voiceless consonants. They are:
>
> /p/, /f/, /h/, /k/, /s/ (<u>s</u>and), /th/ (<u>th</u>ank), /sh/, /ch/, and /wh/.
>
> **Stops or Continuants:**  Consonants that are sounded instantaneously are called stops. For instance, the sound of <u>n</u> can be held for as long as you like, but a sound like <u>d</u> cannot. The stops are:
>
> /b/, /p/, /d/, /t/, and /g/, /k/.

### Vowels

As in the case of consonants, the phonetic principles that regulate the articulation of vowel sounds are also important to understand. English vowel sounds are often more complicated to learn because each vowel has a number of different sounds. Familiarity with the rules for vowel articulation is essential to a reading instruction program. Here and on the following pages we will introduce the fundamentals.

The letters *a, e, i, o, u,* (and sometimes *y* and *w*) are the English vowel sounds. *A, e, i, o,* and *u* all have long and short sounds:

> long vowel sound: ā āche  ē ēven  ī īcicle  ō ōver  ū ūse
>
> short vowel sound: ă ăct  ĕ ĕgg  ĭ ĭnto  ŏ ŏften  ŭ ŭnder

The chart that follows provides a systematic list of long and short vowels in initial and medial positions. It is useful in helping children to master vowel sounds. You might make smaller charts that the children can use or make flashcards to identify trouble spots.

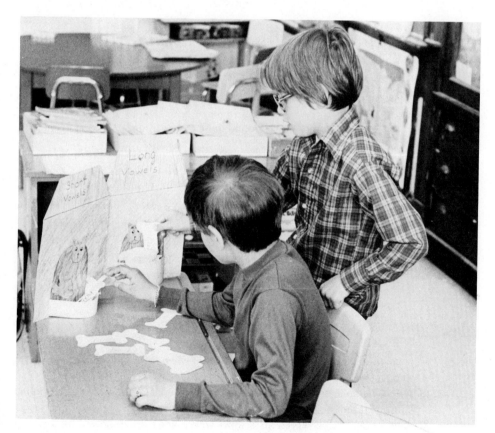

*Figure 70.* You might design attractive games for your children to reinforce concepts of long and short vowel sounds. (Photo by Linda Lungren)

## Long Vowel Sound in the Initial Position

ā    ace, age, ate, angel, Asia, acron, apron, ache
ē    ego, equal, even, east, ecology, each, eve, evil
ī    ice, ivy, icicle, identity, idea, iodine, iota, Ireland
ō    ocean, over, oboe, old, oh, okay, open, oval
ū    unicorn, use, usual, uniform, union, universal, Utah, unicycle

## Short Vowel Sound in the Initial Position

ă    apple, average, act, axle, antelope
ĕ    egg, elephant, elegy, enter, editor
ĭ    in, it, into, igloo, itch
ŏ    ox, of, offer, often, octopus
ŭ    uncle, umbrella, undo, utter, us

## Long Vowel Sound in Medial Position

ā    cape, cake, page, lady, baste
ē    Pete, Steve, neither
ī    mild, while, like, nine, fine
ō    bone, cove, spoke, those, vote
ū    music, amuse, mule, fuse, accuse

## Short Vowel Sound in Medial Position

ă    bat, bad, tact, whack, shack
ĕ    wet, pen, when, tent, spend
ĭ    sick, tip, wick, big, ship
ŏ    cot, box, top, hog, bomb
ŭ    but, tub, scrub, cunning, pun

The following rules may be helpful when introducing vowel usage.

### Short Vowels

1. A vowel grapheme represents a short vowel when it is followed by a consonant unit, such as in cat, pen, sit, not, but.
2. A vowel grapheme represents a short vowel when it is followed by a compound consonant unit, -dg/dj/ or -x/ks/: wedge, exist.
3. A vowel grapheme represents a short vowel when it is followed by a cluster of consonants, tt or spl, as in cattle or split.
4. A vowel grapheme represents a short vowel when it is followed by a double consonant, as in litter, throttle, tall.

## Long Vowels

1. A vowel grapheme represents a long vowel sound when it is followed by a consonant, which in turn is followed by <u>l</u> or <u>r</u> and another vowel, usually a final e, as in <u>stable, cradle.</u>
2. The vowel graphemes <u>oi</u> and <u>oy</u> represent the long vowel sound /y/ in <u>toil</u> and <u>toy</u>. The vowel graphemes <u>ou</u> and <u>ow</u> represent the long vowel sound /aw/ in <u>shout</u> and <u>cow</u>.
3. When the vowel grapheme occurs as the last unit of a syllable and when it is preceded by a consonant unit, the grapheme will represent the long vowel sound, as in <u>spree, knee, tree.</u>

## Schwa Sound

We often see the schwa symbol /ə/ in unaccented syllables of multisyllabic words, and often we see it now in some accented syllables. We can see the schwa in such words as around (ə round), lemon (lemən), circle (cərcle). The schwa may be found as any vowel letter if the vowel is in an unaccented syllable. It may also be seen as the short *u* sound and the vowel sound in *er, ir,* and *ur.*

## Y As a Vowel

When *y* appears in a syllable that does not contain a vowel letter, it has a short *i* sound and acts as the vowel for that syllable. Examples are *system* and *myth*. When the letter *y* is the final sound in a one-syllable word, it has a long-*i* sound. Examples are *try, why,* and *cry*. When *y* appears as the last letter in a multisyllabic word, it has a long-*e* sound. Examples are *hairy, dainty,* and *busy*. When *y* appears as the last letter of a syllable that is not the last syllable in a multisyllabic word, it has a long-*i* sound. Examples are *dynamic* and *cypress.*

## Vowel Digraphs

There are a number of two-vowel combinations which together are sounded as one vowel. These combinations are called vowel digraphs. Examples are *seat, took, conceive, wait, taught,* and *boat.*

In 1968 study, Burmeister studied the frequency of adjacent vowel pairs acting as vowel digraphs. She concluded that certain vowel pairs consistently acted as digraphs and certain vowel pairs seldom acted as digraphs:

| Grapheme | Example | Pronunciation | Frequency | Per cent |
|----------|---------|---------------|-----------|----------|
| ay | gray | /ā/ | 132/137 | 96.4 |
| oa | road | /ō/ | 129/138 | 93.5 |
| ai | villian | ə | 9/309 | 2.9 |
| ea | sergeant | ə | 3/545 | 0.5 |

Source: Based on information reported in Lou E. Burmeister; "Vowel Pairs," *The Reading Teacher*, 21, 5 (February 1968) 447–448. Reprinted by permission of the International Reading Association and the author.

## Vowel Dipthongs

When a syllable contains two vowels, and both of them are sounded, the two-vowel combination is called a diphthong. The first vowel is sounded strongly, and the second is a glided or semivowel sound. Examples are *ow* in *cow*, *oy* in *boy*, *ou* in *shout*, or *oi* in *coil*.

Burmeister's research (1968) also found similar patterns of consistency and inconsistency in the study of adjacent vowel pairs that act as diphthongs.

| Grapheme | Example | Pronunciation | Frequency | Per cent |
|----------|---------|---------------|-----------|----------|
| oi | hoist | oi | 100/102 | 98.0 |
| au | taut | o | 167/178 | 93.8 |
| oy | coyote | oi | 1/50 | 2.0 |
| oo | blood | ou | 7/315 | 2.2 |

## Additional Vowel Rules

These generalizations may prove helpful when introducing children to the concept of vowel sounds:

1. When a single vowel in a syllable is followed by the letter r, the letter r is the dominant sound recorded and the vowel sound is affected or influenced by it: cart, dollar.
2. When the letter a is followed by ll or lk in a syllable, the a represents the sound of ou or au: balk, hall.
3. When the letter combinations gn, gh, ght, ld, or nd follow the single letter i in a syllable, the i represents a long sound: right, resign, wild.
4. When the letter combination ld follows the single letter o in a syllable, the letter o usually represents a long vowel sound: cold, hold.
5. When the letter combination re followes a single vowel in a syllable, one generally hears an r sound: bore, hire.
6. E's at the end of a monosyllabic word usually make the first vowel a long sound. This is sometimes called the Magic E rule, safe, abode.

You may recognize many of these rules. You may have had to memorize them as children. Some may have been helpful and some may have confused you. Three studies, Clymer (1963), Bailey (1967), and Emans (1967), published comprehensive views of the overall usefulness of traditional phonics rules, presented in the following figures. Rules with 75 per cent frequency are probably worth teaching and will help with decoding skills. Those with low frequencies may not prove helpful and may confuse the children because of the many exceptions.

## FORTY-FIVE PHONIC GENERALIZATIONS

| | Percentage of Utility | | |
|---|---|---|---|
| | *Clymer* | *Bailey* | *Emans* |
| | Grades 1–3 | Grades 1–6 | Grades 4–12 |
| 1. When there are two vowels side by side, the long sound of the first vowel is heard and the second vowel is usually silent. (leader) | 45 | 34 | 18 |
| 2. When a vowel is in the middle of a one-syllable word, the vowel is short. (bed) | 62 | 71 | 73 |
| 3. If the only vowel letter is at the end of a word, the letter usually stands for a long sound. (go) | 74 | 76 | 33 |
| 4. When there are two vowels, one of which is final e, the first vowel is long and the e is silent. (cradle) | 63 | 57 | 63 |
| 5. The r gives the preceding vowel a sound that is neither long nor short. (part) | 78 | 86 | 82 |
| 6. The first vowel is usually long and the second silent in the digraphs ai, ea, oa, and ui. (claim, beau, roam, suit) | 66 | 60 | 58 |
|           ai | | 71 | |
|           ea | | 56 | |
|           oa | | 95 | |
|           ee | | 87 | |
|           ui | | 10 | |
| 7. In the phonogram ie, the i is silent and and the e is long. (grieve) | 17 | 31 | 23 |
| 8. Words having double e usually have the long e sound. (meet) | 98 | 87 | 100 |
| 9. When words end with silent e, the preceding a or i is long. (amaze) | 60 | 50 | 48 |
| 10. In ay, the y is silent and gives a its long sound. (spray) | 78 | 88 | 100 |
| 11. When the letter i is followed by the letters gh, the i usually stands for its long sound and the gh is silent. (light) | 71 | 71 | 100 |
| 12. When a follows w in a word, it usually has the sound a as in was. (wand) | 32 | 22 | 28 |
| 13. When e is followed by w, the vowel sound is the same as that represented by oo. (shrewd) | 35 | 40 | 14 |
| 14. The two letters ow make the long o sound. (row) | 59 | 55 | 50 |
| 15. W is sometimes a vowel and follows the vowel digraph rule. (arrow) | 40 | 33 | 31 |
| 16. When y is the final letter in a word, it usually has a vowel sound. (lady) | 84 | 89 | 98 |
| 17. When y is used as a vowel in words, it sometimes has the sound of long i. (ally) | 15 | 11 | 4 |
| 18. The letter a has the same sound (o) when followed by l, w, and u. (raw) | 48 | 34 | 24 |
| 19. When a is followed by r and final e, we expect to hear the sound. (charge) | 90 | 96 | 100 |
| 20. When c and h are next to each other, they make only one sound. (charge) | 100 | 100 | 100 |
| 21. Ch is usually pronounced as it is in kitchen, catch, and chair, not like ah. (pitch) | 95 | 87 | 67 |
| 22. When c is followed by e or i, the sound of s is likely to be heard. (glance) | 96 | 92 | 90 |

23. When the letter c is followed by o or a,
    the sound of k is likely to be heard.
    (canal)                                         100          100          100

24. The letter g is often sounded as
    the j in jump when it precedes the letters
    i or e. (gem)                                    64           78           80

25. When ght is seen in a word, gh is silent.
    (tight)                                         100          100          100

26. When a word begins with kn, the k is
    silent. (know)                                  100          100          100

27. When a word begins with wr, the w is
    silent. (wrap)                                  100          100          100

28. When two of the same consonants are
    side by side, only one is heard. (dollar)       100          100          100

29. When a word ends in ck, it has the same
    last sound as in lock. (neck)                   100          100          100

30. In most two-syllable words, the first
    syllable is accented. (bottom)                   85           81           75

31. If a, in, re, ex, de, or be is the first syl-
    lable in a word, it is usually unaccented.
    (reply)                                          87           84           83

32. In most two-syllable words that end in a
    consonant followed by y, the first syllable
    is accented and the last is unaccented.          96           97          100

33. One vowel letter in an accented syllable
    has its short sound. (banish)                    61           65           64

34. When y or ey is seen in the last syllable
    that is not accented, the long sound of e
    is heard.                                         0            0            1

35. When ture is the final syllable in a word,
    it is unaccented. (future)                      100          100          100

36. When tion is the final syllable in a word,
    it is unaccented. (notion)                      100          100          100

37. In many two- and three-syllable words,
    the final e lengthens the vowel in the
    last syllable. (costume)                         46           46           42

38. If the first vowel sound in a word is
    followed by two consonants, the first
    syllable usually ends with the first of the
    two consonants. (dinner)                         72           78           80

39. If the first vowel sound in a word is fol-
    lowed by a single consonant, that conso-
    nant usually begins the second syllable.
    (china)                                          44           50           47

40. If the last syllable of a word ends in le,
    the consonant preceding the le usually
    begins the last syllable. (gable)                97           93           78

41. When the first vowel element in a word
    is followed by th, ch, or sh, these symbols
    are not broken when the word is divided
    into syllables and may go with either the
    first or second syllable. (fashion)             100          100          100

42. In a word of more than one syllable, the
    letter v usually goes with the preceding
    vowel to form a syllable.                        73           65           40

43. When a word has only one vowel letter,
    the vowel sound is likely to be short. (crib)    57           69           70

44. When there is one e in a word that ends
    in a consonant, the e usually has a short
    sound. (held)                                    76           92           83

45. When the last syllable is the sound r, it is
    unaccented. (ever)                               95           79           96

Unfortunately, there is no magic formula that will teach all children to read. Some learn well with phonics and some do not. It should be remembered that the ultimate goal of teaching phonics, as well as any other method of instruction, is comprehension. Phonics strategies, then, should be seen merely as aids to help the student comprehend meanings.

In addition to phonics skills and strategies, there are other word analysis techniques that may help children to decode new words. These techniques are *sight word skills, structural analysis skills*, and *contextual skills*. Following are some instructional methods that may help you to aid your students in developing their word analysis knowledge.

## Sight Word Strategies

The *whole-word method*, or *look-say method*, is found in many basal programs. The technique involves teaching high-frequency words that often are not phonetically regular as sight words.

Many children can recognize a number of words before they come to school. Often, they are special words that have meaning for them. They may be names, or whole phrases such as, Happy Birthday, or Merry Christmas. Other sight words in the child's vocabulary may be words or signs that he sees frequently, such as McDonald's, exit, or stop.

Sylvia Ashton-Warner in her book *Teacher,* describes how she taught Maori children in New Zealand to read by utilizing this exciting method of personal words. She asked the children to tell her a word they wanted to know. She then wrote the word on a card and gave it to them. You can adapt this method to your own classroom by having the children keep "secret files" of their own special words. The words should be reviewed every so often, but not in a rote manner.

Short stories can be created using the special words. Have the children use every word in a story, or ask them to write several short stories using one or two of their words in each.

Write language experience charts as a group, and hang them on the walls. In addition to enticing the children to use the words correctly, this activity will also keep the words in view.

Create short plays using the words from storytelling sessions or from a brainstorming session.

These suggestions are based on the language experience method of teaching reading, explained in earlier chapters, but can easily be integrated into other instructional programs.

Some basal programs introduce new sight words in word families, so that rhyming words may be learned at the same time: *mat, cat, fat*. This is an elementary configuration clue. The child learns that when he sees the *-at* configuration the new word will sound like the other *-at* words he has learned.

### Configuration Clues

Often without realizing it, we identify many clues when we are reading. Configuration clues are among them. For example, if the following formation is given to us and we are told that the answer is a holiday greeting, we can find the answer by looking at the configuration.

☐ ☐ P P ☐    ☐ H ☐ ☐ K S ☐ ☐ ☐ · ☐ ☐ ☐

In the following pattern, we are told that the answer is the name of a college:

☐ ☐ ☐ ☐ E ☐ S ☐ ☐ ☐

☐ ☐

☐ E ☐ ☐ S

We use configuration clues to arrive at our two answers, "Happy Thanksgiving" and "University of Texas."

Shapes of words also offer configuration clues for children; for example, bed is different in shape from puppy. Children often attend to and depend upon configuration when they are decoding.

Sometimes, a child realizes ran means *ran*, and then he is introduced to man and is told this says *man*. The child internalizes this information: ran = *ran*. When he sees the word *run* in a sentence, he recognizes the *r* and guesses that the word says *ran*. In other cases, the child who has learned ran = *ran* might even say "ran" when he comes across such words as rooster, rabbit, rye, or rough.

As a teacher, you will need to examine carefully the appropriate words you will select to teach as sight words so that the children's memories do not become overtaxed. For example, children may not be able to learn long words like *nightingale* or *superintendent* as sight words. There are other strategies that will be more appropriate for teaching these longer words to younger children. An appropriate starting point for teaching sight words is the child's own name. Color names and numeral names are also useful because of their visual referents, such as *black, gray, 4 (four)*. Here the teacher can easily enhance student's sight word learning abilities by putting visual representations of different colors and numerals on the classroom walls.

The next step is to determine appropriate criteria for introducing sight words. The single best criterion seems to be to select high-frequency functional words (the words with which young children are most likely to come into contact) such as *the*.

The next step is to determine appropriate criteria for introducing sight words. The best single criterion seems to be to select high-frequency functional words, like *the*, e.g.:

(The) cat (in) (the) hat .

The following is an extended list for use as a sight word vocabulary.

## THE DALE LIST OF 769 EASY WORDS

**A**
a
about
above
across
act
afraid
after
afternoon
again
against
ago
air
all
almost
alone
along
already
also
always
am
American
an
and
animal
another
answer
any
anything
apple
are
arm
around
as
ask
at
away

**B**
baby
back
bad
bag
ball
band
bank
basket
be
bear
beat

beautiful
because
bed
bee
been
before
began
begin
behind
being
believe
bell
belong
beside
best
better
between
big
bill
bird
bit
black
bless
blind
blood
blow
blue
board
boat
body
bone
book
born
both
bottom
bow
box
boy
branch
brave
bread
break
breakfast
bridge
bright
bring
broken
brother
brought
brown

build
building
built
burn
busy
but
butter
buy
by

**C**
cake
call
came
can
cap
captain
car
care
careful
carry
case
catch
cause
cent
center
chair
chance
change
chief
child
children
choose
Christmas
church
circle
city
class
clean
clear
clock
close
cloth
clothes
cloud
coal
coat
cold
color
come

coming
company
cook
cool
corn
corner
cost
could
count
country
course
cover
cow
cried
cross
crowd
crown
cry
cup
cut

**D**
dance
dark
day
dead
dear
deep
did
die
different
dinner
do
doctor
does
dog
done
don't
door
double
down
draw
dream
dress
drink
drive
drop
dry
dust

**E**
each
ear
early
earth
east
easy
eat
edge
egg
eight
either
else
end
England
English
enough
evening
ever
every
everything
except
expect
eye

**F**
face
fair
fall
family
fancy
far
farm
farmer
fast
fat
father
feed
feel
feet
fell
fellow
felt
fence
few
field
fight
fill
find
fine

finger
finish
fire
first
fish
fit
five
fix
floor
flower
fly
follow
food
foot
for
forget
fourth
found
four
fresh
friend
from
front
fruit
full

**G**
game
garden
gate
gave
get
gift
girl
give
glad
glass
go
God
going
gold
golden
gone
good
got
grain
grass
gray
great
green

grew
ground
grow
guess

**H**
had
hair
half
hall
hand
hang
happy
hard
has
hat
have
he
head
hear
heard
heart
heavy
help
here
herself
hid
high
hill
him
himself
his
hold
hole
home
hope
horse
hot
house
how
hundred
hunt
hurry
hurt

**I**
I
ice
if
in

| | | | | | | |
|---|---|---|---|---|---|---|
| Indian | **M** | night | post | see | speak | think |
| instead | made | nine | pound | seed | spot | this |
| into | mail | no | present | seem | spread | those |
| iron | make | noise | press | seen | spring | though |
| is | man | none | pretty | self | square | thought |
| it | many | noon | pull | sell | stand | thousand |
| its | march | nor | put | send | star | three |
| **J** | mark | north | **Q** | sent | start | through |
| jump | market | nose | quarter | serve | station | throw |
| just | matter | not | queen | set | stay | tie |
| **K** | may | note | quick | seven | step | till |
| keep | me | nothing | quiet | several | stick | time |
| kept | mean | now | quite | shake | still | tire |
| kill | measure | number | **R** | shall | stone | to |
| kind | meat | **O** | race | shape | stood | today |
| king | meet | oak | rain | she | stop | together |
| kiss | mean | ocean | ran | sheep | store | told |
| knee | met | of | rather | shine | storm | tomorrow |
| knew | middle | off | reach | ship | story | tongue |
| know | might | office | read | shoe | straight | too |
| **L** | mile | often | ready | shop | street | took |
| lady | milk | old | real | short | strike | top |
| laid | mill | on | reason | should | strong | touch |
| lake | mind | once | red | shoulder | such | town |
| land | minute | one | remember | show | sugar | trade |
| large | miss | only | rest | shut | suit | train |
| last | money | open | rich | sick | summer | tree |
| laugh | month | or | ride | side | sun | true |
| lay | moon | other | right | sign | suppose | try |
| lead | more | our | ring | silk | surprise | turn |
| learn | morning | out | river | silver | sweet | twelve |
| leave | most | outside | road | sing | **T** | twenty |
| left | mother | over | rock | sir | table | two |
| leg | mountain | own | roll | sister | tail | **U** |
| lesson | mouth | **P** | roof | sit | take | uncle |
| let | move | page | room | six | talk | under |
| letter | Mr. | paint | rose | size | tall | until |
| lie | Mrs. | pair | round | skin | taste | up |
| lift | much | paper | row | sky | teach | upon |
| light | music | part | run | sleep | teacher | us |
| like | must | party | **S** | slow | tear | use |
| line | my | pass | said | small | tell | **V** |
| lion | myself | path | sail | smile | ten | valley |
| lips | | pay | salt | smoke | than | very |
| listen | **N** | pen | same | snow | thank | visit |
| little | name | people | sand | so | that | **W** |
| live | near | pick | sat | soft | the | wait |
| load | neck | picture | save | sold | their | walk |
| long | need | piece | saw | soldier | them | wall |
| look | neighbor | place | say | some | then | want |
| lost | neither | plain | school | something | there | war |
| lot | nest | plant | sea | sometime | these | warm |
| loud | never | play | season | song | they | was |
| love | New York | please | seat | soon | thick | wash |
| low | next | point | second | sound | thin | waste |
| | nice | poor | | south | thing | |
| | | | | space | | |

| | | | | | | |
|---|---|---|---|---|---|---|
| watch | well | where | whose | wing | word | year |
| water | went | whether | why | winter | work | yellow |
| wave | were | which | wide | wish | world | yes |
| way | west | while | wild | with | would | yesterday |
| we | what | white | will | without | write | yet |
| wear | wheat | who | win | woman | wrong | you |
| weather | wheel | whole | wind | wonder | XYZ | young |
| week | when | whom | window | wood | yard | your |

Repetition of sight words is essential for the child who is beginning to read. Dolch (1936) prepared a list of 220 words, which constitute nearly half of the words that a mature reader encounters in print. Many of the words that are included on this list almost literally defy phonics generalizations. Therefore, it seems sensible to teach these words as sight words.

### THE DOLCH BASIC SIGHT VOCABULARY OF 220 WORDS

| | | | | | | |
|---|---|---|---|---|---|---|
| a | call | from | jump | on | sing | under |
| about | came | full | just | once | sit | up |
| after | can | funny | | one | six | upon |
| again | carry | gave | keep | only | sleep | us |
| all | clean | give | kind | open | small | use |
| always | cold | go | know | or | so | very |
| am | come | goes | laugh | our | some | walk |
| an | could | going | let | out | soon | want |
| and | cut | good | like | over | start | warm |
| any | did | got | little | own | stop | was |
| are | do | green | live | | take | wash |
| around | does | grow | long | pick | tell | we |
| as | done | had | look | play | ten | well |
| ask | don't | has | | please | thank | went |
| at | down | have | made | pretty | that | were |
| ate | draw | he | make | put | the | what |
| away | drink | help | many | | their | when |
| | | her | may | ran | them | where |
| be | eat | here | me | read | then | which |
| because | eight | him | much | red | there | white |
| been | every | his | must | ride | these | who |
| before | | hold | my | right | they | why |
| best | fall | hot | myself | round | this | will |
| better | far | how | | run | those | wish |
| big | fast | hurt | never | | three | with |
| black | find | I | new | saw | to | work |
| blue | first | if | no | say | today | would |
| both | five | in | not | see | together | write |
| bring | fly | into | now | seven | too | yes |
| brown | for | is | of | shall | try | you |
| but | found | it | off | she | two | your |
| by | | its | old | show | | |

### Contractions

Contractions should also be taught as sight words because of their formation patterns. When two or more words combine to form a new, shorter word, an apostrophe is substituted for one or more letters in the new word. This is an easy rule for children to remember. Following is a list of common contractions:

| I have | I've | she is | she's | must not | mustn't |
|--------|------|--------|-------|----------|---------|
| I am | I'm | has not | hasn't | they have | they've |
| I will | I'll | are not | aren't | have not | haven't |
| he will | he'll | | | will not | won't |
| she is | she's | it is | it's | of the clock | o'clock |
| she will | she'll | he is | he's | would not | wouldn't |
| did not | didn't | he will | he'll | there is | there's |
| was not | wasn't | cannot | can't | is not | isn't |
| does not | doesn't | do not | don't | should not | shouldn't |
| will not | won't | had not | hadn't | could not | couldn't |
| they are | they're | has not | hasn't | you are | you're |

## Whole Word Method

Many words that students encounter have a complete lack of correspondence between spelling and pronunciation. Such words of course, will appear throughout a student's education, and these whole words must be taught as sight words. Common examples of words that cannot be taught according to phonics rules are *pneumonia, phlegm,* and *mnemonic.*

A number of words have entered our usage from other languages. These must often be taught as sight words because they may have retained their foreign spellings. Ruddell (1974) has provided the following list.

| Language Source | Plants and Animals | Food | Culture | Miscellaneous |
|-----------------|--------------------|------|---------|---------------|
| American Indian | sequoia catawba cayuse | supawn pemmican | manitou kayak | chautauqua |
| French | caribou | brioche a la mode parfait sazarac | bureau bateau pirogue | Cajun charivari rotisserie |
| Spanish | mesquite marijuana mosquito palomino | frijol tequila enchilada | sombrero serape lariat pueblo | conquina hombre savvy |
| German | | blutwurst schnitzel zwieback | pinochle rathskeller turnverein | katzenjammer phooey spiel |
| Italian | | spaghetti ravioli | duet opera piano virtuoso | granite balcony |
| Persian | lilac lemon | sherbet | caravan khaki borax | paradise check |

| Language Source | Plants and Animals | Food | Culture | Miscellaneous |
|---|---|---|---|---|
| Greek | | | acrobat | tactics |
| | | | barometer | tantalize |
| | | | catastrophe | elastic |
| Russian | | vodka | ruble | steppe |
| | | | droshky | |

Regardless of the grade level or the content you are teaching, you will be introducing and reinforcing sight word skills. As you observed in the Dolch or Dale word lists and the list of contractions, many of the words you will be teaching as sight words do not lend themselves to visual representation, such as *the* and *I'm*. Therefore, they must be taught in context. The following rules may aid you to help your children to develop their sight word vocabularies:

*Figure 71.* When it is appropriate show a picture of the word or concept being introduced. (Photo by Linda Lungren)

1. When it is appropriate, show a picture of the word or concept being introduced. Present a sentence containing the sight words you wish to introduce or reinforce. Encourage your students to study the picture and the number of words on the page and to try to guess what will be said in the passage. You can also ask the child to guess the word by first reading the sentence context.

2. Ask the students to look at the words as you read them. This helps children to decide if their guesses are correct.

3. Point to the picture and reread the passage while the children follow the story visually.

4. Encourage the children to read the passage with you.

5. Ask individual children to read the sentences while the other children follow the story visually.

6. After reading the sentence, point out the individual words you are introducing.

7. Discuss the meaning of each word. Explain that some words, such as *the, is,* and *am,* often serve as helpers to complete sentences.

8. "Tell" children certain words that have extremely irregular patterns: *sight, of, who, laugh, though, the, should.*

9. As you frame each word, assist students in recognizing the length and configuration, initial letter(s), and ascending letter features.

10. Finally, encourage students to reread the sentence with you.


## Structural Analysis Skills


As helpful as sight word strategies are in word recognition, readers at all levels must have some *structural analysis skills* to analyze unfamiliar words. The ability to divide words into their smallest parts is an aid in comprehension as well as in decoding. For example, children who can syllabicate parts of the word *un-sports-man-like* by knowing that the prefix *un* = *not* and the suffix *like* = *as* will be able to say the word and know that it means "not as a sportsman." When you are establishing the structural analysis segment of your word analysis program, a thorough knowledge of all the rules of morphology will prove helpful to you.

When linguists discuss the contents of structural analysis, they usually include a description of the following:

Morphology

affixes (suffixes and/or prefixes)

<u>Variants</u>
inflectional endings
  plural(s)
  tenses (ed)
  comparatives (est)
grammatical usage
compound words

As you begin to develop your students' structural analysis skills, it is important that you become acquainted with a description of morphology.

## *Morphology*

The morpheme is the smallest structural unit of meaning in any language. The morpheme should not be confused with a word. A word may be a single morpheme or it may be composed of several morphemes: *back* or *back-ward*. Morphemes may be free, such as the word *back*, or bound, like *ing*, in *back-ing*. The following chart illustrates examples of bound and free morphemes.

| Bound Morpheme | Free Morpheme | Bound Morpheme |
|---|---|---|
| pre | view | |
| re | view | |
| | view | er |
| | view | ing |
| pre | view | er |
| re | view | ing |
| pre | test | |
| re | test | |
| | test | er |
| | test | ing |
| pre | test | ing |
| re | test | ing |

Free morphemes are sometimes called *root words* or base words. Examples of root words with which your beginning readers are likely to come into contact follow.

| | | | |
|---|---|---|---|
| play | sleep | agree | fear |
| box | cover | part | push |

Can you add bound morphemes to these root words to create new words? Ernst (1955) gave us an insight about root words:

> Words are interesting . . . When you begin to know which ones belong to the same families and who their forefathers were, they become fascinating.

It is extremely important that the teacher include instruction on the construction of words within the students' initial reading program. Understanding how words are put together will help young readers to unlock word meanings. To learn word construction, children must be introduced to the affixes of English. Affixes are called bound morphemes, and they include prefixes and suffixes. The following chart illustrates the affixes of the English language.

| Word Class | Affix | When Affix Is Added To | Example |
|---|---|---|---|
| ADVERB | -ly | ADJ | slowly |
| | | derived ADJ | carelessly |
| | -wise | N | otherwise |
| | -wards | N | backwards |
| | a- | N | ahead |
| | | V | afloat |
| | | ADJ | aloud |
| | | STEM | aghast |
| | al- | ADV | almost |
| | -fore | ADV | therefore |
| | -most | N | foremost |
| ADJECTIVE | -y | N | lengthy |
| | | STEM | pretty |
| | -al | N | functional |
| | | STEM | terminal |
| | -ible | V | reversible |
| | | STEM | fallible |
| | -able | V | adorable |
| | | STEM | viable |
| | -ful | N | careful |
| | -less | N | guileless |
| | -en | N | wooden |
| | -ive | V | possessive |
| | | N | defective |
| | | STEM | native |
| | -ar | N | particular |
| | | STEM | linear |
| | -ary | N | honorary |
| | | STEM | ordinary |
| | -ic | N | aromatic |
| | | STEM | arctic |
| | -ish | N | foolish |
| | | STEM | squeamish |
| | -ous | N | mischievous |
| | | STEM | fabulous |
| | -ent | V | abhorrent |
| | | STEM | resident |
| | | | grandiose |
| | -ose | ADJ | morose |
| | | STEM | spotted |
| | -ed | N | determined |
| | | V | |

| Word Class | Affix | When Affix Is Added To | Example |
|---|---|---|---|
| | -id | STEM | morbid, lucid |
| | -ing | N | conflicting |
| | | V | hanging |
| | -ate | N | proportionate |
| | | STEM | literate |
| | -ile | STEM | juvenile |
| | -ory | V | contradictory |
| | | STEM | illusory |
| | -ant | N | concordant |
| | | STEM | rampant |
| | -some | V | meddlesome |
| VERB | -ate | N | fabricate |
| | | STEM | separate |
| | -ize | N | idolize |
| | | ADJ | vitalize |
| | | STEM | emphasize |
| | -ify | N | citify |
| | | ADJ | simplify |
| | | STEM | liquify |
| | -ish | STEM | finish, polish |
| | -en | N | hasten |
| | | ADJ | moisten |
| | | STEM | glisten |
| | en- | N | engulf, enjoy |
| | | V | enliven, enjoin |
| | em- | ADJ | embitter, |
| | -le | N | handle |
| | | STEM | amble |
| | -er | V | loiter, saunter |
| NOUN | -age | V | spoilage |
| | -ance | V | condonance |
| | -cy | N | hypocrisy |
| | | ADJ | obstinacy |
| | -ee | V | employee |
| | -er | N | boxer |
| | | V | skier |
| | | STEM | matter |
| | -ian | N | historian |
| | -ile | N | projectile |
| | -ism | N | despotism |
| | | STEM | paroxism |
| | -ist | V | typist |
| | | N | pianist |
| | | ADJ | socialist |
| | -ive | N | objective |
| | | V | relative |
| | | STEM | missive |
| | -ity | STEM | animosity |

| Word Class | Affix | When Affix is Added To | Example |
|---|---|---|---|
| | | ADJ | generosity |
| | -ment | V | payment |
| | -ness | ADJ | goodness |
| | -old | N | cuckold |
| | -ship | N | citizenship |
| | | ADJ | hardship |
| | -ster | N | gangster |
| | | ADJ | oldster |
| | | STEM | monster |
| | -um | V | continuum |
| | | ADJ | ultimatum |
| | | STEM | curriculum |
| | -us | N | modulus |
| | | STEM | stimulus |
| | -tion | derived V | solution |
| | | V | eruption |
| | -hood | N | statehood |

## Prefixes

Some of the most frequently recurring prefixes and their meanings in English are the following:

dis (not, a part)          em (in)
in (not)                   de (from)
mis (wrong)                inter (between)
anti (against)             ex (out, from)
non(not)                   en (in)
com (with)                 op, ob (against)
con (with)                 pro (in front of)
pre (before)               per (fully)
super (over)               im (not, in)
tri (three)                un (not, opposite of)

## Suffixes

When the meaning of a word is modified by the addition of a new ending, a suffix has been added to the root word. Thorndike's text *The Teaching of English Suffixes* (1932) provides some insight into the frequency with which some suffixes appear. For example, the five most common suffixes in English are the following:

ion        decoration
er         harder

|      |           |
|------|-----------|
| ness | <u>awareness</u> |
| ity  | <u>purity</u> |
| y    | <u>rainy</u> |

Other suffixes that appear frequently are:

|      |              |
|------|--------------|
| able | <u>objectionable</u> |
| ant  | <u>pleasant</u> |

More examples of recurring English suffixes include the following:

| | |
|---|---|
| ness (being) | wise (ways) |
| ment (result of) | ling (little) |
| ward (in direction of) | ty (state) |
| our (full of) | ity (state) |
| ious (like, full of) | ure (denoting action) |
| eous (like, full of) | ion (condition or quality) |
| et (little) | ian, or, ist, er (one who does) |
| able, ible, ble (capable of being) | en (made of, to become) |
| ic (like, made of) | ly (similar in appearance or manner) |
| ish (like) | ful (full of) |
| ant (being) | ness (quality or state of being) |
| ent (one who) | less (without) |
| age (collection of) | y (like a, full of) |
| ance (state of) | al (pertaining to) |
| ence (state or quality) | man (one who) |

In addition to affixes, including prefixes and suffixes, certain other elements of the English language add meaning to words and are also called bound morphemes. These elements include inflectional endings (plurals, possessives, and markers for third person singular verbs), tense markers, and pronoun markers (number, case, and possession).

## *Inflectional Endings*

### 1. Plural, Possessive, and Third Singular Verb Markers

A. If the word ends in any of these phonemes (/s, z, c, j/), the inflectional ending is /z/.

| | | | |
|---|---|---|---|
| barrage | /bəraj/ | barrages | /bərajəz/ |

B. If the word ends in a voiceless consonant, the appropriate ending is /s/.

| | | | |
|---|---|---|---|
| bit | /bit/ | bits | /bĭts/ |
| sip | /sip/ | sips | /sĭps/ |

C. If the word ends in either a voiced consonant or a vowel, the appropriate ending is /z/.

| crib | /krib/ | cribs | /kribz/ |
|------|--------|-------|---------|
| rid  | /rid/  | rids  | /ridz/  |

### 2. Tense Markers

#### A. Past Tense and Past Participle

Both of these forms use the same rules to produce their appropriate endings.
1. If the verb ends in /t/ or /d/, the ending is /əd/.

| rate | /ret/ | rated | /retəd/ |
|------|-------|-------|---------|

2. If the verb ends in a voiceless consonant, the ending is /t/.

| dip | /dIp/ | dipped | /dIpt/ |
|-----|-------|--------|--------|

3. If the verb ends in a voiced consonant or a vowel, the ending is /d/.

| rib | /rIb/ | ribbed | /rIbd/ |
|-----|-------|--------|--------|

#### B. The Progressive

When the progressive is used, that is, *ing*, as in "He is going," /Iŋ/ is added to the verb form, following the BE.

| he will sell | /hi wIl sel/ |
|--------------|--------------|
| he will be selling | /hi will bi selIŋ/ |

### 3. Pronouns

Pronouns in English are also inflected for number, case, and gender:

| Singular | | | Plural | | |
|----------|--|--|--------|--|--|
| Subject | Object | Possessive | Subject | Object | Possessive |
| 1st I/aI | me/mi/ | my/maI/ mine & main/ | 1st we/wi | us/əs/ | our/aUr/ ours/aUrz/ |
| 2nd you/yu/ | you/yu/ | your/yor/ yours/yorz/ | 2nd you/yu/ | you/yu/ | your/yor/ yours/yorz/ |
| 3rd he/hi/ | him/him/ | his/hiz/ | 3rd they/ðe/ | them/ðEm/ | their/ðErǂ/ theirs/ðErz/ |
| she/si/ | her/hr | her/hr/ hers/hrz/ | | | |
| it/It/ | it/It/ | its/Its/ | | | |

## *Compound Words*

As part of structural analysis, children need to be made aware of their innate knowledge of compound words. In doing this, children are able to extract meaning quickly from compound words. Gleason (1969) conducted a study of children's definitions of compound words. She offers the following definitions for the words *airplane, breakfast,* and *Friday.*

> They knew what the words referred to and how to use them, but their ideas about the words were rather amusing. One little boy said that an airplane is called an airplane because it is a plain thing that goes in the air. Another child said that breakfast is called breakfast because you have to eat it fast to get to school on time. Several children thought that Friday is called Friday because it is the day you eat fried fish.

During beginning reading programs children may be taught to identify many compound words as sight words.

| | |
|---|---|
| grandmother | football |
| grandfather | doghouse |
| thanksgiving | toothpick |
| breakfast | seaweed |
| outcome | filmstrip |

Structural analysis is an extremely useful tool for you as a teacher of reading. When you translate this knowledge into an instructional program, your children will be able to use the rules of morphology to unlock the meanings of words. When implementing your structural analysis program with beginning readers, you may want to follow some of these rules:

1. Encourage children to analyze the ending of each word, such as *s, ed* as tense markers, "'s" as possession, and *s* as a plural marker.

2. Encourage children to split words into parts with which they are already familiar, re/*heat*/ing.

3. Encourage children to guess the pronunciation of a new word by looking at the parts of the word that are familiar to them.

4. Encourage children to make their own "new" compound words and share these words with the class. This will help them better understand how compound words are formed.

An understanding of structural analysis will help your young children deal with many new words. Structural analysis, like phonics and sight word strategies, is only one way of helping children to learn to decode words. Each strategy is useful only as an aid to learning.

## Contextual Analysis

The process of word recognition also involves the analysis of the printed language within a given context.

> All language . . . concerns itself with meanings. Or, perhaps, we should say rather that human beings are basically concerned with meanings and use language as their tool to

grasp, to comprehend, and to share meanings. It is the linguist's business to turn the spotlight on the tool-language-itself in order to examine the physical material of which it is composed and to determine the ways this material has been selected and shaped to accomplish its function of mediating meaning. (Fries [1963], p. 97)

Earlier in this chapter we examined the application of phonic strategies, sight word strategies, and structural analysis strategies. The contextual structure of sentences, passages, and stories, however, can often provide the easiest clues to the meanings of unknown words. Children should be exposed to all the available clues within a text, because they learn to read in so many different ways. There are a number of different kinds of contextual clues. They are definitions, synonyms, summaries, similes, examples, appositives, antonyms, and groupings. Examples of each follow:

**Definition:** The word is introduced and defined in the same context.

Example. Knights were medieval gentlemen-soldiers; usually of high birth.

**Synonym:** The idea is repeated in another way.

Example. She has a yen to go back to Maine. This yearning never seems to end.

**Summary:** The idea is enlarged upon, repeated, or described.

Example. This child is very precocious. She hasn't started school yet, but can already read at a second-grade level, and converses easily with older children.

**Simile:** The idea is compared to something else by using like or as.

Example. The little dog was as black as night.

**Example:** Evidence is presented to support the idea.

Example. Tom is industrious. Every morning he checks in fifteen minutes early, and he never leaves until everything is done.

**Apposition:** The word is elaborated upon in a short phrase, set off by commas.

Example. Shakespeare, an Elizabethan playwright and poet, wrote *Romeo and Juliet.*

**Antonym:** The opposite of the idea is denied.

Example. Mr. Smith is not easily annoyed. No matter what we do, he never seems to lose his patience.

**Groupings:** The word is grouped with things in the same category.

Example: Her new dress was a combination of blue, red, yellow, and magenta.

Spache maintains that teaching children contextual analysis strategies is extremely important.

> Apparently most context clues demand some degree of inferential thinking. As a result some teachers assume that contextual analysis is not much more than guesswork and therefore should not be promoted. The truth is that such inferential thinking is an essential part of the reading process at all maturity levels and should be strongly encouraged. Pupils should not be burdened with learning the technical terms which might be employed to describe the types of context clues. Rather the emphasis should be placed upon helping the reader use the sense of the sentence or the surrounding sentences as an aid in identifying the probable meaning of a difficult word. The goal of contextual analysis is not always an exact recognition of a word or its pronunciation. These may be approached by other means such as phonic or structural analysis. But when these techniques are successful, they do not necessarily result in the derivation of the meaning of the word, for it may not be encompassed in the reader's auditory vocabulary. Thus contextual analysis takes the reader beyond pronunciation to meaning, which in many situations is more significant for his ultimate comprehension. (1973, p. 497)

Other contextual clues that help the beginning reader with understanding unknown words are *italics, footnotes, capitalization, boldface type, quotation marks,* and *parenthetical statements.* The best way to begin teaching children to use these kinds of context clues are exercises in which they identify and extract these clues from their reading material. A teacher might give out a story and tell the class that there are fifteen capital letters in the story. The students then try to "beat the clock," to pick out the words that begin with capital letters. This is a simple exercise, but very adaptable to higher-level skills that may later be encountered.

Unfortunately, even a thorough knowledge of contextual analysis strategies will not guarantee that a child will comprehend every word he sees in print. He will, however, be much better equipped to attempt a new word than will a child who has never been taught these skills. Other contextual analysis strategies include picture clues, lexical clues (word and sentence meaning of clues), relational clues (word order clues in a sentence), and interpretation clues. These can be accomplished by using such exercises as the following:

1. Deleting words from sentences:
   As soon as she could struggle free, she _____ away as fast as she could.
2. Deleting words from language experience stories:
   We played in the snow. I made a snow angel. Michael made a _____. Patricia made a _____.

**Picture Clues**

1. Bob got a new _____ for his birthday.

2. I would love to ride in a _____ .

## Lexical Clues

1. We always go to the _____ in the summer. I love to play in the sand and salt water.
2. It's time for _____ . I'm glad, because I'm so tired.

## Rational Clues

1. The little white _____ meowed her thanks for the dinner I gave her.
2. She had to_____ her car to come here.

## Interpretive Clues

1. The bright _____ of the car in the dark told us it was coming.
2. The puppy wagged his _____ with joy.

The mature reader depends a great deal upon context clues to aid him in speeding up his reading and to increase his understanding of difficult material. We can easily understand, then, that these skills are not only beginning reader aids to be dismissed later on. Context skills well learned will be of the utmost importance when reading material becomes more and more complex. If students are having trouble with an unfamiliar word, they should be encouraged to ask themselves the following questions:

1. Are there clues to the meaning of this word in the surrounding words?
2. Will I understand this word if I continue to the end of the sentence?
3. Have I examined the pictures for clues to the meaning?

In the next few pages, we will present several activities that may be useful reinforcements for your word analysis program.

## VISUAL DISCRIMINATION ACTIVITIES

### Match Game

Goal: Visual discrimination

Age level: 2-3

Construction: Write the child's name in large letters on a piece of paper. Using another piece of cardboard, write the child's name and cut the letters into individual cards.

Utilization: The child should match the letter cards in the proper order beneath his name on the piece of paper.

### Tops and Bottoms

Goal: Visual Discrimination

Age level: 1–2

Utilization: Place an assortment of bottles and lids in front of the child. The child should then try to match up the appropriate lid with each bottle.

## Funny Faces

Goal: Visual discrimination

Age Level: 1–2

Construction: Draw a large face with three or four features, or cut out felt shapes

on a felt board          . Leave out one of the features—an eye, for example.

Utilization: Have the child tell you or point to what is missing. The same can be done with pictures of objects, such as a car with three wheels, or a dog without a head.

## Jigsaw Puzzle

Goal: Visual discrimination

Age level: 1–2

Construction: Paste a colorful magazine picture onto a piece of cardboard. Cut the picture into three or four large shapes.

Utilization: The child should attempt to put the pieces back together in the proper places to make the picture whole again.

## Mobile

Goal: Visual discrimination

Age level: 0–1

Utilization: To assist in the development of visual skills, a colorful mobile (musical, if possible) can be hung over an infant's crib or bassinet. It will help the child to develop focusing abilities and to distinguish different shapes and colors. Also, keep in mind that studies have shown an infant's favorite object to view is a human face.

# PHONICS ACTIVITIES

## Calling

Goal: Auditory discrimination

Age level: 4–8 months

Utilization: While the infant is lying in his crib or playpen, arrange to have the room quiet and devoid of people for about five minutes. Then call the child from different locations in the room and let the infant turn his head to try and locate the source of the sound.

### Making a Consonant Poster

Goal: Recognition of initial consonant sounds

Age level: 5-6

Construction and Utilization: After students are familiar with five to ten consonant sounds, assign each student a consonant. The child then looks through magazine, cuts out objects beginning with the same consonant sound, and pastes them on a large sheet of paper.

### Sewing Cards

Goal: Recognition of initial consonant sounds

Age level: 5-6

Construction: On large cards made out of oak tag, paste pictures on one side of the card. On the other side, write the beginning consonant sound in a different order. Punch holes to the right of the pictures and to the left of the letters.

Utilization: The child takes colored yarn and "sews" the pictures to the corresponding consonant sound, by threading left to right.

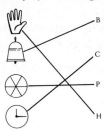

### Lotto

Goal: Reinforcement of consonant sounds

Age level: 5-6

Construction: Lotto boards can be used to reinforce a variety of skills. On a piece of oak tag or cardboard, draw nine squares with a letter in each. Make nine smaller cards each pasted with a picture from old workbooks or magazines.

Utilization: The child places the small cards face down and, one by one, matches the picture to the corresponding consonant sound.

### Beginning Sound

Goal: To reinforce sound/symbol relationships

Age level: 4, 5

Construction: Fill a barrel with objects that begin with the b sound, such as ball, book, belt. Include a box filled with cardboard squares on which are written the letter b and a box of beans.

Utilization: Take out the barrel and label it with a letter b. Pulling one item at a time from the barrel, call on the children to identify it. Encourage use of the word in context, continually reinforcing its beginning sound. Have the children tape the cardboard squares to classroom objects that begin with that sound. Finally, give each child a b and let him glue beans on the letter shape.

## Scavenger Hunt

Goal: Decoding

Age level: 7–8

Construction: On small pieces of paper, write a list of five to ten objects that can be found in the area. The words used can be those to which the class has just been introduced, such as those containing vowel diagraphs, and so on.

Utilization: Establish a time limit. Whoever has collected the most objects on his list wins.

## Phonics Baseball

Goal: Sound/symbol relationship recognition

Age level: K–1

Construction: Draw a large baseball field on the board or on a large piece of oak tag. Supply markers for each team. (Suggestion: Use yogurt tops for the "Yogurt Yankees," playing cards for the "Third Grade Cardinals". Divide the class into teams.

Utilization: The teacher acts as umpire by giving each team a letter or combination of letters on the board. Each member of the group has to sound out a letter combination correctly for a single, or use the letter combination's sound in a word correctly for a double. Failure to do so constitutes an out; three outs per team and then another team is "at bat." The letter combinations should become progressively harder, and the team with the most runs at the end of the game wins.

## Listen for the Sounds

Goal: Auditory discrimination

Age level: 3–4

Utilization: Hand out whistles, symbols, and bells to the class and have them use the instruments whenever they hear two words that begin with the same sound. If the child uses the instrument when the words do not begin with the same sound, he or she is disqualified. Whoever is left after everyone else has been disqualified wins the game.

## Concentration

Goal: Letter recognition

Age level: 4–5

Construction: Make up a deck of fifty-two cards with a letter of the alphabet on each. Spread the cards out and place them face down on a table or floor.

Utilization: A small group of students take turns turning over two cards and trying to make a match. If a match is made, the player names the letters and keeps the cards. Whoever has the most pairs when all the cards have been taken wins.

### Cooking Letters

Goal: Letter recognition

Age level: 4–5

Utilization: Have children make letter shapes out of prepared dough. Each child makes a different letter. While the dough is baking, the students are shown flashcards and must identify the name of the letter they were making, when it is shown.

### The Billboard Game

Goal: Letter recognition

Age level: 4–5

Utilization: When riding in a car on class field trips, play the billboard game. Players take turns locating an A on a sign, a B, and so on.

### Bingo

Goal: Word recognition

Age level: 6–7

Construction: Bingo can be played in different ways for all levels. Make up cards with five columns across and five rows down. In each square, print a word or letter.

Utilization: The teacher calls out the word or letter and students place a marker over the square if the word is on their card. Whoever fills up his card first shouts "Bingo!" and wins the game.

### Syllable Clap

Goal: Syllabication of given words

Age level: K–2

Construction: Prepare a list of words, ranging from two syllable words to more complicated ones.

Utilization: Arrange the class into groups that form circles. Model the proper clapping procedure for them by saying a word, such as elephant, and have the whole class clap with you on each syllable. Then, begin putting the words on the board, give each group time to sound out the word to themselves and plan out a clapping pattern, and then go around the room and have each group clap out a syllable pattern. Award points for each correct response.

## CONTEXTUAL ANALYSIS ACTIVITIES

### Complete the Elephant

Goal: Utilizing contextual appositions

Age level: 7–9

Construction: On the board, draw two outlines of an elephant's body minus trunk, tail, feet, and legs.

Utilization: Divide the class into two teams. In turn, a member from each team is given a sentence that contains a word in apposition. However, the main word has been replaced by a blank line. Each time a player is correct, he may add a new part of the elephant. Whichever team completes the elephant first wins. Later, more complicated animals could be used.

Example:

> The _____, an instrument used in a baseball game, was thrown by the pitcher. (ball)
>
> The _____, a soft sweet mixture, began to drip from the cone. (ice cream).

## Show Me

Goal: Utilizing Contextual similes

Age level: 7–9

Construction: Divide large pieces of drawing paper into sections. Design a series of sentences using similes with one word omitted.

Example: His voice sounded like the roar of a _____.

Utilization: A child selects a sentence and mentally fills in the blank. He then illustrates the sentence on a piece of drawing paper and labels the picture with the completed sentence.

## SIGHT WORD ACTIVITIES

Goal: To reinforce the relationship between the written word and its referent

Age level: 4–5

Construction: Make label cards for as many objects in the classroom environment as possible. For example, make a word card for door, window, plant, paints, blocks, sandbox, and so on.

Utilization: Ask the group to locate each item as you name it. Call on a child to tape each label to the object until many of the objects in the environment are labeled. As new materials and equipment are acquired, continue the labeling procedure with the children.

### Familiar Objects

Goal: To identify high-frequency, familiar sight words

Age level: 3–4

Construction: Gather together a collection of cereal boxes, traffic "stop" signs, milk cartons, or any other food container familiar to the children.

Utilization: Hold up the box or sign and have the children take turns identifying the name on the label. Call attention to those that begin with the same letter so they have the same sound. Then place all the containers in the "house corner" where children can use them for experience playing.

### Copy Cat

Goal: Memory

Age level: 3–4

Utilization: Have each child repeat various clapping patterns, starting with short, simple ones and increasing in complexity.

### Treasure Hunt

Goal: Sight words

Age level: 6–7

Construction and Utilization: To reinforce color sight words, draw a design on a ditto master, labeling each section with the name of a color. After the student has correctly colored in each section, he will be able to see the "treasure," which could be any sort of treasure chest filled with coins.

## Sight-Word "Go Fish"

Goal: Discrimination of function sight word

Age level: 5–8

Construction: Write a list of function sight words on separate index cards. Write sentences leaving out one word spaces. Ask the children to supply the correct sight words.

Function words:

| of | the | off | if |

| then | over | above |

Sentences:

| Keep _____ the grass. |

| The sky is _____ the earth. |

Utilization: This game can be played like Go Fish. Deal each player seven cards and put the rest of the deck in the middle of the table. The object of the game is to match two cards, | Keep _____ the grass | and | off | . If a player cannot make a match, he asks the player to his right: "Do you have an off card?" If he does not have it, he tells the original player to Go Fish!

## Sight-O

Goal: Recognizing sight words

Age level: 5–8

Construction: Draw a Bingo card using the word S I G H T - O. Write sight words in each of the boxes.

| S | I | G | H | T | O |
|-------|-------|------|-------|--------|-------|
| of | every | off | sight | how | would |
| the | is | FREE | might | should | where |
| each | as | from | what | who | when |

Utilization: The caller draws the sight words from a pile of prepared sight words. He names the card as each student examines his board to see if he has the word. If he has, he covers it with a chip. The first to have all the spaces covered wins the game.

## STRUCTURAL ANALYSIS ACTIVITIES

### Concentration

<u>Goal</u>:  Word recognition

<u>Age level</u>: 6–7

<u>Construction</u>: Make up two decks of cards with C-V-C words that are identical except for the middle vowel. Each word should have a pair. Place cards face down on a floor or table.

<u>Utilization</u>: A small group of students take turns turning over the cards to make a match. Students must read the word after they turn it over. If the words match, the student keeps the cards, and when all the cards have been taken, whoever has the most pairs wins.

### Old Monster Digraphs

<u>Goal</u>:  Vowel digraphs

<u>Age level</u>: 7–8

<u>Construction</u>: Make up a deck of cards containing one word on each that has a vowel digraph. Pairs should be made that have the same common element.

<u>Utiilization</u>: All of the cards are dealt out and players take turns drawing a card from each other's hands, without looking. When a pair is made of two words that have the same vowel digraph, they are placed down on the table. Play continues until all the cards have been paired. Whoever is left holding the Old Monster loses the game.

### Crosswords

<u>Goal</u>:  Understanding plurals

<u>Age level</u>: 8–9

<u>Construction</u>: Design a crossword puzzle in which students choose a word from a list to complete the sentences. The words should be in singular form. The sentence clues will require the student to make plural forms of the words.

<u>Utilization</u>: The student completes the sentence by choosing a word from the list and pluralizing it. The correct letters are then written into the appropriate puzzle boxes.

fly     mouse     candy

There are so many _____ in our attic we'll have to set some traps.

### Fishing

<u>Goal</u>:  Word analysis

<u>Age level</u>: 4–5

Construction: Cut different shapes of different colors out of construction paper. Attach a paper clip to each shape. Tie a long string to any pole or branch and attach a bar magnet to the end of the string. The class is seated in a circle with the shapes on the floor in the middle.

Utilization: The teacher asks each child in turn to catch a "small yellow triangle," and so on. The same activity can be used with upper- and lower-case letters.

## Match the Shapes

Goal: Word analysis

Age level: 4–5

Utilization: The teacher draws a shape on the board, and students take turns stating other shapes in the room that are also triangles, circles, and so on. After the matching activity has been mastered, the teacher calls out the name of a shape, and students identify those objects of that shape in the room.

## Cans, Cans, Cans

Goal: Development of visual and motor coordination

Age level: 0–1

Construction: Gather together a collection of empty cans. Remove the sharp edges and cover them with contact paper. The cans should be of different circumferences so that the child can put the smaller cans inside the larger cans.

Utilization: The child must decide what is the proper sequence. The cans can also be turned upside down to build a tower.

## Spoons

Goal: Altering word structures with inflectional endings

Age level: 7–8

Construction: Make up a deck of playing cards containing families of four words each. These should show words that are changed because of inflectional endings. For example, lie, lay, lain, lying, and buy, bought, buying, buys.

Utilization: For five players arrange four spoons on the floor or on a table in the middle of the group. Players are dealt five cards each. The dealer then starts passing the cards one by one to the person next to him. That player either keeps the card and discards one of his own, or passes the card to the next player. The next player does the same. The object of the game is to acquire four of the same word family. When this is accomplished, the player grabs a spoon. All other players then quickly grab a spoon and the player left without one gets an "s." The next time he doesn't reach a spoon he gets a "p." The first player to spell SPOONS loses the game.

## Checkers

Goal: Contractions

Age level: 8-9

Construction: Draw a checker board on a piece of oak tag. In each square write a contraction twice, having it face both directions. Also needed are checkers, chips, or beans.

Utilization: Before a player can land on a square, he must state the two words that the contraction was taken from. For example, if the square contains "won't", the player must say "will not." Follow the rules for playing checkers.

## A Quiz Show

Goal: Antonyms

Age level: 8-9

Construction: Make up a series of sentences containing a word that has an antonym. Checkers or some sort of noisemakers will also be needed.

Utilization: Divide the group into two teams, with three players on each team. The Master of Ceremonies reads a sentence such as, "It was so funny I just had to laugh." If a player can substitute an antonym for one of the words in the sentence, he signals with his clicker and restates the sentence: "It was so funny I just had to cry." If he is correct, he scores five points for his team. If he is incorrect, the other team has a chance to acquire the points. The team with the most points at the end of the game wins.

## Fishing for Homonyms

Goal: Understanding and recognizing homonyms

Age level: 7-8

Construction: Make up a deck of cards containing pairs of homonyms.

Utilization: Five cards are dealt to each player, with the rest in the middle face down as the fish pond. The first player asks any other player, "Do you have the homonym for fir?" If the other player does, he must hand it over to the first player. If he does not have it, player 1 must draw a card from the fish pond. Player 1 can continue to ask for cards until another player says "Go Fish." Players lay down pairs of homonyms as soon as they receive them. Whoever has the most pairs when all the cards have been drawn wins.

## BIBLIOGRAPHY

Ashton-Warner, S. *Teacher*. New York: Bantam Books, 1967.

Bailey, M. "The Utility of Phonic Generalizations in Grades One Through Six." *The Reading Teacher*. (February 1967) 20:412–18.

Burmeister, L. *Words—From Print to Meaning*. Reading, Mass.: Addison-Wesley Publishing Co., Inc., 1975.

Burmeister, L. *Words—From Print to Meaning.* Reading, Mass.: Addison-Wesley Publishing Co., Inc., 1975.

Burmeister, L. "Vowel Pairs." *The Reading Teacher.* (February 1968) 21:447–498.

Coleman, E. *Collectiong a Data Base for an Educational Technology,* Parts I and III. El Paso, Texas: University of Texas, 1967.

Clymer, T. "The Utility of Phonics Generalizations in the Primary Grades." *The Reading Teacher.* (January 1963) 16:252–258.

Dolch, E. "A Basic Sight Vocabulary." *Elementary School Journal.* (February 1936) 36: 456–460.

Durkin, D. *Teaching Them To Read.* Boston: Allyn & Bacon, Inc., 1974.

Emans, R. "The Usefulness of Phonics Generalizations Above the Primary Grades." *The Reading Teacher.* (February 1967) 20:419–25.

Ernst, M. *Words.* 3rd ed. New York: Alfred A. Knopf, Inc., 1955.

Fairbanks, G. *Experimental Phonetics: Selected Articles.* Urbana, Ill.: University of Illinois Press, 1966.

Fries, C. C. *Linguistics and Reading.* New York: Holt, Rinehart and Winston, 1963.

Gibson, E., and H. Levin. *The Psychology of Reading.* Cambridge, Mass.: MIT Press, 1975.

Gleason, J. B. "Language Development in Early Childhood." In J. Walden (Ed.) *Oral Language and Reading.* Champaign, Ill.: National Council of Teachers of English, 1969.

Groff, P. *The Syllable: Its Nature and Pedagogical Usefulness.* Portland, Ore.: Northwest Regional Educational Laboratory, 1971.

Guszak, F. *Diagnostic Reading Instruction in the Elementary School.* New York: Harper & Row, Publishers, 1972.

Heilman, A. *Principles and Practices of Teaching Reading.* Columbus, Ohio: Charles E. Merrill Publishing Company, 1972.

Hoover, K. "The Effect of Sequence of Training in Kindergarten Children." Unpublished Ph. D. thesis, Standford University, 1975.

Jenkins, J., R. Bausel, and L. Jenkins. "Comparison of Letter Name and Letter Sound Training as Transfer Variables," *American Educational Research Journal* (1972) 9:75–86.

Kucera, H., and W. Francis. *Computational Analysis of Present-Day American English.* Providence, R. I.: Brown University Press, 1967.

Lapp, D. and Flood, J. *Teaching Reading To Every Child.* New York: Macmillan Publishing Company, Inc., 1978.

Marchbanks, B., and H. Levin. "Cues by Which Children Recognize Words." *Journal of Educational Psychology.*(1965), 56:57–61.

McHugh, J. "Words Most Useful in Reading." Compiled at California State University, Hayward, 1969.

Murphy, H., and D. Durrell. *Letters in Words.* Wellesley, Mass.: Curriculum Associates, Inc., 1970.

Murphy, H. and D. Durrell. *Speech to Print Phonics.* New York: Harcourt Brace Jovanovich, Inc., 1972.

Pollard, R. S. *Pollard's Synthetic Method.* Chicago: Western Publishing House, 1880.

Ruddell, R. *Reading-Language Instruction.* Englewood Cliffs, N.J.: Prentice-Hall, Inc., 1974.

Shuy, R. "Some Relationships of Linguistics to the Reading Process." Teachers' Edition of *How It Is Nowadays,* by T. Clymer and R. Ruddell Reading 360 Series, copyright 1973, by Ginn and Company. Used with permission.

Silberberg, N., M. Silberberg, and I. Iverson. "The Effects of Kindergarten Instruction in Alphabet and Numbers on First Grade Reading." *Journal of Learning Disabilities* (1972). 5:254–261.

Spache, G.D., and Evelyn Spache. *Reading in the Elementary School.* Boston: Allyn & Bacon, Inc., 1973.

Thorndike, E. *The Teaching of English Suffixes.* New York: Bureau of Publications, Teachers College, Columbia University, 1932.

*Webster Collegiate Dictionary.* "Vocabulary of Rhymes." Springfield, Mass.: G & C. Merriam Company, 1970.

# 13

# Comprehending Stories and Texts

*Figure 72.* Reading is not a passive process; it demands active participation. The reader has to decode, search his memory, and think, think, think while processing a text. (Photo by Linda Lungren)

Reading is comprehension. If you have not comprehended, you have not read. It is important to always ask your students to read for a purpose, for a goal. To realize this purpose or reach this goal, the reader has to extract meaning from the text. The meaning that readers extract from written discourse can be acquired from explicit text information, from implicit relationships in the text, and/or from knowledge and experience of the world. Because young children have experienced the world in only a limited way, you are actually aiding the development of their comprehension abilities every time you help them to experience the world in which they live.

### What Is Reading Comprehension?

Although researchers are not positive about every aspect of reading comprehension, they are certain that the child who comprehends a story or text is the child who is actively involved in the written material. Reading is not a passive process; it demands active participation. The reader has to decode, search his memory, and think, think, think while processing a text.

Stauffer (1969) has stated that reading is a thinking process in which the reader has to be an active participant. Passivity and successful reading comprehension are mutually exclusive. Jenkins (1974) maintains that reading comprehension is closely linked with memory. He suggests that what is best remembered is that which has been experienced:

> I think we will eventually conclude that the mind remembers what the mind *does* not what the word does. That is, experience is the mind at work, not the active world impinging on a passive organism—and experience is what will be remembered. (p. 11)

The proficient reader processes written material by performing many operations while he is reading. This processing, an interaction between the reader's mind and the text, is an indivisible whole. Let us look at the following example:

Suppose the text says:

TEXT

Spinning tops can be fun.

READER

"I wonder which meaning is correct. Let me look at more of the text."

READER

"Oh, that means to spin a top."

READER

"I see an ambiguity."

Possibility #1        Possibility #2

To spin a top        Tops that spin
can be fun.           can be fun.

TEXT

Spinning tops can be fun. First, put the top on the ground, then rotate it clockwise . . .

*Figure 73.* You can influence the active participation of young readers by providing interesting materials and teacher-generated activities that foster concentration and observation. (Photo by Linda Lungren)

All of this happens in the reader's mind in a moment. The time that it takes may not be the critical element in the reading process; the critical element may be the *active participation* of the reader. You can influence the active participation of your young readers in three essential ways:

1. *Motivation*: by providing interesting materials, and provoking interest by setting clear, worthwhile goals.

2. *Strategies Development*: by providing readers with the strategies that are necessary for comprehending stories and texts. These strategies must exist within the reader before he can become a full participant in reading.

3. *Concentration*: by providing teacher-generated activities that foster concentration and observation by the young reader. The activities can help your children to "zero in" on the materials that they are reading. Thorndike (1917) discussed the importance of recognizing reading as an active, participatory process when he wrote:

> Understanding a paragraph is like solving a problem in mathematics. It consists in selecting the right elements of the situation and putting them together in the right relations, and also with the right amount of weight or influence or force for each. The

mind is assailed as it were by every word in the paragraph. It must select, repress, soften, emphasize, correlate and organize, all under the influence of the right mental set of purposes or demands. (p. 329)

## Theories of Reading Comprehension

Although we know that reading comprehension has to be an active process—the reader must work—we still do not have a totally adequate explanation of how reading comprehension works. In recent years, many researchers have attempted to explain the processes involved in comprehending written discourse.

Currently, there are three positions that are held on the nature of the reading process. Each is a point on a continuum, stressing one particular facet of the process. The continuum stretches from one end where it is believed that reading is essentially text based, i.e., the text defines the act of the reading, to the other end where it is believed that reading is essentially knowledge based (in the mind of the reader); this view has been called the schema view of reading based on Bartlett's (1932) notion that we have cognitive schema operating during the reading process. The text-based position is frequently referred to as a bottom-up process view of reading, i.e., the text is the starting point of the reading act. The schema or knowledge-based position is frequently referred to as topdown process view of reading.

In the middle of the continuum there is a third view of reading, one that suggests that reading is both text-based (bottom-up) and knowledge-based (top-down). This position is called the interactive process view of reading.

In the next few pages, we will present several views of reading. Each of the designers of these theories espouses an interactive view of reading. However, each can be placed on in the continuum in approximately the following places:

Gough, LaBerge and Samuels    Trabasso, Rumelhart, Frederiksen    Smith

| text-based | interactive | knowledge-based |
| bottom-up | view of | top-down |
| view of | reading | view of |
| reading | | reading |

In the next few pages, we will present some current theories. It is extremely important for us to attempt to understand as much as we can about the nature of reading comprehension in order to plan appropriate reading curricula.

### *Gough's Theory (1972)*

Gough proposed a model that is serial in nature. He believes that readers start with graphemic input and go through each of the steps illustrated in the following diagram in order to comprehend written discourse.

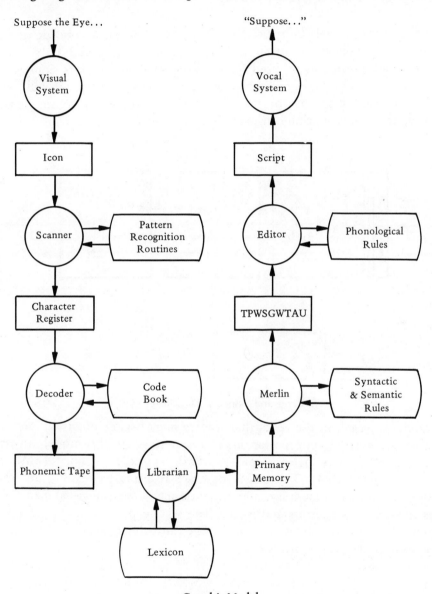

Gough's Model

Gough might suggest that reading instruction should begin with letter-by-letter teaching and then progress to words. He might argue that lexical meanings are grouped into meaningful units and interpreted by the reader in conjunction with the syntactic and semantic knowledge that he possesses. According to

Gough, after a sentence is understood, it is stored in *The Place Where Sentences Go When They are Understood* (TPWSGWTAU). Higher levels of comprehension (such as inferences) are not included in his model.

### LaBerge and Samuels' Theory (1974)

LaBerge and Samuels base their theory of reading on a concept of automaticity. They believe attention is important to reading and only a small amount of attention can be used for decoding skills if one is to comprehend fully. It is important for decoding to become automatic so that it will not require attention. Once this occurs, attention can focus on comprehension. Following is a representation of the model.

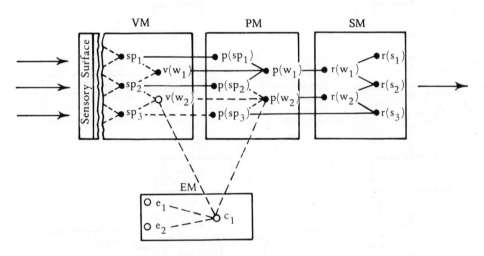

LaBerge and Samuels' Theory (1974)

This model is based on the belief that reading must begin with visual input and end with the meaning interpretation. The four stages in this model are visual memory (VM), phonological memory (PM), episodic memory (EM), and semantic memory (SM). The stages that are relevant to reading are visual memory, phonological memory, and semantic memory. The visual memory includes recognition of letters and words. The second part of the process is the mapping of sounds to letters and words. The third step occurs when the reader associates meaning with written words.

### Trabasso's Theory (1972)

Trabasso defines comprehension as:

> a set of psychological processes consisting of a series of mental operations which process linguistic information from its receipt until an overt decision. Two main operations are

noted: 1) encoding the information into internal representations and 2) comparing these representations . . . Comprehension may be said to occur when the internal representations are matched. The overt responses (true) is an end result of the act of comprehension. (1972), p. 113)

Trabasso envisions comprehension as a series of mental operations (stages) through which the reader must progress in order to understand the material. The item (letter, word, phrase, etc.) is encoded during the first major operation, whereas during the second major operation, the item is matched with an internal structure (an internal template).

The following illustrates Trabasso's stage theory. The reader is asked to compare a sentence that is provided, for example:

> The table is yellow.
> or
> The table is not yellow.

with the table in a picture. If the table is yellow, the first sentence is encoded and then quickly matched to the picture. On the other hand, if the table is not yellow, additional processes will be required before a match can be made. Processing time of a sentence is dependent upon the number of operations (stages) that are required of a reader by the material.

Trabasso has identified three stages through which he believes a reader must progress in order to achieve understanding.

> Stage 1: The reader encodes the sentence in the form of an internal representation. A sentence expressed as a negation may involve the encoding of "False" as a separate property.
>
> Stage 2: The reader encodes the picture and then compares the graphic and pictorial representations to determine if they match. If they do not match, the reader may have to recode.
>
> Stage 3: The reader formulates a "True" or "False" response.

A breakdown in the comprehension process is possible whenever a reader misses a link in the sequence of stages.

## Rumelhart's Theory (1976)

Rumelhart has generated a theory of reading comprehension that is based on a principle of *interactive* stages. He believes that the occurrences of one stage influence the other stages. His theory is represented as follows:

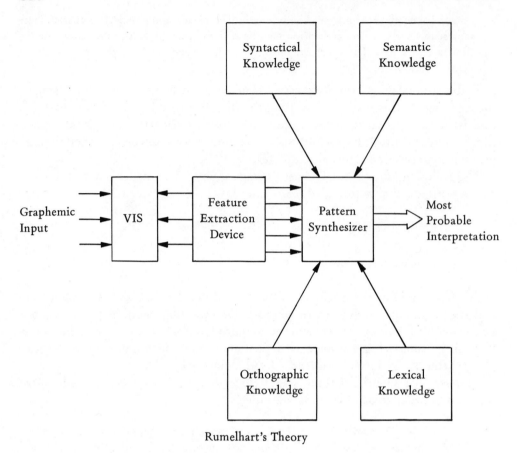

Rumelhart's Theory

The unique feature of Rumelhart's theory is that it discusses reading as a top-down and bottom-up process. He suggests that the reader begins with graphemic input (that which is printed on the page) and advances through all of the stages to obtain meaning. The reader either begins with the lower-level processes, those that happen before the higher-level processes (this is bottom-up processing), or the reader begins with the pattern synthesizer stage, working through the stages to the graphemic features of the page (this would be top-down). The theory is predicated on the belief that a reader will begin with graphemic input and advance to complete understanding. But the theory allows for the reader to begin at any point and then work in any direction.

### Frederiksen's Theory (1976)

Another theory of comprehension was presented by Frederiksen in 1976. This model is flexible because it operates from both the top-down (the reader begins with the high-level skills of comprehension and progresses to the low-level skills of decoding) and bottom-up mode. In addition, it considers the higher-level comprehension skills, e.g. inferencing, disambiguating unclear referents.

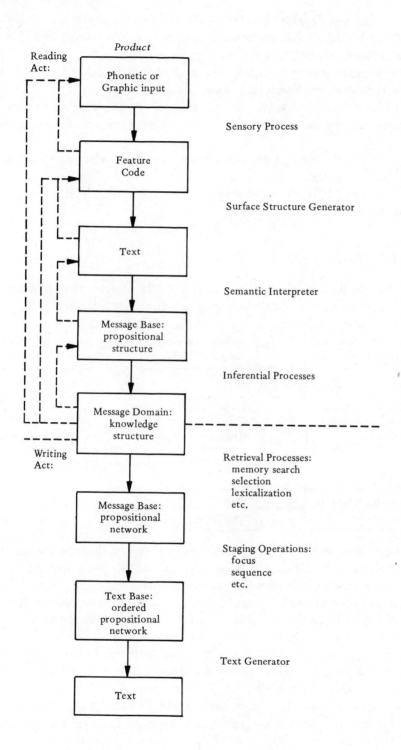

Fredriksen's Theory

This model was developed based on the following assumptions:

1. Skilled reader's comprehension is based on the interaction between the high- and low-level skills in a top-down manner.

2. If a reader encounters difficulty in decoding or other low-level skills, he will revert to the bottom-up technique.

Based on these assumptions of the comprehension act, Frederiksen believes that early reading instruction should be oriented toward achieving two main goals:

1. Teaching children to process written material in the same manner as they process oral language.

2. Decoding skills should be taught so the reader is not bound by the bottom-up mode.

### Smith's Theory (1971)

In Smith's theory of reading, he rejects the notion that reading is a decoding of printed words to spoken language, for example,

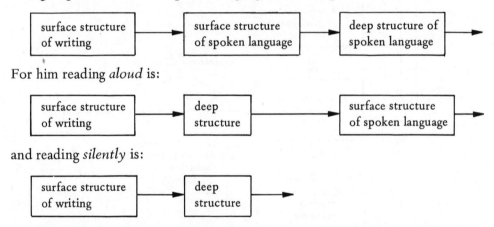

For him reading *aloud* is:

and reading *silently* is:

He believes comprehension must take place first and that the identification of individual words comes second. As an example of this phenomenon, he uses the following sentence: "We should *read* the *minute* print on the *permit*." None of the italicized words can be articulated until they have been understood in context. He believes that a reader sees four to five words ahead of and behind the actual word that he is reading. Research has shown that when lights are turned out on an oral reader, the reader is able to recite the next four or five words of the passage that he is reading. Smith reasons that this occurs because the eye is ahead of the voice by four or five words.

Smith also believes that a reader's world knowledge enriches the printed word. He states, "The more that is known behind the eyeball, the less that is required to identify a letter, word, or meaning from the text." When the material is familiar to the reader, it is quickly comprehended. On the other hand, when the material is more unfamiliar and the vocabulary is more complex, the reader has difficulty comprehending the passage.

The actual process of reading for the competent adult reader can be illustrated in the following diagram:

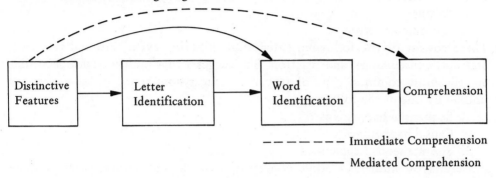

The main limitation of this view, however, is that it does not account for three well-known phenomena:

1. The child who has never seen most of the words that he has in his spoken vocabulary.

2. The fluent reader who encounters words he has never seen before.

3. The second language learner whose aural/oral repertoire exceeds his visual repertoire.


## Story Grammars


In an effort to further understand the comprehension process researchers have been conducting extremely fruitful research on children's understanding of stories. These analyses have been called *story grammars* because they attempt to unravel the complex interrelations of story elements and children's understanding of stories. Stein (1978), in her report for the Center for the Study of Reading, reviewed the current state of the art on story grammar. She reported that, in the past, researchers have maintained that there is a prototype grammatical structure for all stories. She suggests that listeners recognize the structures of stories they hear (or read). The ultimate question in the research on story grammar is: Does the structure exist in the listener (reader) or in the story itself? Or does the structure exist in both the reader and the text and does the comprehension occur when the two match each other?

Bartlett (1932) argued that a story structure ("an active organization of past reactions and experiences which are always operating in any well-developed organism") would be effected by the listener's schema when the story structure was beyond the experience of the listener. He argued that prototypical structures exist primarily in the mind of the listener.

According to Stein and Glenn (1977), the acquisition of schematic story structures is the result of having stories told or read to the young child. The child who is read to frequently is able to generate rules about story structures, and this child is able to change the actual story in such a way that it fits with his scheme for stories.

Stein (1978) analyzed two types of stories: simple stories and multiple-episode stories. She maintains that simple stories have two parts:

1. Setting
2. Episodic structure

These consist of the following categories: initiating event, internal response, attempt, consequence, and reaction. She suggests that multiple-episode stories are the most common type of story. The most common of these stories are unified by one of the following:

1. Sequential happenings
2. Causal happenings
3. Simultaneous happenings

Results of studies of adult conceptions of "good" stories, conducted by Stein and Nezworski (1978) and Mandler and Johnson (1977), suggested that adults would consistently reorganize stories that failed to correspond with an expected sequence into recalled stories that fit an expected pattern. This research found that young children seldom make this connection because most stories are too long for them to reconstruct in an expected pattern. Therefore, the young child may chunk a sequence into smaller units, thereby losing the essence of the prototypical structures.

Studies of second- and sixth-graders' abilities to recall stories that contained inverted sequences (deviations in story schema) found that the reorganization of text sequence into expected structures occurred almost all the time. These findings are significant because of the frequency with which temporal inversions occur in stories used in school textbooks. Many of these temporal inversions are *marked* inversions ("This happened because . . .") which provide a signal that a deviation is occurring in the normal sequence of events. While these inversions may facilitate the reader's recall process by elevating an unfamiliar text structure to the level of an expected sequence, stories containing inversions are still more difficult for readers to recall because they require increased memorization.

In an attempt to investigate the "controversy" over marked temporal inversions, Stein and Nezworski (1978) conducted a study with six- and ten-year-old children. They discovered that the ten-year-olds recalled inverted stories as well (or better) than stories containing the expected sequence of events. With the six-year-olds, the majority of inversions significantly decreased recall, thereby pointing to a significant difference between younger and older children. The primary explanation for this decreased recall ability in younger children is that they are less familiar with deviant text structures.

Accepting the belief that deviant text structures heavily influence young children's recall, one may query, "How do children acquire strategies or rules that allow them to maintain a high level of recall when inversions do occur?" Presently, no conclusive evidence exists to accurately pinpoint the order in which children acquire recall strategies to deal with text inversions primarily because investigation needs to be done into just what events children perceive as being *directly* related to one another.

## *Recalling Story Events*

Stein and Glenn (1977) suggested that children who listened to stories that had been organized in a normally expected sequence could recall certain categories of information which were related to the organizational structure of the story more frequently than other categories. This increased accuracy of recall in certain categories has been attributed to the prototype story schema itself. The most frequently recalled categories across all grade conditions evaluated were: setting statements introducing the protagonist, initiating events, and consequence statements. The least frequently recalled categories were setting statements describing contextual information, internal responses, and reactions statements.

Two factors that may affect the categories of information that are recalled are the following:

1. Two or three statements in a story are summarized or otherwise integrated by a listener when he is asked to recall story information.

2. Certain story statements are redundant, so the information in one category may be logically omitted to avoid semantic redundancy.

Studies by Stein and Nezworski (1978) have indicated that the temporal position of statements can also affect their frequency of recall. In stories in which a positive intent is stated before a negative outcome, young children will infer that the character's original intentions were negative. But, when the intentions are moved to the end of the story, children will recall that the character's intentions were good, despite the negative outcome. So, the inclusion of temporal inversions in a story can ensure that children make certain kinds of recall inferences. These inversions can increase recall of certain statements and constrain the recall of other, less important information. Use of a "flashback" writing technique could even increase story recall by getting major obstacles out of the child's way so that he can attend more efficiently to subsequent story events.

It was also found that children and adults expect specified types of information to be explained in a fixed order within the framework of a story. When information is not presented in an appropriate order, children tend to reorganize the information to fit their preconceived notions of appropriate story structure. Because researchers have demonstrated that the manipulation of temporal sequence within a story can negatively affect children's processing, we, as teachers, can use this information to create stories that are memorable to children. We can help children to organize information by creating story structures that match children's current level of development. The level of structural story complexity that children can comprehend increases with age.

## Literal, Inferential, Critical Reading Comprehension

The preceding theories illustrate some of the most current thinking about reading comprehension. Many of these theories have been translated into practices based on the idea that there are three levels of comprehension; these levels are usually called *literal* (on the line) comprehension, *inferential* (between the lines) comprehension, and *critical* (beyond the lines) comprehension. This distinction had limited usefulness because it divided comprehension into three manageable categories. But many problems arose from this three-level design because educators began to think linearly about these three levels, assuming that they represented three levels of difficultly. They assumed that these three levels were hierarchically ordered, and that literal comprehension was easier than inferential comprehension, which in turn, was easier than critical comprehension.

The idea was probably the result of reading educators' attempts to model comprehension processes in a manner similar to the way that Bloom modeled levels of cognitive functioning. The following illustrates Bloom's notions about levels of cognition.

Bloom's taxonomy of educational objectives

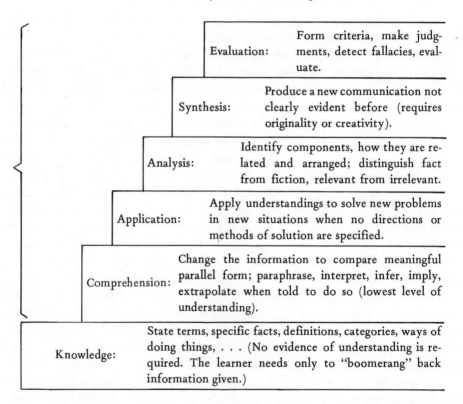

| Evaluation: | Form criteria, make judgments, detect fallacies, evaluate. |
|---|---|
| Synthesis: | Produce a new communication not clearly evident before (requires originality or creativity). |
| Analysis: | Identify components, how they are related and arranged; distinguish fact from fiction, relevant from irrelevant. |
| Application: | Apply understandings to solve new problems in new situations when no directions or methods of solution are specified. |
| Comprehension: | Change the information to compare meaningful parallel form; paraphrase, interpret, infer, imply, extrapolate when told to do so (lowest level of understanding). |
| Knowledge: | State terms, specific facts, definitions, categories, ways of doing things, . . . (No evidence of understanding is required. The learner needs only to "boomerang" back information given.) |

Bloom's taxonomy presented learning as a developmental process in which each category of the hierarchy became progressively more difficult. Mastery of one category was thought to be dependent upon the preceding category.

It has been suggested that Bloom's taxonomy of educational objectives is closely related to the hierarchy of learning that encompasses the reading comprehension processes. In the past, researchers in reading have based reading comprehension taxonomies on Bloom's taxonomy. These schemata were similar to the following:

| Level of cognitive development | Reading comprehension |
|---|---|
| Knowledge (recall) | **Text Explicit Information** (literal comprehension) |

**Text Explicit Information** (literal comprehension)

Identification of
  sounds
  letters
  phrases
  sentences
  paragraphs
Recognition and recall of
  details
  main ideas
  sequence
  comparison
  cause-and-effect relationships
  character traits
  patterns

Comprehension (understanding)

Translation of ideas or
information explicitly stated:
  classifying
  generalizing
  outlining
  summarizing
  synthesizing

Application (abstracting)

**Text Implicit Information** (inferential comprehension)

Realization of one's experiences and
Textual exposures

Inferring:
  details
  main ideas
  sequence
  comparisons
  cause-and-effect relationships
  character traits

Analysis (analyzing)

Predicting outcomes

Synthesis (production)

Interpreting figurative language,
Imagery, character, motives, and
responses
Synthesizing:
  convergently
  divergently

| Evaluation | **World Knowledge Information** (critical comprehension) |
| --- | --- |
| (judging) | Making evaluative judgments of |

reality or fantasy
fact or opinion
adequacy and validity
appropriateness
worth, desirability, and
acceptability
Valuing
Propaganda detection:
euphemism
fallacy of reasoning
statistical fallacy (maps, charts)
stereotyping
oversimplification

Appreciation

Emotional response to content
Identification with characters or incidents
Reactions to the author's use of language
Reactions to the author's word pictures

Reprinted with permission from Lapp, D. & Flood, J. *Teaching Reading to Every Child.*
New York: Macmillan Publishing Company, 1978.

## Sources of Reading Comprehension

Because the three-part division of literal, inferential, and critical comprehension is still used by many teachers and publishers of reading comprehension tests and reading texts, it may be useful for you to think of this categorization scheme as an attempt to divide the sources of reading comprehension into three important components:

Literal comprehension—comprehension that results from the *extraction of text explicit information*

Inferential comprehension—comprehension that results from the *extraction of text implicit relationships*

Critical comprehension—comprehension that results from *world knowledge* and *previous experiences.*

There are two major objections to a three-level (literal, inferential, and critical comprehension) classification scheme:

1. It is assumed by some that there is a linear progression of difficulty in these three levels of comprehension, and it is assumed that tasks that measure comprehension can be correctly labeled as literal, inferential, or critical.

2. This scheme takes only the source of comprehension into consideration. It does not take into account the dynamic, active process of comprehension in which the reader participates. In short, the operations of the learner during the reading process are ignored in this three-level scheme.

It is extremely important to begin to unravel some of the processes involved in proficient comprehension. An appropriate way to begin this unraveling is to examine the operations of the reader during reading episodes. We know the following facts about readers:

1. A reader processes propositions and not sentences. A proposition is a relational structure established by a predicate term and one or more argument terms. For example, in the sentence *Annette's daughter, Alicia, is an intelligent girl*, there are at least six propositions.

> Annette is a mother.
> Annette has a daughter.
> The daughter is Alicia.
> Alicia has a mother.
> Alicia is a girl.
> Alicia is intelligent.

These propositions are not consciously articulated by the reader. In this view of reading, it is suggested that the reader is ready to accept anything that follows logically from these propositions, such as, Alicia can count backwards, but the reader is also prepared to carefully examine new information that does not logically follow from these propositions, such as, Alicia is a boy.

2. All readers process (infer) regardless of memory demands (Flood and Lapp, 1977).

3. Readers attend to certain semantic and/or syntactic elements in the initial propositions of texts (Flood, 1978; Trabasso, 1972). An example of this phenomenon was reported by Flood (1978) when he asked proficient readers to supply the second sentence for two passages that began in the following ways:

| Passage A | Passage B |
|---|---|
| Christmas always meant going to Grandma's house. | One of the oldest drinks known to man is milk. |

In Passage A, all readers wrote in a personal narrative (reminiscent) style, supplying a second highly descriptive sentence about the event of Christmas. In Passage B, all readers supplied a second data-filled sentence using a formal, non-narrative style.

All proficient readers seem to participate in similar operations during comprehension. Most proficient readers, after being exposed to the following two sentences:

> Thomas is laughing, smiling, and squealing.
> He is hugging the Master of Ceremonies.

will probably infer something like "Thomas is happy because he won the prize."

The operations in which the reader participates can be described in the following way:

| Type | Example: |
|---|---|
| 1. Clarification of anaphoric referent. | he = Thomas. |
| 2. Superordination of strings of lexical items. | laughing, smiling, squealing = happy. |
| 3. Inferring causality. | Thomas is laughing, smiling, and squealing and hugging the Master of Ceremonies BECAUSE he won the prize. |

Frederiksen (1977) suggests that there are at least twenty-six types of inferences that readers generate. These inferences are important for proficient reading, and there are certain conditions that elicit these operations. Some of the conditions that elicit these twenty-six inferences in reading are the following:

| Type | Example |
|---|---|
| 1. Ambiguity in sentences and clauses. | Flying planes can be dangerous. I like her cooking. She fed her dog biscuits. |
| 2. Unclear anaphoric referents. | Zoe and Zeke were masons. They were paid by Vera and Velma. They were inflexible. |
| 3. Unclear cataphoric referents. | It was a beautiful day in spring when it happened. |
| 4. Unclear deictic referents. (person, place, time). | Paula and Phyllis were meeting in the afternoon. She was so late that she left. |
| 5. Unclear topical referents. | It was always this way. They had so much fun when they went there that they decided to go again. |
| 6. Partial lexicalization. | The set disappeared. |
| 7. Missing connective. | Tony drove too fast. The police didn't care about the emergency. |
| 8. Unclear segmentation. | Mary went to the fire station. Bernard and Mary lived happily ever after. They got the firemen to help them put out the fire. |
| 9. Need for reduction. | Danny was whining, coughing, vomiting, crying, tossing, bleeding, shouting, moaning. |
| 10. Need for extensions. | Emma lost her tooth. Her father put her quarter in her piggy bank. |
| 11. Pragmatic considerations. | The house was 80 years old and the crew arrived. |

Although we are only at the threshold of our understanding of reading comprehension, we are coming to some agreement that we need to specify the operations that the readers must perform if they are reading with proficiency. Frederiksen (1977) has offered us a first step over the threshold by specifying twenty-six types of inferencing operations which are listed on pages 367-69.

| TYPE OF OPERATION | DEFINITION | EXAMPLE | |
|---|---|---|---|
| | | Actual Text | Recalled Text |
| *Lexical Operation* | | | |
| 1. Lexical expansion | Expanding a concept into one or more propositions | The child is sick. | The child is vomiting, sore, feverish. |
| 2. Lexicalization | Replacing a proposition with a lexical concept | The child is vomiting, sore, feverish. | The child is sick. |
| *Identification Operation* | | | |
| 3. Attribute inference | Specifying an attribute | The boy has a bicycle. | The boy has a big bicycle. |
| 4. Category inference | Classifying an object or action | Joan is buying an outfit. | Joan is buying a skirt and sweater outfit. |
| 5. Time inference | Specifying a time | She is watering the roses. | She was watering the roses. |
| 6. Locative inference | Specifying location | She is watering the roses. | Mary is watering the roses in the garden. |
| 7. Part structure | Specifying part of an object | She is watering the roses. | She is watering the roots of the roses. |
| 8. Degree inference | Specifying the degree of an attribute, e.g., very | We'll put them in a vase. | We'll put them in a nice vase. |
| *Frame Operation* | | | |
| 9. Act inference | Filling in an action | Father will be sad. | Father will feel sad. |
| 10. Case inference | Inferring agent or instrument | a. Agent—Now the junk is all put away | a. Agent—Karen was putting away the party favors. |
| | | b. Instrument—Tom hit the boy. | b. Instrument—Scott hit the boy with the bat. |
| 11. Instrumental inference | Generating a cause of an event | Paula got well. | Dr. Ryan made Keith well. |
| 12. Result inference | Generating the result of an action | Take some of mine. | Sadie, you can have some of mine. |
| 13. Source inference | Inferring a prior state | Jimmy, you don't have a soda. | Take some of mine. |
| 14. Goal inference | Generating a goal for an action | Bobby cleaned his room. | Bobby cleaned his room so his father wouldn't get mad. |

| TYPE OF OPERATION | DEFINITION | EXAMPLE Actual Text | Recalled Text |
|---|---|---|---|
| 15. Theme inference | Generating a theme | Let's fix the mistake. | Mitchell rebuilds the structure. |
| 16. Frame transformation | Transforming a frame of one type into a frame of another type | $N_1VN_2$—John bought shoes. | $VN_2N_1$—Buy shoes, John. |
| 17. Disembedding operation | Removing a proposition from an event frame | He wants to take a vacation. | He . . . went to New England. |
| 18. Embedding operation | Inserting a proposition into an event frame | This is Pearl. She is buying a boat. | Pearl went to buy a boat. |
| *Event Generation* | | | |
| 19. Event inference | New, more general proposition | He is sick. | He is vomiting, feverish, and cranky. |
| | More specific propositions | He is vomiting, feverish, and cranky. | He is sick. |
| *Macrostructure Operation* | | | |
| 20. Superordinate inference<br>21. Subordinate inference | Ten subtypes, corresponding to the different slots (processive and resultive event frames) | The parade was held on Tuesday. | The parade of the clowns was postponed until Tuesday because it rained on Monday. |
| *Algebraic Operation* | | | |
| 22. Algebraic inference | Metric (degree) or nonmetric | A little boy was watering the flowers and then he ran down the lane. | A little boy watered the flowers and ran down the lane |
| *Dependency Operations* | | | |
| 23. Causal inferences | Connect unconnected events with causal relations | Tony was washing the windows and crashed and broke the vase. | Because Tony was washing the window carelessly, he fell and broke the vase. |
| 24. Conditional inferences | Specify antecedent conditions for an event | Now Sara thinks that Bootie will be sad. She wants to hug him. | She thought he might be sad. |
| 25. Logical inferences | Specify the logic of the inferences | It's lightning outside. | It's lightning outside; it must be raining. |
| *Truth Value Operation* | | | |
| 26. Truth value operation | Qualification or negation | Peter hurt Amy. | He thought she might be mad. |

## Teaching Reading Comprehension

### *Planning a Program*

With these realizations, it might be useful to follow these 9 steps in planning your teaching program:
1. Encourage children to read diversified types of writing.
2. Analyze the tasks of comprehension.
3. Encourage children to deal with many different response modes.
4. Plan an interactive language arts curriculum.
5. Analyze your student texts.
6. Plan an effective questioning program.
7. Develop your student's concept formation strategies.
8. Develop a literacy program for coping with life situations.
9. Encourage students to detect forms of propaganda.

Each step will be discussed in greater detail in the remainder of this chapter.

### *Step I: Encourage Children to Read Diversified Types of Writing*

As early as possible children should be encouraged to develop comprehension strategies in several contexts, i.e., they should read many types of writings. The following types of writing should be part of the program:

1. Narrative Writings — tales, fables, short stories, novelettes
2. Poetry Writings — poetry, song lyrics, nursery rhymes, proverbs
3. Textual Writings — textbooks: science, social studies
4. Dramatic Writings — drama, plays
5. Editoral Writings — magazines, newspapers, diaries, journals
6. Representational Writings — charts, graphs, tables, figures, maps
7. Functional Literacy Writing — cartoons, propaganda, advertisements, applications, schedules.

The emphasis at each level should reflect each child's developmental stage and should address his specific needs, e.g., the acquisition of comprehension strategies in narrative writings should be emphasized for very young children.

### *Step 2: Analyze the Tasks of Comprehension*

Pearson and Johnson (1978) discuss comprehension tasks of the concept level, proposition level, and level of longer discourse. In the following chart, Pearson and Johnson outline the tasks of comprehension at the concept level. The tasks of comprehension at the propositional level are presented on page 371.

Table 13.1  Concept Level Comprehension

| Category | Relation | Examples | Task |
|---|---|---|---|
| Simple Associations | 1. synonymous | Assist-help | Recognize that two words have similar meanings |
| | 2. antonymous (antonyms) | help-hinder | Recognize that two words can have opposing meanings |
| | 3. associative (associations) | green-grass run-fast walk-slow | Recognize that pairs of words often occur together in the language (often the words are linked by an attribute relation) |
| | 4. classificatory (classes) | animal-dog cat horse | Recognize that a class label has various examples that belong to that class |
| Complex Associations | 5. analogous (analogies) | dog is to bark as cat is to meow | Recognize that two pairs of words can be related in a similar way |
| | 6. connotative-denotative | I strolled walked sauntered | Recognize that words that denote the same class of things or behaviors connote different meanings or feelings |
| Ambiguous Words | 7. multiple meanings | fly—to soar fly—an insect | Recognize that a given word can refer to different concepts (have different meanings) |
| | 8. homographic (homographs) | proJECT— PROJect | Recognize that words alike in spelling can differ in pronunciation and meaning |
| | 9. homophonous (homophones) | fair-fare | Recognize that words alike in sound differ in spelling and meaning |

Reprinted with permission from Pearson, D. and D. Johnson. *Teaching Reading Comprehension.* New York: Holt, Rinehart and Winston, 1978.

## Step 3. Encourage Children to Deal With Many Different Response Modes

Your text presentations should contain several responses modes as a motivating element as well as a sound instructional procedure. All of the following response modes should be used: true/false, multiple choice, cloze, short answer, paraphrase, Wh questions, drawing a picture, matching, manual (manipulating), written comprehension.

## Step 4. Plan An Interactive Language Arts Curriculum

It is critical to integrate the language arts into an interactive instructional program. Children should be asked to listen, read, and write in order to maximize their involvement and understanding of the strategies that are involved in reading comprehension. In addition to answering questions about texts, children should be asked to rewrite (paraphrase) texts, e.g., children might be asked if the following sentence could have two meanings:

$\left(\begin{array}{l}\text{Resolving} \\ \text{Ambiguity}\end{array}\right)$ The duck is ready to eat.

*Table 13.2 Propositional Level Comprehension*

| Task | Word Level Analogue | Example | Description |
|---|---|---|---|
| 1. Paraphrase | Synonym | The lady shut the door = The door was closed by the woman. | Recognize the equivalence in meaning between two or more sentences. |
| 2. Association | Association | | Student reads paragraph. Selects the one sentence that is out of place in the paragraph. |
| 3. Main Idea— | Classification | | Student reads paragraph. Then 1. Selects the main idea, *or* 2. Selects details that support a main idea. |
| 4. Comparison | Analogies | One paragraph is about bicycles, a second about canoes. Question: How are the pedals on a bicycle like the oars in a canoe? | After reading a paragraph, student compares relationships therein to relationships in another paragraph, story, or experience. |
| 5. Figurative Language | Connotation-Denotation | 1. John is a veritable gazelle = John can run fast. | 1. Recognizes the equivalence between a figurative and a literal statement, *and* 2. Recognizes the difference in tone and feeling communicated by the two sentences. |
| 6. Ambiguous Statements | Multiple Meanings | Flying planes can be dangerous = 1. It can be dangerous to fly planes. 2. It can be dangerous to be around where airplanes are flying. | 1. Recognizes that a single sentence can have more than one meaning, *and* 2. Selects the appropriate meaning for a given paragraph context. |
| 7. Causal | | The people revolted because the new king was a tyrant. 1. Why did the people revolt? 2. What happened because the new king was a tyrant? | 1. Can identify causes or explanation (answer *why* questions), *or* 2. Can identify effects (answer *what happened because* or *what will happen next* questions). |
| 8. Sequence | | John went into the store. He bought a new tire. Then he went home to put it on his bike. What happened after John bought a new tire? | After reading a paragraph. 1. Places events in the sequence explicated in the paragraph, *or* 2. Answers *when* or *what happened after* or *what happened before* questions. |
| 9. Anaphora | | *John* is my friend. *He* is kind. I *play ball*. So *does* Henry. | Recognizes the logical equivalence between an anaphoric (substitute) term and its antecedent. |

Reprinted with permission from Pearson, D. and D. Johnson. *Teaching Reading Comprehension*. New York: Holt, Rinehart and Winston, 1978.

If yes, they might be asked to rewrite the sentence twice to convey the two meanings, e.g.

1. We are ready to eat the duck for dinner.
2. The duck is hungry, and he is ready to eat his dinner.

or

Read the following sentence and answer the question: "What is Betty doing?"

(Ellipsis) Ausra is dancing and singing, so is Betty.

Answer: Betty is dancing and singing.

or write a sentence that means the same as:

(Lexical Transform)          The mechanical man shot the poisonous ray. e.g.,
                             The robot shot the poisonous ray.

(Syntactic Transform)        The Cheshire cat chased the toy poodle, e.g.,
                             The toy poodle was chased by the Cheshire cat.

or

children might be asked to create writing samples that demonstrate their comprehension of a specific text, e.g., "If you were the girl in the story, what would you say to the baker?"

The intent of this approach would be to demonstrate the interrelatedness and interdependence of the language arts. Each lesson could simultaneously contain exercises in several comprehension strategies. The lessons might show that vocabulary skills, comprehension skills, and study skills are necessary for the total acquisition of meaning.

A model lesson might resemble the following:

Lesson: Understanding Words in Context

Exercise 1     Goal: Disambiguating ambiguous lexical items within sentences.

               Read the following sentences and explain the meaning of the word "crew."

               The "crew" arrived.
               The "crew" arrived to paint the house.

Exercise 2     Goal: Understanding multiple meanings.

               Write as many examples for the meaning of "crew" as you know: e.g.

               The crew rowed the boat.
               The wrecking crew tore the house down.
               The whole crew (gang) was there.

Exercise 3     Goal: To improve writing skills.

               Compose a story using one of the following as your starter.

               1. The crew staggered out of the smoking car . . .
               2. "I never had a worse crew," shouted . . .
               3. The rains kept coming as we watched the crew . . .

Exercise 4   Goal: Understanding multiple meanings.

Write two examples for each of these multiple meaning words.

bomb
lemon
star

Exercise 5   Goal: Understanding words in context.

Read these sentences and tell the meanings that each word has in the sentence below:

1. He bought a Chevy. What a lemon.
2. That play was a bomb.
3. I want to be a star.

## Step 5. Analyze Your Student's Texts

We suggest that you analyze your student's storybooks and textbooks for difficulties that they may encounter. Ask yourself:
"Are the passages clearly written; do they make sense?"
"Are there frequent illustrations, offering clues to the meaning of the passage?"
"Is the text's vocabulary appropriate for young readers?"
"Is the story structure appropriate for young readers?"
"Do the passages contain material about things that interest young children?"
If you think the storybook or textbook is too difficult, you can do the following:
1. Abandon the storybook and select an alternate one that is more appropriate for your children.
2. Rewrite the text, correcting it to clarify potentially troublesome areas. For example, if the text says, "Dan and Dee are playing basketball, but Don is not. Don and Del are roller skating," you may want to:
1. Change the names to avoid confusion.
2. Make the unclear reference to Don in the second sentence less ambiguous. The reader could rightly wonder if the Don in the second sentence is the Don in the first sentence.
A corrected, more readable version of the text that adheres closely to the original intent might be: "Mike and Patti are playing basketball, but Anthony is not, because he is roller skating with Debbie."

## Step. 6. Plan an Effective Questioning Program

In addition to clarifying unclear texts, you can direct students' reading by developing comprehension tasks. The most commonly used directive task is *questioning*. Although questions are useful tools for stimulating thinking and learning, you must remember that questions do not automatically produce a certain type of thinking. Reading is performed by readers as they activate their thinking processes; reading is not performed by a question. We, as teachers, have spent a great deal of time and effort labeling questions as literal,

*Figure 74.* In addition to clarifying texts that are unclear, you can direct students' reading by developing comprehension tasks. The most commonly used directive task is questioning. (Photo by Linda Lungren)

inferential, and critical (evaluative). Much of this time and effort has been futile; if we want to understand the effect of our questions, we should turn our attention to examining the processes that are involved during reading as the direct result of the questions that we ask.

Because teacher-generated questions can stimulate a student's thinking, it is important to analyze the questions that we ask, remembering that students *interpret* questions in many different ways; it is possible for students to give different answers than those that teachers had intended. For example:

Jane Turner, rushing through the door, expecting to find a surprise party, found a quiet meeting taking place.

Question: What did Jane Turner expect to find?

Intended answer: A surprise party.

Possible answers:  1. Her birthday celebration.
2. Friends.
3. She was the laughingstock of the meeting.

Each of the possible answers is relatively correct. Although each strays farther from the text and the actual question, it is important to appreciate an interpretive answer such as, "She was the laughingstock of the meeting," if we want to fully understand the way in which students make sense of texts. You, as the teacher of young children, should be aware of the types of questions that your students ask. These can give you clues about childrens' comprehension abilities at any given moment.

Another way to look at questioning as a stimulant for thinking is to think of questions as a tool for ordering thinking, for putting together many pieces of a puzzle. When a student misinterprets or miscomprehends a question, what do we know? We only know that something went awry; we need to go back to the passage and discover, with the child, the pieces of the puzzle that were misunderstood or forgotten. This retracing procedure can be performed through systematic questioning that is based on the logical propositions within the text or story. Consider, for example, the beginning of the book, *Where the Wild Things Are* by Maurice Sendak:

1. The night Max wore his wolf suit and made mischief of one kind
2. and another
3. his mother called him "Wild Thing!"
4. and Max said, "I'll eat you up!"
5. so he was sent to bed without eating anything.

Let us suppose that you asked your children to answer one question: Why did Max's mother send him to bed without eating? The answer that you might expect from your students would be similar to the following:

Max was sent to bed without eating

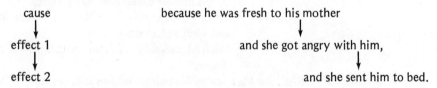

In order to give you such a response, the child has to attend to the text and perform numerous mental processes. For example, the child has to do the following:

| Text | Processes |
|---|---|
| and Max said, "I'll eat you up!" | 1. Understanding synonyms—Max was "fresh" <br> "fresh" means the reader has been able to understand: <br> a. tone (Max's intent) <br> b. dialogue rules between his mother and him. <br> c. his mother's intention in her reply |

| | |
|---|---|
| his mother called him "Wild Thing" and (so, therefore) Max said | 2. Understanding conjunctions—and, so, or therefore there is a cause-and-effect relationship |
| "I'll eat you up" (to her) (his mother) | 3. Understanding that Max was speaking to his mother |
| (so his mother said "Go to your room without eating anything") so he was sent to bed without eating anything. | 4. Understanding cause-and-effect inferences |

If your students are unable to answer the question correctly, you can retrace their steps by asking logically ordered questions that require them to process one bit of information at a time. A set of questions like this may help your children:

Question 1:   What did Max's mother call him on the night he made mischief of one kind and another?

         Text source:  1. The night Max wore his wolf suit and made mischief of one kind
                      2. and another
                      3. his mother called him "Wild Thing!"

         Operation:    syntactic transformation of question to subject-verb-object sentence, i.e., Max's mother called him "Wild Thing!"

Question 2:   Why did Max's mother call him "Wild Thing?"

         Text source:  1. The night Max wore his wolf suit and made mischief of one kind
                      2. and another
                      3. his mother called him "Wild Thing!"

         Operations:   syntactic deletion— . . . Max . . . made mischief of one kind and another
                          inferred causality—(so) his mother called him "Wild Thing."

Question 3:   What did Max say to his mother when she called him "Wild Thing?"
         Text source:  4. and Max said "I'll eat you up!"
         Operation:    elongation—I'll eat you up (to her)

Question 4:   What do you think Max's mother thought of that?
         Text source:  5. so he was sent to bed without eating anything.
         Operation:    extracting Max's purpose/tone
                        application of world knowledge

Question 5:   Then what did Max's mother say/do?
         Text source:  5. so he was sent to bed without eating anything.
         Operations:   passive to active transformation—he was sent
                        _____ sent Max to bed. syntactic substitution
                        (elongation——Mom sent Max to bed.
                        world knowledge of (rule)—Mom's turn to talk—"I send you to bed without dinner"
                        deleted imperative—Go to bed.)

This procedure can be used with all children's books. For example, in *Sylvester and the Magic Pebble* by W. Steig; the first episode is as follows:

> Sylvester Duncan lived with his mother and father at Acorn Road at Oatsdale. One of his hobbies was collecting pebbles of unusual shape and color.
>
> On a rainy Saturday during vacation he found a quite extraordinary one. It was flaming red, shiny, and perfectly round, like a marble. As he was studying this remarkable pebble, he began to shiver, probably from excitement, and the rain felt cold on his back. "I wish it would stop raining," he said.
>
> To his great surprise the rain stopped. It didn't stop gradually as rains usually do. It CEASED. The drops vanished on the way down, the clouds disappeared, everything was dry, and the sun was shining as if rain had never existed.

If we want to ask a single question that adequately assesses the child's comprehension to this point in the story, we might ask, "Why did the rain stop?" The intended response might be similar to the following:

| Necessary Process for the Response | Response |
| --- | --- |
| Critical event from text | The rain stopped |
| Cause of critical event | because Sylvester found a pebble and the pebble was remarkable |
| Action 1 | While he held the magic pebble |
| Temporal inference | he simultaneously |
| Action 2 | wished for the rain to stop. |
| Consequences of actions | This (procedure) caused his wish to be granted. |

If the child answers correctly, proceed with the rest of the story. If the child answers incorrectly, you must analyze the question. It requires the following operations:

| Text Source | Processes |
| --- | --- |
| Sylvester Duncan lived with his mother and father at Acorn Road in Oatsdale. One of his hobbies was collecting pebbles of unusual shapes and color.<br><br>On a rainy Saturday during vacation he found a quite extraordinary one. It was flaming red, shiny, and perfectly round, like a marble. As he was studying this remarkable pebble, he began to shiver, probably from excitement, and the rain felt cold on his back. "I wish it would stop raining," he said. | 1. Inferring the cause of the action. |

To his great surprise the rain stopped.
It didn't stop gradually as rains usually
do. It CEASED.

On a rainy Saturday during vacation
he found a quite extraordinary one.

2. Disambiguating one
   one = pebble

As he was studying this remarkable
pebble, he began to shiver, probably
from excitement, and the rain felt
cold on his back. "I wish it would
stop raining," he said.

3. Vocabulary: Finding   a   figurative
   synonym
   remarkable = magic

   extraordinary

"I wish it would stop raining," he
said
            (while)
he was holding/studying the pebble.

4. Inferring temporal inference simul-
   taneity
                  while

It didn't stop gradually as rains
usually do. It CEASED.

5. Inferring results of the action.

   The rain stopped (and things
   happened)

For the child  who answered the original question incorrectly, the following
six sequential questions, with their appropriate text sources, may enhance the
child's comprehension.

| Question | Text Source |
|---|---|
| 1) What did Sylvester find? | Sylvester Duncan lived with his mother and father at Acorn Road in Oatsdale. One of his hobbies was collecting pebbles of unusual shape and color.<br><br>On a rainy Saturday during vacation he found a quite extraordinary one. It was flaming red, shiny, and perfectly round, like a marble. As he was studying this remarkable pebble, he began to shiver, probably from excitement, and the rain felt cold on his back. |
| 2) What did the pebble look like? | It was flaming red, shiny, and perfectly round, like a marble. |
| 3) What kind of pebble was it? | As he was studying this remarkable pebble. . . . |
| 4) What did he do with the re-markable pebble? | He was holding/studying the pebble. |
| 5) What did he say while he was studying the pebble? | "I wish it would stop raining," he said. |
| 6) What happened as he said, "I wish it would stop raining." | To his great surprise the rain stopped. |

Leading children through the text in this step-by-step manner may be a productive procedure for helping them to understand the interrelatedness of the entire text.

### Step 7. Develop Your Students' Concept Formation Strategies

In addition to remembering that asking questions is a means of helping children to develop their comprehension strategies, it is also important for you to remember that reading comprehension is an interactive process that takes place as the reader interprets the text. This interpretation is based on the experience and background of each child. You have to help your students develop knowledge and experiences that will enhance their reading. One way to develop this background is through instruction in *concept formation*. In helping children learn how to form concepts, you are helping them to develop their critical thinking skills.

In order to help children to form a concept, you should share with them a broad general experience. With your relatively inexperienced younger students, you may wish to involve them in an activity they have never done before (for instance, making homemade ice cream, a short introduction to modern dance movements, or visiting a nearby cheese factory). This can be followed by organizing the many details of the experience into a workable grouping of simple "research topics." The following process will help you to develop strategies for such grouping so your children can form general concepts.

1. Ask students, "What did you see?" "What did you hear?" "What did you smell?" This line of questioning will stimulate your young students' awareness of their senses. An excellent method for increasing sensory awareness is the "blindfold walk." It was first popularized by nature guides who wanted to increase their students' capacity for absorbing the whole realm of their environment. The "blindfold walk" is carried out in the following manner:

> Divide your students into pairs.
>
> Each pair receives a blindfold from the teacher.
>
> Each member of the pair takes a turn at being blindfolded and led around by the hand. The partner who is not blindfolded does the leading through the environment (nature trail, school grounds, school corridors). It is the leader's job to guide the blindfolded person carefully and to ask questions like, "What does this feel like? Can you guess what it is? What can you smell?"

In addition to being a useful group activity based on mutual trust, the "discoveries" of a "blindfold walk" can easily be turned into a classroom writing exercise.

2. As students begin to group the items of their experience, they will be engaged in the process of identifying common properties. They will be beginning to engage in abstraction processing.

3. After they have established categories, ask students, "How would you label these groups?" As students begin this labeling process, they are involved in hierarchical ordering of superordinates and subordinates. The acquisition of each of these processing skills is extremely important in the development of reading comprehension skills.

Concept formation can begin with the listing of discrete items. For example, after viewing a film about the Pilgrims, one group of students listed the following items:

| | | |
|---|---|---|
| Pilgrims | Massachusetts | furs |
| churches | utensils | tobacco |
| meeting houses | fireplaces | lumber |
| houses | slaves | schools |
| gardens | plantations | haystacks |
| farmers | Indians | shoes |
| clothing | water wheels | rock walls |
| maps | goats | mills |
| ships | canoes | ministers |

To actually get the list on the board, a number of subquestions may be necessary. Children sometimes get stuck on a category and name many similar items. Look at the preceding list for an example. The students had listed meeting houses and houses. If they had continued with sheds or houses for the cattle, it would have been good to shift their thinking by saying, "Did you see any other things in the film that interested you?" This questioning strategy often breaks the imitative responses. All students should be encouraged to participate. Everyone has seen something worth recording.

The students categorized the preceding list under the following concept headings:

| | | |
|---|---|---|
| people | travel, transportation | buildings |
| tools | things to wear | industries |

Some of the items did not fit into any of these broad categories. The students then re-examined the list to determine what other labels would be needed to include the disparate items.

Another technique for developing concepts is called question-initiating. As with the first technique, an "opener" or introductory broad experience is provided as motivation. Following this opener, the student is asked to work in a small group or choose a partner and "brainstorm" all the questions that occurred to him as he watched the film or took the walk. Each group will list the questions for which they would like to find answers. With younger children, you may find that you have to go from group to group to generate ideas and keep the group on task. You should provide writing paper on which the students can write their questions; for your younger students, you will do most of the writing. After the questions have been written down, sorting and grouping into categories follows.

Using either one of the techniques suggested will help students determine the specific, concrete details that are subsumed under the category label. Once the category has been formed, it will be necessary to re-examine the variation within the category so that a general statement can be developed about the concept. It is important for the students to gather a large fund of information about the category they have chosen so that they can organize the data and, on the basis of the organized information, develop some general statements. Stauffer (1969) explains:

> The principal outcome of all this is the plea that the children be required to do their own learning. Teachers must present children with reading situations in which the children experiment by trying out ideas to see what happens, by manipulating things and ideas, by positing questions and seeking answers, by reconciling what they find at one time with what they find at another, and by comparing their findings with each other. Children must be active and required to act on material things as well as hypothetical ideas, and they should do this in social collaboration or in a group effort. Such children are required to communicate with each other. Intelligent functioning—which equilibrium obtains—requires a fine balance between a person and his milieu and stresses the paramount importance of interaction, so that a realistic and a meaningful support is secured, and so that a child can acquire the rationality and objectivity which only a multiperspective view can offer. Then he can sort particulars into a set of classes to order their diversity and form a concept. (p. 351)

### *Step 8. Develop a Literacy Program for Coping with Life Situations*

Instructing your students in concept formation is instrumental in preparing them for the task of reading. However, the demands of comprehension are so complex and varied in today's world that it is important for you to go beyond this preparatory process. After you have effectively introduced your students to a new concept and prepared appropriate questions for stimulating thinking, your task is to help your students through new, varied materials from life situations that require the transfer of the reading strategies they have acquired. If you are successful in assisting in this transfer of concept to reality, you are helping your students learn how to deal effectively with the world in which they live.

If you are developing a program that is designed to foster literacy, you may want to include the development of basic mathematics skills. You may also want to provide application strategies that are necessary for making decisions in life-coping situations. The following outline is presented in an attempt to further explain this duality:

| I. DO YOU HAVE THE ACADEMIC SKILLS OF LITERACY? | II. CAN YOU APPLY THESE SKILLS TO LIFE-COPING SITUATIONS? |
|---|---|
| A. Lanugage arts<br>  1. Spoken<br>     Are you able to communicate in the dominant language of the culture? | A. Personal<br>  1. Restaurant functioning<br>  2. Driver's license application<br>  3. Transportation schedules |

2. Written language
   Can you express yourself through
   the written language of the culture?
   (syntax, semantics, spelling)
3. Reading
   Can you critically comprehend the
   printed materials of the dominant
   culture? (perceive, infer, evaluate,
   apply)
B. Computation
   Can you add, subtract, multiply, divide,
   compute fractions and percentages,
   interpret graphs and thermometers?

4. Instruction manuals
5. W2 forms
6. Grocery slips
7. Bank slips
8. Insurance forms
9. Savings accounts
10. Home purchases
B. Career
   1. Employment ads
   2. Pension plans
C. Health
   1. Medications
   2. Health care
D. Civic responsibilities
   1. Community resources
   2. Consumer economics
   3. Environmental issues

### Step 9: Encourage Students to Detect Forms of Propaganda

Although the processes involved in critical thinking have been clearly outlined for decades, many people still make faulty evaluations, exhibit a lack
of problem-solving strategies, and are unable to detect propaganda. It might
seem that these are higher-level skills that need not be taught until children
have mastered the basic processes of reading. Such is not the case; critical
thinking must be taught in connection with beginning reading skills. In a con-
sumer-oriented world, we must *all* possess critical reading/thinking skills if
we are to be considered literate.

An understanding of propaganda is essential to good reading. You may want
to explain each of the following propaganda techniques to your students:

| Type | Example |
| --- | --- |
| Bandwagon | Everyone is buying Bunny Bimbos. |
| Prestige | Debbie Gombar, ace pitcher, chews ZOZO gum. |
| Testimonial | John Sexton, ace tennis pro, says "Drink Limiade." |
| Repetition | ZOZO gum is good to pop, pop, pop. |
| Plain Folks | I'm a cabbie and I like ZOZO gum. |
| Snob Appeal | Everyone in Snob Heights plays the Boo Game. |
| Simple | I love ZOZO gum. |
| Emotional Appeal | Good mothers use UPY, do you? |
| Authority | All lawyers recommend Speigile. |
| Ego | Are you strong enough to be a mason? |
| Image | You'll be another Dr. J. if you chew ZOZO gum. |
| Oversimplification | Life is better with ZOZO gum. |
| Buckshot | ZOZO is chewy, chewy, chewy. |

As suggested earlier, we believe strongly that the prime goal of all reading instruction is comprehension. All other reading skills are steps toward this goal;

it is comprehension that allows the student to mature intellectually. This chapter has introduced both the theory and implementation strategies of reading comprehension. In order to be a successful reading teacher, you must understand the intricacies of reading comprehension. Because it is extremely important to assimilate theory (the models of reading presented in the beginning of this chapter) into practice (the appropriate strategies for teaching comprehension), we have suggested a few activities that may help you in a comprehension program.

## COMPREHENSION STRATEGIES

### Copy Me

Strategy development: Recall

Age level: 0-1

Procedure: Have the child imitate your movements, such as patting your head, rubbing your stomach, clapping your hands. Try two movements in a row, then three, increasing in complexity.

### Who Doesn't Belong Here?

Strategy development: Categorizing/Classifying

Age level: 1-2

Construction: Develop sets of objects containing four items. Spread them horizontally in front of the child. For example, three shoes and a carrot, three apples and a toy truck, three pencils and a pen.

Procedure: The child should point to the object that doesn't belong.

### Story Time

Strategy development: Comprehension of explicitly illustrated information

Age level: 1-2

Procedure: Frequent reading of picture books to children in this age group is crucial for the development of their future reading skills. Have the child point to characters or objects while you are reading about them, ask simple questions, or have the child repeat the names of objects after you.

### Find the Treat

Strategy development: Memory

Age level: 2-3

Construction: Give the child some raisins or candy to eat. Arrange four cups of different shapes and colors face down in front of the child. While he or she is watching, place a piece of candy under one of the cups and then place a screen in front of the cups.

Procedure: After ten seconds, lift the screen, and the child should be able to find the treat at the first attempt. Repeat the activity, using the same color and shape of the cups and increasing the time the screen is lowered.

### Touch and Feel

Strategy development: Vocabulary

Age level: 2-3

Construction: Collect materials that show different textures.

Procedure: Let the child feel and examine the materials and help him to describe them, using such words as "hard, soft, rough, smooth." Then put a duplicate of each of the materials into a bag. The child is given a soft piece of wool, for example, and then must reach into the bag and find the other soft piece.

### What Goes With What?

Strategy development: Classifying/Categorizing

Age level: 2-3

Construction: Prepare sets of objects; for example, a cup and saucer, sock and shoe, pencil and paper. Scramble the objects.

Procedure: Have the child tell which two belong together. He may have a perfectly good reason for pairing two objects that you had never thought of.

### Story Time

Strategy development: Recall

Age level: 2-3

Procedure: Children love to hear the same books read to them over and over. After reading a story, go back to the beginning of the book. Have the child retell the story just by looking at the pictures.

### Hide and Seek

Strategy development: Memory

Age level: 2-3

Construction: Collect a small group of objects or toys and place them in front of the child.

Procedure: Review the name of each of the objects and have the child repeat the name after you. Have the child close his eyes and remove one of the objects. He should then be able to tell you what is missing. Start out with a small number of objects and gradually increase the number, removing more than one object.

## Listening is Fun

Strategy development: Memory

Age level: 3-4

Procedure: Provide many listening experiences, using records and tapes of stories, songs, and nursery rhymes. Especially valuable are those that ask children to sing along, answer questions, match pictures with sounds, or perform movements.

## Let's Make a Book

Strategy development: Writing/Reading

Age level: 3-4

Procedure: Have the child dictate a story to you after which the child can illustrate the story. This can be made into a book to be read again and again.

## Detective Work

Strategy development: Listening comprehension

Age level: 3-4

Procedure: The teacher or another child locates an object in the room and then gives the other children clues. For example, "I see something yellow we use to write with." The first person to identify the object can give the next clue.

## Simon Says

Strategy development: Listening comprehension (following directions)

Age level: 3-4

Procedure: The teacher gives three directions and the class must follow them in the correct sequence. For example, "Touch your toes, clap your hands, and blink your eyes." Increase the number of directions as the children become more efficient. Children can also take turns giving the directions.

## Blocks

Strategy development: Classifying

Age level: 3-4

Construction: Place approximately fifteen blocks of different sizes, shapes, and colors in front of the child.

Procedure: After demonstrating, have the child group the blocks by color, then shape, then size. The same can be done with buttons, coins, shoes, crayons.

## One Step at a Time Drawing

Strategy development: Following directions

Age level: 4–5

Construction: Give students a blank piece of paper and a pencil or crayon. Tell the class they are going to draw a picture, one step at a time.

Procedure: Give them specific directions such as, "Place a dot in the middle of the page. Draw a line above it. Make a circle below it." At the end of the game, students can compare their pictures.

### You Are an Actress/Actor!

Strategy development: Recall

Age level: 4–5

Construction: Read a children's story such as "The Three Little Pigs" or "Little Red Riding Hood" to the class.

Procedure: Have members of the class act out the story. They should be able to remember the proper sequence of events and the dialogue, with perhaps a little prompting from the class and teacher.

### How Are We Alike?

Strategy development: Sequencing

Age level: 4–5

Construction: Have five or six students come to the front of the room. These students should be chosen so that they all have something in common: blue eyes, black hair, brown shoes, and so on.

Procedure: The class must guess what is the common characteristic. Another activity would be to set up a pattern with the students such as black hair, blond hair, black hair, blond hair, and then have students continue the pattern.

### Finish The Story

Strategy development: Story sequence

Age level: 4–5

Construction: Read a simple story aloud to the group. Choose students to assume parts in the re-enactment of the story for the rest of the group.

Procedure: On the following day, have the children listen to another simple story, but do not relate the story ending. Instead, have the children assume the various roles and act out their own ending.

### Complete the Pattern

Strategy development: Logical thinking

Age level: 4–5

Construction: On strips of paper, draw or use stamp pads to show various shapes and designs.

Procedure: The child must complete the pattern, drawing in four more designs.

For younger children, the students can just repeat the pattern.

## You Make Up the Ending

Strategy development: Prediction

Age level: 5–6

Construction: Record short stories on a tape recorder cassette, leaving out the ending.

Procedure: The student listens to the story and dictates to the teacher an appropriate ending to the story. The student then illustrates the ending on drawing paper.

## Emotions

Strategy development: Classifying

Age level: 5–6

Construction: Give students several magazines and have them cut out pictures of people. Attach a large chart to a wall or blackboard and label it with various emotions: happy, sad, frightened, helping, and so on. To give students assistance, draw expressive faces next to each heading:

Happy  Sad  Frightened  Helping

Procedure: Students must paste each of their magazine pictures under the appropriate heading.

## Story Time

Strategy development: Recall

Age level: 5–6

Construction and Procedure: Children at this age level can answer more complicated questions about books that have been read to them. In the middle of the story, ask, "What do you think will happen next? What are the names of the characters? How would you have ended the story?"

## A Picture Story

Strategy development: Sequencing

Age level: 5-6

Construction: Mount individually on small cards four or five pictures that tell a story. For example, a child could be shown putting on ice skates, skating on the ice, the ice cracking, and so on.

Procedure: The student must then put the cards in the correct left to right sequence.

## It Could Go On Forever!

Strategy development: Memory

Age level: 6-7

Construction and Procedure: Students sit in a circle. One consonant sound is chosen and the teacher starts the game by saying "On my summer vacation I packed a ball." for example, if b was the consonant chosen. The next student repeats "On my summer vacation I packed a ball and a bat." The next student must repeat the entire sentence, adding a word beginning with that consonant. Continue around the circle.

## Comic Strips

Strategy development: Sequencing

Age level: 6-7

Construction: Laminate comic strips taken from the Sunday newspaper. Cut the strips into sections and mix them up.

Procedure: The student must put the comics into the proper sequence and tell what is going on in the story when completed.

## Small to Large

Strategy development: Comprehending relative size

Age level: 6-7

Construction: Take vocabulary words from the students' reading selections and write them on small index cards. Put them into groups of five or six cards each. The cards should contain names of objects found in the reading selections such as raindrop, house, bush, bird, shoes, and so on.

Procedure: The student must read the names of the object and place the cards in the proper order, smallest to largest. He should then give the cards to another student and compare answers.

## The Riddle Game

Strategy development: Recall

Age level: 6-7

Construction and Procedure: Make up riddles to describe characters from stories the class has read. They can be written or read aloud. For example, "I live in the North Pole. I bring gifts to children all over the world. I have a long white beard. Who am I?" Then let members of the class make up riddles.

## Puppet Show

Strategy development: Comprehending theme

Age level: 7-8

Construction and Procedure: Have a group of students read the same book, and then develop a puppet show illustrating the main ideas of the book for the rest of the class. The class should then be able to retell what happened in the story.

## Treasure Hunt

Strategy development: Following instructions

Age level: 7-8

Construction: Hide imitation gold coins or other valuable-looking objects throughout the classroom. There should be one "treasure" for every two students. Make up a series of clue cards that the students must follow exactly in order to find the treasure. For example, walk ten feet, turn left and look in the fifth shelf of the closet. Clues should be placed accordingly throughout the classroom.

Procedure: Tell students they are to find a buried treasure, and give them the location of the first clue.

## Who Am I?

Strategy development: Recall

Age level: 7-8

Construction and Procedure: After the class has read a series of five or six short stories, have members of the class act out a character from any of the stories. The rest of the class can be divided into two teams. In turn, a member from each team has the opportunity to identify the character acted out. Score five points for each correct answer. The characterization can be pantomime or with dialogue.

## Post Office

Strategy development: Classifying

Age level: 7-8

Construction: Acquire several liquor bottle boxes that are sectioned off with cardboard. Label each box with different ideas such as Places Visited, Famous People, Hobbies and Activities, Kinds of Animals. Make up a series of short notes containing information that would apply to one of those categories. The notes could be made to sound as if someone was writing to his parents, telling them about the various activities in which he is taking part.

Procedure: The student reads the notes and puts them into the appropriate slot under each category.

## Find the Information

Strategy development: Comprehending explicitly stated information and implicit relationships

Age level: 8–9

Construction: Prepare a booklet containing baseball cards. Laminate each page of cards. Include in the booklet a laminated sheet of paper with questions about the cards such as, "Who had the best batting average in 1976? Who do you think is the best all-round player?"

Procedure: The student answers the questions on a separate piece of paper.

## Be A Door-to-Door Salesperson

Strategy development: Understanding propaganda

Age level: 8–9

Construction and Procedure: Give each student the name of a particular product and have all do research about the product—cost, efficiency, what it does, and how well it does what it was made to do. Each student then goes in front of the class and pretends to be a door-to-door salesperson. The student should include facts in the presentation, as well as exaggerations and opinions. After the presentation, students should be able to tell which statements were facts and which were opinion.

## BIBLIOGRAPHY

Bartlett, J. R. *Remembering: A Study in Experimental and Social Psychology.* Cambridge, England: University Press, 1932.

Bloom, B. *Stability and Change in Human Characteristics.* New York: John Wiley and Sons, 1964.

Brown, A. L. "The Development of Memory, Knowing, Knowing about Knowing, and Knowing How to Know." In H. W. Reese (ed.) *Advances in Child Development and Behavior.* New York: Academic Press, Inc., 1975.

Brown, A. L. "Recognition, Reconstruction and Recall of Narrative Sequences by Preoperational Children." *Child Development,* 156–166, 1975.

Flood, J. "The Effects of First Sentences on Reader Expectations in Prose Passages." *Reading World,* May 1978.

Flood, J. and D. Lapp. "Prose Analysis and the Effects of Staging on Prose Comprehension." Paper presented at the Second Annual Reading Association of Ireland Conference, Dublin, Ireland, 1977.

Frederiksen, C. H. "Inference and Structure of Children's Discourse." Paper for the Symposium on the Development of Processing Skills, Society for Research in Child Development Meeting, New Orleans, 1977.

Gough, P. B. "One Second of Reading." In J. F. Kavanaugh and I. G. Mattingly *Language by Eye and Ear*. Cambridge, Mass.: MIT Press, 1972.

Guilford, J. P. "The Three Faces of Intellect." *American Psychologist,* (1959), **14**: 469–479.

Jenkins, J. J. "Can We Have a Theory of Meaningful Memory." In R. L. Solso (Ed.) *Theories in Cognition Psychology: The Loyola Symposium*. Hillsdale, N.J.: Earlbaum 1974.

LaBerge, D., and S. J. Samuels. "Toward a Theory of Automatic Information Processing, in Reading." *Cognitive Psychology* (1974) **6**:293–323.

Lapp, D. and Flood, J. *Teaching Reading To Every Child*. New York: Macmillan Publishing Company, 1978.

Mandler and Johnson. "Remembrance of Things Parsed: Story Structure and Recall." *Cognitive Psychology* (1977) **9**:111–151.

Pearson, D. and D. Johnson. *Teaching Reading Comprehension*. New York: Holt, Rinehart and Winston, 1978.

Rumelhart, D. E. "Toward an Interactive Model of Reading." Technical Report No. 56, Center for Human Information Processing, University of California-San Diego, 1976.

Sendak, M. *Where The Wild Things Are*. New York: Harper and Row, 1969.

Smith, N. B. *Reading Instruction for Today's Children*. Englewood Cliffs, N.J.: Prentice-Hall, Inc., 1963.

Smith, F. *Understanding Reading*. New York: Holt, Rinehart and Winston, 1971.

Stauffer, R. G. *Directing Reading Maturity as a Cognitive Process*. New York: Harper & Row, Publishers, 1969.

Steig, W. *Sylvester and the Magic Pebble*. New York: E. P. Dutton & Co., 1970.

Stein, N. "How Children Understand Stories: A Developmental Analysis," in L. Katz (ed). *Current Topics in Early Childhood Education* (Volume 2), Hillsdale, N.J.: Ablex, Inc. In press.

Stein and Glenn. "The Role of Structural Variation in Children's Recall of Simple Stories." Paper presented at the Society for Research in Child Development, New Orleans, 1977 (a); "A Developmental Study of Children's Construction of Stories." Paper presented at the Society for Research in Child Development, New Orleans, 1977 (b).

Stein and Nezworski "The Effects of Organization and Instructional Set on Story Memory," *Discourse Processes* (1978) **1**:177–193.

Thorndike, E. L. "Reading as Reasoning: A Study of Mistakes in Paragraph Reading." *Journal of Educational Psychology* (1917) **8**: 323–332.

Trabasso, T. "Mental Operations in Language Comprehension." *Language Comprehension and the Acquisition of Knowledge*. Washington, D.C.: V. H. Winston, 1972.

# 14

# Language and Reading in the Content Areas

Often the child who tries the hardest suffers most in reading textbooks. He thinks he must read carefully and remember all the information. He starts into a textbook chapter on Plains Indians. The first paragraph names nine different tribes. He rereads and "studies" trying to memorize all nine. The second paragraph names five rivers and two mountain ranges. Again "study," memorize. By this time he's getting pretty well fed up with the Plains Indians and with reading in general. The next paragraph describes the buffalo. It is high shouldered, shaggy. He thinks it looks like his brother and then goes on. The buffalo has hair like a lion and a hump like a camel. Picture that! By this time he has been reading for fifteen minutes and has covered three paragraphs.

*(Ireland, 1973, p. 586)*

As you read this quote and reflect on the many difficulties a reader has with content area materials and classroom experiences, you are probably picturing a reader who is at least ten years of age. Your mental picture may be of this older child because we often equate content area experiences with middle-age or older-age students. Many believe that the early years must be spent in mastering basic mathematics, reading, and writing skills. Although this is absolutely true, there must be a *context* for the mastery of reading skills. Therefore, we propose that content area experiences begin in the *preschool*, thus providing the appropriate context for beginning reading experiences. If you are skeptical about this proposition, think for a minute about many of the early preschool experiences, that children encounter everyday, such as pouring, measuring, molding, cutting, pasting. All of these activities could be categorized as early mathematics and science experiences. This chapter is designed to help you in understanding how to utilize these and similar activities as an appropriate content area context for extending the language/reading skills of the young child.

*Figure 75.* Many activities in preschool could be categorized as early mathematics and science experiences. (Photo by Linda Lungren)

## Social Studies in the Early Childhood Curriculum

The development of a social studies curriculum for children in early learning programs must be designed to accomplish the following goals:

1. Introduce social science concepts.
2. Apply social science concepts to life situations.
3. Socialize the child through simulated situations.

These goals may be easily simulated through life experiences because social science information is a composite of information from six different disciplines: psychology, sociology, geography, anthropology, economics, and civics. Examples of integrated social science curricula that stress the cognitive/affective dimensions of learning follow.

1. The University of Minnesota Project Social Studies.
2. Taba Elementary Social Studies.
3. Materials and Activities for Teachers and Children (MATCH).

Four other early childhood social studies programs, which stress the affective dimensions of learning, have been analyzed by Peter Martorella. (1975). An analysis of these programs, which include *Developing Understanding of Self and Others* (DUSO-1): *First Things: Values; Human Development Program;* and *Dimensions of Personality,* are presented in Table 14–1.

*Table 14–1*

**Summary Comparisons of Early Childhood Affective Programs**
**Peter Martorella, 1975**

|  | Developing Understanding of Self and Others (DUSO-1) | First Things: Values | Human Development Program | Dimensions of Personality |
|---|---|---|---|---|
| Basic Teaching Models | Awareness training; Laboratory method; conditioning | Developmental | Awareness training; conditioning | Laboratory method |
| Basic Affective Theme(s) | Emotion arousal; focus on self | Emotion arousal | Focus on self | Focus on self |
| Key Student Role(s) | Spectators, actors, role playing | Taking, justifying, and defending moral stands; considering and challenging competing arguments | Group participant | Group participant |

| | Developing Understanding of Self and Others (DUSO-1) | First Things: Values | Human Development Program | Dimensions of Personality |
|---|---|---|---|---|
| Key Teacher Roles | Group discussion leader; clarifier and summarizer; puppeteer and dramatizer; behavior reinforcer | Organizing discussion groups; encouraging role taking; "devil's advocate"; diagnosing stages of moral reasoning | Organizing discussion groups; group discussion leader; behavior reinforcer | Organizing discussion groups; group process observer |

Martorella, P.H. "Selected Early Childhood Affective Learning Programs: An Analysis of Theories, Structure, and Consistency," *Young Children*, Vol. 30, No. 4 (May 1975) p. 300.

Numerous social studies programs are available, but the selection or development of one that is appropriate for your children will depend upon the curriculum goals that you have established. Taba (1967) provided the following four general categories from which your curriculum goals may be further delineated:

1. Basic Knowledge
2. Thinking
3. Attitudes, feelings, and sensitivities (affective dimensions)
4. Skills

*Figure 76.* Development of academic skills such as map reading, graphing, and charting are a major part of the basic skills goals. These students are studying a model of their own city. (Photo by Linda Lungren)

The development of goals that are intended to expand each child's *basic knowledge* about social studies includes main ideas, facts, and concepts from any of the social sciences. Goals designed to extend *thinking skills* include those goals that are related to the development of deduction, application, concept formation, synthesis, and analysis. Goals that are designed to extend the *affective dimensions* of learning include the development of an understanding of tolerance, acceptance, and self-appraisal. Development of academic skills such as map reading, graphing, and charting is a major part of the *basic skills* goals.

As you attempt to integrate these goals into a beginning social studies/language arts curriculum, it will be necessary to 1) provide a wide content area base for the learner as he attempts to explore the social sciences and 2) equip students with the literacy skills they will need to interpret the social sciences.

Because this is not a text related to any one content area, we will focus on the second item in an attempt to provide you, the teacher, with a thorough understanding of the language arts skills related to the development of a beginning knowledge of social studies, and with an understanding of the implementation strategies that are necessary to achieve the pragmatic aspect of your curriculum.

One of the first themes that can be explored in the early childhood classroom is "the child as part of the family structure." As you discuss and view pictures of various types of family structures, children will become acquainted with the social, psychological, and economic distinctions of their individual family.

How are the families of the children in the classroom similar? Different? Are the families in the community alike? As you begin to explore the intricacies of these answers, you will be expanding the experiential and language base of each young child. It is easy to incorporate geography into this topic as you extend your discussion to include an investigation of families in other states, countries, and continents.

Agriculture can be investigated as you explore the eating habits of the children in your class. Study of the values, customs, and traditions of various families around the world will give students insights about themselves, their families, and others. Remember to maintain openness in the discussion. It is a wise teacher who realizes that everyone has biases, but you must work toward openness in your thinking and your discussions with your students. While it is important not to criticize the ideas of your students, you must feel free to demand from your children rationales that substantiate opinions. In this way, you will be encouraging the development of critical thinking skills.

Social studies issues arise as children work and play together. A democratic classroom involves discussion and provides a format from which the teacher can develop a language experience program. There are many books available that introduce children to multiple social studies concepts. Following is a list of some of these books:

*Figure* 77. Social studies issues arise as children work and play together. A democratic classroom involves discussions and provides the teacher with a format from which to develop a language experience program. (Photo by Linda Lungren)

Baker, B. *What Is Black?* New York: Franklin Watts, Inc., 1969. A frank discussion of the color black as a positive entity.

Clark, A. N. *In My Mother's House.* New York: The Viking Press, Inc., 1941. This text explores the life of the Tewa Indians in New Mexico.

Evans, E. K. *People are Important.* New York: Capital Publishing Co., 1957. Presents the notion of the importance of human beings regardless of race, customs or dwelling.

Foster, D. V. *A Pocketful of Seasons.* New York: Lothrop, Lee & Shepard Co., 1971. As the title suggests, this text delightfully examines the concept of season changes.

Hoethe, L., and R. Hoethe. *Houses Around the World.* New York: Charles Scribner's Sons, 1973. This text provides an introduction to the type of houses that are lived in by people throughout the world.

Keats, E. J. *Peter's Chair.* New York: Harper & Row, Publishers, 1967. Presents some of the traumatic feelings experienced through "growing pains."

Liang, Y. *Tommy and Dee Dee.* New York: Henry Z. Walck, Inc., 1953. A wonderful glimpse into the Chinese New Year's Festival.

McGovern, A. *Why It's A Holiday*. Eau Clair, Wis.: E. M. Hale and Co., 1960. The customs, traditions and history of "holiday."

Patterson, L. *Christmas in Britain and Scandinavia*. Champaign, Ill.: Garroid Publishing Co., 1970. A merry glimpse into Christmas in other cultures.

Simon, N. *Hanukkah*. New York: Thomas Y. Crowell Company, 1966. An extraordinary examination of the customs of Hanukkah.

## Mathematics in the Early Childhood Curriculum

The young child's world is filled with many words including the names of numbers. These words are heard on television, in games, and in songs. Children learn the content and sequential order of these words. Although this task may seem simple, it is often quite difficult for the young child, who may be overwhelmed by the infinite quantity of numbers and their concrete referents. In order to master this early concept, children should be aided in their acquisition of a one-to-one correspondence between a number word and its referent.

When presenting these examples to the young child, it is necessary to orally read the number and the word, and to point and count the appropriate referents. Young children often point to the same object more than once when they are counting. This occurs because they tend to forget which objects they have counted.

Piaget (1953) once presented a tray filled with six bottles and many smaller glasses to several young children. He told each child to take from the tray an equal number of bottles and glasses. The four- to five-year-old child produced arrangements similar to the following:

All of the children made their bottle line and their glass line equal in length, disregarding the number correspondence of the lines. When these same children were presented the six bottles in a circle, they matched the arrangement with a circle of glasses that corresponded in size but not in number. Their circles looked like the following:

Clearly, children of this age experience difficulty matching objects in a one-to-one correspondence. This difficulty is also evidenced between objects and words. The classroom environment of the early learner should be rich with experiences that provide these correspondences.

The children involved in the Piaget (1953) experiment discussed earlier are in the *preoperational stage* of cognitive development. During this stage of development, the thought process of the child is governed by perception rather than by logical reasoning. Children are unable to hold a constant quantity of objects, regardless of their arrangements in the physical world. The child of this age is able to tell which group has more or less even though absolute answers to the "how many" questions may be difficult to obtain.

Once a learner advances beyond the preoperational stage, he realizes that if he begins with eleven blocks he will always maintain eleven, regardless of the arrangement. For the child in the preoperational stage who has not mastered this concept, the arrangement of the objects dictates quantity. As the spatial arrangement is altered, the child believes the quantity is altered. As you may have already realized, the child at this age has difficulty understanding the operations that are involved in adding and subtracting.

Through manipulating objects and teacher direction, the young children may learn a specific realtionship but, in the preoperational stage, they will be unable to apply abstract principles to a new situation. By the time children are approximately six years of age, they are more capable of applying logical reasoning to more concrete situations than they are at an earlier age.

Six- to nine-year-old children no longer confuse number with space. They can understand the logical rationale for an action. They can see the relationship between actions, and they can deduce information from one experience and apply it to another. They are able to understand the principles of addition and subtraction. Children of this age are thought to be in the stage of *concrete operations* (Piaget, 1953).

During the concrete operational stage, which spans the early elementary grades, children are better able to understand an abstract principle if they are able to perform physical actions on objects. In order to facilitate this process, you as the classroom teacher must provide an environment that is rich with manipulative objects.

*Figure 78.* Children need vast experience in counting manipulative objects before they can begin to combine and separate sets. (Photo by Linda Lungren)

As an early childhood education teacher, you will be planning curriculum for children who are either in the preoperational or concrete operational stage of development. Once the children aged four and five have had experiences with the skills of *matching sets, equivalences,* and *nonequivalences,* they will be ready for experiences that involve recognizing and *naming* the *properties of numbers.* What frequently occurs at this point is that the child who has an understanding of sets and numbers cannot match sets of objects and numbers. Children need vast experience in counting manipulative objects before they can begin to *combine* and *separate* sets.

The ability to understand the processes involved in combining and separating sets is the same type of ability that is needed for mastering addition, multiplication, subtraction, and division. The bases of this understanding can be provided if children have concrete manipulative objects upon which they can experiment. Children in the primary grades should be given ample experiences in combining sets (addition), separating sets (subtraction), and combining equal sets (multiplication). Most children are not ready to engage in separating equal sets (division) until after the third grade.

As young children work with manipulatives, they should be encouraged to use verbal representations for each object. As the verbal symbols are understood, children are anxious to read and write numerals. Reading and writing numerals should not be stressed until the child has had many manipulative and counting experiences.

Examples of accepted ways to write numerals should be part of the classroom decoration. Children often write numerals backwards. Continued exposure and practice with the writing process often is sufficient to eliminate backward writing. The following examples demonstrate some of the reversals that young children make when they write numerals:

$$2 \ \text{S}, \ 4 \ \text{T}, \ 6 \ \text{ᵭ}$$

You might want to have a decorative chart on one of your walls to serve as a model for correct numeral writing.

$$\boxed{1 \ 2 \ 3 \ 4 \ 5 \ 6 \ 7 \ 8 \ 9 \ 10}$$

As children manipulate and combine sets, they may say "one and one makes two." Once the child has gained some understanding of this concept through teacher-directed working with manipulatives, he is ready to be introduced to the representational signs (+) (−).

Children enjoy these early writing experiences. They are creating. Help them by being their audience and by providing classroom space to "show off" their masterpieces. Be careful not to scorn a backward number. Children, like adults, correct their mistakes quickly if they receive positive reinforcement and if they are reintroduced to the correct symbol or answer. If children leave your classroom with strong self-concepts, they have gained the most important variable needed for later success in life.

The introduction of *place value*, which indicates the value of a written numeral, occurs easily after the child has begun to write numbers. The child who can write

3
30
300

can be introduced to the value of 3 as ones, tens, and hundreds. Classroom illustrations can provide constant reinforcement.

| I can write | Thousands | Hundreds | Tens | Ones |
|-------------|-----------|----------|------|------|
| 3          |           |          |      | 3    |
| 30         |           |          | 3    | 0    |
| 300        |           | 3        | 0    | 0    |
| 3000       | 3         | 0        | 0    | 0    |

Children in the second grade often experience difficulty with algorithms (the rules governing carrying in addition and borrowing in subraction) because they do not have a thorough understanding of place value.

*Figure 79.* During the preschool and early elementary years young children are exposed to many geometrical concepts through their manipulative objects. (Photo by Linda Lungren)

## Geometry

During the preschool and early elementary years, young children are exposed to many geometrical concepts through their manipulative objects. As children sort shapes into squares, triangles, rectangles, circles, and trapezoids, they should be told the appropriate names and alerted to the differing dimensions. Illustrations containing such information should be part of your classroom environment.

square

triangle

rectangle

circle

trapezoid

---

A trapezoid has 4 sides.

A square has 4 equal sides.

A rectangle has 4 sides which do not have to be equal.

A circle is a curved figure.

A triangle has 3 sides.

*Money*

Young children should be helped in developing an understanding of the monetary value of various coins and bills. An easy way to encourage this understanding is through the development of a classroom store. Through purchasing, children are able to begin to conceptualize the exchange rate of one coin for another, coins for bills, or smaller bills for larger ones. As the child gains competence in monetary exchanges, he is becoming skillful at counting, addition, subtraction, base ten operations, and conservation.

Your store should be labeled with as many words and numbers as possible. The following signs could easily be part of your classroom store.

| GUM: 1¢ A STICK |
| --- |

| COMICS: 10¢ |
| --- |

| BASEBALL CARDS: 3 for 5¢ |
| --- |

| SHAUN CASSIDY POSTERS: 15¢ |
| --- |

*Measurement of Space and Time*

As young children engage in activities that require them to determine "how much" and "how many," they are determining nonstandard units of measurement. Children often find it quite intriguing to measure their rest mats, puzzle boards, or body length with toothpicks or popsicle sticks before using a standard measuring instrument. An activity that involves both standard and nonstandard measuring tools enables the child to see the validity of measuring with a standard instrument because measurement with nonstandard instruments varies according to the length of the toothpick or popsicle stick.

During the preschool years children have a very basic understanding of measurement of space and time. Piaget (1971) suggests that the young child is unable to differentiate *objective* and *subjective* time. Children believe that time is controlled by *their* actions. The preschool child, unlike the primary-age child, believes that the faster he pours sand, the faster it will fall through a sand timer.

Although primary-age children may understand the process of the sand timer, they will tell you that the hands on a large-faced clock move more quickly than the hands on a smaller-faced clock. It is not until around the age of nine or ten that children develop a stable conception of time.

Throughout the early years children are exposed to mathematical concepts that can only be explored in an environment designed by a teacher who is attuned to the development of young children.

Through and through, the world is infected with quantity. To talk sense is to talk in quantities. It is no use saying that the nation is large—how large? It is no use saying that radium is scarce—how scarce? You cannot evade quantity. You may fly to poetry and music, and quantity and numbers will face you in your rhythms and your octaves. (Whitehead, 1929, p. 7)

## Science in the Early Childhood Curriculum

"Why is it dark when we go to sleep?"
"What makes flowers grow?"
"Where does the sun go at night?"
"Where does rain come from?"

These are some of the first scientific questions that are asked by the young child. But even before children begin to ask questions about scientific occurrences, they have begun to explore these phenomena. Such explanations may include the young toddler who approaches the hot iron, burner, or radiator and is cautioned of its danger; the young child who pushes a toy car slowly up an incline and watches with glee at its quick return; or, the excitement that young children experience when they watch a balloon fly around as it loses its air.

These young children are experiencing science. Through the questions and situations posed by adults in their environment, they can be aided in developing and refining their basic scientific skills: *observing, classifying, hypothesizing, experimenting, recording, interpreting,* and *generalizing.*

*Observation* is the basis of all scientific inquiry. As children observe objects, they become skillful at seeing similarities and differences. Once the ability to observe is refined, the child is able to *classify* objects according to size, shape, color, texture, function, and situation. As well as developing the ability to classify according to physical attributes, the children learn how to react to certain situations, for example, materials and animals may be classified according to function as well as physical property. Subcategories also emerge as points of reference for the young child. Although young children are not totally skillful at *hypothesizing*, they are able to explain situations that involve two or more facts that occur simultaneously ("We can't play outside because it is raining"). Parents and teachers who encourage young children to verbalize observations can also help them to predict or hypothesize, by asking them questions similar to the following: "What would happen if we went outside in the rain?"

Through experimenting, the child is able to test the prediction ("Put your hand out the window and see if you do get wet"). Children love experimentation as long as they never completely lose their feeling of security. As children attempt basic experiments that may test classroom observations, it is important

*Figure 80.* Observation is the basis of all scientific inquiry. Once the ability to observe is refined the child is able to classify objects according to size, shape, color, texture, function, and situation. (Photo by Linda Lungren)

to *record* the results so they may have accurate accounts and so the information may be shared with others who are not present at the experiment.

The act of recording provides an exciting means by which the child may begin basic reading and writing activities. Records may include experience charts, picture charts, graphs, and booklets. For example, as seen in Figure 82, children may observe the growth rate of a class plant during the first week of growth and then predict its growth during the remaining weeks. Each week the actual growth rate can be recorded and the validity of the prediction tested.

The abilities to *interpret* information and make *generalizations* are scientific skills that are more obvious in the behavior of the primary-aged child than in the preschool child. The more experiences the child has, the better he becomes at interpreting and generalizing.

The classroom teacher should capitalize on actual classroom experiences in attempting to develop these skills ("If we know that plants grow better in sunlight, where should we place the plants in our classroom?").

*Figure 81.* Children love experimentation as long as they never completely lose their feeling of security. As children attempt basic experiments which may test classroom observation it is important to record the results to share later. (Photo by Linda Lungren)

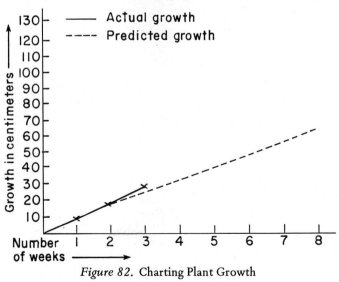

*Figure 82.* Charting Plant Growth

## The Expressive Arts in the Early Childhood Curriculum

*Figure 83.* The young child's early experiences with the expressive arts occur through music, painting, sculpture, drama, and dance. (Photo by Linda Lungren)

The young child's early experiences with the expressive arts occur through music, painting, sculpture, drama, and dance. Growth in most of the expressive arts is dependent upon physical growth.

The elements of musical composition include tempos, rhythms, intensities, and tones. Children gain continued understanding of these musical aspects as they sing songs, dance, and create their own music. The early childhood curriculum can facilitate such growth by providing experiences with drums, bells, triangles, and cymbals. In conjunction with the development of musical skills, young children are quick to "pretend" and engage in drama interpretations. They dress up in adult clothing, they pretend to eat, cry, and sleep. They soon project these pretend behaviors on their toys; the doll or stuffed animal eats, sleeps, cries, and talks; the block becomes a car; and the bicycle becomes a motorcycle.

Three- and four-year-olds are anxious to engage in role-playing activities. In their role-playing situations they model the behaviors of the significant others in their environment, such as baby, father, mother, older sibling, fireman,

*Figure 84.* Three and four year olds are anxious to engage in role playing activities. They model the behaviors of the significant others in their environment. (Photo by Linda Lungren)

policeman, doctor, nurse. During this stage of development, young children play *separately together* for hours; this phenomenon has been termed *parallel play*. You may wonder how it is possible for children to play separately, yet together. Picture the following interchange:

Shannon (age four):  "You go to work, and while you're gone, I'll do the laundry, mow the lawn, and fix the car."

Eric (age five):  "OK, and when I get home, I'll feed the children while you get ready to go to work."

The results of this interchange could involve hours of independent activity. This transaction probably was previewed as an actual home encounter between their parent models.

**Children are Creative.**  Children's creativity can be fostered in a classroom, designed by a teacher who appreciates the talents of children. Such a classroom provides experiences that promote the development of self-expression and aesthetic appreciation.

The drawings on pages 412–414, which have been created by children of various ages, represent attempts to communicate personal thoughts and feelings.

*Figure 85.* Children's creativity can be fostered in a classroom designed by a teacher who appreciates the talents of children. (Photo by Linda Lungren)

Singing games and folk dancing provide children opportunities for developing coordination. Rhythm can be explored by adding various types of music to skipping, hopping, running, and walking exercises.

Because teachers have limited experiences with the expressive arts, it may be beneficial for you to visit craft shops and to critically analyze the books and activities that are available for use with your children. Most activities contain possibilities for language exploration through speech, reading, or writing.

A section of your classroom should be equipped to entice children to explore the expressive arts. As well as housing the musical instruments in this section, you may wish to include a trunk filled with a variety of adult clothes—shoes, dresses, ties, hats, pants. The trunk might also include the following:

easels with water-mixed paints
writing and drawing paper
records and record player
crayons

Becky    (Age 2 years 10 months)
Subject: "What makes me happy?"
"These are trees."

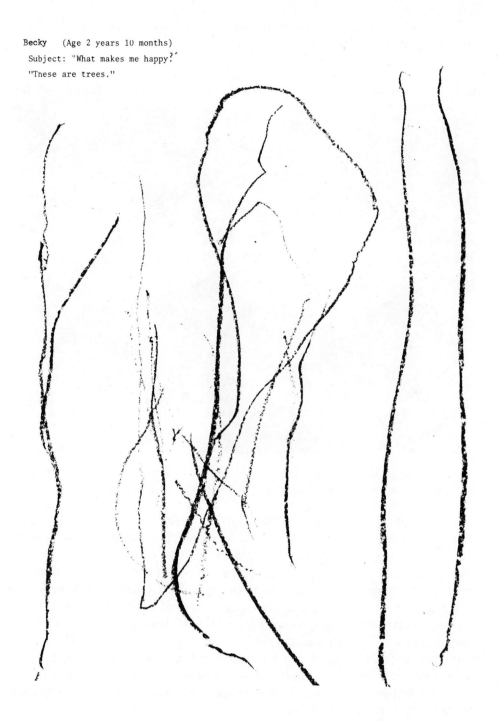

Stephanie Harris. Age 5 (Birthday in September she says) Picture of self.

Stacy  (Age 2)

What makes you happy, Stacy?

"Friends."

Each line seems to represent a friend--or the same line
can change and become a boat or Duke (the family dog).

*Figure 86.* Singing games and folk dancing provide children with opportunities for developing coordination. (Photo by Linda Lungren)

(Exploration materials continued)
   magic markers
   clay
   materials for cutting and pasting work
   construction paper
   paint brushes
   pipe cleaners
   tissue paper
   paper plates
   wallpaper
   yarn
   carpenter bench and tools
   junk (egg cartons, plastic bottles)
   magazines

Encourage children to use various media to express themselves. Not everything the child produces will be brilliant and wonderful. However, it is far more encouraging if you respond to a child's efforts by saying, "Susan, you pounded a lot of nails," than to say, "Susan, you wasted so many nails and produced nothing." Engage children in conversations about their work. They will be

*Figure 87.* Encourage children to use various media to express themselves. Not everything the child produces will be brilliant and wonderful. (Photo by Linda Lungren)

eager to evaluate it. But never, never damage the children's self-concepts by blatant criticism of their efforts. You probably won't have many Reniors or Bachs in your classroom. The goals of the expressive arts curriculum should be *appreciation* and *self-expression*. With your help your students can attain these goals.

### The Integration of the Language Arts Throughout the Early Childhood Curriculum

Language arts activities are living experiences. The language arts provide the communication skills and the content areas provide the parameters needed to explore and extend communication skills.

This chapter has introduced several content areas and offered a variety of classroom situations that integrate the language arts and content area subjects. Throughout this text we have attempted to introduce you to the theoretical constructs of the various language arts: *listening, speaking, reading,* and *writing.*

We do not believe that skill in the language arts can be extended without the content area framework because a literate person is able to communicate *about* something. Therefore, we encourage you to use content area topics to extend the communication skills of all of the young children with whom you interact.

## BIBLIOGRAPHY

Anderson, P., and D. Lapp. *Language Skills In Elementary Education.* New York: Macmillan Publishing Co., Inc., 1979.

Baldwin, B. T., and L. I. Stecher. *The Psychology of the Pre-School Child.* New York: Appleton-Century-Crofts, 1925.

Bessell, D., and P. Palomares. *Human Development Program.* San Diego: Human Development Training Institute, 1970.

Brittain, W. L. *Creativity, Art, and the Young Child.* New York: Macmillan Publishing Co., Inc., 1979.

Copeland, R. W. *How Children Learn Mathematics,* 3rd ed. New York: Macmillan Publishing Co., Inc., 1979.

Court, S. R. A. "Numbers, Time, and Space in the First Five Years of a Child's Life." *Pedagogical Seminary,* (1920) 27:71–87.

Court, S. R. A. "Self-Taught Arithmetic from the Age of Five to the Age of Eight." *Pedagogical Seminary* (1923) 30:51–68.

Desort, H., and T. Unabelle. "Geographic Readiness in the Kindergarten." *Journal of Geography* (1961) 60:331–335.

*Dimensions of Personality.* Dayton, Ohio: Pflaum/Standard, 1972.

Dinkmeyer. D. *Developing Understanding of Self and Others.* Circle Pines, Minn.: American Guidance Service, 1970.

Dunfee, M. *Elementary School Social Studies: A Guide to Current Research.* Washington, D.C.: Association for Supervision and Curriculum Development, 1970.

Durgin, H. J. "From Curiosity to Concepts: From Concepts to Curiosity—Science Experiences in the Preschool." *Young Children* (1975) 30:249–256.

Durkin, D. *Teaching Young Children To Read.* Boston: Allyn & Bacon, Inc., 1972.

Erlwanger, S. H. "Case Studies of Children's Conceptions of Mathematics," Part I, *Journal of Children's Mathematical Behavior* (1975) 1:157–283.

Fantz, R. L. "Visual Perception from Birth as Shown by Pattern Selectivity," *Annals of the New York Academy of Sciences,* (1963) 118:793–814.

*First Things: Values.* Pleasantville, N.Y.: Guidance Associates, 1972.

Freud, S. *Totem and Taboo.* Vienna: Hugo Heller, 1913. Copyright 1950 by Routledge and Kegan. Published in 1962 in New York by W. W. Norton & Company, Inc.

Furth, H. G. *Piaget and Knowledge.* New York: Ballantine Books, 1971.

Ginnsburg, H. *Children's Arithmetic.* New York: D. Van Nostrand Company, 1977.

Good, R. G. *How Children Learn Science.* New York: Macmillan Publishing Co., Inc., 1977.

Hawkins, D. "Messing About In Science," *Science and Children* (1965) 2:5–9.

Inhelder, B., and J. Piaget. *The Growth of Logical Thinking*. New York: Basic Books, Inc., 1958.

Ireland, R. J. "Let's Throw Out Reading!" *Reading Teacher* (March 1973) 26:584–588.

Jarolimek, J. "Skills Teaching In The Primary Grades." *Social Education* (1967) 31:222–223; 234.

Kresse, H., and R. Green. *MATCH*. Boston: American Science and Engineering, 1968.

Krown, S. *Threes and Fours Go to School*. Englewood Cliffs, N.J.: Prentice-Hall, Inc., 1974.

Liberman, J. N. "Playfulness and Divergent Thinking: An Investigation of Their Relationship at the Kindergarten Level," *Journal of Genetic Psychology* (December 1965) 107: 219–224.

Martorella, P. "Selected Early Childhood Affective Learning Programs: An Analysis of Theories, Structure, and Consistency," *Young Children*, Vol. 30, No. 4 (May 1975), 300.

Matterson, E. M. *Play and Playthings for the Preschool Child*. Baltimore: Penguin, 1965.

McLaughlin, K. L. "Number Ability In Preschool Children," *Childhood Education* (1935) 11:348–353.

Mitchell, E., and B. S. Mason. *The Theory of Play* (rev. ed.) Cranbury, N.J.: A. S. Barnes & Co., Inc., 1948.

Mugge, D. J. "Are Young Children Ready to Study the Social Sciences?" *Elementary School Journal* (February 1968) 68:36–38.

Omwake, E. "The Child's Estate." In A. I. Solnit and S. A. Provence (Ed.) *Modern Perspectives in Child Development*. New York: International Universities Press, 1963.

Piaget, J. *The Moral Judgment of the Child*. New York: Harcourt Brace Jovanovich, Inc., 1932.

Piaget, J. *The Child's Conception of Numbers*. London: Kegan Paul, Trench, Trubner & Co., 1953.

Piaget, J. *The Child's Conception of the World*. London: Kegan Paul, Trench, Trubner & Co., 1971.

Piaget, J. *Mental Imagery in the Child*. New York: Basic Books, 1971.

Piaget, J. *Biology and Knowledge: An Essay on the Relations Between Organic Regulations and Cognitive Processes*. Chicago, Ill.: University of Chicago Press, 1971.

Piaget, J. "Piagetian Theory and Its Implications for the Helping Professions." (Proceeding of the annual interdisciplinary seminar) Los Angeles: Publications Dept., University of Southern California 1971.

Piaget, J. *Insights and Illusions of Philosophy*. New York: William Collins & World Publishing Co., Inc., 1971.

Piaget, J. *Psychology and Epistemology*. New York: Grossman, 1971.

Richardson, L. I., K. L. Goodman, N. N. Hartman, H. C. Le Pique. *A Mathematics Activity Curriculum for Early Childhood and Special Education*. New York: Macmillan Publishing Co., Inc., 1980.

Schaeffer, B., V. H. Eggleton, and J. L. Scott. "Number Development in Young Children," *Cognitive Psychology* (1974) 6: 357–379.

Serdus, M., and M. Tank. "A Critical Appraisal of Twenty-Six National Social Studies Projects." *Social Education* (April 1970) 34:383–449.

Smith, R. *Music In The Child's Education.* New York: The Ronald Press Company, 1970.

Spodek, B. "Social Studies for Young Children: Identifying Intellectual Goals." *Social Education* (January 1974) 38:40–53.

Stern, C., and M. Stern. *Children Discover Arithmetic.* New York: Harper & Row, Publishers, 1971.

Strickland, R. G. "The Language of Elementary School Children: Its Relationship to the Language of Reading Textbooks and the Quality of Reading of Selected Children." *Bulletin of the School of Education,* Indiana University (1962), pp. 1–131.

Taba, H. *Elementary Social Studies.* Reading, Mass.: Addison-Wesley Publishing Co., Inc., 1967.

Taba, H. *Teacher's Handbook for Elementary Social Studies.* Reading, Mass.: Addison Wesley Publishing Co., Inc., 1967.

Taylor, B. L., and T. L. Groom. *Social Studies Education Projects: An ASCD Index.* Washington, D.C.: Association for Supervision and Curriculum Development, 1971.

Tough, J. *Talking, Thinking, Growing.* New York: Schocken Books, Inc., 1973.

Vergara, W. C. *Science In The World Around Us.* New York: Harper & Row, Publishers, 1973.

Walsh, H. M. *Introducing the Young Child to the Social World.* New York: Macmillan Publishing Co., Inc., 1980.

White, B. L., J. C. Watts, and others. *Experience and Environment: Major Influences on the Development of the Young Child,* Vol. 1, Englewood Cliffs, N.J.: Prentice-Hall, Inc., 1973.

Whitehead, A. N. *The Aims of Education.* New York: Macmillan Publishing Co., Inc., 1929.

# Section

# V

# Developing a Language/Reading Program for Every Young Child

# 15

## Developing the Language/Reading Strategies of Bilingual Children

*Figure 88.* Listening experiences in the form of records and tapes of stories, songs, and nursery rhymes can be helpful to the bilingual student. (Photo by Linda Lungren)

In most American classrooms there are bilingual children who may not be receiving appropriate language/reading instruction. With this realization, it probably comes as no great surprise to you that a very high percentage of non-English speakers never graduate from high school (Zamora, 1968). Although some of the causes for this high dropout rate are not language- or culture-related, the bulk of them are. Many well-intentioned teachers have taken incorrect steps with bilingual and second-language speakers and, inadvertently, have frustrated them to the point of total withdrawal. However, it is not our intention to dwell on the failings of schools. Rather, it is our intention to present a concise body of information about bilingual and English-as-a-second-language (ESL) students that will help you to improve your students' language and reading skills.

While it may seem obvious, it is important to underscore the fact that bilingual children are *not* disadvantaged. In fact, they have the privilege of two languages. You will have to deal with this language abundance when you are teaching children who are learning English. Sometimes the situation will call for instruction in the native language, sometimes in English, and sometimes in both languages.

## Special Needs of the Bilingual and ESL Student

The needs of bilingual children are often special because of their ethnic heritage (Ching 1976). Zintz (1975) aptly explains some cultural interference problems that teachers and students may experience.

> Too many teachers are inadequately prepared to understand or accept these dissimilar cultural values. Teachers come from homes where the drive for success and achievement has been internalized early, where "work for work's sake" is rewarded, and where time and energy are spent building for the future. Many children come to the classroom with a set of values and background of experiences radically different from that of the average American child. To teach these children successfully, the teacher must be cognizant of these differences and must above all else seek to understand without disparagement those ideas, values, and practices different from his own.

Perhaps the most important characteristic of any good teacher is his or her ability to accept each child without prejudice or preconception. Children quickly and thoroughly sense rejection by their teachers. In the case of the bilingual child, the teacher must be quick to accept children's language because it is the language of their homes and their parents. Language and self-concept are so closely intertwined that children can be made to feel foolish and worthless when their "accent" or dialect is ridiculed by their teacher or peers. Trust and confidence between teachers and children must precede linguistic corrections. Through positive interactions with teachers and peers, a child's self-concept will improve tremendously.

## Bilingual/Bicultural Early Education Programs

Many early education programs have not been designed for bilingual/bicultural children. Some of the elements of these programs are appropriate without any specific changes, and other elements need substantive changes to be appropriate for bilingual children. Let us analyze one early education program, The Montessori Program, for its appropriateness for bilingual/bicultural children.

Maria Montessori was one of the first educational innovators to combine a concept of liberty with a structure of work. She rebelled against the conventional wisdom of her time and provided children with freedom of movement and expression in their classroom, believing that freedom must exist within limits. Her educational method attempted to create a learning environment in which children were able to acquire the "tools" of their culture without losing their sense of initiative. In this way, she believed that children would strive to master their environment. They would act on natural impulse and explore their surroundings, organizing their experiences in such a way that they would lead themselves to a mastery of their own culture. The Montessori program made its way to the United States, and its supporters maintained its educational rationale and mission. In order to adequately evaluate the American Montessori program, a series of cultural questions should be asked to assess the contemporary effectiveness of this program in meeting the needs of children and parents of the 1980s.

In answering the question, "Can the Montessori program be adapted for the bilingual child?" one is immediately struck by the evaluative thrust of the question. You are actually being asked to make two judgments:

1. Is the overall program acceptable?

2. If not, what are the acceptable elements of the program, and what elements of the program need to be adjusted or omitted?

In part, the original query is a moot point because Montessori programs abound in the United States, and many bilingual children attend these preschools. Because there seems to be little movement away from the Montessori program by parents of bilingual children, the question, "Can the Montessori program be adapted for the bilingual child?" more appropriately should be, "How can the program be altered to meet the needs of bilingual children in the United States?"

In order to sensibly answer this question, the reviewer must evaluate the program, using a four-dimensional assessment scheme that includes the following:

1. Aspects of the Montessori program that are acceptable in their present form for a bilingual/bicultural early education program.

2. Elements of the Montessori program that are appropriate in an early education center but need adaptation to be used in a bilingual/bicultural early education program.

3. Aspects of an appropriate bilingual/bicultural early education program that are absent in the Montessori program.

4. Elements of the Montessori program that are inappropriate in a bilingual/bicultural early education program.

The evaluation of the Montessori program is presented in the chart on p. 427.

Each of these assessment categories will be further explained in the succeeding pages.

**Category 1:** Aspects of the Montessori program that are acceptable in their present form for a bilingual/bicultural early education program

The first category does not seem to need extended explanation. In general, the Montessori materials and activities, which are used as exercises for the cognitive development of the child, are both acceptable and appropriate for a bilingual/bicultural early education program. These materials stress the importance of self-discovery, and they are intended to be self-correcting. The assessment component of the materials, the self-correcting aspect, however, may not be totally in keeping with the values and customs of all cultural backgrounds. Thus, it becomes important to make a distinction between the materials and the use of the materials as an assessment of the child's current cognitive development. The materials—rods, golden beads, pegs—are acceptable in their current form, but the rigidity of the assessment needs serious re-evaluation in a bilingual/bicultural program. With the works of many educators, psychologists, anthropologists, and sociologists, it becomes increasingly obvious that we must investigate a series of questions connected with culture and children's performance.

**Category 2:** Aspects of the Montessori program that are appropriate in an early education program but need adaptation to be used in a bilingual/bilcultural early education program

As suggested in the chart, two Montessori activities fall into this second category: gardening activities and circle time activities. In the gardening activities where children are exposed to principles of cultivation and growth, there seem to be possibilities for introducing acceptable activities for a bilingual/bicultural early education program. A teacher or aide who speaks the first language of the child may explain the technical aspects of gardening (terminology, names of tools) in the child's first language. When decisions are made concerning the selection of vegetables/plants to grow, the children's cultural backgrounds may be used as a criterion for selection (if many children are from a Mexican cultural background, it may be appropriate to grow jalopeno peppers). That would lend itself naturally to a cultural lesson when the jalopenos were harvested. Teachers could explain to the children that some cultural groups use certain spices extensively in their food preparation. The lesson could be extended to talk about nutrition and diet; one of its goals may be to reduce stereotypical thinking about "balanced diets," consisting only of products from a single, albeit dominant, cultural group.

Circle time activities also lend themselves to adaptation within a bilingual/bicultural early education program. If there is a place in the Montessori

| Aspects of Montessori Program | Aspects of the Montessori Program that are acceptable in their present form for a bilingual/bicultural early education program | Aspects of the Montessori Program that are appropriate in an early education center but need adaptation to be used in a bilingual/bicultural early education program | Aspects of an appropriate bilingual/bicultural early education program that are absent in the Montessori Program | Aspects of the Montessori Program that are inappropriate in a bilingual/bicultural early education program |
|---|---|---|---|---|
| 1. Cognition activities | | | | |
| a. (numeration and attributes) | | | | |
| Golden Beads | X | | | |
| Rods | X | | | |
| Cubes | X | | | |
| Prisms | X | | | |
| b. Auditory discrimination | | | | |
| Tone Bells | X | | | |
| Sound Boxes | X | | | |
| c. Tactile/Kinesthetic discrimination | | | | |
| Sandpaper letters | X | | | |
| Water temperature | X | | | |
| d. Matching/Naming Colors/Visual discrimination | | | | |
| Color squares | X | | | |
| Puzzles | X | | | |
| 2. Cross-Age grouping in one classroom | X | | | |
| 3. Gardening activities | | X | | |
| 4. Circle time activities | | X | | |
| 5. Teachers from mixed/various language background | | | X | |
| 6. Integrated/formulated/structured language components | | | X | |
| 7. Self-expression/creative dramatics | | | X | |
| 8. Teacher/adult-child interaction | | | X | |
| 9. Child-child interaction | | | X | |
| 10. Story time/sharing time activities | | | X | |
| 11. Private space | | | | X |
| 12. Emphasis on washing hands/cleaning tables, room/rearranging room | | | | X |
| 13. Phonics approach to reading | | | | X |

program where cooperation among children is accepted or encouraged, it is during this activity. It should be noted however, that cooperation is *not* an explicit objective of the Montessori program. This activity lends itself to discussions of children's different perceptions about such topics as weather, daily activity, jobs, family, holidays. Children who have experienced a specific kind of weather pattern—heat and humidity, for example—may not describe a particular day as "hot," whereas other children in the group may say, "It's the hottest day ever." These differences in perception may lend themselves to effective lessons on cultural backgrounds and personal experience.

**Category 3**: Aspects of an appropriate bilingual/bicultural early education program that are absent in the Montessori program

The Montessori program seems to be most seriously deficient in providing learning opportunities in three areas: language development, sharing/cooperation among individuals, and creative dramatics/self-expression. More specifically, chart items 6–10 (integrated/formulated/structured language components; self-expression/creative dramatics; teacher/adult-child interaction; child-child interaction; story time/sharing time activities) are conspiciously absent in the Montessori program.

The Montessori program lacks an integrated and structured language component, a critical element in any bilingual/bicultural early education program. The Ypslanti Early Education Program provides an effective model for a curriculum stressing language development. According to Rochelle Mayer, in her article "A Comparative Analysis of Preschool Curriculum Models," the verbal-cognitive preschool models, of which the Ypslanti program is an example, provide children with excellent language activities: "Throughout the day the teacher is continuously speaking to the children, questioning them, and responding to them."

An appropriate bilingual/bicultural program might necessitate some of the following objectives and strategies that are not present in the Montessori program:

OBJECTIVES:

1. Enjoyment of books and an understanding of books as resources by teachers and children. Books should represent a wide variety of cultural and linguistic backgrounds. Children whose first language is not English should have the opportunity to have stories read to them in their first language.

2. Comprehension of material related orally, such as understanding directions or a story that has been read.

3. Appreciation of the relationship between oral and written language Words in print are a form of talk written down.

4. Confidence in children's ability to create written materials, such as stories dictated to a teacher.

5. Sight vocabulary of words that are familiar and important to the child, such as the child's name and the names of frequently used classroom materials.

6. Letter-sound associations, particularly initial phonemes, consonants, and recognition of familiar sounds.

STRATEGIES:

1. Reading to children individually and in small groups in the child's first language (when appropriate) and in English. Asking questions related to the story and encouraging children to retell the story in their own words.

2. Listening experiences in the form of records and tapes of stories, songs, and nursery rhymes provided in Spanish (when appropriate) and English. Listening experiences that result in the following of simple directions (games such as "Simon Says").

3. Films of familiar stories.

4. Use of labels in the classrooms to indicate names of things and places for their storage.

5. Use of children's names on cubbies, lockers, tote boxes, art work, and so on.

6. Taking down of children's dictated stories and helping children make their own books.

7. Trips to libraries and museums and other neighborhood places of interest.

8. Use of recipe charts for cooking activities.

9. Language experience approaches. Children who show interest in beginning reading instruction will be given the opportunity to begin a personalized language experience reading program. These children will make word cards and will be taught to "read" single words.

A second area in which the Montessori program is deficient is the cooperation/sharing component that should be found in bilingual/bicultural programs. It should be noted that children may play together or work together in the Montessori program; there is certainly no restriction against children talking to one another. However, a critical distinction must be made between effect and purpose. Clearly, the objectives of the Montessori program are not directed toward cooperation among children *per se*. This is an important component in any bilingual/bicultural program because the cultural experiences of many bilingual children are intricately interwoven with a concept of sharing and cooperation.

A third area that needs attention in an appropriate bilingual/bicultural program is the self-expression/creative dramatics component. Teachers of children from diverse cultural programs have a special opportunity to build on individual competence through relevant forms of creative dramatics, which will enable children to express themselves freely within their own cultural constraints. A model lesson may include the children's enactment of fear. Children from different backgrounds might be able to deal with their own fears when it becomes clear to them that children from other cultural backgrounds do not necessarily share these anxieties. (This lesson, however, could be counterproductive—the teacher may introduce a whole new set of fears and anxieties.)

> **Category 4:** Aspects of the Montessori program that are inappropriate in a bilingual/bicultural early education program.

There are many components in the Montessori program that are inappropriate for the bilingual child. Foremost among these is the creation of a "private space" for each child; a place that is the possession of an individual child; a place where other children cannot enter without permission. Ignoring for the moment the fact that many three-year-olds simply cannot grasp a concept of ownership from a cognitive point of view, it is particularly offensive and inappropriate in the bilingual/bicultural program because it is alien to some cultural groups (for example, Navajo) and in direct violation of community values to other cultural groups (Hopi).

A second component of the Montessori program that may need to be eliminated in a truly bicultural program is the emphasis placed on "practical life experiences." The practical life experiences include such activities as cleaning and caring for oneself and one's surroundings. The buttoning and lacing frames are examples of materials used as practical life exercises in addition to washing hands and face, brushing teeth, cleaning and dusting the classroom. It should be noted here that we are not particularly opposed to each of these activities as important life experiences for children, but the criticism is directed toward the emphasis placed on these activities. Again, the rationale for eliminating this emphatic structure is to guard against the violation of cultural values. In the Montessori program individual children are held accountable for cleaning, dusting, and rearranging. Frequently, when these activities are actualized , they become sources of competitive behavior among children.

Finally, the introduction of a phonics approach to reading as the exclusive teaching/learning methodology seems to violate the finds of a great body of current reading research (Thonis, 1976, O'Brien, 1973). In a bilingual/bicultural program, several beginning reading methodologies should be used simultaneously: whole word, linguistic, and language experience methodologies. The sole emphasis on phonics does not take into account the phonological interference of first and second language that many bilingual children experience.

As a final point, it should be stressed that parents and teachers of bilingual children should be particularly attentive to their special needs. The Montessori program, in the United States, is probably here to stay, and it should be evaluated from a contemporary knowledgeable point of view. Although it may be an extremely effective program for most children, its proponents must be flexible enough to add and delete in order to meet the needs of all children.

### Differences Among Bilingual Students

To suggest that there is one route, one introduction to language/reading methodology for all bilingual or English-as-second-language (ESL) students is utter folly. The complexity of the situation is often overwhelming for the new teacher. However, the following matrix may help you to understand some of the differences among bilingual and ESL children with regard to their ability to read and write. There are six different combinations represented in the following matrix:

|  | Student 1 | Student 2 | Student 3 | Student 4 | Student 5 | Student 6 |
|---|---|---|---|---|---|---|
| **SPEAKS** | Spanish | Spanish | — | Spanish | Spanish | Spanish |
|  | — | English | English | — | English | English |
| **READS** | — | — | — | Spanish | — | Spanish |
|  | — | — | — | — | English | English |

You will note that students 4, 5, and 6 have no problem *per se* because each speaks and reads at least one language. Teaching student 4 to read in English or student 5 to read in Spanish depends upon several factors: his age, the level of the child's progress in English at the present time, and the need for reading in a second language.

### Linguistic Influences on Second Language Teaching

Effective instruction in beginning reading has changed considerably with the current findings of linguistic reasearch. Traditionally, psycholinguists have emphasized that children learn language by imitating what they hear. Incorrect usage and incorrect punctuation were self-corrected when speakers failed to communicate effectively.

Second-language teachers, who were influenced by this theory, began teaching oral language by having children mimic and memorize. Rather than teaching grammatical rules for future independent speaking, they emphasized proper sounds and the acquisition of nativelike accents by language learners. The assumption of this approach was that in memorizing enough samples of natural speech, the learner would be able to make proper use of these structures in the appropriate context. Although this approach failed to produce bilinguals, it did demonstrate that learners could perfect their accent in a second language even if they learned it after childhood.

In contrast transformational/generative grammarians have stressed the ability of all children to generate sentences in their native language that they have neither imitated nor memorized. These linguists have changed many of the objectives of second-language teachers. Instead of emphasizing either reading or speaking exclusively, the second-language teacher explores the many dimensions of language with the students. The key is to create meaningful contexts that stimulate communication in the new language. Although reading is not to be ignored in this approach, it has been assumed that one cannot, in the early stages, read what one cannot produce orally. As the child moves to a more advanced level in the new language, reading reinforces language and develops it through exposure to new vocabulary, syntactic structures, and cultural contexts.

## What the Teacher of Language/Reading Needs to Know About other Languages

### *Spanish*

Spanish is the second most frequently spoken language in the United States. It is possible that you will eventually work with a Spanish-speaking child. The following information about the Spanish language may help you to develop a successful language/reading program for your children from a Spanish speaking background.

#### Sounds of Spanish and English

| Phoneme | Initial | | POSITION Medial | Final |
|---------|---------|---------|--------|-------|
| /f/ | (Sp.) | Fuerte | zaFa | — |
|     | (Eng.) | Fine | saFer | leaF   saFe |
| /s/ | (Sp.) | Siento | meSa | veS |
|     | (Eng.) | Some | faCing | priCe |
| /p/ | (Sp.) | Paso | taPa | — |
|     | (Eng.) | Pen | taPer | floP |
| /d/ | (Sp.) | Donde | toDo | — |
|     | (Eng.) | Done | toDay | carD |

Some children may experience difficulty in producing some of the sounds of English. Some of these possible difficulties are as follows:

| Sound | Example | Possible Error |
|-------|---------|----------------|
| Vowels: | | |
| 1. long e | leave, feel | live, fill |
| 2. short e | live, fill | leave, feel |
| 3. short i | mate, bait | met, bet |
| 4. long a | met, bet | mate, bait |
| 5. short a | hat, cat | hot, cot |
| 6. long o | hot, cot | hat, cat |
| 7. short o | coal, hole | call, hall |
| Consonant Blends: | | |
| 8. th | thin, then, path | sin, den, pass |
| 9. sh | shoe, show, wash | sue, choe, bus or bush |
| 10. ch | chew, chop, witch | choe or jew, cash, wish |

| Sound | Example | Possible Error |
|---|---|---|
| Consonant: | | |
| 11. b | bin, beer, tab, rabbit | pin, pear, tap, rapid |
| 12. g | goat, wing | coat, wink, duck |
| 13. w | way, wash | gway, gwash (with more proficiency pronounced gwash or watch) |
| 14. y | yellow, yale | jello, jail |
| 15. v | vote, vail | boat, bail |

## *Chinese*

While there are many dialects of Chinese, including Mandarin which is the National dialect in the People's Republic and Taiwan, *Cantonese* is the dialect we have chosen to present since it is spoken by most Chinese families who imigrate to the United States from Hong Kong, Kowloon, or Macao.

1. The Chinese language does not have as many vowels as English; therefore, a Chinese child learning to speak English may have difficulty. For example;

/ay/buy      /iy/meat      /ey/gait

2. Chinese speakers seldom use consonants in final positions.

3. There is not a direct correspondence between English and Chinese sounds:

rich      shed

4. Many Chinese dialects are devoid of the sounds of consonant clusters:

calf      swish

5. In Chinese dialects that do not contain consonant clusters, it may be impossible for the child to develop English plurals:

calves      swishes

6. Chinese speakers may indicate plurals through the use of numerical designations or auxiliary words:

three dogs = three dog

7. The Chinese speaker expresses grammatical relationships by auxiliary words and word order:

She gave me two cars.
Yesterday she give I two cars.

8. Chinese speakers use tone or pitch to distinguish *word* meanings, whereas speakers of English combine pitch and intonation to present *sentence* meaning.

9. The Chinese speaker may exclude subjects of predicates if the context alone is understandable:

| English | Chinese |
| --- | --- |
| It is raining. | It rains. |
| The car is shiny. | Car shiny. |

10. English speakers invert the noun and verb forms when asking questions. The Chinese speaker does not follow this inversion but, instead, adds empty words *ma* or *la* to the sentence:

| English | Chinese |
| --- | --- |
| Are you happy? | You are happy <u>ma</u>? |

11. Chinese speakers use a time word or phrase to indicate the tense of a verb:

She go "jaw" means "She went."

## Assessing Language Proficiency

The first questions you will ask when you are working in English with a second-language child is, "How much English does the child know?" The first issue is to assess the child's proficiency in English. It should be emphasized that children have different proficiencies within their language ability. In most cases it may be advantageous for you, as the teacher, to conduct a structured, but informal, nonthreatening interview with the child in order to determine his proficiency and ease in speaking English.

Most tests that have been designed to assess language dominance have ignored the fact that children have many variations in their language abilities. Sometimes their native language is their dominant, preferred language for a particular task, but sometimes it is not. This seems logical, because many adults experience the same phenomenon; that is, a Spanish-speaking adult who studies Advanced Statistics in England may prefer to use English when he is discussing statistics. Therefore, before globally assessing a child's language dominance, we need to ask, What is the specific task that the child is being asked to perform? What is the language of the person to whom the child will speak during the instructional period? The answers to these questions will provide a great deal of useful information that will enable you to begin your instructional program.

In determining the language proficiency of a preschool child, you will want to extract information about several aspects of language so that you can design a program for each student. You can make up your own test, which gathers information about the speaking and listening skills of the bilingual child. Be sure to keep in mind the following guidelines as you administer any kind of test.

1. The child should be tested on two separate occasions by separate examiners, unless the teacher is bilingual in English and in the child's native language.

2. Be certain that you and the child are seated in a quiet corner, free from distraction.

3. Make every effort to gain the child's complete attention and tell him that you are going to ask each question only once.

4. Speak in a conversational tone; do not hurry.

5. Do not give emphasis to any of the material that would distort it for the child.

If you plan to design your own test, you could include tasks such as repeating words or syllables, writing alphabet letters from English, or writing the child's native language, listening to a story and answering questions, and identifying pictures. Useful tests for assessing the language efficiency of children of this age group include the following:

Bilingual Syntax Measure, 1973 (grades K–2)
Harcourt Brace Jovanovich, Inc.
Testing Department
757 Third Ave.
New York, NY 10017

James Language Dominance Test, 1974 (grades K–1)
Learning Concepts
Speech Division
2501 N. Lamar
Austin, TX 78705

### Language Assessment

Boston University Speech Sound Discrimination Picture Test. Boston: Boston University.

Monroe, Marion, and Bernice Rogers. *Foundations for Reading.* Glenview, Ill.: Scott, Foresman and Company, 1964. (The assessment procedures designed by Monroe were adapted and administered in Spanish to Head Start enrollees in the Tempe, Arizona, Elementary Program.

### Perceptual Abilities

Frostig, Marianne. *Development Test of Visual Perception.* Palo Alto, Calif.: Consulting Psychologists Press, 1966.

Kephart, Newell C., and Eugene C. Roach. *The Purdue Perceptual Motor Survey.* Columbus, Ohio: Charles E. Merrill Publishing Company, 1966.

Kirk, Samuel A., and James J. McCarthy. *The Illinois Test of Psycholinguistic Abilities.* Champaign, Illinois: University of Illinois Press, 1968.

Mertens, Marjoire H. *Mertens Visual Perception Test.* Tempe, Arizona: Arizona State University, 1966.

### Learning English As a Second Lanugage

One of the best ways to teach young children English, if their first language is not English, is to let them play and learn with children whose first language is English. Young children are less encumbered by introspection and self-consciousness than older children and adults. They are willing to create new words and to decipher the complex and often unintelligible speech of their peers. However, not all children learn a second language spontaneously. It is foolhardy to think every second-language child will learn English merely because he is young. Some children may need rather direct instruction in English-as-a-second-language.

*Figure 89.* One of the best ways to teach young children English if their first language is not English, is to let them play and learn with children whose first language is English. (Photo by Linda Lungren)

Although you may not be teaching any bilingual children at the present time, you may have to do so in the future. If you decide that you need to give direct instruction in English-as-a-second-language and you are unsure how to do it, you may want to refer to the following scope and sequence chart:

Scope and Sequence Chart

## BEGINNING LEVEL

Syntactic Structures

A. Declarative and question sentence structures.
   1. Word order of declaratives contrasted with different word order of questions with BE verbs. (They are leaving, Are they leaving?)
   2. Use of contracted forms of BE verbs: (he's, they're, I'm) Use of pronouns with corresponding form of BE verb: (she is, they are)
   3. Use of BE verbs to show action:
      (a) in progress
      (b) of repetitive nature
   4. Use of determiners: (THE, A, AN)
   5. Affirmative and negative short answers to questions with BE verbs. (I'm going, He's not going.)

B. Verbs other than BE.
   1. Word order for declaratives compared to order for questions with DO and DOES.
   2. Affirmative and negative short answers to questions with DO and DOES.
   3. -S forms of third person singular used with pronouns (he, she, it) and other singular nouns in declaratives, contrasted to plural nouns. (he runs, we run).

C. Expression of time (tense).
   1. Use of BE in expressions of past tense in statements and questions. (I was walking, Were they singing?)

Articulation

A. Contrasted intonation contours of declarative sentences, questions, and short answers.
B. Stress and accent patterns of requests.
C. Articulation of contracted forms of BE with pronouns HE, SHE, WE, YOU, IT, THERE.
D. Articulation of the /s/, /z/, and /-ðz/ of third person singular verbs and plurals as in words like EATS, WINS, SMASHES, and contractions such as IT'S, THERE'S.
E. Unstressed forms of A, AN, THE.
F. Articulation of /k/, /g/, /n/. KICK, GO, SING.
G. Stress the accent patterns of compound words.
H. Articulation of /t/, /d/, and -ed endings as in FOOT, WOOD, HUNTED.
I. Articulation of /p/, and /b/ as in PAY, BOY.
J. Articulation of /f/ and /v/ as in CALF, MOVE.
K. Articulation of /θ/ and /ð/ - THIN, THOSE.
   (a) Contrasting /t/ with /θ/ - BOAT, BOTH.
   (b) Contrasting /d/ with /ð/ - DAY, THEY.
L. Articulation of /s/, /z/, /c/ and /j/ - MASH, PLEASURE, CHOOSE, FUDGE.
M. Articulation of /m/ and /n/ - MOON, NO.
N. Articulation of /l/ and /r/ - LOSE, READ.

| Syntactic Structures | Articulation |
|---|---|

Syntactic Structures

2. Irregular verbs which form past tense without-ED (Use of vowel & consonant contrast).
3. Formation of verbs other than BE to express past tense using regular rule (-ED).
   (a) Past tense forms and placement of verbs other than BE in declaratives and questions.
4. Forms of short responses to questions asked in past tense (use of BE or DO appropriately).
5. Use of BE verbs + GOING TO to express future tense. (She is going to ride home. They are going to sing.)

D. Formation of questions with interrogative words or word order.
E. Negatives.
   1. Use and placement of NOT in declaratives (past, present, future) with verb BE.
   2. Use of NOT in questions with BE.
   3. Use of NOT in sentences (declarative and question) with DO and verbs other than BE.
   4. Use of ANY, RARELY, SELDOM, FEW,
F. Frequency words.
   1. Different positions of frequency words with BE contrasted with positions with verbs other than BE (He sometimes walks. He is always late.)
   2. Use of EVER in question patterns; NEVER in declarative sentences.

Articulation

O. Articulation of /w/ and /y/ - WOOD, YELLOW.
P. Articulation of front vowels.
   (a) /i/ and /I/ - SEAT, SIT
   (b) /e/ and /ə/ - SAY, PET
   (c) Contrast of /ə/ with /I/ - SET, SIT.
   (d) Contrast of /I/, /ə/, and /i/ - SIT, SET, SEAT
   (e) /æ/ - HAT
Q. Articulation of middle vowels.
   (a) /ə/ and /a/ - NUT, HOT
   (b) Contrast of /a/ with /æ/ - HOT, HAT
   (c) /ai/ - TIE
   (d) /ər/ - HURT
R. Articulation of glides and back vowels.
   (a) /u/ and /U/ - FOOD, FOOT
   (b) /aU/ - COW
   (c) /o/ and /ə/ - Boat, BOUGHT
   (d) /oI/ - TOY

## INTERMEDIATE LEVEL

The following skills should be an extension of a solid foundation in beginning level materials.

Syntactic structures

A. Review of patterns introduced at beginning level.

Articulation

A. Articulation of consonant cluster. /sp/ as in SPECIAL.

B. Modification constructions: use of substitute words
   1. How OTHER and ANOTHER can be substituted for nouns, contrasted with their use as modifiers of nouns.
   2. Use of objective forms of personal pronouns in object position.
C. Structures in which ME, TO ME, and FOR ME are used with certain verbs.
D. Patterns of word order when expressing manner. John runs quickly.
E. Modals: Use of MUST, CAN, WILL, SHOULD, MAY, and MIGHT in appropriate place in sentence.
F. Techniques for connecting statements.
   1. AND. . .EITHER contrasted with AND. . .TOO.
   2. Use of BUT.
G. Structures with two-word verbs (verb + particle) CALL UP, PUT ON.
   1. Structures in which they are unseparated.
   2. Structures in which they are separated.
H. Patterns for answers to Why and How questions.
I. Special patterns using TO and FOR.
   1. FOR and TO + other words as modifiers following some terms of quality.
   2. Placement of VERY, TOO, ENOUGH.
   3. Patterns in which nouns or pronouns are used after certain action words.
J. IT or THERE as subject of the sentence.
K. —'S as a contraction and as a possessive marker.
L. Comparisons.
   1. Structures for comparisons with DIFFERENT FROM, SAME AS, LIKE, THE SAME. . . AS AS. . . AS.

B. Articulation of consonant cluster. /st/, /sk/, /sn/, /sm/, /sl/, and /sw/ as in STEP, SKIP, SNAP, SMELL.
C. Articulation of final consonant clusters. Consonant +/s/, consonant + /t/, consonant + /d/, as in CATS, DROPPED, USED.
D. Articulation of final consonant clusters (two consonants + /s/, as in HELPS.)
E. Articulation of final consonant clusters (two consonants + /t/, as in JUMPED.)
F. Intonation patterns used in comparisons.

    2. Patterns of comparison using
-ER THAN and MORE THAN,
OF THE. . .-EST, and THE MOST.

## INTERMEDIATE-ADVANCED LEVEL

### Syntactic structures

A. Review structures introduced at
earlier levels.
B. Word order pattern and use of
relative clauses or embedded
sentence to modify nouns.
    1. Words used as subject of the
embedded sentence (THAT,
WHICH, WHO, etc.).
    2. THAT and related words in
other positions.
C. WHAT, WHEN, WHO, in
object position.
D. Embedded sentences of different
statement pattern type used in
object positions.
E. Patterns with HAVE and BE in the
auxiliary.
    1. Present-perfect complete
HAVE (HAS) + -ED/-EN form
of verb.
    2. BE + ing verb form (used with
YET, ANYMORE, STILL).
    3. HAVE + BEEN + -ing verb
forms in continuous present-
perfect structures.
    4. Using BE + -ED/-EN verb forms.
    5. Using BE with -ED/-EN and -ing
in descriptions.
    6. Special cases:
      (a) BE + two-word verbs and
-ing form.
      (b) Use of HAD in those
structures.

### Articulation

A. Articulation of final consonant cluster:
(two consonants + /z/ as in HOLDS).
B. Articulation of final consonant cluster:
(two consonants + /d/ as in SOLVED).

*Special structural patterns:*

A. Verb modification.
    1.  WISH     (that) + declarative
        HOPE     sentence.

    2. TO omitted after certain verbs.

B. Conditionals.
    1. Patterns with SHOULD, MIGHT, COULD, MUST.
    2. Cause-and-effect sentence structures.

C. Object structures and modification.
    1. Use of -ing endings of verbs.
    2. Patterns for verbs followed by an object and one or more describing words, and/or an -ing form.
    3. Verbs followed by two nouns with the same reference.
    4. -ING endings used in subject position contrasted to their use at the beginning of sentences (referring to the subject).

D. Logical order of sentences in sequence.
    1. Ordering for sentences related by HOWEVER, THEREFORE, ALSO, BUT.
    2. Ordering for sentences related by terms of time or place (before, after that, then).

## ADVANCED LEVEL

### Syntactic structures

A. Review of all levels.

B. Review of function words.
    1. Auxiliaries: WILL, MAY, CAN, COULD, SHOULD, MIGHT, WOULD, MUST, HAVE, BE, SHALL, DO.
    2. Preposition adverbs:
        (a) Frequently used: AT, BY, IN, INTO, FOR, FROM, WITH, TO, ON, OF, OFF.
        (b) Location
        (c) Direction
        (d) Time
        (e) Comparison

C. Conjunction patterns with BUT and OR.

D. Other complement structures.
    1. believe

### Articulation

Spelling vowel sounds:
/I/ and /i/:
glides /aI/ and /r/;
glides /aU/ and /oI/

Intonation and stress patterns used with comparisons, manner and time words, and prepositions.

Intonation patterns for modals:
COULD, WOULD, MUST, SHOULD.

Conjunction and intonation pattern with OR and BUT.

Words for degree and for generalizing.

Articulation of TO and TOO.

1. believe
   want
   think     + declarative sentence.
   expect
2. Use of appropriate comple-
   mentizer words.

## VOCABULARY DEVELOPMENT

### Beginning Level

A basic flexible-content vocabulary should include items relevant to the students' everyday experiences, that is:

| | |
|---|---|
| eating and cooking utensils | colors |
| common foods | name of occupations |
| parts of the body | days of the week |
| articles of clothing | months of the year, seasons |
| furniture | common animals |
| telling time | various materials: wood, plastic. |
| numbers: cardinal, ordinal | holidays |
| family relationships | most important geographic names |
| | words used to ask directions |

Pictures and/or objects should be used to explain all of these.

In addition:

Several basic two-word verbs (verbs + particle) for example, PICK UP, WAIT FOR, HANG UP, GET UP.

Concepts of directionality: IN FRONT OF, BEHIND, BEFORE, AFTER
Countable and noncountable nouns: CUP as opposed to CEREAL.

Following simple directions:

Simple synonyms, antonyms, especially adjectives and prepositions such as GOOD - BAD, ON - OFF.

### Intermediate Level

Extension of vocabulary introduced plus:

| | |
|---|---|
| Shopping expressions | Family names of more distant relatives |
| Further occupations and | Government agencies |
| responsibilities | Clothing materials |
| Health and health practices | |
| Further synonyms and antonyms | |

### Intermediate-Advanced Level

| | |
|---|---|
| Daily living skills | Directions involving choice |
| Purchasing suggestions | Derivations |
| Driving | Structural analysis: prefixes, suffixes, |
| Traffic regulations | hyphenation of words |
| Postal procedures | Synonyms, antonyms, homonyms |
| Insurance procedures | (more advanced) |

Music, literature, the arts
Educational opportunities
Leisure-time activities
Travel
Government

Advanced Level

Study skills information—locating and organizing information, synthesis of information, and making cross-comparisons

Propaganda techniques—discerning fact and fiction

The human body and its actions
   Evening and morning activities

Special problems: Idiomatic expressions
   Multiple meanings of words

Advanced descriptive terminology
   Attributes of objects (size, shape)
   Attributes of people (including personality)

Buying and selling

Transportation and communication

Personal and professional contacts (job applications)

Further government interaction (law, courts, taxes)

Oral and written reports   (books, movies, trips)

Discussions on American history, geography, climate.

## WRITING

### Beginning Level

In beginning English, writing is quite limited. It should be directly related to the student's understanding and use of vocabulary and structures in the class. At this level, the comma, period, question mark, and apostrophe should be taught in order to develop proper intonation. The use of capital letters at the beginning of sentences should be introduced.

The following is a suggested guide for allotting time for the teaching of language skills at this level: Listening—40 per cent; Speaking—40 per cent; Reading—15 per cent; and Writing—5 per cent.

### Intermediate Level

As in the beginning, writing should be a direct outgrowth of the student's mastery of the spoken work in class. Simple dictation and writing answers to questions generated by reading and conversation materials can be used as effective exercises.

Reading activities should include silent reading, group oral reading, and individual oral reading, with emphasis on the intonation patterns of language, such as rhythm and stress.

Proportions of time that might be spent in developing skills: Listening and Speaking—45 per cent; Reading—35 per cent; Writing—20 per cent.

Intermediate-Advanced Level

At this stage, more time should be devoted to reading and writing. Advanced reading comprehension should be evaluated both orally and in written form, and should include knowledge of literal, interpretive, and critical levels of cognition.

Writing skills should be directly related to the needs of daily living as well as the more formal requirements of education. Reference and study skills should also be emphasized.

Suggested proportions of time: Listening and Speaking—40 per cent; Reading—40 per cent; Writing—20 per cent.

Advanced Level

At this stage emphasis should be on the expansion of the material introduced at previous levels. The student should be encouraged to use his reading and writing skills to enable him to gain insight into all realms of our society.

Reprinted with permission from Lapp, D. and J. Flood. *Teaching Reading to Every Child*. (New York: Macmillan Publishing Co., Inc., 1978).

## Language Experience Method

One of the most effective methods of teaching language/reading to bilingual speakers is the language experience method because it elicits language from the child. The teacher or the child, when he is able, transcribes the oral language, and the child *reads* what he has spoken.

All children bring to school many language skills: listening, comprehension, and speaking. The tasks of the reading teacher are to help children develop those skills further and to teach them the visual appearance of the language that they already understand. Developmentally, all children learn to listen and to speak before they learn to read and to write. It is clear that oral language conveys meaning if the speaker and listener share the same set of oral symbols for objects and relationships in their experience. The reading teacher must remember that oral language is the base of the reading process and until it is developed, reading seems a senseless, futile exercise for the child.

### Adapting the Language Experience Method for Young Bilingual Students

1. Use simple stories and poems for listening exercises and as language models.
2. Provide opportunities for first-hand experiences—outings to the country or city, museums, zoos, bus or train rides.
3. Have children make phrase books describing their experiences by drawing a picture and writing a short caption beneath it.

*Figure 90.* Have children make phrase books describing their experiences by drawing a picture. (Photo by Linda Lungren)

Young children can dictate their story to you and you can write their words under the picture.

4. Provide model sentences individually or on the board or a large chart.

Today we visited _____ .

We saw _____ .

My favorite animal was _____ .

We traveled by _____ .

You may also want to ask, How do I implement a language experience method for ESL children when they have limited English? The following lesson presents a language experience approach with primary-grade children who are not proficient in speaking English.

---

**Lesson Plan**

**Topic and Group**

The following is a Halloween language experience lesson, designed to introduce new vocabulary words about Halloween to a full-time ESL primary class in which children have different oral and written language skills.

## Objectives

A. Classroom objective

The teacher will introduce the children to the theme of Halloween, emphasizing Halloween vocabulary.

B. Behavioral objective

After being introduced to the vocabulary associated with Halloween, each child will be able to read at least two words related to Halloween that have been added to their word bank, and each child will correctly identify in context the word Halloween and any other word(s) of his/her choice.

## Diagnosis

Teacher Observation:

The fall season has arrived, and the teacher heard children talking about an American holiday known as "Halloween." He observes the limited descriptive vocabulary being utilized by the children. Halloween books and pictures are then placed around the room to stimulate Halloween vocabulary development.

## Strategies

The theme of Halloween will be introduced by the teacher as he reads a Halloween picture book to the entire class. An experience chart will be written by the teacher and dictated by the children. The teacher will elicit responses by asking questions such as the following:

What do children do on Halloween? What will you dress up as for Halloween? What will you wear? What do you say when someone answers the door? What are some things we have to be careful of on Halloween?

Each child who is able will dictate a word or phrase for the chart. The chart would be similar to the following:

### Things That Remind Us Of Halloween

| | |
|---|---|
| Jaime: | scary |
| Wolfgang: | monsters |
| Cullen: | costumes |
| Denny: | candy |
| Soo-Lin: | parties |
| Pillar: | trick-or-treat |
| Tommy: | cold |
| Nicole: | pumpkins |
| Johann: | excited |

Each child will be given a word card with Halloween written on it. The children will be given a piece of drawing paper to illustrate whatever they like best about Halloween. While the children are drawing, the teacher will individually help each child write another word card of his/her choice for the word bank. The more advanced readers could write several of their own word cards.

> When each child finishes his drawing, he will label it or be helped in label-
> ing by dictating to the teacher a descriptive word, phrase, sentence, or several
> sentences.

## Program

In designing and planning your program for young children, it is important
to review the designs of other programs. O'Brien recommends the program on
page 448 for young bilingual children.

### *Spanish Native Language Programs*

If you are teaching Spanish-speaking children, you may need to begin your
instruction in the child's native language. The following list of words on pp.
449–59 are those that young Spanish-speaking children acquire early in their
language/reading development. This list may serve as the basis for your initial
language/reading program.

### *Planning Your Bicultural Program*

In planning your program, it is extremely important to remember that you
are the teacher for every child in your care. Your program must include
activities for every child. The information contained in this chapter is only a
beginning to understanding the abundance of bilingualism. A first step that all
teachers should take is to make their classrooms bicultural, exploring and
celebrating the diversity that your children will bring to you.

## A SUGGESTED PROGRAM FOR EARLY PRIMARY LEVELS*

| Structured activities | Semistructured activities | Unstructured activities |
|---|---|---|
| *Large group* | *Large group* | *Large group* |
| Planning time: Teacher-directed discussion of | Total class working on such projects as | Sharing time period provided for |
| 1. plans for the day | 1. social living unit activities (charts, displays, talking murals, bulletin boards, indoor/outdoor construction projects, experience charts) | 1. show and tell experience |
| 2. classroom goals | | 2. reporting on individual or group activities |
| 3. preparation for class projects, field trips, social activities, etc. | | 3. showing art work, reading creative stories, poems. Library period set aside for independent reading or "picture reading" and listening to "talking books," etc. |
| 4. classroom rules and regulations | 2. science activities (collections, labeled displays, experience charts, records of experiments, indoor/outdoor gardens, science word dictionaries or files) | |
| 5. housekeeping task assignments | | Demonstration period provided for |
| *Small group* | 3. a classroom newspaper or news sheet | 1. creative dramatic presentations |
| Ability-group instruction in beginning language and reading: | 4. literary experiences, story reading, story telling, poetry, recordings, creative writing | 2. puppet shows |
| 1. oral language | 5. creative dramatics | 3. individual talent opportunity |
| 2. vocabulary building | | 4. choral reading |
| 3. visual and auditory skill building activities | *Small group* | *Small group* |
| 4. concept building | Groups "cycled" through learning centers for specific learning experiences: | Clusters of children involved in cooperative work or play activity |
| 5. language experience activity | 1. library center | *Individual* |
| *Individual* | 2. listening-viewing station | Free-choice activity in learning center Playhouse area, toy or game area, art or crafts area |
| Teacher-directed individual learning experiences such as | 3. reading skills center (games and manipulative devices) | |
| 1. programmed instruction in silent reading, and perceptual skill development | 4. creative writing center | Individual-choice work tasks related to plans of the day |
| 2. teacher-constructed tapes and work sheets | 5. science center | |
| | *Individual* | |
| | Individuals assigned to learning centers for specific learning experiences | |

*C. O'Brien, *Teaching the Language Different Child to Read* (Columbus, Ohio: Charles E. Merrill Publishing Company, 1973), p. 57. Reprinted by permission.

## List I

a - a
abajo - under
abandonar - abandon
abcorrecer - to abhor
abrazar - to hug
abrir - to open
absoluto - absolute
abuelo - grandfather
aća - here
ascabar - finish
acaso - change - adv. maybe
acción - action
aceite - oil
acento - accent
aceptar - accept
acerca - about - with regard to
acercar - approach - to bring near
acertar - to find - to figure out
acompanar - to accompany
aconsejar - to advise
acordar - to agree upon
acostumbrar - to accustom
actitud - attitude
acto - act
actual - actual - present

acudir - to respond to come to rescue
acuerdo - agreement
adelantar - advance - to move forward
adelante - ahead
además - also
adiós - goodbye
admirable - admirable
admiracion - admiration
admirar - to admire
admitir - to admit
adonde - where
adorar - to adore
adquirir - to aquire
advertir - to warn
afan - eagerness - zeal
afecto - fond
afirmar - affirm
afligir - to afflict
agitar - to agitate - shake
agradable - agreeable
agradar - to please
agradecer - to thank
agregar - to add
agua - water
aguardar - to await - to wait for

ahi - there
abogar - to drown
abora - now
aire - air
ajeno - another's
al - cont. of ael
ala - wing
alcalde - mayor
alcanzar - to reach
alegrar - make happy
alegre - happy
alegria - happiness
alejar - to move away
algo - something
alguien - someone
algún (-o) - some, any
aliento - breath
alma - soul
alrededo - around
alterar - to alter
alto - high, tall
altura - height
alumbrar - to light
alzar - to raise
allá - over there
alli - there
amable - amiable
amante - lover

amar - to love
amargo - bitter
amargura - bitterness
ambos - both
amenazar - daybreak
americano — American
amigo - friend
amistad - friendship
amo - I love, n. boss
amor - love
amoroso - amorous
anciano - old person
ancho - wide
andar - to walk
ángel - angel
angustia - anguish
animal - animal
animar - to anticipate
animo - spirit covered
anteior - previous
antes - before
antiguo - antique
anunciar - announce
añadir - to add
año - year
apagar - to turn off
aparecer - appear
apartar - to separate

aparte - apart
apenas - scarcely
aplicar - apply
apoyar - to support
aprender - to learn
apretar - squeeze
aprovechar - take advantage of
aquel - that
aquél - that one
aquí - here
árbol - tree
arder - to burn
ardiente - burning
arma - weapon
armar - to arm
arrancar - to root
arrastrar - to drag
arreglar - to fix
arriba - upstairs
arrojar - to throw
arte - art
articulo - article
artista - artist
asegurar - insure
asi - thus
asiento - seat
asistir - assist
asomar - to peep into

*s. = substantivo (noun); adv. = adverbio; adj. = adjetivo; v. = verbo; prep. = preposicion; pron. = pronombre.

color - color
columna - column
combatir - to combat
comedia - comedy
comenzar - to begin
comer - to eat
cometer - to commit
comida - food
como, cómo - How, as, like
compañero - companion
compañia - company
comparar - compare
complacer - to please
completo - complete
componer - compose
comprar - to buy
comprender - to understand
común - common
comunicar - communicate
con - with
concebir - conceive
conceder - concede
concepto - concept
conciencia - conscience
concluir - conclude
conde - count
condenar - condemn
condesa - countess
condición - condition

conducir - to conduce
conducta - conduct
confesar - confess
confianza - confidence
confiar - confide
conforme - in agreement
confundir - confuse
confusion - confusion
confuso - confused
conjunto - joined
conmigo - with me
conmover - affect
conocer - to know
conocimiento - knowledge
conque - condition
conquista - conquest
consagrar - to consecrate
consecuencia - consequence
conseguir - obtain
consejo - advice
consentir - to allow
conservar - conserve
considerar - consider
consigo - with him
consistir - to consist
constante - constantly
constituir - constitute
construir - contract
consuelo - consolation

consumir - to consume
contar - to count
contemplar - contemplate
contener - to contain
contento - glad
contestar - to answer
contigo - with you
continuar - to continue
continuo - continuous
contra - against
contrario - contrary
contribuir - to contribute
convencer - to convince
convenir - convene
conversación - conservation
convertis - convert
convidar - to invite
copa - cup
corazón - heart
corona - crown
correr - run
corresponder - correspond
corriente - current
cortar - cut
corte - court
corto - short
cosa - thing
costa - coast
costar - to cost

costumbre - custom
crear - to create
crecer - to grow
creer - to believe
criado - bred, raised
criar - to raise
criatura - child
cristal - glass
cristiano - Christian
cruel - cruel
cruz - cross
cruzar - to cross
cuadro - picture
cual, cuál - which, which one
cuando - since
cuándo - when
cuanto, cuanto - how much - as much as
cuarto (s.) - room
cubrir - to cover
cuello - neck
cuenta - account
cuento - story
cuerpo - body
cuestión - dispute
cuidado - care
cuidar - to take care of
culpa - blame
culto - cult

cumbre - top
cumplir - to fulfill
cura - cure
curiosidad - curiosity
curioso - curious
curso - course
chico - a boy
dama - a lady
daño - harm
dar - to give
de - prep. of, from
debajo - under
deber (v.o s.) - duty
débil - wear
decidir - decide
decir - to say
declarar - declare
dedicar - dedicate
dedo - finger
defecto - defect
defender - defend
defensa - defense
dejar - to leave
del - of
delante - in front of
delicado - delicate
demás - others
demasiado - too much
demonio - demon

asombrat - to astonish
aspecto - aspect
aspirar - to aspire
asunto - subject
atar - to tie
atención - attention
atender - to attend
atento - attentive
atrás - behind
atravesar - to go through
atreverse - to dare
aumentar - increase
aun, aun - even, still
aunque - although
ausencia - absence
autor - author
autoridad - authority
auxilio - help
avanzar - advance
ave - bird
aventura - adventure
avisar - notify
ay - alas!
ayer - yesterday
ayudar - to help
azúcar - sugar
azul - blue

bailar - to dance
bajar - to lower

bajo - low
balcón - balcony
bañar - to bathe
barba - beard
base - base
bastante - enough
bastar - to suffice
batalla - battle
batir - shake
beber - drink
belleza - beauty
bello - beautiful
bendecir - to bless
bendito - blessed
besar - to kiss
beso - a kiss
bestia - beast
bien (s., adv.)* well
blanco - white
blando - soft
boca - mouth
boda - wedding
bondad - goodness
bonito (adj.) - pretty
bosque - forest
bravo - brave
brazo - arm
breve - brief
brillante - brilliant
brillar - to shine

buen(-o) - good
burla - mockery
burlar - to ridicule
buscar - to seek

caballero - gentleman
caballo - horse
cabello - hair
caber - to go in or into
cabeza - head
cabo - cape
cada - every, each
cadena - chain
caer - to fall
café - coffee
caída - fall, tumble
caja - box
c(u)alidad - quality
calma - calmness
calor - heat
callar - to keep silent
calle - street
cama - bed
cambiar - to change
cambio - change, barter
caminar - to walk
camino - path, road
campana - bell
campaña - campaign
campo - country, field

cansar - to tire out
cantar - to sing
cantidad - quantity
canto - I sing
capa - cape
capaz - capable
caapital - capital
capitan - captain
capitulo - chapter
cara - face
caracter - character
carcel - jail
cargar - to carry
cargo - burden
caridad - charity
cariño - affection
carne - meat
carrera - career
carro - car
carta - letter
casa - house
casar - to marry
casi - almost
caso - case, event
castellano - Castillian
castigar - castigate
castigo - punishment
causa - cause
causar - to cause
ceder - cede, to yield

celebrar - celebrate
celebre - famous
centro - center
ceñir - surround
cerca - near
cercano - neighboring
cerebro - brain
cerrar - to close
cesar - to cease
ciego - blind
cielo - sky
ciencia - science
cireto (-amente) - certainly true
circumstancia - circumstance
citar - to convoke
ciudad - city
civil - civil
claridad - clarity
claro - clear
clase - class
clavar - to nail
cobrar - to collect
cocer - to sew
coche - coach
coger - to catch
cólera - anger
colgar - to have
colocar - arrange

demonstrar - demonstrate
dentro - inside
derecho (-a) - the right to
derramar - to spill
desaparecer - to disappear
descansar - to rest
desconocer - not to know
describir - to describe
descubrir - to discover
desde - since
desear - to desire
deseo - a wish
desesperar - become desperate
desgracia - disgrace
desgraciado - unfortunate
deshacer - to undo
desierto - desert, deserted
despedir - to emit
despertar - to awaken
despreciar - to scorn
despues - after
destinar - to destine
destino - destiny
destruit - destroy
detener - detain
determinar - determine
defras - in back of
día - day
diablo - devil

diario - diary
dicha - luck
dicho (s.) - saying
dischoso - lucky
diente - tooth
diferencia - difference
diferente - different
difícil - difficult
dificultad - difficulty
difunto - dead
digno - worthy
dinero - money
dios - God
direction - address
directo - direct
dirigir - to direct
discreto - discrete
discurrir - contrive
discurso - disourse
disgusto - displeasure
disponer - dispose
disposición - disposition
distancia - distance
distinguir - to distinguish
distinto - distinct
diverso - diverse
divertir - to divert
dividir - to divide
divino - divine
doblar - to fold

doble - fold
doctor - doctor
dolor - pain
dominar - dominate
don, D. - Mr.
donde, done - wherever, where
dona, Da. - Mrs.
dormir - to sleep
drama - drama
duda - doubt
dudar - to doubt
dueño - owner
dulce - candy, sweet
dulzura - sweetness
durante - during
durar - to last
duro - hard

echar - to throw
edad - age
edificio - building
educacion - education
efecto - effect
ejecutar - execute
ejemplo - example
ejercer - to execute
ejército - army
el, el - he, the
elegir - to elect

elemento - element
elevar - to elevate
ella - she
emoción - emotion
empenar - to pawn
empezar - to begin
emplear - to employ
emprender - to undertake
empressa - enterprise
en - in
enamorar - to make love to
encantador - enchanting
encanto - enchantment
encargar - to order
encender - to light
encerrar - to enclose
encima - on top
encontrar - to find
encuentro - encounter
enemigo - enemy
energia - energy
enfermedad - sickness
enfermo - sick
engañar - to fool
engaño - deception
enojo - anger
enorme - large
enseñanza - teaching
enseñar - to teach
entender - to understand

enterar - to bury
entero - complete
entonces - then
entrada - enter
entrar - to enter
entre - between
entregar - to turn in
entusiasmo - enthusiasm
enviar - to send
envolver - to envolve
época - era
error - error, mistake
escapar - to escape
escaso - scarce
escena - scene
escalvo - slave
escoger - to select
esconder - to hide
escribir - to write
escritor - writer
escuchar - to liten
escuela - school
ese, ése - that, that one
esfuerzo - spirit, vigor
eso - that
espacio - space
espada - spear
espalda - back, shoulders
espanol - Spanish
esparcir - to scatter

especial - special
especie - spice
espejo - mirror
esperanza - hope
esperar - to wait
espeso - thick
espíritu - spirit
esposo - husband
establecer - to establish
estado - state
estar - to be
estatua - statue
este, éste - this, this one
estilo - sytle
estimar - to estimate
estrecho - narrow
estrella - star
estudiar - to study
estudio - studio
eterno - eternal
evitar - avoid
exacto - exact
examinar - examine
escelente - excellent
exclamar - to exclaim
exigir - demand
existencia - existence
existir - exist
experiencia - experience

experimentar - to experiment
explicar - to explain
exponer - expose
expresar - express
expresión - expression
extender - extend
extensión - extension
extranjero - foreigner
extrañar - to banish
extraño - strange
extraordinario - extraordinary
extremo - extreme

facil - easy
facultad - faculty
falda - skirt
falso - false
falta - lack
fama - fame
familia - family
famoso - famous
fantasía - fantasy
favor - a favor
favorecer - to favor
fe - faith
felicidad - happiness
feliz - happy

fenomeno - phenomenon
feo - ugly
fiar - to ball
fiel - faithful
fiesta - party
figura - figure
figurar - to figure
fijar - to make firm
fijo - firm
fin - end
final - final
fingir - to fake
fino - fine
firme - firm
fisico - physical
flor - flower
fondo - fund
forma - form
formar - to form
formidable - formidable
fortuna - fortune
frances - French
franco - Frank
frase - phrase
frecuente - frequently
frente - front
fresco - fresh
frio - cold
fruto - fruit

fuego - fire
fuente - fountain
fuera - outside
fuerte - strong
fuerza - strength
función - function
fundar - to raise
futuro - future

galán - courtier
gana - desire
ganar - to win
gastar - to spend
gato - cat
general - general
género - class, kind
generoso - generous
genio - genius
gente - people
gesto - gesture
gitano - gypsy
gloria - glory
glorioso - glorious
gobernar - govern
gobierno - government
golpe - stroke, hit
gota - drop
gozar - to enjoy
gracia - grace

gracioso - funny
grado - grade
gran (-de) - grand, big
grandeza - grandeur
grave - ponderous
griego- Greek
gritar - to scream
grito - shriek
grupo- group
guapo - handsome
guardar - to keep
guerra - war
guiar - drive
gustar - to like
gusto - taste

haber - to have
habitacion - residence
habitar - to swell
hablar*
hacer - to do
hacia - toward
hacienda - estate
hallar - to find
hambre - hunger
harto - satiate
hasta - until
he acquí - here is
hecho (s.) - made or done

*Habiar: word misspelled or does not exist.

helar - to freeze
herida - wound
herir - to wound
hermano - brother
hermoso - handsome
hermosura - beauty
hervir - to boil
hierro - iron
hijo - son
hilo - thread
historia - history
hogar - home
hoja - leaf
hombre - man
hombro - shoulder
hondo - deep
honor - honor
honra - reverence
honrar - to honor
hora - hour
horrible - horrible
horror - horror
hoy - today
huerta - irrigated land
hueso - bone
huevo - egg
huir - to escape
humanidad - humanity
humano - human
humilde - humble

humo - smoke
hundir - to submerge

idea - idea
ideal - ideal
idioma - language
iglesia - church
ignorar - ignore
igual - equal
iluminar - illuminate
ilusión - illusion
ilustre - illustration
imagen - image
imaginación - imagination
imaginar - imagine
imitar - imitate
impedir - to hinder
imperio - empire
imponer - to impose
importancia - importance
importante - important
importar - to matter
imposible - impossible
impresion - impression
impreso - printed matter
imprimir - to print
impulse - impulse
inclinar - incline
indicar - indicate
indiferente - indifferent

individuo - individual
industria - industry
infeliz - unhappy
infierno - infernal
infinito - infinite
influencia - influence
ingenio - inventive
inglés - English
inmediateo - immediate
inmenso - immense
inocente - innocent
inquieto - restless
inspirar - inspire
instante - instant
instrumento - instrument
inteligencia - intelligence
intención - intention
intentar - intent
interés - interest
interesante - interesting
interesar - to interest
interior - interior
interrumpir - interrupt
íntimo - intimate
introducir - introduce
inútil - useless
invierno - hell
ir (-se) - go, to go
ira - wrath
isla - island

izquierdo - left

jamás - never
jardín - garden
jefe - chief
joven - young
juego - game
juez - judge
jugar - to play
juicio - judgement
juntar - to join, connect
junto - together
jurar - promise
usticia - justice
justo - just
juventud - youth
juzgar - judge

la - fem. the
labio - lip
labor - work
labrador - farmer
lado - side
ladrón - thief
lágrima - tear
lance - cast, throw
lanzar - to throw
largo - long
lástima - pity
lavar - to wash

lazo - bow
lector - reader
lecho - bed, couch
leer - to read
legua - league
lejano - distant
lejos - far
lengua - tongue
lento - slow
letra - letter
levantar - to lift
level - of little weight
ley - law
libertad - liberty
librar - to set free
libere - free
libro - book
ligero - fast
limitar - to limit
límite - limit
limpio - clean
lindo - pretty
línea - line
líquido - liquid
lo - art. neut., the
loco - crazy
locura - insantity
lograr - to gain
lucha - struggle
luchar - to struggle

leugo - later on
lugar - place
luna - moon
luz - light
l'ama - call
llamar - to call
llano - even
llanto - flood of tears
llave - key
llegar - to arrive
llenar - to fill
lleno - full
llevar - to take
llorar - to cry

meadre - mother
maestro - teacher
magnifico - magnificent
majestad - majesty
mal (-o— (adj., bad, badness s. o adv.)
mandar - to command
manera - manner
manifestar - manifest
mano - hand
mantener - maintain
manana - tomorrow
máquina - machine
mar - sea
maravilla - wonder

marcar - to mark
marchar - to march
marido - husband
mas, más - more conj. but
masa - dough
matar - to kill
materia - matter
material - material
matrimonio - matrimony
mayor - greatest
me*
medico - doctor
medida - measure
medio - half
medir - to measure
mejor - better
mejorar - to improve
memoria - memory
menester - need, want
menos - less
mentir - to lie
mentira - a lie
menudo - small
merced - mercy
merecer - to deserve
mérito - merit
mes - month
mesa - table
meter - to put in
mezcla - mixture

mi, mí*
miedo - fear
mientras - while
military - military
ministro - minister
minuto - minute
mio - mine
mirada - glance
mirar (v.) to look
misa - mass
miserable - miserable
misena - misery
mismo - same
misterio - mystery
misterioso - mysterious
mitad - half
moderno - modern
modesto - modest
modo - mode
molestar - molest
momento - moment
montaña - mountain
montar - mount
monte - mountain
moral - moral
morir - to die
mortal - mortal
mostrar - to show
motivo - motive
mover - move

movimiento - movement
mozo - young man
muchacho - boy
mucho - much
mudar - move
muerte - death
mujer - woman
mundo - world
murmurar - murmur
musica - music
muy - very

nacer - to be born
nación - nation
nacional - national
nada - nothing
nadie - no one
natural - natural
naturaleza - nature
necesario - necessary
necesidad - necessity
necesitat - to need
necio - stupid
negar - to deny
negocio - business
negro - black
ni - neither, nor
ninguno - none
niño - boy
no - no

noble - noble
noche - night
nombrar - to name
nombre - name
norte - north
nota - grade, mark
notable - notable
notar - to note
noticia - news
novio - bride groom
nube - cloud
neuvo - new
numero - number
numeroso - numerous
nunca - never

obedecer - obey
objeto - object
obligación - obligation
obligar - obligate
obra - work
obscuridad - obscurity
obscuro - obscure
observación - observation
observer - observe
obtener - obtain
ocasion - occasion
ocultar - conceal
oculto - hidden

*me: 1st person, per. pron. dative, accusative and reflexive of Yo.     mi = pers. pron. oblique case of pronoun Yo, used after a prep.
*mi, mi: mi = sing. poss. pron. my

ocupacion - ocupation
ocupar - occupy
ocurrir - occur
odio - hatred
ofender - offense
oficial - official
oficio - occupation
ofrecer - offer
oido - ear
oir - hear
ojo - eye
olor - odor
olvidar - forget
opinión - opinion
oponer - oppose
oración - prayer
orden - order
ordenar - order
ordinario - ordinary
oreja - ear
orgullo - pride
origin - origen
orilla - shore
oro - gold
otro - other

paciencia - patience
padecer - to suffer
padre - father
pagar - to pay

página - page
país - country
pájaro - bird
palabra - word
palacio - palace
pan - bread
papel - paper
par - equal, on a par
para - for
parar - to stop
parecer (v.) - to seem
pared - wall
parte - part
particular - particular
partida - divided, broken
partido - broken
partir - to divide
pasado - past
pasar - to pass
pasear - to take a walk
paseo - stroll
pasión - passion
paso - pace, step
patria - native country
paz - peace
pecado - sin
pecho - chest
pedazo - piece
pedir - to ask
pegar - to stick

peligro - danger
peligroso - dangerous
pelo - hair
pena - penalty, pain
penetrar - penetrate
pensamiento - thought
pensar - to think
peor - worse
pequeño - small
perder - to lose
perdón - pardon
perdonar - to forgive
perfecto - perfect
periódico - newspaper
permanecer - to stay
permitir - to permit
pero - but
perro - dog
perseguir - to follow
persona - person
personaje - character
personal - personal
pertenecer - to pertain
pesar (v. o s.) - to weigh, or cause regret
peseta - quarter
peso - weight
picar - to prick, pierce
pico - beak
pie - foot

piedad - piety
peidra - rock
piel - skin
pieza - piece
pintar - to paint
pisar - to step on
placer - pleasure
planta - plant
plata - silver
plato - dish
plaza - market
pluma - pen
problación - population
pobre - poor
poco - scanty
poder (v. or s.) to be able, power
poderoso - powerful
poeta - poet
política - politics
politico - political
polvo - dust
poner - to put
poquito - a little bit
por - prep. by, for
porque - because
porqué - why
porvenir - time to come
poseer - possess
posesion - possession

posible - possible
posición - position
precio - price
precioso - precious
preciso - precise
preferir - prefer
prequnta - question
preguntar - to ask
premio - prize
prenda - piece of jewelry
prender - to turn on
preparar - to prepare
presencia - presence
presentar - to present
presente - present
presidente - president
prestar - lend
pretender - pretend
primero - first
primo - cousin
principal - principal
principe - prince
principio - principle, beginning
prisa - in a hurry
privar - to deprive
probar - to try
proceder - proceed
procurar - ask for
producir - produce
profundo - profound

prometer - promise
pronto - soon
pronunciar - pronounce
propiedad - property
propio - own
propener - propose
proporcion - proportion
proporcionar - to proportion
proposito - purpose
proseguir - to pursue
protestar - to protest
provincia - province
próximo - next
prueba - proof
publicar - publish
publico - public
pueblo - town
puerta - door
puerto - port
pues - conj. because
punta - point
punto - dot, period
puro - pure

que, qué - that - what!
quedar (-se) - to stay
queja - complaint
quejarse - complain
quemar - to burn

*Respectar = to concern, regard
*Respecto = relation, proportion

querer - to love
querido - loved one
quien, quién - who? - who is
quienquiera - whoever
quitar - take away
quizá, quiza(s) - maybe perhaps
rama - branch
rapido - fast
raro - strange
rato - a while
rayo - ray
raza - race
razon - reason
real - real
realidad - reality
realizar - realize
recibir - receive
recién - recent
reciente - recently
reclamar - reclaim
recoger - pick up
reconocer - to know
recordar - remember
recorrer - to go over
recuerdo - remembrance
reducir - reduce
referir - refer
regalar - give away
region - region

Respetar = to respect, revere
Respeto = respect

regla - rule
reina - queen
reinar - to rule
reino - kingdom
reir - to laugh
relación - relation
relativo - relative
religión - religion
religioso - religious
remedio - remedy
remoto - remote
rendir - subdue
reñir - quarrel
reparar - to repair
repartir - to divide
repetir - to repeat
replicar - to reply
reposar - to rest
reposo - repose
representar - represent
republica - Republic
resistir - resist
resolucion - resolution
resolver - resolve
respe(c)tar*
respe(c)to*
respirar - breathe
responder - respond
respuesta - answer
resto - rest

resultado - result
resultar - to result
retirar - retire
retrato - picture
reunión - meeting
reunir - to meet
revolver - resolve
rey - king
rico - rich
ridiculo - ridiculous
riesgo - risk
rigor - rigor
rincón - corner
rio - river
riqueza - richness
risa - laughter
robar - to steel
rodar - to move
rodear - to surround
rodilla - knee
rogar - to plead
rojo - red
romper - to break
ropa - clothes
rosa - rose
rostro - face
rubio - blond
rueda - wheel
ruido - noise
ruina - ruins

rumor - rumor
saber (v.) - to know
sabio - wise
sacar - to take out
sacerdote - priest
sacrificio - sacrifice
sacudir - to shake
sagrado - sacred
sal - salt
sala - living room
salida - exit
salir - to go out
saltar - to leap
salud - health
saludar - to greet
salvar - to save
sangre - blood
sano - healthy
santo - saint
satisfacer - satisfy
satisfecho - satisfied
se - to know
seco - dry
secreto - secret
seguida - continued, successive
seguir - to follow
segun - according to
segundo - second
seguridad - security

457

seguro - insurance, sure, certain  
semana - week  
semejante - similar  
sencillo - simple  
seno - breast  
sensación - sensation  
sentar - to sit  
sentido (s.) - sense  
sentimiento - sentiment  
sentir - to feel  
seña - signal  
señal - a signal  
señalar - to signal  
señor (-a) - Mr. Mrs.  
señorito (-a) - miss, young gentleman  
separar - seperate  
ser (v. o s.) - to be  
sereno - serene  
serio - serious  
servicio - service  
servir - to serve  
severo - severe  
si, sí - if, yes  
siempre - always  
siglo - century  
significar - signify  
siguiente - the following  
silencio - silence  
silla - chair  

*Ti = pron. 2nd pers. sing (oblique case of tu) thee

simple - simple  
sin - without  
sin embargo - however  
sincero - sincere  
singular - singular  
sino - conj. but, except  
siquiera - at least, though  
sistema - system  
sitio - place  
situación - situation  
situar - to place  
soberano - sovereign  
soberbio - haughtiness  
sobre (prep.) - on, upon  
sobrino - nephew  
social - social  
sociedad - society  
sol - sun  
soldado - soldier  
soledad - solitude  
soler - to be in the habit  
solicitar - to solicit  
solo, solo - alone, only  
soltar - to untie  
sombra - shadow  
sombrero - hat  
someter - to subject  
sonar - to sound, to ring  
sonido - sound  
sonreir - to smile  

soñar - to dream  
sordo - deaf  
sorprender - to surprise  
sorpresa - surprise  
sospechar - to suspect  
sostener - to sustain  
suave - soft  
subir - to climb  
suceder - to happen  
suceso - event  
suelo - floor  
suelto - lose  
sueño - a dream, sleepy  
suerte - luck  
suficiente - sufficient  
sufrir - suffer  
sujeto - subject  
suma - sum  
sumo - supreme  
superior - superior  
suplicar - implore  
suponer - suppose  
supremo - supreme  
supuesto - supposed  
suspender - to suspend  
suspirar - to sign  

tabla - tablet  
tal - such  
tal vez - perhaps  

talento - talent  
también - also  
tampoco - neither  
tan - as, so, so much  
tanto - so much  
tardar - to delay  
tarde (adv. o s.) - late - afternoon  
te (pron.) - old case of tú  
teatro - theatre  
tema - theme  
temblar - tremble  
temer - to fear  
temor - fear  
templo - temple  
temprano - early  
tender - to hang clothes  
tener - to have  
terminar - to end  
termino - term  
terreno - land area  
terrible - terrible  
terror - terror  
tesoro - treasure  
testigo - witness  
ti*  

tiempo - time  
tienda - store  
tierno - tender  
tierra - earth  

tio - uncle  
tipo - type  
tirano - tyrant  
tirar - to throw  
titulo - title  
tocar - touch  
todavia - not yet  
todo - all  
tomar - to drink  
tono - tone  
tonto - sully  
torcer - twist  
tornar - to turn  
torno - spinning wheel  
toro - bull  
torre - power  
total - total  
trabajar - to work  
trabajo - work  
traer - to bring  
traje - suit  
tranquilo - tranquil  
tras - behind  
trasladar - transfer  
tratar - try  
trato - treaty  
traves - reverse, misfortune  
triste - sad  
tristeza - sadness  
triunfar - to triumph

vender - sell
venganza - revenge
venir - to come
venta - sale
ventana - window
ventura - fortune
ver - see
verano - summer
veras - reality
verbo - verb
verdad - truth
verdadero - truthful
verde - green
verguenza - sham
verso - verse
vestido - dress

vestir - to dress
vez - turn, time
viaje - trip
vicio - vice
victima - victim
vida - life
viejo - old
viento - wind
vino - wine
violencia - violence
violento - violent
virgen - virgin
virtud - virtue
visión - vision
visita - visit
visitar - to visit

vista - view
visto - obvious, clear
viudo - widower
vivir - to live
vivo - live
volar - to fly
voluntad - voluntary
volver - to return
voto - vote
voz - voice
vuelta - turn

y - and
ya - already, right away
yo - I

triunfo - triumph
tropezar - stumble
tu, tú*
turbar - confuse

ultimo - last
un, uno (-a)*
unico - only one
unión - union
unir - white
usar - to use
uso - use
usted - you
útil - useful

vacio - empty

vago - lazy
valer - to protect
valiente - valiant
valor - value
valle - valley
vanidad - vanity
vano - vain
vapor - vapor
variar - vary
vario - various
varón - boy
vaso - glass
vecino - neighbor
vela - candle
velar - to watch
vencér - conquer

*Tu = per. pron. 2nd person, m. or f. thou

*Tu = poss. pron. m. or f. (pl. tus) thy

*Un, una: indef. art. a, an

## BIBLIOGRAPHY

Ching, D. *Reading and the Bilingual Child.* Newark, Del.: International Reading Association, 1976.

Hirsch, S. "Informal Diagnostic Instruments of English Language Skills" In J. Flood (Ed.) *Proceedings of the Boston University Bilingual Reading Laboratory.* Boston: Boston, University School of Education, 1976.

Lapp, D. and Flood, J. *Teaching Reading to Every Child,* New York: Macmillan Publishing Company, Inc., 1978.

Montessori, M. *The Montessori Method.* New York: Schocken Books, 1964.

National Education Association. *The Invisible Minority,* Washington, D.C., 1966.

O'Brien, C. *Teaching the Language Different Child to Read.* Columbus, Ohio: Charle E. Merrill Publishing Company, 1973.

Ruddell, R. *Reading-Language Instruction.* Englewood Cliffs, N.J.: Prentice-Hall, Inc., 1974.

Spaulding, S. "A Spanish Readability Formula." *Modern Language Journal* (December 1956) 40:435.

Thonis, E. W. *Teaching Reading to Spanish-Speaking Children.* Newark, Del.: International Reading Association, 1976.

Thonis, E. W. *Teaching Reading to Non-English Speakers.* New York: Macmillan Publishing Co., Inc., 1970.

Zamora, J. *The Educational Status of a Minority,* Washington, D.C.: Office of Education, 1968.

Zintz, M. *The Reading Process.* Dubuque, Iowa: William C. Brown Company Publishers, 1970.

# 16

# Diagnostic/Prescriptive Teaching
# of Language/Reading

*Figure 91.* Children are unique in many, many ways. As a teacher you will need to develop and implement curricula which fosters their unique qualities. (Photo by Linda Lungren)

461

Don't you see my rainbow, teacher?
Don't you see all the colors?
I know that you're mad at me.
I know that you said to color the cherries red
    and the leaves green.
I guess I shouldn't have done it backwards.
But, teacher, don't you see my rainbow?
Don't you see all the colors?
Don't you see me?

*(Cullum, 1971, p. 34)*

As Cullum's poem suggests, children are unique. They are unique in many, many ways. As a teacher you will need to develop and implement curricula that fosters their unique qualities. When asked to state their educational philosophy, the majority of teachers are very quick to recite the well-worn cliche: "create an environment which fosters the development of individual differences." However, as one observes classroom settings, it becomes quite obvious that a dichotomy exists between educational theory and practice. Attempts to individualize and personalize the curriculum have met with little success. The many rationalizations for student failure have included large classes, insufficient funds, authoritative administrators, disruptive children, parental opposition, and social injustice. To this list we would like to add *unacceptable teacher preparation.* In our varied encounters with teachers, we have found them to be *willing* but *unprepared* to personalize and manage their curricula. If you feel you are like these teachers, an understanding of the procedures delineated on page 463 may provide you with the strategies needed to eliminate the dichotomy between your beliefs and practices.

## Classroom Management

The system that is outlined on page 463 is designed as a guide to aid you in implementing a personalized, integrated early reading/language arts content area curriculum. Extended use of management systems in curriculum planning has become widespread because of the ever-growing use of technology in schools today. The use of a management system provides a procedural structure that encourages program flexibility and individualization.

## Understand Program Context

The development of your *classroom* curriculum must successfully adhere to larger working units, *the school* and *the community.* In order to establish compatability among these three elements, it is important that you become

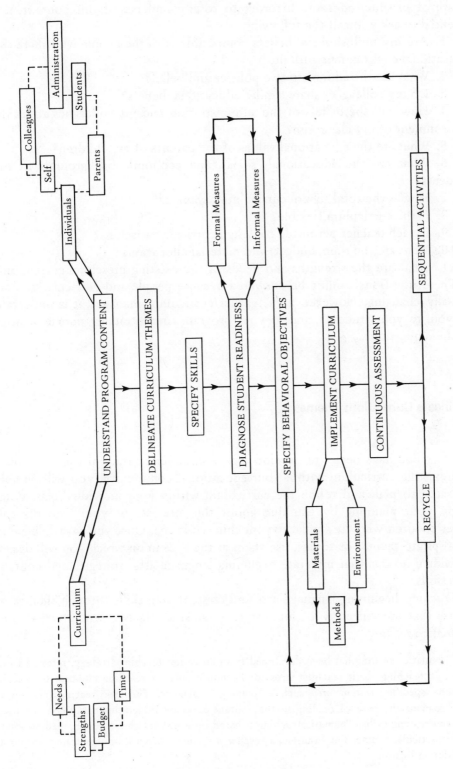

Classroom Management System

aware of *program context*. In order to totally understand this context, it is essential to ask yourself the following:

1. Are my philosophical beliefs compatible with the people who share this educational environment with me?

2. What are the administrative policies and beliefs?

3. Do my colleagues share similar educational beliefs?

4. How will the beliefs of the administration and my colleagues affect the environment of my classroom?

5. What are the educational values of the parents of my children?

6. What are the educational, social, and economic backgrounds of my students?

7. How is the total school curriculum organized?

8. Is the curriculum flexible?

9. Is each teacher permitted to design curricula variations?

10. What are the time, budget, and material allocations?

11. What are the strengths and needs of the existing preschool curriculum?

These questions cannot be answered because people and curricula are continually changing. However, as a teacher/curriculum manager, it is important to you, to your students, and to your program to continually pursue answers to these questions.

## Delineate Curriculum Themes

After you have begun to develop a general understanding of the individuals and existing curriculum within your educational community, you will be able to begin to plan and refine the curriculum within your individual classroom. Begin your planning by thinking about the interests of your students and other children who are similar to your children in age. Once you have delineated appropriate themes or topics, use them as the base upon which you will design individual lessons that integrate beginning language arts strategies and content area skills.

Teaching beginning language arts and content area skills through themes or topics that are currently of interest to your students is often referred to as *thematic teaching*.

> Thematic teaching has been developed from an earlier teaching strategy, referred to as unit teaching. Unit teaching stressed the importance of teaching children to read in one specific *content area* such as reading in science. Thematic teaching, however, broadens the base of reading in the content areas by integrating many content areas and reading skills. Thematic teaching is based on a natural phenomenon, reading about a particular theme. For example, a teacher may introduce a lesson on train transportation in Boston.

(Lapp and Flood, 1978, pp. 377–78)

While the children are studying such a theme, they can discuss the use of trains in Boston, their experiences with trains, and train use throughout Massachusetts (social studies). They can construct cardboard trains (measurement-mathematics), while verbally listing and copying all the new vocabulary words associated with train transportation (language arts). They might also have an elementary discussion about train construction and the mechanics of building an engine (science). A concluding activity related to this theme is to have children paint, draw, or color pictures related to their new knowledge of trains. These pictures could easily become the basis for further experiences with spoken and written language activities.

*Figure 92.* Thematic teaching provides the context needed to integrate the language arts and content area subjects into life situation teachables. (Photo by Linda Lungren)

Thematic teaching provides the context needed to integrate the language arts and content area subjects into life situation teachables. Such integration, it is hoped, will result in usable, transferable skills.

Students need to learn far more than the basic skills. Children who have just started school may still be in the labor force in the year 2030. For them, nothing could be more wildly impractical than an education designed to prepare them for specific vocations or professions or to facilitate their adjustment to the world as it is. To be practical, an education should prepare a man for work that doesn't yet exist and whose nature cannot even be imagined. This can be done only by teaching people how to learn, by giving them the kind of intellectual discipline that will enable them to apply man's accumulated wisdom to new problems as they arise, the kind of wisdom that will enable them to recognize new problems as they arise. (Silberman, 1970, pp. 83–4.)

As you select appropriate themes, be sure that they are broad enough to allow for the integrated incorporation of science, social studies, math, and language arts lessons. Some possible topics might include the following:

1. Pets
2. Clowns
3. "Sesame Street" characters
4. Theatrical idols

Once the themes have been initially delineated, they can be altered as students' interests change. You are now ready to specify the general skills your students are to accomplish in the language arts content areas.

## Specify Skills

When working with classroom teachers who are attempting to implement an integrated thematic curriculum, one initial problem seems to exist for all— *Skills*. Teachers initially ask, "How can I have an integrated program and still teach the skills that pertain to my grade level?" The answer to this is, teach your skills through the delineated theme. For example, in a kindergarten program, you may wish to accomplish the following skills as well as many others.

*Language Arts*

1. Letter identification
2. Basic writing skills
   a. Names
   b. Labels
3. Read names and classroom labels
4. Extend language skills
5. Extend listening skills

*Mathematics*

1. Count
2. Basic understanding of number sequence

*Social Studies*

1. Extend positive self-concept
2. Develop awareness of self and others in one's environment

*Science*

1. Understanding concept of time (second, minute, hour, day, month, year)
2. Awareness of weather (seasons, temperature)

*General*

1. Recognition of colors
2. Development of motor skills
3. Identification of left and right

Many of these skills can be accomplished through the earlier discussed lessons that pertained to train transportation in Boston by simply showing a picture of a modern train and discussing the following:

1. Who can name the different parts of the train?
   (Language Arts Skill 3, 4, 5)
2. How many parts have we named?
   (Language Arts Skills 4, 5
   Mathematics Skills 1, 2)
3. How close is the nearest train station to our school?
   (Social Studies Skills 1, 2
   Language Arts Skills 4, 5
   Mathematics Skill 2)

Now present a picture of an older train and ask

4. How do these trains differ?
   (Science Skill 1
   Language Arts Skills 4, 5)
5. Let's draw a picture of a train we would like to ride on.
   (General Skill 2)
6. After you have finished drawing your picture, let's each tell a story about it.
   (Language Arts Skills 4, 5)

The skills you wish to accomplish are often general enough to be developed through any theme. It is important to specify the skills to be accomplished. Once they have been specified, you will feel more at ease when you attempt to integrate your thematic program.

## Diagnose Student Readiness

*Which children* need instruction? *Which skills* are needed? These questions may be answered thourgh the use of *formal* measures such as standardized reading tests and *informal* measures such as observation scales, teacher-made checklists, and textbook exams.

Examples of *informal* measures are presented in the following pages. Russell's check list was developed in 1967 to aid teachers in organizing their knowledge about general student behavior.

### Checklist for Reading Readiness*

#### Physical Readiness

|  |  | Yes | No |
|---|---|:---:|:---:|
| 1. Eyes |  |  |  |
| a. Does the child seem comfortable in the use of his eyes (does not squint, rub eyes, hold materials too close or too far from eyes)? | 1. | ☐ | ☐ |

*Figure 93.* Which children need instruction? Which skills are needed? A teacher must use a combination of formal and informal evaluation methods. (Photo by Linda Lungren)

      b. Are the results of clinical tests or an oculist's examination favorable?     2. ☐ ☐

2. Ears
    a. Is it apparent through his response to questions or directions that he is able to hear what is said to the class?     3. ☐ ☐

3. Speech
    a. Does he articulate clearly?     4. ☐ ☐
    b. Does he speak in a group with some confidence?     5. ☐ ☐
    c. Does he speak without gross errors in pronunciation?     6. ☐ ☐
    d. Does he respond to suggestions for speech improvement?     7. ☐ ☐

4. Hand-eye coordination
    Is he able to make his hands work together in cutting, using tools, or bouncing a ball?     8. ☐ ☐

5. General health
    a. Does he give an impression of good health?     9. ☐ ☐
    b. Does he seem well nourished?     10. ☐ ☐
    c. Does the school physical examination reveal good health?     11. ☐ ☐

**Social Readiness**

1. Cooperation
    a. Does he work well with a group, taking his share of the responsibility?     12. ☐ ☐

    b. Does he cooperate in playing games with other children?    13. ☐ ☐

    c. Can he direct his attention to a specific learning situation?    14. ☐ ☐

    d. Does he listen rather than interrupt?    15. ☐ ☐

2. Sharing

    a. Does he share materials, without monopolizing their use?    16. ☐ ☐

    b. Does he offer help when another child needs it?    17. ☐ ☐

    c. Does he await his turn in playing or in games?    18. ☐ ☐

    d. Does he await his turn for help from the teacher?    19. ☐ ☐

3. Self-Reliance

    a. Does he work things through for himself without asking    20. ☐ ☐
       the teacher about the next step?

    b. Does he take care of his clothing and materials?    21. ☐ ☐

    c. Does he find something to do when he finishes an assigned    22. ☐ ☐
       task?

    d. Does he take good care of materials assigned to him?    23. ☐ ☐

## Emotional Readiness

1. Adjustment to task

    a. Does the child seek a task, such as drawing, preparing?    24. ☐ ☐

    b. Does he accept changes in school routine calmly?    25. ☐ ☐

    c. Does he appear to be happy and well adjusted in school-    26. ☐ ☐
       work, as evidenced by relaxed attitude, pride in work,
       and eagerness for a new task?

    d. Does he follow adult leadership without showing resent-    27. ☐ ☐
       ment?

2. Poise

    a. Does he accept a certain amount of opposition or defeat    28. ☐ ☐
       without crying or sulking?

    b. Does he meet strangers without displaying unusual shy-    29. ☐ ☐
       ness?

## Psychological Readiness

1. Mind set for reading

    a. Does the child appear interested in books and reading?    30. ☐ ☐

    b. Does he ask the meanings of words or signs?    31. ☐ ☐

    c. Is he interested in the shapes of unusual words?    32. ☐ ☐

2. Mental maturity

    a. Do the results of the child's mental test predict probable    33. ☐ ☐
       success in learning to read?

    b. Can he give reasons for his opinions about his own work    34. ☐ ☐
       or the work of others?

    c. Can he make or draw something to illustrate an idea as    35. ☐ ☐
       well as most children his age?

    d. Is his memory span sufficient to allow memorization of    36. ☐ ☐
       a short poem or song?

    e. Can he tell a story without confusing the order of events?    37. ☐ ☐

    f. Can he listen or work for five minutes without rest-    38. ☐ ☐
       lessness?

3. Mental habits

a. Has the child established the habit of looking at a suc-    39.   □   □
cession of items from left to right?

b. Does his interpretation of pictures extend beyond mere    40.   □   □
enumeration of details?

c. Does he grasp the fact that symbols may be associated    41.   □   □
with spoken language?

d. Can he predict possible outcomes for a story?    42.   □   □

e. Can he remember the central thought of a story as well    43.   □   □
as the important details?

f. Does he alter his own method to profit by another child's    44.   □   □
example?

4. Language Patterns

a. Does he take part in class discussions and conversations?    45.   □   □

b. Is he effective in expressing his needs in classroom situa-    46.   □   □
tions?

c. Are the words used in the preprimers and the primer    47.   □   □
part of his listening and speaking vocabulary?

d. Does he understand the relationship inherent in such    48.   □   □
words as up and down, top and bottom, big and little?

e. Does he listen to a story with evidence of enjoyment and    49.   □   □
the ability to recall parts of it?

f. Is he able to interpret an experience through dramatic    50.   □   □
play?

*Reprinted from pages 55-7 of the *Manual for Teaching the Reading Readiness Program* rev. ed. Ginn Boston, 1967 by David H. Russell, Odille Ousky, and Grace B. Haynes.

**Prereading Rating Scale.** To use the prereading rating scale, place a check in the appropriate box in front of the following questions. The test manual describes the use and interpretation of this scale in detail.

## I.   Facility in Oral Language

Yes   No

□   □   1. Does the child take part in class discussions and conversations?

□   □   2. Is he effective in expressing his needs in classroom situations?

□   □   3. Can he tell a story or relate an experience effectively?

## II.   Concept and Vocabulary Development

□   □   4. Is he familiar with the words and concepts related to his environment: for example, people, places, things, and activities?

□   □   5. Does he have a knowledge of nursery rhymes and traditional children's stories and can he talk about them?

□   □   6. Has he travel experiences within the community and to other places and can he describe them?

### III.   Listening Abilities

☐  ☐  7. Is the child able to understand directions read or told to him?
☐  ☐  8. Does he possess the ability to recall stories heard by providing the essential information and a sequence of events?
☐  ☐  9. Is he able to memorize a short poem or story?
☐  ☐  10. Is he a retentive and responsive listener?

### IV.   Skills in Critical and Creative Thinking

☐  ☐  11. Does the child's interpretation of pictures extend beyond mere enumeration of details?
☐  ☐  12. Can he predict possible outcomes for a story?
☐  ☐  13. Does he express unique ideas about personal experiences, classroom happenings, and stories he has heard?
☐  ☐  14. Does he demonstrate flexibility in his thinking patterns or does he have a "one-track mind"?

### V.   Social Skills

☐  ☐  15. Is the child accepted by other children?
☐  ☐  16. Can he play competitively with others?
☐  ☐  17. Does he listen rather than interrupt?
☐  ☐  18. Does he await his turn for help from the teacher?

### VI.   Emotional Development

☐  ☐  19. Can the child accept some opposition or defeat?
☐  ☐  20. Is he eager for new tasks and activities?
☐  ☐  21. Can he accept changes in routine?
☐  ☐  22. Does he appear to be happy and well adjusted in schoolwork?

### VII.   Attitude Toward and Interest in Reading

☐  ☐  23. Does the child ask questions about letters, words, and numbers?
☐  ☐  24. Has he grasped the fact that "writing is talk written down"?
☐  ☐  25. Is he enthusiastic about beginning to learn to read?

### VIII.   Work Habits

☐  ☐  26. Can the child work by himself?
☐  ☐  27. Can he see a task through to completion?
☐  ☐  28. Can he find something to do when he finishes an assigned task?

### Informal Teacher Checklist

Student's name: _____

Date: _____

| Skill | Definitely Yes | To a Degree | No | Comment |
|---|---|---|---|---|
| a. Can recognize letters | | | | |
| b. Can rhyme | | | | |
| c. Has memorized alphabet | | | | |
| d. Can describe actions & pictures | | | | |
| e. Can sound out words | | | | |
| f. Can tell story about picture | | | | |
| g. Can hold a pencil | | | | |
| h. Can match objects that are the same or different | | | | |
| i. Knows that written words mean spoken words | | | | |
| j. Can put pictures in order | | | | |
| k. Can write letters of alphabet | | | | |
| l. Knows numbers | | | | |
| m. Can write numbers | | | | |
| n. Can name the colors | | | | |
| o. Knows words about time (before, after, until) | | | | |
| p. Can "read" simple stories | | | | |
| q. Knows abstract words (happy, brave) | | | | |
| r. Knows words about space (front, back, above) | | | | |
| s. Knows common nouns (dog, lake) | | | | |

Before assessing specific cognitive competencies, teachers should be certain that the child's vision and hearing are adequate for the task of reading. Auditory and visual acuity may often be initially assessed through observation.

*Vision.* Although there are many factors involved in the reading process, the subject of vision is certainly of prime importance because reading is basically a visual act. Seeing is central to reading because the printed stimulus enters the mind through the eye.

Spache (1973) describes the visual aspect of the reading process:

> His eyes hop or glide from one stop to the next, from left to right. He does not read in a smooth sweep along the line but only when the eyes are at rest in each fixation. During the sweeps or swings from one fixation to the next, the reader sees nothing clearly for his eyes are temporarily out of focus. Each fixation, during which reading actually occurs, lasts from about a third of a second in young children to about a quarter of a second at the college level. In all probability most of the thinking that occurs during reading is done during this fractional part of a second, for a number of studies show that the duration of the fixation often lengthens if the reading material is very difficult. The fixations are the heart of the visual reading act, for they occupy about 90 per cent of the time for reading, while interfixation and return sweeps account for the rest.
>
> If the reader fails to recognize what he sees in a fixation, or to understand the idea offered, he tends to make regression. That is, he makes another fixation at approximately the same place or he swings backward to the left to read again. He may regress several times until the word is recognized or the idea comprehended before resuming the normal left-to-right series of fixations. Then near the end of each line he makes one big return sweep to a fixation close to the beginning of the next line. (p. 9)

*Hearing.* The development of *hearing* acuity precedes vocabulary development and may be viewed as a reading readiness base. Even the smallest impairment of auditory ability *may* cause problems with both language development and reading. Because research in this area is inconclusive, it is not obvious to what degree the reading process may be hindered by lack of auditory ability. Auditory discrimination relates to reading because a child's ability to hear small sound units and add meaning to the units is a word-analysis skill that is essential in reading. Readiness programs must provide tasks that help children perceive partial word utterances as well as whole word utterances.

The classroom teacher needs to be alert in order to detect symptoms that might suggest that a child is having hearing difficulty. Some common symptoms are *slurred or inaudible language, turning one's ear toward the speaker, interchanging words with similar sounds, inability to discriminate like or unlike sounds, cupping one's ear when listening, requesting that statements be repeated, earaches, frequent colds, and unnatural tonal quality of the voice.*

## Santa Clara Unified School District Inventory of Developmental Tasks

Here is an example of a comprehensive inventory checklist, designed by the Santa Clara Unified School District, Santa Clara, California to assess vision and hearing and language/thought development. It has been used to assess certain aspects of readiness.

The following extremely comprehensive instrument has been described by its creators in terms of sequential and hierarchical skills. Before using this instrument, it is important to point out the taxonomic approach used in its creation. If you look at the scoring sheet first, the ordering will be quite clear.

Santa Clara Unified School District

Name    _Jim N._    Date _____

Birthdate _____ School _____

Teacher _____ Grade/Type of Class _____

## INVENTORY
### of
### DEVELOPMENTAL TASKS
An Observation Guide

0  1  2           40

**Conceptual**

| 9.9 assign number value | 9.10 identify position | 9.11 tell how 2 items are alike | 9.12 sort objects 2 ways |
|---|---|---|---|

**Language**

| 8.8 give personal informa-tion | 8.9 describe simple objects | 8.10 relate words and pictures | 8.11 define words | 8.12 use correct grammar |
|---|---|---|---|---|

**Auditory Memory**

| 7.7 perform 3 commands | 7.8 repeat a sentence | 7.9 repeat a tapping sequence | 7.10 repeat 4 numbers | 7.11 recall story facts | 7.12 repeat 5 numbers |
|---|---|---|---|---|---|

**Auditory Perception**

| 6.6 discrimi-nate between com. sound | 6.7 identify common sounds | 6.8 Locate source of sound | 6.9 match beginning sounds | 6.10 hear diff. between words | 6.11 match rhyming sounds | 6.12 screen sounds |
|---|---|---|---|---|---|---|

**Visual Memory**

| 5.5 recall animal pictures | 5.6 name objects from memory | 5.7 recall 3 color sequence | 5.8 recall 2 picture sequence | 5.9 reproduce design from memory | 5.10 recall picture sequence | 5.11 recall 3 part design | 5.12 recall word forms |
|---|---|---|---|---|---|---|---|

**Visual Perception**

| 4.4 match color objects | 4.5 match form objects | 4.6 match size objects | 4.7 match size and form on paper | 4.8 match numbers | 4.9 match letter forms | 4.10 match direction on design | 4.11 isolate visual images | 4.12 match words |
|---|---|---|---|---|---|---|---|---|

**Visual Motor**

| 3.3 follow target with eyes | 3.4 string beads | 3.5 copy a circle | 3.6 cut with scissors | 3.7 copy a cross | 3.8 copy a square | 3.9 tie shoes | 3.10 copy letters | 3.11 copy sentence | 3.12 form patterns |
|---|---|---|---|---|---|---|---|---|---|

**Coordination**

| 2.2 creep | 2.3 walk | 2.4 run | 2.5 jump | 2.6 hop | 2.7 balance on one foot | 2.8 skip | 2.9 balance on walking beam | 2.10 show left and right | 2.11 jump rope assisted | 2.12 jump rope alone |
|---|---|---|---|---|---|---|---|---|---|---|

| 1.1 | 1.2 | 1.3 | 1.4 | 1.5 | 1.6 | 1.7 | 1.8 | 1.9 | 1.10 | 1.11 | 1.12 |
|---|---|---|---|---|---|---|---|---|---|---|---|

Level 1   Pre-School        Level II 5–5½ yrs        Level III 6–6½ yrs        Level IV 7– yrs

Each of the skills from coordination to conceptualization is ordered by ascending difficulty. Each of the tasks on the horizontal axis (2.2 creep to 2.12 jump rope alone) are also ordered by ascending difficulty. The complete list of tasks is presented with a model page from the *Santa Clara Guide*. This example page demonstrates the scoring procedure for each task; task 5.8, 5.9, and 5.10 are presented as examples.

### Instructional Activities

Level

1. Attending Behavior

2. Coordination

I.
  - 2.2 Can creep—crawling in homolateral, then cross-pattern
  - 2.3 Can walk—timed: Rooster walk, Elephant Walk, Bear, Ostrich
  - 2.4 Can run—3-legged race, Bird run, Crab run, Dog run, Horse gallop
  - 2.5 Can jump—chairs, blocks, hopscotch
  - 2.6 Can hop—height, time
  - 2.7 Can balance on one foot

II.
  - 2.8 Can use hands and arms—right/left: Follow the Leader, Simon Says, Twister, teach body parts
  - 2.9 Can skip and play skip-ball tag, lean while skipping

III.
  - 2.10 Can balance on walking beam—hands behind back
  - 2.11 Can jump rope, assisted

IV.
  - 2.12 Can jump rope, unassisted

3. Visual motor

I.
  - 3.3.1 Walking—A sitting student watching is able to follow a teacher walking around the room
  - 2 Skipping—A sitting student watching is able to follow another child skipping around the room
  - 3 Object focus — Look at _____ until I count to 5
  - 4 Ball roll count aloud until ball stops
  - 5 Gliders
  - 6 Thumb focus
  - 7 Pencil tracking—Practice directional objects
  - 3.4 String beads, thread needles, sorting tasks (timed) make chains of colored strips (own patterns)
  - 3.5 Can copy circle—Simple forms, complex forms, mazes

II.
  - 3.7 Can copy cross—Follow numbers (dot-to-dot)
  - 3.8 Can copy square—The Clock Game

III.
  - 3.6 Can use scissors—Zigzag strips, geometric forms
  - 3.10 Can copy letters—Copy-speed tests
  - 3.11 Can copy simple words, then cut up and rearrange
  - 3.12 Form Patterns—Tinker Toy construction projects (Play Tiles), ball and jacks, drawing people, catching the ball (see Bayne Hackett and Robert Jenson, A Guide to Movement Exploration. Palo Alto, Calif.: Peck Publication, 1966.)
  Can Copy diamond

**Level**

4. <u>Visual perception</u>

I.    4.4  Can match color objects—Color-code typing
      4.5  Can match form objects—Use shape to make pictures
           Child has to match shapes to build the picture:

                      tree

      4.6  Can match size objects—Parquetry blocks to have child work a design
           on top of a marked paper
      4.7  Can match size and form on paper—have child match a shape on
           on paper

II.   4.8  Can match numbers
      4.9  Can match letters

III.  4.10 Can match direction of design toy card (same direction?) Mirror
           patterns (see <u>Frostig's Manual</u>, pp. 149-150) Play camera, obstacle
           course

IV.   4.11 Can isolate visual images—cloud pictures
      4.12 Can match words

5. <u>Visual memory</u>

I.    5.5  Recalls animal pictures
      5.6  Can name objects from memory—chalk, button
      5.7  Reproduce a visual sequence of three colors from memory, five color
           chips, three color flashcards: tell child to reproduce the order you
           just gave him/her
      5.8  Can recall a picture sequence
           One tachistoscope for building visual memory in one frame:

      5.9  Can reproduce design from memory
           Draw from memory:

           | c | a | t |    Have children put one letter in a square

III.  5.10 Can reproduce a sequence of three pictures from memory
      5.11 Can recall impart design

IV.   5.12 Can recall word forms:

      Arzo    |  Arpo  Arno  Arzo  |

      Expose target word for five seconds
      Internal design
      Match words in a list

Level

    6. <u>Auditory perception</u>

        6.6  Can discriminate between common sounds
             Have children close eyes and listen for familiar sounds.
        6.7  Can identify common sounds—Cross the Road game
        6.8  Can locate source of sounds
        6.9  Can match beginning sounds
            1  I'm going to the _____ and I'm taking _____
            2  Rissen-Act game (aural version of Simon Says)
            3  Come Letter game
            4  Shopping at the Supermarket game
            5  Lost Squirrel game

III.      6.10 Can hear fine differences between similar words
            Badder-Lantern/Sheep Sleep/Cub Cup
IV.      6.11 Can match ending sounds

    7. <u>Auditory memory</u>

        7.7  Can perform three commands
II.      7.8  Can repeat a sentence—Play Echo, rote poem
        7.9  Can repeat a tapping sequence
            Worksheet .  ...  .  ..  ..   .
III.     7.10 Child repeats a series of four numbers:
            6    2    9    7  forward, backward
       7.11 Can recall story facts—($imple comprehension)
IV.     7.12 Can repeat five numbers:
            2 – 4 – 2 – 7 – 8  or  A – R – C – K – L

    8. <u>Language</u>

II.      8.8  Can give personal information—Who am I?
        8.9  Can describe simple objects
            The gift box
            Who was it?
            Come and find it
            What do I have in my hand?
            Feel box
            The Mystery box
III.     8.10 Can relate words and pictures—Giraffe/tall   Rabbit/hop
       8.11 Can define words
IV.     8.12 Can use correct grammar
            Improve usage of see/saw
            (see <u>And to Think I Saw It on Mulberry Street</u>, Dr. Seuss)
            Improve usage of was/were

    9. <u>Conceptual</u>

II.      9.9  Can assign number value
            Which is bigger?  5 or 8
III.     9.10 Can identify first, last, or middle
       9.11 Can tell how two things are alike
            Riddles
            Grouping/card-sorting tasks

Find identical objects in a room
Subclasses—e.g., animals, dogs, collies
Complete functional sentences—e.g., Knives are to cut with.
9.12 Can sort objects two ways:
Place things in categories
Learning-to-think series

---

**Sample Sheet from Guide**

*Visual Memory      Level II      Task 5.8*

5.8   Reproduce a sequence of two pictures from memory.
Material:  Five picture cards, three flashcards.
Procedure:  Show child a flashcard for five seconds. Say: "First this, then this." Remove card from view. Say: "Make one just like mine." Child reproduces the sequence seen on the flash card by arranging two pictures in the proper order.

**Scoring Procedure**
Scoring:

| 0 | 1 | 2 |
|---|---|---|
| Child has two or more errors. | Child has one error. | Child has all correct. |

---

*Visual Memory      Level II      Task 5.9*

5.9   Reproduce designs from memory
Material:  Three picture flash cards
Procedure:  Say: "I'm going to show you a card with a drawing on it. After I turn the card over, you draw one just like the one on the card." Show child the card for five seconds.

Scoring:

| 0 | 1 | 2 |
|---|---|---|
| Child cannot reproduce two or more designs. | Child fails to reproduce one design. | Child can reproduce the three forms accurately. |

---

*Visual Memory      Level III      Task 5.10*

5.10   Reproduce a sequence of three pictures from memory.
Material:  Five picture cards and three picture flash cards.
Procedure:  Show child a flashcard for five seconds. Say: "First this, then this, then this." (Point left to right.) Remove card from view. Say: "Make one just like mine." Child reproduces the sequence seen on the flashcard by arranging three pictures in the proper order.
Scoring:

| 0 | 1 | 2 |
|---|---|---|
| Child has two or more errors. | Child has one error. | Child has them all correct. |

## *Formal Reading Readiness Tests*

You may also wish to use formal reading readiness tests. If so, the Appendix of this text has been designed to aid you in selecting one that is appropriate.

Most formal reading readiness tests include items designed to assess the following areas:

1. Auditory discrimination:

   Can the child discriminate between same and different sounds?

2. Copying.
3. Word recognition.
4. Counting and writing numbers.
5. Drawing a human figure.
6. Sentence comprehension.
7. Visual discrimination:

   Can the child identify same and different pictures?

8. Auditory and visual associations:

   The child is shown four pictures.

He is asked to circle the cat.

## *Diagnosing Student's Attitudes and Interests*

In addition to diagnosing children's readiness skills, you may also find it useful to investigate their attitudes about reading. Sometimes young children acquire negative attitudes about reading and sometimes these attitudes go unnoticed or unchecked. If children continue to have negative attitudes, their reading can be affected, and they can "refuse" to learn. It is extremely important to try to "get to" these children, but in order to intervene and change these attitudes, you will have to assess their attitudes. The following instruments may help you in your assessment:

### Reading Attitude Inventory
**Paul Campbell, 1966**

Name _____ Grade _____ Teacher _____

1. How do you feel when your teacher reads a story out loud?

2. How do you feel when someone gives you a book for a present?

3. How do you feel about reading books for fun at home?

4. How do you feel when you are asked to read out loud to your group?

5. How do you feel when you are asked to read out loud to the teacher?

6. How do you feel when you come to a new word while reading?

7. How do you feel when it is time to do your worksheet?

8. How do you feel about going to school?

9. How do you feel about how well you can read?

10. How do you think your friends feel about reading?

11. How do you think your teacher feels when you read?

12. How do you think your friends feel when you read out loud?

13. How do you feel about the reading group you are in?

14. How do you think you'll feel about reading when you're bigger?

Following is an alternate form of the first measure.

## Reading Interest/Attitude Scale

**Right to Read Office, Washington, D.C. 1976**

Date _____ Grade _____ Name _____

Directions: Read each item slowly twice to each child. Ask him/her to point to the face which shows how he/she feels about the statement. Circle the corresponding symbol. Read each item with the same inflection and intonation.

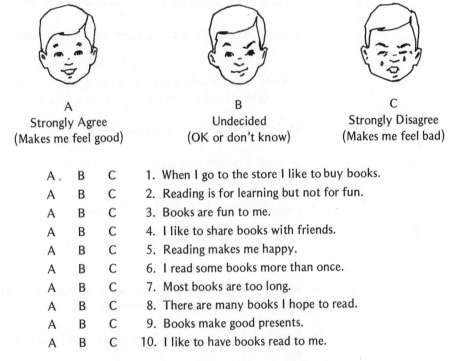

| A | B | C |
|---|---|---|
| Strongly Agree | Undecided | Strongly Disagree |
| (Makes me feel good) | (OK or don't know) | (Makes me feel bad) |

| | | | |
|---|---|---|---|
| A | B | C | 1. When I go to the store I like to buy books. |
| A | B | C | 2. Reading is for learning but not for fun. |
| A | B | C | 3. Books are fun to me. |
| A | B | C | 4. I like to share books with friends. |
| A | B | C | 5. Reading makes me happy. |
| A | B | C | 6. I read some books more than once. |
| A | B | C | 7. Most books are too long. |
| A | B | C | 8. There are many books I hope to read. |
| A | B | C | 9. Books make good presents. |
| A | B | C | 10. I like to have books read to me. |

This second measure can be used with older students. You can read some of the following statements to your students in order to assess their attitudes toward reading.

## Reading Attitude Inventory

**by Molly Ransbury, 1971**

Yes     No

_____ _____   1. I visit the library to find books I might enjoy reading.

_____ _____   2. I would like to read a magazine in my free time.

Yes    No

_____  _____    3. I cannot pay attention to my reading when there is even a little noise or movement nearby.

_____  _____    4. I enjoy reading extra books about topics we study in school.

_____  _____    5. I would like to read newspaper articles about my favorite hobbies or interests.

_____  _____    6. I feel I know the characters in some of the comic books I read.

_____  _____    7. My best friend would tell you that I enjoy reading very much.

_____  _____    8. I would like to belong to a group that discusses many kinds of reading.

_____  _____    9. I would enjoy spending some time during my summer vacation reading to children in a summer library program.

_____  _____   10. My ideas are changed by the books I read.

_____  _____   11. Reading is a very important part of my life. Every day I read many different types of materials.

_____  _____   12. I read magazines for many different reasons.

_____  _____   13. My friends would tell you that I'd much rather watch TV than read.

_____  _____   14. When I listen to someone read out loud, certain words or sentences might attract my attention.

_____  _____   15. I would only read a book if my teacher or my parents said I had to.

_____  _____   16. Magazines, comic books, and newspapers do not interest me.

_____  _____   17. I do not enjoy reading in my free time.

_____  _____   18. I would enjoy talking with someone else about one of my favorite books.

_____  _____   19. I might go to the library several times to see if a special book had been returned.

_____  _____   20. I am too busy during vacations to plan a reading program for myself.

Yes    No

_____ _____   21. Sometimes the book that I'm reading will remind me of ideas from another book that I've read.

_____ _____   22. If my only reading was for school assignments, I would be very unhappy.

_____ _____   23. Reading is not a very good way for me to learn new things.

_____ _____   24. I think reading is boring.

_____ _____   25. If I see a comic book or magazine I would usually just look at the pictures.

_____ _____   26. I sometimes read extra books or articles about something that we have discussed in school.

_____ _____   27. I enjoy going to the library and choosing special books.

_____ _____   28. I do not read during any of my vacations from school.

_____ _____   29. I would not want to help set up a book exhibit.

_____ _____   30. It would be very, very nice for me to have my own library of books.

_____ _____   31. I don't try to read many different kinds of books.

_____ _____   32. If I do not read many things when I'm an adult, I will miss many important ideas about life.

_____ _____   33. I read because the teacher tells me to.

_____ _____   34. I read only because people force me to.

_____ _____   35. I must shut myself in a quiet room in order to read almost anything.

_____ _____   36. I never do extra reading outside of school work because reading is so dull.

_____ _____   37. I only read extra books if my parents say I have to.

_____ _____   38. Reading certain newspaper articles might make me happy, or sad, or even angry.

_____ _____   39. I should spend some of my time each day reading so that I can learn about the world.

Yes    No

_____  _____  40. Before I make up my mind about something, I try to read more than one writer's ideas.

_____  _____  41. When I read, I sometimes understand myself a little better.

_____  _____  42. Some characters I have read about help me to better understand people I know.

_____  _____  43. Reading is a very important part of my life. I read nearly every day in books or newspapers and I enjoy doing so.

_____  _____  44. I would like to read some of the novels my teacher reads to the class.

_____  _____  45. I would like to read more books if I had the time.

_____  _____  46. I might keep a list of the books that I wish to read during the next few months.

_____  _____  47. My parents force me to read.

_____  _____  48. If people didn't tell me that I had to read, I would probably never pick up a book.

_____  _____  49. Sometimes I think ahead in my reading and imagine what the characters might do.

_____  _____  50. I wish I could buy more books for myself.

_____  _____  51. Sometimes I wish the author of the book had written the story a different way.

_____  _____  52. Much of my free time is spent in reading, library browsing and discussing books.

_____  _____  53. I read lots of different newspaper articles so that I can learn more about the world.

_____  _____  54. Reading is as much a part of my life as eating, sleeping, and playing.

_____  _____  55. A story that I see on television might also be interesting to read in a book.

_____  _____  56. Even a little reading makes me feel tired and restless.

Yes        No

____    ____    57. I try to read many different types of materials in my free time.

____    ____    58. I would always rather talk about things, than to read about them.

____    ____    59. I have never wanted to read a book twice.

____    ____    60. When I am an adult and work all day, I will not read.

____    ____    61. I would feel disappointed if I could not find a book that I was very interested in reading.

____    ____    62. I have sometimes told my friends about a really good book that they might like to read.

____    ____    63. I look for some main ideas that the writer presents when I read a magazine article.

____    ____    64. Reading is a very important part of my life when I am not in school.

These are only a few of the many available instruments which purport to measure reading attitudes. Others which may be of interest to you include:

Powell, A., *Primary Attitude Reading Index with Administrator's Directions,* 1971, (Grades 1-3).

Powell, A., *Intermediate Attitude Reading Index with Administrator's Direction,* 1971, (Grades 4-6).

Estes, Thomas H., "Assessing Attitudes Toward Reading," *Journal of Reading,* November, 1971, (Grades 4-6).

Koch, R. E., "What Do You Think About Reading?", 1974, (Grades 4-6).

Huntington, Bett, "Scales to Measure Attitudes Toward Reading," 1975, (Grades 1-6).

### *Determining Student's Interests in Reading*

The development of student's positive interest in reading may depend upon the success with which you are able to know and understand the child's background and the experiences that have led him to his present state. It also suggests that some understanding of individual personality is required. How are such understandings acquired?

As you attempt to implement a reading program, you may wish to talk to the child about the things he enjoys doing. Ask him to explain what he does in his free time. You should observe the things which hold his interest and the things which seem to have little impact on him. It may also be useful to assess a student's reading interests by collecting information from an informal survey. Two surveys which may help you to collect this information are presented in the following pages. The first is a "complete the sentence" type of survey, and the second is a reading/responding survey.

### Interest Inventory

Name _____ Age _____

Date _____

1. My favorite day of the week is _____ because

   _____ .

2. The television programs I like the most are _____

   _____ .

3. The most fun I ever had was when _____

   _____ .

4. The person I would most like to meet is _____ because

   _____ .

5. My favorite course in school is _____ .

6. The one course in school I don't like is _____ .

7. I dislike it because _____ .

8. On a sunny day I like to _____ .

9. Reading is _____ .

10. The things I like to read are _____ .

11. The best story I ever read was _____ .

12. In my spare time I like to _____ .

13. The chores I do at home are _____ .

14. My brothers and sisters _____ .

15. My hobbies are _____ .

16. I get really mad when _____ .

17. When I grow up I'd like to be _____

      because _____ .

18. Poetry makes me _____ .

19. Music is _____ .

20. Places I'd like to visit are _____ .

21. My favorite sport is _____ .

22. Libraries are _____ .

23. During the summer I like to _____ .

24. On a winter day I like to _____ .

25. I wish my parents would _____ .

26. Animals are _____ .

27. I'd like to have a _____ for a pet because

    _____ .

28. The best food in the whole world is _____ .

29. My favorite color is _____ .

30. Right now I'd like to _____ .

The following survey calls for direct verbal interaction between the student and the teacher. The child listens as the teacher reads each of these items and then responds to them orally.

## Interest Inventory

Name _____ Age _____

Date _____

1. What do you like to do when you have free time?
2. How do you usually spend your summers?
3. How much reading do you do on your own?
4. How much television do you watch each day?
5. What are your favorite TV programs?
6. What movies have you seen that you really liked?
7. Do you ever read a book after you have seen the television or movie version?
8. Have you ever visited any of these places?

| | | |
|---|---|---|
| Art Museum | Circus | Theater |
| Science Museum | National Park | Library |
| Concert Halls | Zoo | |

9. What other countries have you visited or lived in?
10. What other cities or states have you visited or lived in?
11. Circle the school subjects you like, cross-out the subjects you don't like:

| | | |
|---|---|---|
| Arithmetic | Science | Gym |
| Spelling | Social Studies | Health |
| Reading | Music | English |
| Art | Other languages | |

12. Circle the kinds of books and stories you like, cross-out the books and stories you don't like:

| | | |
|---|---|---|
| Adventure | Mystery | Magazines |
| Animal stories | Motorcycles | Comic books |
| Hobby stories | Love and romance | Ghost stories |
| Biography | Science fiction | Family stories |
| Autobiography | Car magazines | Riddles and jokes |
| Science | Fables and myths | Horse stories |
| Western stories | Sports | Humor |
| Art and music | Religion | Fantasy |
| Fairy tales | People of other lands | History |
| Poetry | Newspapers | Geography |

13. What is it that you do well?
14. What is it that you do not do well?

In addition to assessing your children's attitudes, you may find it useful to assess your students' interests. In discovering your students' interests, you will be able to personalize the curriculum for each of them.

### Films for Promoting Interest in Reading

The following films may help you to promote your children's interest in reading:

### Films for Parents and Teachers*

| | | |
|---|---|---|
| Reaching Your Reader | 17 minutes | Centron |
| Reading On Series | (varies) | ACI |
| (And Then What Happened, From Left to Right, From Start to Finish, One and More Than One, Put Them Together, Tell Me all About It) | | |
| Reading for Pleasure | 11 minutes | Coronet |
| Reading Growth: Reading Creatively | 14 minutes | Coronet |
| Reading Is Fun—Black Kids In White Schools | 60 minutes | Garfunkle |
| Reading to Enrich Your Classwork | 14 minutes | Coronet |
| Reading to Remember | 18 minutes | Syracuse |
| Reading with a Purpose | 11 minutes | Coronet |
| Mature Reader | 10 minutes | Coronet |
| Maurice Sendak, The Work of | 14 minutes | Weston Woods |
| Lively Art of Picture Books | 57 minutes | Weston Woods |
| Libraries Are Kids' Stuff | 15 minutes | Weston Woods |
| Library—The Reading Program | 19 minutes | Syracuse |
| What Is Effective Reading? | 12 minutes | McGraw-Hill |

Children may be grouped according to the areas of need that you had identified in the chart on page 492.

For example, a class might be studying the parts of a train. The teacher could ask the children to name the parts of the train, listing on the board the names of the train sections.

| | | |
|---|---|---|
| Engine | Caboose | Wheels |
| Windows | Steam | Light |
| Doors | Seats | Whistle |

Group I: Susan, Kostas, Bobby, Roger, David, Manoush, Harold, Jay, Erin, Remo.

As reflected in the preceding chart, these students are ready to engage in activities that would require them to identify and write the letters contained in the names of the train sections.

*All films selected from Boston University's Film Library Listings 1978-1980, Copyright 1978, Trustees of Boston University.

| Remo | Erin | Enrico | Nancy | Jay | Denise | Mary | Harold | Virginia | Manoush | David | Roger | Gina | Bobby | Debbie | Sheryl | Kostas | Susan | |
|---|---|---|---|---|---|---|---|---|---|---|---|---|---|---|---|---|---|---|
| + | + |  | + |  |  |  | + | + | + | + | + |  |  |  |  | + | + | Letter Identification |
| + | + |  | + |  |  |  | + | + | + | + | + |  |  |  |  | + | + | Writing Letter |
| + | + |  | + |  |  |  | + | + | + | + | + | + |  |  |  | + | + | Writing Name |
| + | + | + | + |  |  |  | + | + | + | + | + | + | + |  |  | + | + | Writing Labels |
| + | + |  | + |  |  |  | + | + | + | + | + | + |  |  |  | + | + | Read Name |
| + | + | + | + |  |  |  | + |  | + | + | + | + | + |  |  | + | + | Read Labels |
|  |  |  |  |  |  |  | + |  | + | + |  |  |  |  |  |  |  | Language Skills |
|  |  |  |  |  |  |  | + |  | + | + |  |  |  |  |  |  |  | Listening Skills |
|  |  |  |  |  |  |  | + |  | + | + |  | + |  |  |  |  | + | Counting |
|  |  |  |  |  |  |  | + |  | + | + |  | + |  |  |  |  | + | Number Sequence |
|  |  |  |  |  |  |  | + |  | + | + |  |  |  |  |  |  |  | Self-Concept |
|  |  |  |  |  |  |  | + |  | + | + |  |  |  |  |  |  |  | Others |
| + |  | + | + | + | + | + | + | + | + | + | + | + | + | + | + | + | + | Time |
| + | + | + | + | + | + | + | + | + | + | + | + | + | + | + | + | + | + | Seasons |
| + | + | + | + | + | + | + | + | + | + | + | + | + | + | + | + | + | + | Temperature |
|  |  | + |  | + | + |  | + |  |  | + | + |  |  | + | + | + | + | Colors |
|  |  |  |  |  |  |  | + |  | + | + |  |  |  |  |  |  |  | Motor Skills |
|  |  |  |  |  |  |  | + |  | + | + |  |  |  |  |  |  |  | Left-Right |

+ refers to area of need

Group II. Sheryl and Nancy

These two children could be given an activity that required them to write, read, and label the train.

Group III: Gina, Virginia, and Mary

Because these children have the initial language arts skills, they would need to be assigned to activities which developed their concept of time.

Group IV: Denise and Enrico.

These children could be assigned to activities that extend their concept of time or color.

Although we have delineated four groups of children who have various beginning skills through the initial diagnosis, it should not be taken to indicate that there may be only four groups within any given class, or that four is the magical number of any group.

Children should be grouped according to the skills they have for a particular task. There may be some students who possess the terminal skills of the intended instruction prior to the initiation of instruction. These children should be provided more difficult work that is related to the same theme, or they should be encouraged to begin the work within another thematic area.

Other students may be unable to complete a prescribed task because they lack the skills necessary to deal with the content. In order to design an appropriate program for them, you must revise the program to capitalize on the skills they already possess and to build the skills that are needed to master the original program activities.

There may also be some children who can handle the materials and instructional program but who still require teacher guidance and instruction. Your classroom should contain as many groups as are necessary to meet the needs of the students.

You're probably wondering, "How can I manage so many groups with so many different needs?" In order to be able to maintain flexible classroom grouping practices, you must view your role as a classroom manager. You must plan all programs using a variety of techniques for instruction. If you view yourself as the verbal dispenser of all information, a program that requires flexible grouping practices will be quite difficult for you to maintain.

Flexible grouping must be based on students' thematic interests whenever possible. Groups must also be modified according to specific instructional objectives. As a child progresses through the program and acquires the knowledge necessary to fulfill the objective, the group for which that program has been formed may become unnecessary. If the program objective has been met, or if it is determined to be unrealistic, the group may be dissolved. New objectives may then be formed for different purposes and different instructional methods. The same individuals may or may not be part of both groups. Some children who progress very rapidly may profit from working independently. Effective grouping practices are dependent upon well-specified instructional objectives and continuous evaluation of student progress.

*Figure 94.* Flexible grouping must be based on students' thematic interests whenever possible. (Photo by Linda Lungren):

Because groups vary according to acquired skills, the materials used for instruction may not be necessarily uniform for all groups. Your teaching method as well as your educational materials should be modified to meet the needs of the students in a specific group. Successful grouping practices are contingent upon your assessment of what is to be taught, how it is to be taught, and the anticipated behavioral outcomes. It is also dependent upon continuous assessments of student behavior, on flexibility of established groups, and on altering the instructional program to meet the needs of *all* students.

## Specify Behavioral Objectives

Once you have specified the skills to be accomplished through your program of instruction, assessed student readiness, and determined beginning instructional groups, you will need to specify the behavioral objectives to be accomplished by each group.

Although the relative importance of behavioral objectives to thematic program planning continues to be debated (Lapp, 1972), a review of the literature on this topic concluded that acceptance or rejection of behavioral objectives is based on speculation and guesswork that has often been a replacement for research.

After observing many teacher education programs, one may conclude that prospective teachers are often provided instruction in how to write behavioral objectives, but are seldom taught how to utilize them in program planning and evaluation.[1]

According to Gilpin (1962), an adequately prepared teacher can develop instructional objectives more effectively if the following questions and procedures[2] are followed:

1. What is it that we must teach?
2. How will we know when we have taught it?
3. What materials and procedures will work best to teach what we want to teach? (p. viii)

Guidelines such as these may encourage you, as a teacher, to define objectives before beginning to teach a lesson. Mager (1962), for example, specified five steps to follow in the development and use of behavioral objectives:

1. A statement of instructional objectives is a collection of words or symbols describing one of your educational intents.
2. An objective will communicate your intent to the degree you have described what the learner will be doing when demonstrating his achievement, and how you will know when he is doing it.
3. To describe terminal behavior (what the learner will be doing);
   a. Identify and name the overall behavior act.
   b. Define the important conditions under which the behavior is to occur (given and/or restrictions and limitations).
   c. Define the criterion of acceptable performance.
4. Write a separate statement for each objective: the more you have, the better chance you have of making clear your intent.
5. If you give each learner a copy of your objectives, you may not have to do much else. (p. 32)

There are many instances when a general objective is contrived and then designed into a behavioral objective. For example, a classroom objective may be to introduce children to the theme of community helpers. The following example is a behavioral objective derived from such a broad objective:

Given a lesson which introduces the topic of community helpers, the child will be able to name at least one such community helper and describe his role in the community with complete competency.

Why is an objective of this type needed or used by the teacher? When the teacher is asked to state in specific behavioral terms what he or she wants to accomplish by a specific lesson, she will be able to determine the following:

1. If the accomplishment of the stated objective is really of any value to the total development of the child.

---

[1] A behavioral objective is composed on three criteria: (1) the operational *conditions* existing when the behavior occurs, (2) the terminal *behavior* occurring as a result of planned instruction, and (3) the level of *performance* needed for mastery.

[2] Reprinted with permission from D. Lapp, and J. Flood. *Teaching Reading To Every Child.* (New York: Macmillan Publishing Co., Inc.), 1978.

2. If the child has accomplished the objective:
   a. If there are related objectives within the theme that are to be designed and utilized at this time.
   b. Methods of instruction and performance level needed for implementation of related objectives.
3. If the child has not accomplished the objective:
   a. Whether the objective can be accomplished by this child at this time.
   b. Whether the performance level of the objective was too difficult.
   c. What new methods of instruction are needed to better enable the child to accomplish the objective.

Curricular program evaluation depends on clear explanation and explication of the behaviors that you are attempting to measure. Although the teacher may choose from a variety of evaluative modes, she must be careful not to base her total evaluation on a few specified behaviors that have been previously outlined in behavioral terms. We should never be so naive as to believe that measured behaviors are the only positive occurrences within classroom settings. The teacher must be so aware of her children and their programs that she can intelligently estimate growth that has not yet been planned and/or objectively measured.

When the classroom teacher becomes skilled at using behavioral objectives, an abbreviated system may be used, and once the terminal behavior has been clarified, the rest becomes relatively simple. The reluctance to use objectives is quite similar to the reluctance of many educators to use instructional technology, such as teaching machines and audiovisual equipment.

Many educators believe that if children are in a classroom setting that allows technology to "dehumanize" them, it is the fault of technology rather than the person determining the objectives and the procedures for meeting the objectives. Television sets, radios, phonographs, programmed machines, and other such technological hardware serve only as mechanical teacher aids. The planning does *not* come from the machine. The hardware is value-free. The teacher must distinguish between reality and fraud. If we consider textbooks and chalkboards as teacher aids, perhaps we could say that technology has always been part of the classroom. Materials and objectives *should not dictate* curricula. Teachers should plan thematic curricula using aids that facilitate the learning process.

The following frames are presented in an attempt to help you to develop skill in writing behavioral objectives.

---

**Frame 1**

**Behavioral Objectives**

A behavioral objective is a statement that describes the
1. setting under which a specified behavior will occur.

                                              External conditions
2. type of behavior that is to occur.

                                              Terminal behavior
3. level of success that must be achieved.

                                              Acceptable performance

---

Frame 2

<u>External conditions</u>: The setting under which a specified behavior will occur.

Examples of correct statements of external conditions are
1. Given a list of basic sight words ...
2. Following a lesson on vowel digraphs ...
3. After discussing various English words borrowed from German ...
4. After comparing the basal and linguistic methods ...
5. Given a simulated phonic rule ...
6. Following a discussion of the history of standardized readiness tests ...

An acceptable statement of <u>external condition</u> is one that describes the exact settings or conditions that will exist during or will precede the learner's display of the terminal behavior.

---

Frame 3

Examples of incorrect statements of external conditions are
1. To be able to ...
2. To have knowledge of ...
3. To enjoy ...
4. To learn by ...
5. To discuss ...

These examples are incorrect because they do not state the exact conditions under which the terminal behavior will occur.

What must precede the occurrence of the desired behavior?

---

Frame 4

<u>Terminal behavior</u>: The type of behavior that is anticipated.

Examples of correct statements of terminal behavior are
1. The student will be able to identify ...

   (Verbally, visually)
2. The student will be able to recite ...
3. The student will be able to list ...

   (In writing, verbally)
4. The student will be able to read ...

An acceptable statement of <u>terminal behavior</u> is one that describes the anticipated behavior with such specificity that it cannot be misinterpreted.

---

**Frame 5**

Examples of incorrect statements of terminal behavior are

1. The student knows ....
2. The student will enjoy ....
3. The student appreciates ....
4. The student believes ....

These examples are incorrect because the behaviors are not stated in a manner that can be adequately interpreted and measured.

What type of behavior will be accepted as evidence that the learner has achieved the stated objective?

---

**Frame 6**

Acceptable performance: The level of performance that must be evidenced before a specified behavior can be **accepted**.

Examples of correct statements of acceptable performance are

1. .... at least ten of the following sight words.
2. .... both initial phonemes.
3. .... five vocabulary words in three minutes.
4. .... 40 per cent of the basic sight words.
5. .... all of the addition problems on page 126.

An appropriate statement of acceptable performance is one that describes how well the learner must perform before his behavior will be accepted.

---

Please complete the following activities. If you have difficulty, refer to frames 1 through 6.

## ACTIVITIES

### Activity 1: Developing a Behavioral Objective—Reading

You are preparing a unit of study that attempts to facilitate understanding of hypothesis and supporting details. Throughout this unit you plan to rely heavily on the language experiences of the children.

Attempt to develop a statement of external conditions (the setting under which a specified behavior will occur) for the preceding brief unit description.

External conditions (Refer to frames 2 and 3.)

Now can you add a statement of terminal behavior (a type of behavior that is to occur as a result of planned instruction)?

Terminal behavior  (Refer to frames 4 and 5.)

Finally, add a statement of acceptable performance (degree of competency).

Acceptable performance  (Refer to frame 6.)

Now put your sections together and decide what role this behavioral objective has in curriculum planning.

### Activity 2:  Developing a Behavioral Objective—Poetry

You are preparing a unit of study that attempts to facilitate the language process by introducing children to haiku. Throughout this unit you plan to rely heavily on the language experiences of the children.

Please attempt to develop a statement of external conditions (the setting under which a specified behavior will occur) for the preceding brief unit description.

External conditions (Refer to frames 2 and 3.)

Now can you add a statement of terminal behavior (a type of behavior that is to occur as a result of planned instruction)?

Terminal behavior  (Refer to frames 4 and 5.)

Finally, add a statement of acceptable performance (degree of competency).

Acceptable performance  (Refer to frame 6.)

Now put your sections together and decide what role this behavioral objective was in curriculum planning.

Once the behavioral objectives for your program have been designed, you are ready to implement the curriculum.

## Implement Curriculum

After determining the composition of each group and specifying behavioral objectives, it is possible to determine the *methods of instruction* that are to be used as you implement your curriculum. Decisions concerning curriculum implementation will be dependent upon available materials, the instructional *methods* that permit ease of implementation, and the existing classroom *environment*.

### *Instructional Materials*

It is important to assess children's texts in order to determine their difficulty and their appropriateness for each child. Although it is extremely difficult to accurately assess the readability of a text, you can approximate a text's difficulty by observing your children as they attempt to read. Many researchers have attempted to scientifically measure readability and have designed instruments that can give you a rough grade-level estimate of textbooks that children read.

We have included the Fry Readability Formula in an effort to help you quickly (and roughly) assess your students texts.

Classroom materials may include models, films, records, puzzles, maps, magazines, trade books, and reference books. Selection of materials should be based on the following criteria: safety, educational qualities, durability, and cost.

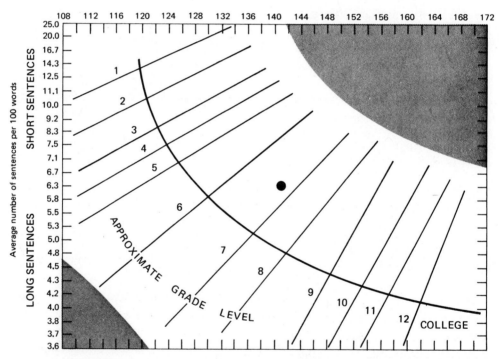

Average number of syllables per 100 words

Short words          Long words

DIRECTIONS: Randomly select three one-hundred word passages from a book or an article. Plot average number of syllables and average number of sentences per 100 words on graph to determine the grade level of the material. Choose more passages per book if great variability is observed and conclude that the book has uneven readability. Few books will fall in gray area but when they do, grade level scores are invalid.

EXAMPLE:

|  | SYLLABLES | SENTENCES |
|---|---|---|
| 1st Hundred Words | 124 | 6.6 |
| 2nd Hundred Words | 141 | 5.5 |
| 3rd Hundred Words | 158 | 6.8 |
| AVERAGE | 141 | 6.3 |

READABILITY 7th GRADE (see dot plotted on graph)

**Safety.** As you select classroom materials, it is important to remember that as well as being easily adaptable to your instructional program, materials must be safe. They must be inspected to determine if they have been painted with lead paint or designed with other toxic materials, or if they have exposed nails, pins, or sharp, pointed edges. Think about the age of the children who will be using the materials. Safety features should be consistent with student age.

*Figure 95.* Selection of materials should be based on safety, educational qualities, durability and cost. Discarded purses and utensils make interesting play materials for young children. (Photo by Linda Lungren)

**Educational Qualities.** When selecting curricular materials you may find it beneficial to ask, What are the educational qualities of this material? and Is this material flexible enough to be used in a variety of situations? It is easy to be misled by advertisements. Be sure not to select sets of pictures designed to teach initial consonants that contain a picture of a *church* to teach the *c* sound. Too often, consonant clusters of digraphs are used to teach singular sounds. If the materials you are selecting have wide flexibility, it may be wise to purchase several units of those materials.

**Durability.** Children play with vigor. The equipment they will use in your classroom will undoubtedly receive a great deal of wear and tear. Remember:
1. Wooden materials are more durable than cardboard or plastic.
2. Paint brushes left to stand in paint overnight are often ruined.
3. Loose pieces result in lost pieces.
4. Adequate storage containers may affect the life of the material.

**Cost.** Unfortunately, the materials that have the greatest durability often initially cost the most. It may be wise to construct your own cardboard blocks and puzzles and put your money into other more expensive materials with greater durability. Buy a few good, durable pieces of equipment each year. You may also be able to secure a variety of free materials from local agencies (lumber yards, pharmacies, stores, factories, travel agencies) in your community.

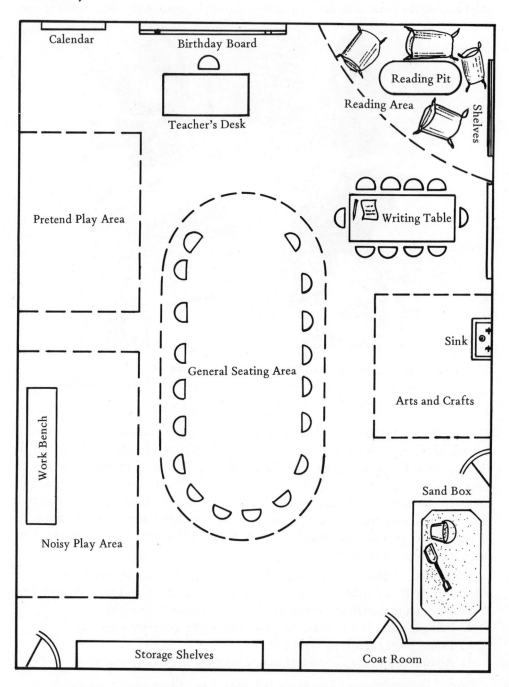

*Figure 96.*

## Environment

Personalized classrooms may be better managed if they are arranged as *learning centers* where a variety of activities may be occurring simultaneously. A classroom utilizing this design might be arranged as illustrated in Figure 96.

*Figure 97.* No matter how large or small the room, it can be sectioned off into smaller areas to be used for different kinds of activities and learning centers. (Photo by Linda Lungren)

There can be many ways to incorporate reading into children's play, just by the way you set up and utilize your classroom. No matter how large or small the room, it can be sectioned off into smaller areas to be used for different kinds of activities and learning centers. Reading "props" can be used in each area to incroporate sight words and language experiences. As evidenced in Figure 96, an effective classroom can be set up to include the following areas:

1. Arts and crafts— should have a large table, storage space with shelves, and be close to a sink. Also arrange to have a place to display children's drawings.

2. Large play area—for active play; building blocks, playing with large toys.

3. Quiet area—for writing and playing individual games.

4. Reading corner—this could be located in a loft-type area, a corner of the classroom, or even in an old bathtub. Include thick rugs and lots of big, soft pillows. A display of books should be included in this area.

5. Workbench—asks parents for donations of pieces of wood and nails, and small tools. Locate this area away from the reading and writing areas.

6. Pretend corner—this area can be used for all kinds of dramatic play including a room of a house, a doctor's office, or a place to stage puppet shows. Include dress-up clothes, empty food containers, small dishes, stuffed animals, occupation-type props such as a fire fighters hat, doctor's utensils, etc.

Your classroom should also include storage shelves for games; places to keep animals; a bulletin board showing children's birthdays for each month; a large calendar with space for showing "today's weather," a large metric thermometer and a daily temperature chart, and "cubbies" or storage spaces in which children can keep their belongings.

Language experiences and recognition of sight words can be incorporated into each of the learning areas with corresponding accessories. Some examples follow.

### Arts and Crafts Center

Label the supplies on the shelves by making up small signs saying "paper," "paint," "brushes," "chalk." Introduce color words by displaying posters with a large circle or objects of a particular color, and label the posters "blue," "red," and so on. Ask a child to bring you a piece of paper of the same color as a blue crayon, or, for more advanced children, hold up the card with "blue" written on it and have the child find the crayon of that color. When a child completes a painting or drawing, ask him to tell you about it and then write a short caption. It is always better to say "Tell me about your picture," than to ask, "What is it?" That question can confuse the child as he may have had nothing in mind at all. Keep recent productions on display in the art corner.

### Play Area

Label the boxes and shelves containing the blocks and other games. Children could make a complete town with the blocks, and you can offer to label the various buildings. For example, "Chang's Drug Store," "Church," "Temple," "Car Wash." If the children are playing a game such as Candy Land, you can have them guess the beginning letter of each color they draw from the deck.

### Quite Area

This area should have lots of paper and pencils available, as well as a display of the alphabet. It would also be helpful to locate the writing table near a blackboard so students can write and copy words from the board. Some children enjoy completing old workbooks and ditto worksheets. This area can also be used for playing individual games such as puzzles, lotto, and matching cards. Label each game and puzzle, such as the "Little Miss Muffet" puzzle, or "Lotto Box."

### Reading Corner

Display large posters of book characters and have display shelves to store the books. Each shelf can have a different theme such as "scary," "sad," "animals." Label each shelf and next to it draw a picture to illustrate the theme.

### Workbench

The workbench can be located near the noisy play area. Acquire a pegboard onto which the tools can be hung. Trace the shape of the tools with white paint and label them as "hammer," "saw," "screwdriver," and so on.

### "Pretend" Play Area

The 'pretend' play area can be used for a multitude of purposes. One day the children might want to use it for a house with kitchen sink, table, dishes, and stove; on another day they might want to have a grocery store with empty containers, cereal boxes, a cash register, and play money. Other possibilities are a doctor's office, a zoo, a theatre for puppet shows, or a clothing store. Help the children to make signs for the theme of the day and to label the various props. For example, animal cages in the zoo can be named "kangaroo," "polar bear," or "elephant." Tickets can be made for admission to the theatre, and the price tags can be put on the clothing items.

Other areas in your classroom can be labeled for language experiences. A daily routine can be established in which the class has to show the weather of the day. "Rainy," "snowy," "sunny," and "cloudy" can all be illustrated and labeled. Another part of the routine can be to take the temperature and record it on a temperature chart. At the end of the month, ask, "What was the coldest day?" "What was the warmest day?" A graph can be colored in each day as follows:

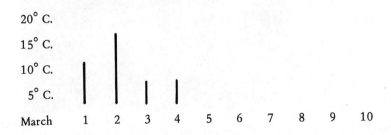

Each child's coat hanger and cubby storage space should be labeled with his or her name. Also, a birthday display board can be made, showing the birthdays of the months:

July Birthdays

Nansi          Diane          Harry

A "mailbox" can be made from a large box with a slot in it or from an old liquor bottle box. Children can "mail" finished worksheets and notes for the teacher and vice versa.

There are unlimited opportunities to incorporate reading activities in a classroom. The more a child can interact with the written word, the more interested he will be in learning to read.

### Children's Personal Space

*Figure 98.* It is a good idea to label each child's cubicle, locker, or box where each child's personal belongings are kept. (Photo by Linda Lungren)

It is a good idea to label each child's cubicle, locker, box, carton, or container where each child's personal belongings are kept. In this way, each child is able to learn to read his own name and the names of some of the other children in his class. Labels, naturally, need to be placed on the child's cubicles in a place and at a height that are comfortably visible to the child. Cubicles can be simply or elaborately labeled:

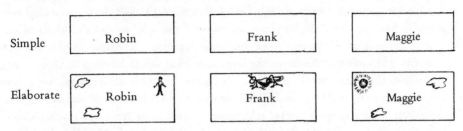

Learning centers contain well-defined physical areas, allowing for needed working space. Each center should be an enticement to learning. The language arts center could contain puppets, felt letters, a record player and records, word games, a radio, and a variety of books. Materials in all centers should be arranged to accommodate a wide range of interests and skills. Materials should be shelved at heights that encourage child exploration.

Learning centers should be as flexible as classroom groups. When the goals of a center have been accomplished or when children have lost interest in the activities of a center, it should be redesigned to introduce new concepts and activities.

The goals of your curriculum will affect the inclusion or exclusion of certain learning centers. If you value art, music, and dramatic play as well as the content areas subjects, your classroom will probably contain learning centers that reflect these curricula beliefs.

The development of classroom learning centers should not preclude the need for classroom areas where children may work, think, or play alone. It is important for a child to learn to function as a member of a group, and it is equally important for him to learn to function independently.

The following guidelines may help you in planning your center:

1. Develop each center as an independent entity. Do not have one center dependent on another for materials or electrical outlets.

2. Determine which centers need to have easy access to the electrical outlets.

3. Determine which center will need a constant water supply. Design these close to a classroom sink or the door nearest the bathroom.

4. Determine which centers need to be closest to natural light. Place these nearer the windows.

5. Arrange all centers so that the activities within are easily visible to you.

6. Consider the traffic flow throughout the classroom. Try to maintain an independent, quiet area that is not easily interrupted.

### Instructional Methods

The best methods and wisest methods lose their effectiveness when we know too little about our pupils. . . . (Durr, 1967, p. 104)

Many studies have attempted to determine the most effective method of teaching reading. Throughout these studies, one variable that appears to be of considerable importance is the *teacher*.

> Our reading research into the effectiveness of various instructional methods in classroom or remedial situations is often pointless. Such comparative research tends to ignore the fact that the dynamic practices of the teacher and the kinds of teacher-pupil interaction she promotes are the most important determinants of pupils' achievements. The collected results of the large-scale First Grade Reading Studies ... strongly reaffirm this fact. Hardly any real differences in pupil achievement were found in comparisons among a half-dozen different approaches in carefully equated populations. Rather, in almost every study, achievement varied more from one teacher's classroom to the next, according to the methods or materials. [G. Spache (1973) p. 43–44]

These statements certainly suggest your importance in the educational setting. The methods of instruction that you employ should emphasize your curricular beliefs. As we have suggested, one very effective method of instruction that encourages the maintenance of a personalized curriculum is thematic teaching. This chapter has been designed to introduce you to the underlying theory of thematic teaching and to provide you with the means for implementing and managing thematic instruction. Within a managed classroom each child is provided with a learning prescription that is simply a note to him that specifies (1) daily/weekly tasks, (2) assignments, and (3) grouping arrangements (see Figure 99).

Each morning you could briefly review the prescriptions with the entire group. Detailed individual reviews may be conducted once the children have begun an activity in a specified center. As you mingle with the children at a particular center, you can quickly determine if any immediate issue needs to take precedence over the prescriptive task. Each child should have individual encounters with you every day.

## Continuous Assessment

You need not be overwhelmed by the evaluation component of this program. You must manage this program in a manner that is workable for you. Although you may greatly enjoy teaching, it is not intended that you devote entire evenings or weekends to school management. In an attempt to design a workable program, it is important to realize that *continuous evaluation* is an essential part of the program, because each succeeding assignment is based on the competencies and needs of each child as he completes his initially assigned task.

Throughout a week, approximately ten to twelve minutes will be required to review each child's prescription. As you complete these evaluations before school, after school, or during the school day it may be expeditious to ask yourself the following questions:

| Center | Task | When | With Whom | Completed |
|---|---|---|---|---|
| Math | (5) (2) (1) Counting Games (3) (4) (6) |  | Bobby<br>Linda | |
| Writing | (D) (E) Practice (C) (B) Letters (A) (F) |  | Alone | |
| Blocks | Building 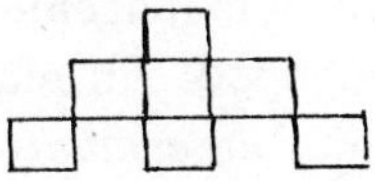 |  | Mary<br>Remo<br>Harold<br>Denise | |
| Rest | Nap  |  | Everyone | |

*Figure 99.*

1. Is the learning task being successfully completed?
2. If not, what additional skills are needed?
3. What is the next learning task for this child?
4. Does the child work effectively alone or as a member of a group?
5. Does the child work more efficiently at long or short assignments?
6. What type of materials seem to be the most interesting to this child?
7. How can I best reinforce this student's learning successes?
8. How can I encourage this child to accept increased responsibility for his learning?
9. How can I best encourage this child to transfer what is learned in one area to other appropriate learning encounters?
10. What activities best aid this child in synthesizing and generalizing newly acquired information?
11. How can I best encourage this child to make evaluative decisions about the validity of newly learned information?

### Sequential Learning or Recycling

As you answer each of these questions you will be able to evaluate *what* has been mastered and to *plan* the next sequential learning task. If the child has mastered the initially prescribed task, you may proceed to the next sequentially related learning experience. If the child has not successfully completed the task you may need to do the following:

1. Provide instruction that addresses the development of readiness skills needed to complete the task.
2. Allot more time for completion of the task.
3. Provide alternate means of instruction.

After making these decisions, you may regroup your students and proceed to the next learning experience. Through the aid of a management system, you will have surveyed, planned, implemented, sequenced, or recycled learning through an integrated theme. Continuous, well-managed *evaluation* is the prime ingredient for success in a program of this type. A system of management enables you, the teacher/manager, to clearly state desired terminal behavior, evaluate instructional effectiveness, and determine sequential learning.

## BIBLIOGRAPHY

Cullum, A. *The Geranium on the Window Sill Just Died But Teacher You Went Right On.* New York: Harlinquist, 1971.

Durr, W. K. *Reading Instruction: Dimensions and Issues.* Boston: Houghton Mifflin Company, 1967.

Fry, E. "Readability Formula that Saves Time," *Journal of Reading*, (April 1968), pp. 513–516, 575–578.

Gilpin, J. G. "Forward." In R. F. Mager *Preparing Instructional Objectives.* Palo Alto, CA: Fearon Publishers, 1962.

Lapp, D. "Behavioral Objectives Writing Skills Test," *Journal of Education* (February 1972), 154:13–24. (This test may be secured from Educational Testing Services, Princeton, N.J.)

Lapp, D. *The Use of Behavioral Objectives in Education.* Newark, Del.: International Reading Association, 1972.

Lapp, D., and J. Flood. *Teaching Reading To Every Child.* New York: Macmillan Publishing Co., Inc. 1978.

Mager, R. F. *Preparing Instructional Objectives.* Palo Alto, Calif: Fearon Publishers, 1962.

Russell, D. H., O. Ousky, and G. Haynes. *Manual for Teaching the Reading Readiness Program,* Revised Edition. Lexington, Mass.: Ginn and Company, 1967.

Russell, D. H., O. Ousky, and G. Haynes. "Inventory of Developmental Tasks," *Santa Clara Guide.* An observation guide.

Schickendanz, J., K. Johnson, and E. Speigler. *Using Reading Everyday in the Preschool: A Curriculum Guide and Discussion for Teachers.* Grant G007-605-403, Right-To-Read, U.S. Office of Education. July, 1977.

Siberman, C. *Crisis in the Classroom.* New York: Random House, Inc., 1970.

Spache, G. D. "Psychological and Cultural Factors in Learning to Read." In R. Karlin (Ed.) *Reading for All.* Proceedings of the Fourth IRA World Congress on Reading. Newark, Del.: International Reading Association, 1973.

# Appendix

**Language/Reading Tests for Young Children**

| Name of Test | For Grades | No. of Forms | Approx. time (in. min.) | Publisher | Author(s) | Vocabulary |
|---|---|---|---|---|---|---|
| ABC Inventory to Determine Kindergarten and School Readiness, 1965 | K-1 | 1 | | Research Concepts | N. Adair | x |
| Academic Readiness and End of First Grade Progress Scales, 1968, 1969 | 1 | 1 | 5-10 | Academic Press | H. Burks | x |
| American School Readiness Test, 1941; rev. 1964 | K-1 | 1 | 45 | Bobbs-Merrill | W.E. Pratt R.V. Young C.A. Whitmer S. Stouffer | x |
| Analysis of Readiness Skills: Reading and Mathematics, 1972 | K-1 | | | Houghton Mifflin | M. Rodrigues W. Vogler J. Wilson | |
| Anton Brenner Development Gestalt Test of School Readiness Test for Kindergarten and First Grade, 1945; rev. 1964 | K-1 | 1 | 3-10 | Western Psychological Services | A. Brenner | |
| Assessment Program of Early Learning Levels, 1969 | Pre K-1 | 1 | 40 | Edcodyne Corporation | E. Cochran J. Shannon | |
| Barclay Early Childhood Skill Assessment Guide, 1973, 1976 | Pre K-1 | 1 | | Educational Skills Development, Inc. | L. Barclay J. Barclay | |
| The Basic Concept Inventory, Field Research Edition, 1967 | Pre K-1 | 1 | 15-15 | Follett Publishing Company | S. Engelman | |
| Binion-Beck Reading Readiness Tests for Kindergarten and First Grade, 1945 | K-1 | 1 | 40 | Acorn Publishing Company | H.S. Binion R.L. Beck | |

| Name of Test | For Grades | No. of Forms | Approx. time (in min.) | Publisher | Author(s) | Vocabulary |
|---|---|---|---|---|---|---|
| A Checklist for the Evaluation of Reading Readiness | Pre K | | | Joseph Sanacore Reading Co-ordinator | J. Sanacore | |
| Childhood Identi-fication of Learn-ing Disabilities, 1974. | Pre K+ | | | Westinghouse Learning Corporation | | |
| CIRCUS: Pre-liminary, 1974 | Pre K | | | Educational Testing Service | | x |
| Clymer-Barrett Pre-reading Battery, 1966, rev. 1967, 1969 | K-1 | 2 | 90 | Personnel Press, Inc. | T. Clymer | |
| The Contemporary School Readiness Test, 1970 | K-1 | 1 | 105 | Montana Reading Clinic Publications | C. Sauer | |
| Delco Readiness Test, 1970 | K-1 | 1 | | Delco Readi-ness Test | W. Rhoades | |
| Diagnostic Reading Tests—Reading Readiness, 1947; rev. 1972 | K-1 | 1 | untimed | Committee on Diagnostic Reading Tests, Inc. | F. Triggs | x |
| Early Detection Inventory | Pre K | 1 | | Follett Publish-ing Company | F. McGahan C. McGahan | |
| Evanston Early Identification Skill, Field Research Edition, 1967 | K-1 | 1 | 10–45 | Follett Publish-ing Company | M. Landsman H. Dillard | |
| First Grade Screening Test, 1966–69 | K | 2 | 30–45 | American Guidance Service, Inc. | J. Pate W. Webb | |

| Compre-hension | Word recognition and attack | Spelling | Listening | Other | Volume and Test in Mental Measurement Yearbooks | Pages in Tests and Review (Buros) |
|---|---|---|---|---|---|---|
| | | | x | Visual discrimination, left- to-right orientation, oral language development, concept development, social and emotional development, motor coordination | | |
| | | | | Visual motor, speech, visual abilities, hearing, fine and gross motor skills, psychological perceptual abilities | | |
| | | | x | Visual discrimination, perceptual motor coordination, letter and numeral recognition, comprehension of oral language, problem solving | | |
| | | | x | Visual discrimination, visual motor performance | 7:744 | 15 |
| | | | x | Colors, science, health, social studies, numbers, handwriting, listening comprehension, reading | | |
| | | | | Visual motor, visual discrimination | | |
| | | | | Relationships, coordination left-to-right approach, visual discrimination | 4:5331 | 160 |
| | | | | School readiness tasks, social-emotional behavior responses, motor performance | 7:746 | 15 |
| | | | | Identifying children expected to have school difficulties | 7:747 | |
| | | | | Intellectual deficiency, central nervous system dysfunction, emotional disturbance | | |

| Name of Test | For Grades | No. of Forms | Approx. time (in. min.) | Publisher | Author(s) | Vocabulary |
|---|---|---|---|---|---|---|
| Gates-MacGinitie Reading Tests— Readiness Skills, 1939; rev. 1969 | K-1 | 1 | 120 | Teachers College Press | A.I. Gates W. MacGinitie | |
| Harrison-Stroud Reading Readiness Profiles, 1949; rev. 1956 | K-1 | 1 | 80-90 | Houghton Mifflin | M.L. Harrison J.B. Stroud | |
| Initial Survey Test, 1970; rev. 1972 | K | 1 | | Scott, Foresman & Co. | M. Monroe J. Manning J. Wepman G. Gibb | |
| An Inventory of Primary Skills, 1970 | K-1 | | | Fearon Publishers | R. Valett | |
| Keystone Ready to Read Tests, 1954 | K | 1 | | Keystone View Company | | |
| Kindergarten Evaluation of Learning Potential, 1963; rev. 1969 | K-1 | 1 | | California Test Bureau/ McGraw-Hill | J. Wilson M. Roebuck | |
| Lee-Clark Reading Readiness Test, 1931; rev. 1962 | K-1 | 1 | 20 | California Test Bureau/ McGraw-Hill | J.M. Lee W.W. Clark | |
| Lippincott Reading Readiness Test (including Readiness Checklist), 1965; Rev. 1973 | K-1 | 1 | | J.B. Lippincott Company | P.H. McLeod | |
| The Macmillan Reading Readiness Test; rev. ed., 1965-70 | K-1 | 1 | 90 | Macmillan Publishing Co., Inc. | A. Harris L. Sipay | x |
| Maturity Level for School Entrance and Reading Readiness, 1950; rev. 1959 | K-1 | 1 | 20 | American Guidance Service, Inc. | K. Banham | |

| Compre-<br>hension | Word<br>recognition<br>and attack | Spelling | Listening | Other | Volume<br>and Test<br>in Mental<br>Measurement<br>Yearbooks | Pages in<br>Tests and<br>Review<br>(Buros) |
|---|---|---|---|---|---|---|
| x | x | | x | Visual discrimination, following direction, letter recognition, visual-motor coordination | 7:749 | 15 |
| | | | x | Using symbols, visual discrimination, using context, names of letters | 5:677 | 265 |
| | | | x | Language meanings, visual ability, letter recognition, sound-letter relationships, mathematics | | |
| | | | | Administered by parent: body identification, alphabet, numbers, draw-a-man, mathematics, class concepts, paragraph reading | | |
| | | | | Readiness skills | | |
| | | | | Association learning, conceptualization, self-expression | 7:751 | |
| | | | | Letter and word symbols, concepts | 7:752 | 373 |
| | | | | Readiness skills | 7:753 | 15 |
| | x | | x | Visual discrimination, rating scale, letter names, visual motor | 7:755 | |
| | | | | Maturity level, behavior | 6:847 | 374 |

| Name of Test | For Grades | No. of Forms | Approx. time (in. min.) | Publisher | Author(s) | Vocabulary |
|---|---|---|---|---|---|---|
| McHugh-McParland Reading Readiness Test, 1966; rev. 1969 | K–1 | 1 | | Cal-State Bookstore | W. McHugh M. McParland | |
| Metropolitan Readiness Tests, 1933; rev. 1969, 1976 | K–1 | 2 | 65–75 | Harcourt Brace Jovanovich, Inc. | G.H. Hildreth N.L. Griffith M.E. McGauvran | |
| Monroe Reading Aptitude Tests, 1935 | K–1 | 1 | 30 | Houghton Mifflin | M. Monroe | |
| Murphy-Durrell Reading Readiness Analysis, 1949; rev. 1965 | K–1 | 1 | 80 | Harcourt Brace Jovanovich, Inc. | H.A. Murphy D.D. Durrell | |
| PMA Readiness Level, 1974 | K–1 | | | Science Research Associates, Inc. | T. Thurstone | |
| Parent Readiness Evaluation of Preschoolers, 1968; rev. 1969 | Pre K-3 | 1 | 60–90 | Priority Innovations, Inc. | A.E. Ahr | |
| Prereading Assessment Kit, 1971–72 | K–1 | | | California Test Bureau/ McGraw Hill | Ontario Institute for Studies in Education | x |
| Prereading Expectancy Screening Scales, 1973 | K–1 | | | Psychologists and Education, Inc. | L. Hartlage D. Lucas | |
| Preschool and Kindergarten Performance Profile, 1970 | | | | Educational Performance Associates, Inc. | A. DiNola B. Kaminsky A. Sternfield | |
| Pre-Reading Screening Procedures, 1968; rev. 1969 | | 1 | 40 | Educators Publishing Service | B. Slingerland | |
| Preschool Screening Instrument, 1973 | K–1 | | | Fort Worth Independent School District | V. Kurko L. Crane H. Willemin | |

| Compre-hension | Word recognition and attack | Spelling | Listening | Other | Volume and Test in Mental Measurement Yearbooks | Pages in Tests and Review (Buros) |
|---|---|---|---|---|---|---|
| | | | x | Visual discrimination, identifying letters, rhyming words, beginning sounds | 7:754 | 15 |
| | | | x | Alphabet, numbers, matching, copying, draw-a-man, word meaning | 7:757 | 194 |
| | | | x | Visual, motor, articulation | 3:519 | 135 |
| | | | x | Sound recognition, learning rate, letter names | 7:758 | 268 |
| | | | x | Verbal meaning, perceptual speed, number facility, spatial relations | | |
| | | | x | Administered by parent: verbal associations and descriptions, motor coordination, visual and auditory memory | 7:759 | |
| | | | x | Symbol perception | | |
| | | | x | Predicting reading problems: visual sequencing, letter identification, visual/auditory spatial awareness | | |
| | | | | Social, intellectual, and physical abilities | | |
| | | | x | Visual discrimination, visual perception memory, letter knowledge | 7:732 | |
| | | | x | Memory-auditory and visual, understanding language, motor skills, closure | | |

| Name of Test | For Grades | No. of Forms | Approx. time (in. min.) | Publisher | Author(s) | Vocabulary |
|---|---|---|---|---|---|---|
| Primary Academic Sentiment Scale, 1968 | Pre K–2 | 1 | 50 | Priority Innovations, Inc. | G. Thompson | |
| Reading Inventory, Probe 1, 1970; rev. 1973 | 1–2 | | | American Testing Company | Diagnostic Reading Committee S. Warner W. Myers | x |
| Reading Readiness Form A, 1953; rev. 1960 | K–1 | 1 | 30–45 | Scholastic Testing Service, Inc. | O. Anderhalter R. Colestock | |
| Riley Preschool Developmental Screening Inventory, 1969 | Pre K–K | 1 | 3–10 | Western Psychological Services | C. Riley | |
| School Readiness Behavior Tests used at the Gesell Institute, 1964; rev. 1965, 1971 | K–5 | 1 | 20–30 | Programs for Education | F. Ilg L. Ames | |
| School Readiness Checklist, research ed. 1963–68 | K–1 | 1 | 10–20 | Research Concepts | J. Austin J. Lafferty F. Leaske F. Cousino | |
| School Readiness Survey, 1967; rev. 1975 | K–1 | 1 | 15–30 | Consulting Psychologists Press, Inc. | F. Jordan J. Massey | x |
| School Readiness Test, 1974–77 | K–1 | | | Scholastic Testing Service, Inc. | O. Anderhalter | |
| Screening Test for the Assignment of Remedial Treatments, 1968 | Pre K–1 | 1 | 60 | Priority Innovations, Inc. | A.E. Ahr | |

| Compre-hension | Word recognition and attack | Spelling | Listening | Other | Volume and Test in Mental Measurement Yearbooks | Pages in Tests and Review (Buros) |
|---|---|---|---|---|---|---|
| | | | | Motivation for learning, level of maturity, and independence from parent | 7:760 | |
| | | | x | Visual discrimination | | |
| | | | x | Uses of things, likenesses in words, listening for "c" and "d" sounds | | |
| | | | | School readiness: design, draw a boy or a girl | 7:761 | |
| | | | | Readiness to start school | 7:750 | 16 |
| | | | | Checklist to be used by parents | 7:762 | 16 |
| | | | | Number concepts, discrimination of form, color naming, symbol matching | 7:763 | 16 |
| x | x | | x | Handwriting and number readiness, letters, visual discrimination | | |
| | | | x | Visual memory, discrimination, copying | 7:764 | |

| Name of Test | For Grades | No. of Forms | Approx. time (in. min.) | Publisher | Author(s) | Vocabulary |
|---|---|---|---|---|---|---|
| Screening Test of Academic Readiness, 1966 | K–1 | 1 | 60 | Priority Innovations, Inc. | A. Ahr | |
| Steinbach Test of Reading Readiness, 1965–66 | K–1 | 1 | 45 | Scholastic Testing Service, Inc. | M. Steinbach | |
| Valett Developmental Survey of Basic Learning Abilities, 1966 | Pre K–1 | | 60–70 | Consulting Psychologists Press, Inc. | R. Valett | |
| Van Wagenen Reading Readiness Scales, 1933; rev. 1958 | K–1 | 2 | 30 | Van Wagenen Psycho-Educational Research Laboratories | M.S. Van Wagenen | x |
| Watson Reading Readiness Test, 1960 | K–1 | 1 | 50–60 | C.S. Hammond and Company | G. Watson | |

| Compre-hension | Word recognition and attack | Spelling | Listening | Other | Volume and Test in Mental Measurement Yearbooks | Pages in Tests and Review (Buros) |
|---|---|---|---|---|---|---|
| | | | | Letters, picture completion, copying, picture description, human figure drawings, relationships, numbers | 7:765 | 16 |
| | | | x | Identifying letters, memory of word forms, language ability | | 16 |
| | | | x | Physical development, tactile discrimination, visual discrimination, language development and fluency, conceptual development | 7:767 | 16 |
| | | | | Range and perception of information, opposites, memory open for ideas, word discrimination | 3:520 | 134 |
| | | | | Subjective, objective (teacher's ratings), physical, social, emotional, and psychological readiness | 6:851 | 377 |

# Index

| Compre-hension | Word recognition and attack | Spelling | Listening | Other | Volume and Test Mental Measurement Yearbooks | Pages in Tests and Review (Buros) |
|---|---|---|---|---|---|---|
| | | | | Readiness, skills-draw a man, characteristics of objects, number, and shapes | 7:739 | 15 |
| x | | | | Perceptual motor, memory, number recognition, word recognition, emotional aspects | | |
| | | | | Alphabet, word matching, discrimination, memory of geometric forms, follow-ing directions | 5:675 | 219 |
| | | | | Visual perception of letters and identification, counting, identification of numbers | | |
| | | | | Number recognition, ten-dot gestalt sentence, gestalt draw-a-man | | |
| | | | | Visual discrimination, letter names, premath skills, language, nouns, verbs | 7:740 | |
| | | | | Sensory tasks, motor per-ceptual skills, environmental exploration, visual and auditory imitation, selfcon-cept, task-order skills, social interaction | | |
| | | | | Basic concepts, pattern awareness, statement repetition | 7:743 | |
| | | | | Picture vocabulary and discrimination, following directions, memory for story, motor control | 3:514 | 128 |